Immigration and Politics in the New Europe
Reinventing Borders

With almost a quarter of the world's migrants, Europe has been attempting to regulate migration and harmonize immigration policy at the European level. The central dilemma exposed in this book is how liberal democracies can reconcile the need to control the movement of people with the desire to promote open borders, free markets, and liberal standards. Gallya Lahav's book traces public opinion and elite attitudes toward immigration cross-nationally and over time to show how and why increasing EU integration may not necessarily lead to more open immigration outcomes. Empirical evidence reveals that support from both elite and public opinion has led to the adoption of restrictive immigration policies despite the requirements of open borders. Unique in bringing together a rich source of original data on European legislators and national elites, longitudinal data on public opinion, and institutional and policy analyses, this study provides an important insight into the processes of European integration, and globalization more broadly.

GALLYA LAHAV is Assistant Professor at the Department of Political Science, State University of New York at Stony Brook, and Visiting Scholar at the Center for European Studies at New York University.

Themes in European Governance

Series Editors
Andrea Føllesdal
Johan P. Olsen

The evolving European systems of governance, in particular the European Union, challenge and transform the state, the most important locus of governance and political identity and loyalty over the past 200 years. The series *Themes in European Governance* aims to publish the best theoretical and analytical scholarship on the impact of European governance on the core institutions, policies, and identities of nation-states. It focuses upon the implications for issues such as citizenship, welfare, political decision-making, and economic, monetary, and fiscal policies. An initiative of Cambridge University Press and the Programme on Advanced Research on the Europeanisation of the Nation-State (ARENA), Norway, the series includes contributions in the social sciences, humanities, and law. The series aims to provide theoretically informed studies analyzing key issues at the European level and within European states. Volumes in the series will be of interest to scholars and students of Europe both within Europe and worldwide. They will be of particular relevance to those interested in the development of sovereignty and governance of European states and in the issues raised by multilevel governance and multinational integration throughout the world.

Other books in the series:

Paulette Kurzer
Markets and Moral Regulation: Cultural Change in the European Union
Christoph Knill
The Europeanisation of National Administrations: Patterns of Institutional Change and Persistence
Tanja Börzel
States and Regions in the European Union: Institutional Adaptation in Germany and Spain
Liesbet Hooghe
The European Commission and the Integration of Europe: Images of Governance

Immigration and Politics in the New Europe

Reinventing Borders

Gallya Lahav

PUBLISHED BY THE PRESS SYNDICATE OF THE UNIVERSITY OF CAMBRIDGE
The Pitt Building, Trumpington Street, Cambridge, United Kingdom

CAMBRIDGE UNIVERSITY PRESS
The Edinburgh Building, Cambridge, CB2 2RU, UK
40 West 20th Street, New York, NY 10011–4211, USA
477 Williamstown Road, Port Melbourne, VIC 3207, Australia
Ruiz de Alarcón 13, 28014 Madrid, Spain
Dock House, The Waterfront, Cape Town 8001, South Africa

http://www.cambridge.org

First published 2004

Printed in the United Kingdom at the University Press, Cambridge

Typeface Plantin 10/12 pt.   *System* LATEX 2$_\varepsilon$ [TB]

A catalogue record for this book is available from the British Library

ISBN 0 521 82814 7 hardback
ISBN 0 521 53530 1 paperback

This book is dedicated:

to the beloved memory of my fathers – Eitan Lahav and Paul Rosenband – whose lives' lessons left me with many questions;

to my parents, Eva and Mike Meyerowitz, and Rosalie Rosenband – who occupy so much of the discourse;

and, especially, to the answers – my Michael and Odeya.

Contents

Figures and tables

Figures

Tables

Preface and acknowledgments

Max Weber, the preeminent social scientist, once said that all scientific inquiry begins with a modicum of subjectivity – merely in the researcher's choice of topic. It is upon this recognition that one can proceed to the true objectivity necessary for scientific investigation. For me, the journey into immigration scholarship took root in my first one-way plane trip from Israel to the United States as a child. It resurfaced over years of shuttling back and forth, and finding a personal safe haven in the middle – Europe – where I could recreate the foreigner context anew. The immigrant story is remarkably familiar to a significant number of immigration researchers I have encountered over the years, and so it is natural that the spin and interpretations we bring to the fore vary so greatly.

This inquiry on immigration attitudes in Europe has its earliest intellectual origins in my initial graduate training at the London School of Economics. Set among the dynamic intellectual commons at Holborn, the LSE provided me with the opportunity to have observer and subject status at one and the same time. From the vantage point of a foreign student in London, and later Paris, where I conducted my thesis work, I had been privy to the fact that Europe had become a multiracial, multiethnic, and multicultural society, perhaps unwittingly, perhaps unacceptingly. But one thing was clear: it lacked a corresponding set of attitudes that resembled the American-pioneered "melting-pot" spirit. What was the common European myth?

At the risk either of appearing to be confused about causal direction or, worse, of being grandiose, I would say that the salience of immigration on the international scene grew with my increasing interest in the issue. In 1986, when I completed my master's work, Jean-Marie Le Pen, leader of France's anti-immigrant extreme-right party, took a seat along with thirty-three other ministers in the Assemblée nationale. In the United Kingdom, where I then lived, Margaret Thatcher, the neo-conservative who in 1979 stole the thunder from her right flank with her "swamped by foreigners" speech, was soon to enjoy her third mandate. Over the years, I have observed similar trends mirrored throughout Europe. One thing became clear: immigration posed a serious dilemma to liberal democracies. It confounded policy-makers who were forced to deal with the increasing agitation of their publics, and with the reality that many foreigners had become permanent residents.

The immigration issue that has evolved over recent years has been further compounded by the increasing insecurity of the changing world. In Europe, immigration has reintroduced cultural, religious, and ethnic diversity at a time when Europeans are witnessing a challenge to the very idea of their nation-state. In the process of finding collective solutions to issues such as immigration, the construction of Europe both unleashes and exposes the deep-seated cultural and political differences on sensitive topics such as immigration, which tap into the core of identity and belonging.

In 1992, the year that touted "Europe 1992" and the completion of a single market "frontier-free" Europe, I took all my theories and conjectures to the hustle-and-bustle streets of Europe. Though I had great resolve to talk to Europe's newly thriving elites in Brussels and Strasbourg about their ideas and understanding of immigration, many of the lessons I was to learn were also unspoken and had to be inferred. One day, on my regular path back from the European Parliament in Brussels, my temporary home, I was struck by the writing on the wall. As I turned the corner of the Grand-place, the central square of Brussels, I saw the unmistakable signs of smoldering social and political unrest: the graffiti that screamed at me (in a snapshot that has sat on my desk every day since) "Immigrés Dehors" – Immigrants Out!! It was the context that impressed me most. It was the young African man passing in front, and glaring almost matter-of-factly; it was Beethoven's 9th Symphony ("Ode to Joy") playing so elegantly and all those beautifully dressed Europeans speaking a cacophony of languages, and those modern buildings superimposed onto a background of stone-paved streets and turn-of-the-sixteenth-century buildings and monuments. In the heart of one of the most cosmopolitan cities of Europe, where the capital of the European Union adorns itself with institutions such as the European Parliament and the Commission, I found one of the most daunting challenges: how can Europe, immersed in the processes of European integration and globalization, deal with the human implications of open borders? Indeed, in the streets of Europe, "the writing was on the wall."

In search of the discourse that captured the range and depth of ideas on immigration, I spent considerable time talking to members of the European Parliament, national elites, media people, experts, and colleagues about the paradoxes unfolding in their midst. It is difficult to exaggerate my indebtedness for a project which possessed me so passionately. I hope to compensate by not appearing underappreciative or shortsighted.

The research for this book was conducted in three parts, and owes its debts to many different people and institutions – unfortunately far too many to mention, but that all nevertheless deserve credit. The construction and implementation of the survey questionnaire with members of the European Parliament and field work itself formed the basis of my doctoral dissertation. It has resulted in one part of the book, and one part of my thinking. Spanning five different European cities and New York, it owes a debt to a very great number of people, who assisted me in some form along the way. Most of them only now realize the importance of their impact – and some never will.

At the Graduate Center of the City University of New York, Christa Altenstetter, Miri Bitton, Bernard E. Brown, Mitchell Cohen, Jill Simone Gross, Hugo Kaufmann, W. Ofuatey Kodjoe, Stanley Renshon, and Henry Wasser contributed to my growth as a scholar and in some form provided me with either moral, intellectual, or organizational support to launch my project. Arthur Goldberg was instrumental in the creation and revisions of both the research design and the survey, and we shared mutual delight in cultivating the fruits of these scientific instruments and watching them ripen. Laurance Bressler personally made the implementation possible; he saw me through the toughest times, and his role transcended the project itself.

In Europe, there were many people who physically, psychologically, and spiritually helped get this project off the ground. Among them are my former teachers and classmates at the LSE, all my great friends who sheltered me or participated in the whirlwind and weight of my research. They include Jennifer Decker, the deBendern/Jurdant/Davis family, and many others, who continue to grow beside me as we turn to new chapters, and as our perspectives develop. Gilles Guilbert fastidiously listened for hours to my sometimes badly spoken French, and worked to make sense out of the interviews by translating much of the data.

And, of course, there are the multitudes of (and particular) people at the European Parliament itself, whose voices can be heard throughout the book, but who for obvious reasons must remain anonymous. Members of the European Parliament shuttle from Brussels to Strasbourg to their home countries; from committee meetings to party group meetings, to national party group committees, to the Hemicycle for voting or question time, to press events, and conferences. The receptivity and participation of so many MEPs, and the active involvement of their assistants, were truly encouraging and inspiring about this democratic forum emerging in Europe. The support and insights of MEPs Rinaldo

Bontempi, Bruno Boissiere, and Bill Newton Dunn irrevocably altered my beliefs in politics and the human spirit. Their generosity and guidance changed this project and my perspective fundamentally and certainly more than can be expressed. Additionally, Antonio Cruz of *Migration News Sheet*, Jan Niessen of the Migration Policy Group, Massimo Pastore, and many other party and media leaders were wonderful sources of information.

Attempting to schedule interviews with members of the European Parliament proved an invaluable and concrete lesson in political culture at work. MEPs have many overlapping interests; however, each orders those interests somewhat differently. Party traditions and ideological principles clearly affect style. Just as the MEPs themselves have collective interests, but individual variations, the Parliament is a forum bringing together a varied but representative group of European elites on a macro-level: a mélange of economists, bankers, civil servants, industrialists, intellectuals, lawyers, judges, scientists, and professional politicians. In all my months at the EP, both in Strasbourg and in Brussels, my conversations with them gave life and meaning to the concept of political culture. Understanding how these political culture indicators affect the variant modes of behavior provided insight into the core issues that questions like immigration raise during these changing times.

But this was only one part of the story. Had I left it there, I would have concluded what many traditional analyses and pundits have suggested, namely that elites (especially those found in ascendant institutions such as the EP) are more progressive and liberal than their diffuse public counterparts. In a second life for the project, I set out to figure out why despite all the differences among elites and policy-makers, and the incredible progress of European integration, immigration policy harmonization was proceeding so guardedly, with outcomes that were far from liberal.

The second part of this research involved extensive data collection and sifting through large Eurobarometer data sets of public opinion. The enormous time consumption and methodological prowess required would not have been possible without the resourcefulness of Joseph Bafumi, whose skills, methodological and intellectual integrity, and perseverance were unsurpassed. Without him, this book would have all looked so different. I am also grateful to Ronald Inglehart and the ICPSR at the University of Michigan, as well as Wesleyan University, for making the data available and digestible.

The third part of this project consisted of intellectual soul-searching, and tracking policy changes that seemed to make the work a moving target. It was the most tortuous, and certainly least indulgent, part, given the quiet walls, computer problems, and lack of sumptuous cafes and pubs.

But it was equally rewarding, and still full of much fortunate support from many people to whom I owe a great deal of gratitude, ranging from computer technicians to Starbucks clerks in the nick of time. While they may remain nameless, they are not forgettable. Hearty thanks also go to my invaluable research assistants at SUNY Stony Brook, Michele Baer, Kate Freitas, Jungseok Kim, and Michael Pisa, who diligently and resourcefully accompanied me at various points of the project.

It was a combination of many people along these three stages that brought this book and me to its deliverance. In this field of enormous interdisciplinary expertise, I have been particularly fortunate to be exposed to the work of sociologists, historians, economists, and demographers – too numerous to mention, but important nonetheless. I found them at the German American Academic Council's (GAAC) two-summer institute in New York and Berlin, the Social Science Research Council (SSRC)/Mellon Foundation, the Center for European Studies at Harvard University, the Center for European Studies at New York University, the European University Institute in Florence – all places where I have been graciously supported and hosted, either with funding and/or shelter.

In this context, I also need to mention the special role of the Population Division of the United Nations, headed by Mr. Joseph Chamie, who hired me for my research expertise. Ironically, I found myself one of the sole political scientists in a demographer's world, and so the learning went both ways. This ongoing relationship has given me new insights into the work that political scientists conduct on migration. I am thankful to Jofred Grinblat, Marta Roig, and Ellen Brennan for keeping me abreast of the substance of our study and for their friendship, and particularly to Hania Zlotnik for showing me the intricate ropes of demographic analysis.

Many have reacted to my arguments and have given me important comments on various works that helped me shape and hone my ideas over the years – and they have become friends in the process. They include Steven Brams, Pauline Cullen, Adrian Favell, Miriam Feldblum, Stanley Feldman, Mark Fischle, Nancy Foner, Terri Givens, Jim Hollifield, Leonie Huddy, Patrick Ireland, Christian Joppke, Rey Koslowski, Mark Miller, Jeannette Money, Rainer Münz, Peter Rutland, Yossi Shain, Karen Stenner, John Torpey, Emek Uçarer, Sarah Wayland, and Patrick Weil.

Over the years, my thinking has evolved, as I have been forced to convince students and colleagues at Wellesley College, Wesleyan University, SUNY Stony Brook, and many others I visited for a far shorter time of the import of this subject. I have benefited from the feedback, and from the lessons taught back to me.

There are a few teachers, colleagues, and friends who, after their reading and re-reading, in some cases spoke more for friendship than "duty"; they will understand their contribution. I am enormously grateful to Phil Cerny, Shari Cohen, Gary Freeman, Carol Gordon, Virginie Guiraudon, Anthony Messina, Kathy Moon, and Mark Schneider for their wisdom and time taken out to give me invaluable comments and guidance. It is difficult to thank Aristide Zolberg for bringing political scientists such as myself to immigration study without also thinking of the greater impact he has made on me generally. It is also not easy to express appropriate gratitude to two people who exceeded all labels and functions of assistance: Asher Arian and Marty Schain were my mentors, my friends, and my human voice of wisdom. Their contributions to this work include all stages of the project's development and more. I am grateful to Asher Arian, my dissertation advisor and guide, for without him the miracle on 42nd Street would not have taken place. Special thanks to John Haslam and his editorial staff, Ashlene Aylward, Karen Anderson Howes, Mike Leach, Karen Matthews, and Jackie Warren at Cambridge University Press for facilitating the transformation of this manuscript into a book. I am also grateful to the anonymous reviewers for awe-inspiring comments that made the ultimate difference. Hopefully, the book speaks to the length of all of their lessons digested. I absolve them all from any responsibility for what remain of my original obstinacies and errors.

On a personal level, I owe my deepest gratitude to my immediate and extended family (my dear friends and neighbors), who shall remain nameless lest I overlook anyone. Many have ridden in tandem with me over time and space – both mental and emotional – and I am so very lucky to have them, I know. I have learned the true meaning of resilience and strength of spirit from my parents, Dr. Eitan Lahav and Eva and Mike Meyerowitz, and my grandparents, Mina and Mordechai Mintz. My mother especially, who put me on this immigrant path, has provided me with the chance to realize my fullest potential, to set goals, and to have visions. I would also like to express special thanks to my sisters, Alona and Marna, their husbands, David Liebling and Eyal Agmon, and the younger generation of the family, Jonathan, Courtney, Dustin, Storm, Neta, Hadar, and Danielle. They have helped put it all in perspective. Rosalie and Paul Rosenband and Debra, Jeff, Joshua, and Leah Franklin have expanded my world of encouragement and support. On the home front, Charles "Danny" Santos made a lot of this possible, and I am enormously grateful. My husband Dr. Michael Rosenband and my divine daughter Odeya stand, like this project, as a testament to the role of perseverance, wonder, and faith in my life.

1   Introduction

Act I, Scene 1: Young dark immigrant boy crosses a bustling city street. As he briskly turns the corner, in front of a kiosk selling newspapers in thirty-five languages, he stops to look up at the European Parliament's new age glass skyscraper that honors Europe's citizens. For the moment, his eyes miss the pop-art covered wall in front of him. Slashing across it, red painted words scream, "Immigrés Dehors!" ["Immigrants Out!"]
(Diary of researcher, Brussels, June 1993.)

Scene 2: In neighboring France, where the European Parliament meets, ideals of "égalité" seem to collide with immigrant realities. Strasbourg, a city of 250,000, is the European Union's capital. It is also home to 14 percent of France's foreign residents, 10 percent unemployment, and a substantial (26 percent of Front National vote) anti-immigrant party.
(New York Times, 23 March 1997.)

Approximately 25 percent of the world's migrants (15 million "foreigners") reside in Europe today. European policy-makers are forced to deal with this reality and the increasing agitation of their indigenous publics. What was once a bureaucratic and post-World War II phenomenon tied largely to reconstruction needs, the introduction of culturally, religiously, and ethnically diverse groups into European society has had an impact in the public and political arenas. This has been marked by electoral campaigns and party contestation, the emergence and consolidation of extreme-right parties, and increasing public support for xenophobic political forces.

The growing politicization of immigration in Europe has occurred at a time when Europeans witness a challenge to the very idea of their nation-states. Despite and because of increasing integration of the European Union (EU), the problems of immigration point to the differences that still exist among the member-states. The construction of Europe, while incorporating attempts to manage issues such as immigration collectively, brings to the fore the existing diversity of cultures and political traditions in the region, particularly in dealing with concepts that are so close to the core of identity: questions of "us" versus "them."

To the extent that the realization of a single-market Europe, anchored in the 1957 Treaty of Rome, rests on the success of freedom of movement, a harmonized immigration policy serves as a major test of founder Monnet's frontier-free Europe. While many believe in the EU's potential in matters of the purse, the sensitive issue of immigration resonates in matters of the heart, where nationalism, racism, and xenophobia persist. Despite the complexity of the migration debate, its resolution (or lack thereof) is a critical test of EU durability.

Efforts to "Europeanize"[1] immigration policy expose a major polemic now being addressed by policy-makers and scholars alike: how can liberal democracies reconcile efforts to control the movement of people with those to promote open borders, free markets, and liberal standards? This conundrum not only serves as the starting point for my inquiry, but also generates a more practical question that drives the rationale of this exploration. Given traditional national differences, the interesting question is not why the immigration issue has become politicized in the EU, but why states would cooperate, and on what bases they would converge, if at all. In studying the normative anatomy of a common immigration policy, I am mainly interested in the constraints and possibilities for collective action problem-solving in a changing and uncertain "playing field." As this story unfolds, the immigration paradox in Europe gives pause to those who suppose that the triumph of global forces makes free movement of persons inevitable.

Questions and considerations

The analytical framework adopted here consists of policy/institutional and attitudinal data that were designed to gauge the viability of European nation-state convergence in a transnational community. It addresses three separate questions. First, what interests (i.e., national, ideological, European) would motivate states to cooperate (or not) on immigration? Second, on what basis would such cooperation be organized (intergovernmental or supranational)? Finally, what would be the nature (liberal or restrictive) of that cooperation?

To a large degree, these questions are empirically grounded in institutional developments and developing norms, and they are measured by what Europeans say and think, and by what policy-makers do. The answers are fundamentally dependent on the extent to which Europeans have coalesced in their thinking, and the way in which policy-makers and institutions have responded.

The organization of this book reflects an attempt to link institutions to norms, and domestic constraints to changing factors in the international

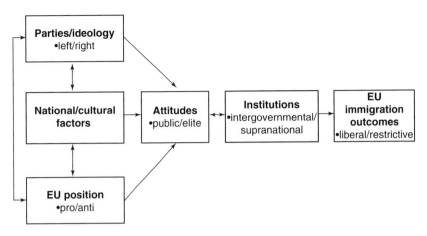

Figure 1.1 Conceptual map

arena. These dynamics illuminate the significant relationship between European regional integration and migration regulation, and they allow us to say something about the future of free movement of people and transnational cooperation. I systematically consider: (1) the interests involved; (2) how they structure public and elite attitudes; (3) their institutional organization; and (4) the link to policy outcomes. These variables are illustrated schematically in figure 1.1.

As figure 1.1 reveals, the linkages between these questions help us understand the conditions under which Europeanization is applicable to immigration issues. In short, we can elucidate the range of behaviors available to policy-makers by linking variables of thinking (i.e., national, ideological, and regional interests) to institutional frameworks and policy preferences.

Immigration and the construction of Europe: the politics of inclusion and exclusion

No analysis of migration in Europe today can avoid the consideration of European integration dynamics. This commonly held assumption derives from international relations theories of globalization and interdependence, and it is supported by immigration scholars trying to explain national "loss of control" (Sassen 1996; Cornelius, Martin, and Hollifield 1994; see also Bhagwati 2003). This book takes issue with these foregone conclusions, but it embraces the premise that immigration is significantly enmeshed in the globalization process. The question is: how?

The drive toward building a common Europe is linked to immigration in two ways: institutionally and attitudinally. First, institution-building and -consolidation present all sorts of struggles – between national and supranational forces; between political parties; between national group actors – that fundamentally involve how Europe should be organized. As discussed in chapter 2, these dynamics channel and frame the entire immigration debate, which is already laden with issues of sovereignty.

The second component of European integration that influences migration thinking is related to the psychological processes that buttress the construction of any new community: the identification of "in-groups" and "out-groups." Can Italians feel kinship with the French, and should people from the United Kingdom feel supranational ties to those living in Belgium? The conflict of identifying with one's nation or Europe as a whole is indeed real and impacts the politics of inclusion and exclusion. "Europeanness," the identification with a larger community, may be seen as a mobilizing force of inclusiveness that inherently *ex*cludes outsiders – foreigners. This attitudinal component of European integration is partic-ularly sensitive to questions of national identity and citizenship, and it is the focus of this book. If we accept the significance of public policy in affecting migration outcomes, we must consider not only the trajectory of institutional developments, but also their normative correlates, the paradigms that policy-makers and publics employ during transitional phases.

Immigration has been traditionally construed as a two-fold dilemma: problems of intake and the nature of incorporation. The first set of questions focuses on the "nuts and bolts" of immigration: yes or no? how many? basis of entry? These issues deal with strategies for control and regulation. The second stream of questions addresses the nature of incorporation, or what should be done with immigrants once they arrive. Policy demands include the kinds of rights to be extended to immigrants and methods of integration (i.e., assimilation, multiculturalism, etc.). Not only do models of integration vary dramatically by country, but many migrants to whom integration programs apply are not migrants at all, but "ethnic minorities," a term generally used to refer to established communities founded by postwar immigrants (Layton-Henry 1990: 6).[2] They are the children or even the grandchildren of migrants, commonly referred to as "second-generation" or "third-generation" immigrants. In the European Union, second-generation Turks residing in Germany have fewer rights than first-generation Irish migrants to the United Kingdom or Macanese in Portugal. As the following chapters show, every country defines intake and incorporation preferences differently, and it is the EU's desire to standardize these policies that has added a new dimension to these incongruities.

The nature of the immigration debate becomes more complicated at the European Union level, as it reflects and magnifies the problems that each nation has confronted internally. With the completion of the single market, citizens of one of the fifteen member-states (soon to be twenty-five), are no longer "foreigners" in the other fourteen. As the EU erases its internal borders, immigration policy and implementation require agreement and trust among members, in addition to some common outlook among nations which have traditionally confronted distinct groups differently. Formulating a common policy involves deciding which outsiders require visas to enter the Union and ensuring that illegal immigrants, drug traffickers, smugglers, and terrorists do not profit from the elimination of borders. It also raises traditional concerns about social welfare policies, integration strategies, asylum histories, and race relations. These concerns are shaped by country-specific and partisan-ideological debates.

Developments at the EU level are indicative of the controversies and limitations that remain concerning immigration and the intergovernmental pillar (the Justice and Home Affairs Council), which has largely left immigration goals and implementation strategies to national and administrative interpretation. Since the adoption of the Treaty on European Union (commonly known as the Maastricht Treaty) in 1993, there has been a formal recognition of the need for a serious common immigration policy. While subsequent EU treaties and summits (including Amsterdam in 1997, Tampere in 1999, Nice in 2000, Laeken in 2001, and Seville in 2002) have attempted to give teeth to a common immigration policy, much of the rhetoric has not been accompanied by any substantive policy changes.

Clearly, the immigration problem at the EU level is about the harmonization of national trends. While the Tampere report issued by the European Council (1999) has gone farther than ever to identify the principles for cooperation, it made a specific plea for strong will and leadership to shape public opinion. How the EU will reconcile the promises of Maastricht, Amsterdam, Tampere, Nice, Laeken, and Seville with the reality of public opinion on immigration remains to be seen.[3] The question persists: can this be done?

Using theories of integration to explain immigration outcomes: institutional explanations

The obstacles that inhibit the free flow of people in a European Union that broadly promotes open borders, free markets, and liberal standards raise fundamental questions about the viability and character of regional integration, cooperation, and globalization at large. These are mainly questions of institutional and attitudinal convergence. What insights do integration theories of cooperation offer immigration researchers? Conversely, what does the attempt to build a common immigration and asylum policy tell us about competing theories of European integration?

The limits to cooperation not only expose the conflict between transnational and domestic mandates in migration regulation, but also reflect the wider gap that remains between *neofunctional* theories of a supranational EU and more realist (state-centric) *intergovernmental* views of governance.[4] While both views envision cooperation taking place, they differ in the extent of changes to national control and policy outcomes that may ensue. Realist, intergovernmental approaches to European policy-making emphasize national differences, limited forms of cooperation, and more protectionist policy outcomes. A neofunctional view endorses supranational governance, which may constrain the behavior of member-states and generate more liberal outcomes. These theoretical trajectories tend to pose a dichotomy between regional norms and national interests – one camp envisions openness and the other protectionism. Prevailing scholarship on migration is divided and thus requires some disaggregation. Based on two competing explanations of cooperation, we may broadly distinguish between *liberal* and *restrictive* immigration policy output.

A supranational view of Europe and liberal immigration

The extent to which the EU is able to operate as a supranational entity (or not) is largely dependent upon its ability to construct and uphold those common policies, such as immigration, which necessarily determine its identity. A unified Europe warrants a common immigration policy to ensure that other common policies it upholds in a number of other realms (e.g., social, economic, etc.) are not undermined by an inconsistent application of immigration and asylum policy in differing member-states. A neofunctional view of Europe posits that cooperation in one issue area is a function of integration in another. And it suggests that, once this process of organization begins, the power of nation-states to act independently is incrementally reduced.[5]

One school, rooted in the international relations theories of interdependence, argues that in an increasingly global world, where the lines between nation-states are becoming blurred, states are indeed seeking international solutions to domestic problems (Keohane and Nye 1977; Art and Jervis 1992). Developments subsumed under the term "globalization" have transformed state sovereignty (Krasner 1993; Ruggie 1993; Sikkink 1993), limited national policy-making (Goldstein and Keohane 1993), and eroded national sovereignty (Evans 1998;

Keohane and Milner 1996). "[T]ransnational and global economic, political, social, and cultural forces, including migration" itself, have weakened national frontiers and decision-making autonomy (Collinson 1993: 103). Economic interdependence and the globalization of the economy have essentially constrained the state's role in regulating migration and have generated more liberal policies (Sassen 1991, 1996). These solutions, in the context of what appear to be immutable global forces, cast doubt on the capacity and/or will of national policy-makers to manage migration unilaterally or according to traditional agendas.

The recent bodies of literature in the fields of international political economy (IPE) and sociology have made impressive contributions to the debate on international constraints on migration regulation. While very different in their assumptions, both schools have challenged the traditional notion of realist politics, bringing into question the state-centric assumptions that states are the sole protectors of territorial integrity, and that national choices are increasingly constrained by the liberal precepts of markets and rights.

Some scholars of political economy have argued that international human rights and the freedom of circulation required by a global economy and regional markets are the two aspects of a liberal regime that undermine the sovereignty and significance of nation-states in regulating migration policy (Hollifield 1992a, 1992b; Sassen 1996). Based on neoliberal theories of twentieth-century norms (see Rosecrance 1986), these theorists of "embedded liberalism" contend that rights expressed in the form of constitutional norms and principles act to constrain the power and autonomy of states. Sociologists and legal scholars have gone even further and declared both territorial sovereignty and national citizenship to be outmoded (Soysal 1994; Bauböck 1994; Jacobson 1996) and devalued (Schuck 1989, 1998)[6] concepts. These arguments lend support to the hypothesis that immigration policy is an area in which states may be expected to cooperate, and to defer to "international regimes," a set of principles, norms, rules, and decision-making procedures around which actor expectations converge in a given area (Ruggie 1982; Krasner 1982, 1983).[7] The implications point to the supremacy of liberal regimes and limited state control over migration interests. They give credence to state-demise and loss-of-control theses.

A national, intergovernmental view of Europe and restrictive immigration

State-centric and (neo)realist critics argue that a view of globalization and international instruments as factors that undermine state capacity to control migration fails to realize the basis from which they derive: the state itself. These theories assume that states have the power to protect and defend territorial integrity, and that they continue to regulate international migration in accordance with their "national interests" (Waltz 1979; Zolberg 1981; Weiner 1985, 1990). While in this view cooperation may occur, its form is intergovernmental, which involves the lowest common denominator of interstate bargaining and strict limits on future transfers of sovereignty.[8]

Indeed, as long as the nation-state is the primary unit for dispensing rights and privileges (Meyer 1980), and for protecting its nationals (Shaw 1997), it remains the main interlocutor for, reference for, and target of interest groups and political actors, including migrant groups and their supporters (Kostoryano 1996). In fact, one does not – yet – find a transnational issue network for migrant rights that includes groups operating at the European level along with others at the national and subnational levels (Guiraudon 2001b). Despite the presence of a few non-governmental organizations (NGOs) in Brussels and the efforts of the European Commission to sponsor a Forum of Migrants, recent studies have revealed a missing link between European-level groups and migrant organizations mobilizing domestically (Favell 1997; Geddes 1998; Kostoryano 1994).

The theoretical debates about the role of the state in migration regulation tend to neglect the mechanisms that are used to effectively manage immigration policy (Lahav 1997b, 1998, 2000). They also tend to ignore national constraints of pluralist societies. Indeed, when we go beyond the realist view of the state as a monolithic unit of analysis and adopt a more pluralist model, there are still questions about domestic constraints on policy-making such as public opinion (Layton-Henry 1992; Thränhardt 1992; Wihtol de Wenden 1988, 1999; Fetzer 2000), including extreme-right and populist pressures (Thränhardt 1997; Givens 2002; Lewis-Beck and Mitchell 1993; Gibson 2002), organized interests (Haus 2002), business/economic actors (Castles and Kosack 1985; Freeman 2002; Kessler 1997), ethnic groups (Abadan-Unat 1997; Esman 1994), or other traditional dominant interests, such as constitutional courts (Joppke 1998b, 1998c, 1999; Legomsky 1987; Schuck 1998).[9] While some have argued that these constraints have led to loss of elite control over the immigration agenda, they fail to explain the increasing will on the part of receiving countries to stem unsolicited migration flows (Brubaker 1994, 1995; Freeman 1994, 1995, 1998; Joppke 1997, 1998b; Lahav 1997b; Guiraudon and Lahav 2000). The presupposition of the unitary state as an administrative actor overlooks the modes of implementation being adopted to regulate migration (Lahav 1998, 2000), as well as the role of law-and-order

Table 1.1 *Summary of theoretical conjectures*

Theory	Form of cooperation	Power	Common immigration policy and immigration outcomes
Realism	Intergovernmental	Nation-state	No, restrictive
Functionalism/ interdependence	Supranational	European Union/ transnational actors	Yes, liberal
Hybrid	Intergovernmental/ supranational	Nation-state and EU	Yes, restrictive

bureaucrats (Guirandon 2000a) and police and security officials (Bigo 1996, 2001; Huysmans 2000).[10] In this scenario, regional disparities reflect important national interests and traditions that are neither necessarily liberal nor readily open to supranational cooperation.

An alternative view: the argument

This book inscribes itself in this theoretical debate by probing the extent to which traditional national tendencies have been supplanted by international and transnational developments. It tests the hypothesis that supranational cooperation or regional integration may be inhibited if national interests and ideological affinities persist in structuring policy preferences. Thus we would expect that the triumph of European integration, particularly in its supranational form, would make the free movement of persons inevitable. In contrast, immigration may prove to remain an area of politics in which nation-states are most assertive about their exclusive claims to sovereignty, and in which governments and political parties will continue to press for stricter physical immigration control.

I attempt to go beyond the well-established sovereignty debate to explain immigration outcomes in Europe. These debates tend to polarize unhelpfully around the decline or resilience of nation-states in regulating immigration. I reject the commonly understood dichotomy between supranational and national constraints (i.e., that one camp promotes openness and the other protectionism). Instead, I argue that increasing interdependence and harmonization at the European level are compatible with growing national influence (see table 1.1).

In general, restrictive cooperation is the likely outcome. This is driven not only by reasons to do with its effectiveness as a policy output but, more importantly, by the powerful policy input of emergent consensual attitudes on restrictive policies, among elites and mass publics alike, regarding how to manage and legislate European immigration problems.

My emphasis on public opinion and its impact on European-level policy-making represents a significant departure from more institution-based analyses of European migration. Recognizing that international regimes and policy outcomes are products of dynamic interaction between institutions, principles, rules, and norms (Krasner 1982; Ruggie 1982; March and Olsen 1984, 1989), I build my argument about cooperation by linking European developments with immigration norms.[11] In this way, the aim is to respond to the growing gap in the immigration literature – a tendency to focus on immigration strictly as policy output, rather than policy input. If we observe that policy outcomes may diverge radically from policy inputs,[12] then it is reasonable to question the missing link. The parameters of long-term policy consequences are likely to be revealed by analyzing the basic norms at work. By delineating the political constellations and constraints on migration cooperation, we may gain some theoretical leverage to predict the portability of Europeanization to policy areas that are sensitive to national interests.

By surveying the prospects for collective policy-making, this book provides a normative portrait of immigration at the European level. It offers a complementary, albeit vital, attitudinal perspective to the work of those who have focused more on policy dynamics such as issues of immigration control, citizenship, naturalization, and integration.[13] I do not pretend to give a comprehensive account of immigration politics in the European Union. Other more politics-based, policy-outcome, or legal works on the subject have provided a much more detailed portrait of migration phenomena and a sense of national dynamics that no elite or public attitudes alone can ever provide.[14] The emphasis on European-level policy-making should be read as a supplement to other more national accounts, as the nation-state is, after all, where the majority of the migration action lies. Together, the data provide evidence that public and elite attitudes provide constraints and possibilities, which have determined some EU-level policy outcomes. Contrary to conventional understanding of regional integration, these dynamics may promote less-than-liberal transnational practices in a global order.

While the challenges of immigration and European integration have been well documented, *how* these dynamics are linked and how they affect the choices available to European policy-makers are yet unclear. Some limited attention has been given to the actual instruments and policies adopted, but there has been little consideration of the attitudes and norms that shape the immigration debate in an emergent Europe. This is important if we want to go beyond descriptive analysis and explain the unevenness of regional integration. This attitudinal perspective begins to help us unravel the larger puzzle that has preoccupied contemporary scholars, namely, why policy-making sometimes wavers from the nation-state level to the EU and why integration proceeds more rapidly in some policy domains than it has in others (see Stone Sweet and Sandholtz 1998: 1).

The attitudinal dimension of immigration cooperation: the analytical framework

Political science theorists of regional integration have, for the most part, neglected mass attitudes as a measure of integration for a long time (for some early exceptions, see Mathew 1980; Hewstone 1986; Feld and Wildgen 1976; Shepherd 1975; Slater 1983). Recently, this public dimension has been taken into account. A few broad studies have made important contributions to the field (Eichenberg and Dalton 1993, 1997; Anderson 1998; Franklin, Marsh, and McLaren 1994; Niedermayer and Sinnott 1995b; Gabel 1998a, 1998b; Green 2000). But we still lack information about the attitudinal relationship between David Easton's "specific" and "diffuse" support distinctions (Easton 1965). We have some understanding of diffuse support (a general reservoir of favorable attitudes or goodwill that helps members to accept or tolerate outputs to which they are opposed).[15] But more research needs to tap into what Easton called "specific support", or support for a particular policy (i.e., immigration). While many of the Eurobarometer surveys gauge general ideals,[16] a concrete assessment of mass integration needs to incorporate some practical applications in order to test the functionalist thesis that a shift in mass loyalties from national to supranational institutions is gradually occurring (Holland 1994: 152).

I attempt to tap into both levels by investigating general attitudes toward community and institutions and measuring them against those specifically applied to immigration policy. By considering institutions both as structures and as norms, we heed caution about gauging the success of European integration in terms of institutional shifts in loyalty (see Hewstone 1986: 13; Inglehart 1977, 1990a), but build on the analytical rigor of empirical research that is offered to us by attitudinal data.

The significance of public opinion and elite attitudes in moving the integration process along the continuum from intergovernmentalism to supranationalism has only recently become more interesting to EU scholars because of issues of "democratic deficit." This concern with the gap between citizens and elites stems from the creation of the EU as a predominantly elite affair, and it has been one of the key stumbling blocks to EU legitimacy (see Gabel 1998a; Thomassen and Schmitt 1999;

Blondel, Sinnott, and Svensson 1998; Steunenberg and Thomassen 2002).[17]

Given that immigration policy-making has long been seen to take place behind closed doors and without public debate, immigration scholars tend to share European integration observers' propensity to discredit public opinion. Noting the divergence between mass and elite attitudes, immigration analysts have corroborated a disjuncture between public opinion and policy developments (Simon and Alexander 1993; Freeman 1995; Guiraudon 2000a; Hansen 2000; Fetzer 2000; Tichenor 2002; Beck and Camarota 2002).[18] They have suggested that liberal immigration policies emerge because (negative) public opinion is not factored into elite decision-making or institutional developments.

These accounts fail to explain why cooperation has been fairly limited and restrictive up to now (Lavenex 1999; Geddes 2000; Lahav 1997b), and how different immigration discourses and public opinion contexts are generating more *restrictive* and protectionist policy responses throughout the EU (Joppke 1998a; Money 1999). More importantly, these liberal paradigms fail to consider that, as the ensuing chapters show, there are more similarities between European elites and publics than previously expected (McLaren 2001).

My approach to bridging these theoretical gaps is premised on several assumptions. First, the assumption that norms, values, and institutions are dynamically linked to policy outcomes is derived from the contributions of literature on new institutions and political psychology. They suggest that decisions and structures, far from being created in a vacuum, actually reflect institutional, historical, and psychological constraints (March and Olsen 1989; Weir and Skocpol 1985; Hall 1986; Powell and DiMaggio 1991; Putnam 1993). Behavior is a function of both environmental situations and attitudinal or psychological predispositions, in what is essentially a "push–pull" relationship (Greenstein 1987: 28–29). Although the relationship between attitudes and behavior is inherently problematic (see appendix B for a discussion on comparing different measurements of attitudes),[19] the two are not randomly associated (Aberbach, Putnam, and Rockman 1981: 31; Putnam 1973; Greenstein 1987; Fishbein and Ajzen 1980; Glynn et al. 1999).[20]

Second, in following the valuable work of students of comparative political behavior in advanced Western democracies, I make the assumption that policy is a result of both popular opinion and elite preferences.[21] A basic premise of this study is that political attitudes, values, and beliefs affect the ways in which decision-makers respond to social change (Aberbach, Chesney, and Rockman 1975). My implicit assumption is that public views help *define* acceptable bounds of politics, but influential elites *refine* the boundaries of policy options (especially on new issues).[22] Although political elites typically differ in the scope of their concerns and the specialty of their knowledge, they are uniquely influential in shaping public policy and setting the agenda (Aberbach, Putnam, and Rockman 1981). Not only is elite thinking more coherently structured and consistent than public opinion (Converse 1964; Jennings 1992), but it is also apt to run ahead of the masses, particularly on topics that are new to national agendas (Putnam 1976; Jacobs and Shapiro 2000).[23] Elite attitudes may thus critically inform issue cleavages and prospects for conflict management in a Europe of changing boundaries.

Finally, as students of democracy and the EU have amply shown, elite beliefs may also tell us about how well the representation process functions in Western democracies.[24] Under representative government, even though the citizens control and the elites rule, the commitment to popular rule sets democracies apart from other political systems. In the broadest sense of the term, the representativeness of elite attitudes is measured by their similarity to the overall attitudes of the public, also called "collective correspondence" (Weissberg 1978; Dalton 2002; Bardi 1991).[25] But the comparison between elite attitudes and public opinion is particularly important in the nascent Union, where the issue of "democratic deficit" has become one of the most common currencies of controversy. Since the evolution of democratic institutions depends on the relationship between leaders and the masses, it is useful to consider attitudes as a measure of the legitimacy and stability of a community.[26]

The congruence between public and elite attitudes illuminates the nature of immigration discourse and European cooperation today. We can begin to formulate this relationship through the lens of competing interests and political cleavages that organize immigration attitudes in the EU. A critical polemic in a Europe that has widened its decision-making fora is: what happens to traditional affinities such as party groups, ideology, and national interests, all of which inform issue attitudes? If issues are about the alleged differences between contending parties (Lipset and Rokkan 1967, 1990; Butler and Stokes 1969, 1974; Lane and Ersson 1999), then the case of immigration presents an interesting policy dilemma to be researched. How will issue cleavages be organized in a supranational Europe whose members represent diverse cultural and historical experiences, different ideological convictions and party affiliations? More particularly, what are the cleavages and affiliations that persist in informing and ordering policy thinking after the Union?

The left–right ideological scheme has provided the most common reference point in Western political space. This spatial dichotomy has prevailed since the 1789 French Revolution, when the liberal, republican, and secular forces seated on the left side of Parliament competed against the conservative and religious forces seated on the right. Political scientists have traditionally used the left–right ideological construct as a yardstick for measuring individual preferences and party positions on the prevalent issues of the day. And policy-makers have been seen to capture diverse interests and manage political conflict in a community organized along the left–right continuum.

To a greater or lesser extent, parliaments throughout Western Europe have been organized along this classic ordinal scheme. This historical rationale, in fact, dictates the European Parliament, the directly elected legislative (and only sovereign supranational) organ of the European Union in the twenty-first century. The founders of the European Parliament and the 1953 Common Assembly earlier hoped that national interests could be transcended through partisan affiliation. They created the first international assembly whose members would sit according to broad political groups, which cut across nationality.[27] Like traditional parliaments, loose party groups organize the controversies, debates, and interests facing the European Union member-states at large.

Emergent controversies and the changing nature of debates, however, led many scholars as early as the 1960s to question the entire framework of conceptualizing conflict in postmodern society (Bell 1962, 1973; Deutsch et al. 1967; Lerner and Gorden 1969). New issues were considered to threaten old political cleavages. The abatement of divisions over policy issues led some to argue that the traditional ideological conflicts and party competition that had emerged from industrialization and had dominated Western party systems for most of the century were no longer relevant. Indeed, the postmodern Inglehart school proclaims that these changes have liberated the citizen from traditional alignments, fidelities, and ties, creating a shift in value systems (Inglehart 1977, 1990a, 1990b, 1990c, 1997; Dalton, Flanagan, and Beck 1984; Flanagan and Dalton 1990; Crewe and Denver 1985; Dalton 2002 [1988]; Kitschelt 1989). This phenomenon has been evidenced by increasing voter volatility, the growth of single-issue movements and non-traditional parties, such as the Greens, and the consolidation of extreme-right parties.

Changing alignments and interests may indeed inform the evolution of the immigration debate in the post-industrial era. There is ample evidence that traditional class conflicts have been supplanted by "new politics" (i.e., environmentalism, gender issues, human rights) and "new security issues" (i.e., ethnic conflict, immigration, terrorism). The immigration issue that surfaced in the 1980s and 1990s in Europe may be representative of a new type of issue that scholars equate with the demise of ideology. As immigration has become increasingly politicized throughout European countries, the divisions in the debate have become decidedly more elusive.

First, the issue has blurred national and international arenas as it has challenged the traditional notion of state sovereignty, or the state's prime tasks of defining citizenship and deciding who shall enter its territory (Papademetriou and Miller 1983; Layton-Henry 1990; Soysal 1994; Hollifield 1992a, 1992b; Sassen 1996; Jacobson 1996; Castles and Miller 1998). Second, beliefs about immigration and racial minorities often cut across normal lines of political battle (Freeman 1979: 101). Contemporary European national debates have shown that this issue may blur differences between mainstream parties. As has been illustrated in the French case, the left–right continuum has revealed signs of convergence and party dealignment (Schain 1987, 1988). In the process of defusing immigration and race politics, the British system has also witnessed party convergence on the issue (Freeman 1979; Messina 1985, 1989). Third, as Germany has experienced, major parties may be internally split on this policy issue (Hoskin 1984; Hoskin and Fitzgerald 1989). Throughout Europe, the immigration issue has torn parties of the left between their own working-class base and foreign workers. Similarly, it has conflicted parties of the right, which have struggled to differentiate themselves from their far-right competitors.[28] Moreover, immigration has been identified as an increasing dilemma for liberals. Many scholars argue that there is only a marginal difference, if any, between liberals and others in terms of support for the flow of immigration – and even those who describe themselves as "liberal" may be somewhat divided on the issue (Simon 1989). Major immigration policy reforms granting (and restricting) rights to foreigners have been associated as much with right-wing coalitions as with left-wing governments (Hammar 1985b; Guiraudon 2002b). This tendency of immigration politics to straddle the ordinary liberal–conservative divide accounts for the often-noted "strange bedfellows" coalitions that emerge around policy reforms (Zolberg 2000). Finally, unlike most political issues that become salient through a struggle of dualistic tendencies, the immigration issue is marked by uneven political contestation (Messina 1990). Whereas on most issues programmatic distinctions among parties generally serve to organize political debate and ultimate policy resolution, on immigration the process has not been so clear.

Empirical data on European mass publics have identified some distinctions. Public opinion polls have provided some insights regarding the nature of divisions in the immigration debate. In 1988/89, the European Commission conducted its first extensive survey on racism and xenophobia. The Eurobarometer survey reported that, among European publics, the degree of importance attached to the problem of immigration surprisingly varies little with age, sex, or educational level, but it becomes distinguishable, if only in a limited way, on the political/ideological level.[29] According to these findings, the more one identifies with the right of the political spectrum, the more importance one attaches to the "problem" of immigration (and vice versa). At the same time, a division on the importance of the issue has emerged on country lines, with traditional European "emigration countries" on one side (i.e., Italy, Spain, Portugal, and Greece) and "immigration countries" (i.e., France, Germany, the United Kingdom, and Belgium) on the other.

European integration adds another dimension to the immigration equation. The emergence of a European cleavage, which consists of a pro- versus anti-Europe division, threatens to cut across many more classical cleavages in politics and society, at the national and regional level (Lahav 1997a; Hix and Lord 1997; Hix 1999a, 1999b; Fetzer 2000). Hix and Lord's analysis of Eurobarometer surveys revealed that, while many issues are still organized along the left–right continuum, the issue of integration inherently undermines the cohesion of the main party families. In their view, the "political interests about the question of European integration are more determined by national and cultural factors than by party affil- iation" (1997: 26). If this is the case – assuming that the connection between increased integration and a common immigration policy is correct, as I claim – then we may expect to predict support for a common immigration policy on the basis of national and cultural factors.

Despite more recent public opinion surveys generated by Euro- barometer reports,[30] and studies on extreme-right movements, we still know very little about attitude cleavages regarding immigration and how competing interests are organized. Analysis of attitudes is critical to understanding today's Europe of changing boundaries. This is especially important in the case of immigration, which has been considered a crisis of elite and mass reactions to foreigners rather than an outgrowth of changes in migrant flows themselves (Baldwin-Edwards and Schain 1994: 7; McLaren 2001). The construction of Europe has presented a new playing field in the political arena of immigration politics, and has given new life to critical issues of the post-Cold War period. More than ever before, immigration patterns are shaped by changing world conditions (i.e., globalization and regional integration) that determine not only the dispositions of individuals toward movement, but also the policies of states toward movement of individuals across their borders

(Zolberg 1999; see Zolberg 1981 for earlier arguments of this kind). The approaches states embrace in reconciling competing interests provide a standpoint from which to evaluate the extent and nature of immigration cooperation.

As this book measures the factors that account for policy preferences, several competing explanations for preferences are put forward and assessed. One explanation focuses on the nation-state as a factor that shapes and organizes policy preferences. Nation-based or cultural theory assumes that each nation's past sets a series of problems for its current leaders and decision-makers. These are shaped by values, cognitive assumptions, and patterns of beliefs that continue to provide a repertoire of familiar responses to political problems (Almond and Verba 1963). While political culture variables may change gradually, they tend to remain stable for a considerable period of time and to be long-enduring (Inglehart 1990a).

Another explanation for policy preferences emphasizes ideological and partisan determinants of attitudes, and these may correlate to regional and transnational constraints. Are there more similarities in the beliefs of a French and a German social democrat than between a French socialist and a French conservative, or between a German social democrat and a German Christian democrat? In this case, we may expect some form of transnational politics based on ideological affinities. It is only logical that political parties, the most general bodies that claim to represent the people, should reflect differences of opinion.

A third cleavage dimension recognizes that, on some issues, the EU position (pro- or anti-integration) may better structure policy preferences than the traditional left–right continuum (Hix 1999a, 1999b; Hix and Lord 1997; Thomassen and Schmitt 1999).[31] In this scenario, an intergovernmental organization of a common immigration policy may be differentiated from more supranational options. In general, the more supportive one is toward European integration, the more likely one is to find immigration outcomes taking place at the supranational level – which is more favorable to a common immigration policy.

Different implications flow from each theory. For example, the persistence of nation-specific norms (i.e., perceptions of history and cultural needs) in immigration policy thinking may indicate that policy options are not easily open to transnational regulation. Cultural variables are not easily influenced, altered, or negotiable, and political culture cannot be legislated or exported. The alternative party explanation assumes that, if the left–right construct is significant in accounting for policy preferences, the immigration issue may have transcended nation-state lines in the European Union. This finding supports the theory that there are more differences within nation-states than between them. It provides a political view of polarizations in a Europe of changing boundaries (namely, that ideological distinctions are relevant to immigration attitudes despite the extent to which the issue cuts across traditional cleavages). If party ideology remains elusive in structuring EU immigration outcomes, then positions on European integration or more national, cultural factors may best predict outcomes. Some individuals think of immigration and asylum as "national" issues, and thus immigration policy may be one of those policy areas in which conflict between champions of national policy and supporters of EU majority-determined policy frequently occurs.[32] These explanations and their individual implications are explored more thoroughly in subsequent chapters.

The plan of the book

This chapter has delineated the complex set of constraints involved in the making of a European immigration regime. Chapter 2 presents the context of the immigration issue as it has unfolded during the construction of a "people's Europe." It investigates the relationship between European integration in the period of rapid "communitari-anization" and the response of EU institutions and member-states to international migration. This chapter represents the institutional/policy dimension of the hypothesis that, despite state reluctance to surrender autonomy, there has been some progress toward harmonization and a common immigration policy. By identifying the character of the system that manages immigration, the chapter provides a background for comparing attitudinal input with policy output. Its longitudinal view helps to identify the factors that spur even limited cooperation.

Chapters 3 through 5 attempt to explain institutional developments by focusing on evolving norms. The chapters provide original empirical data on the cognitive and normative components of immigration policy as revealed by elected European legislators, national elites, and public opinion polls. The attitudinal framework incorporates survey research on both mass and elite attitudes, which are used to capture national, European, ideological, and party dimensions of interest organization (see appendices A and B for comprehensive treatment of data collection and methodology). Analysis of public opinion derives from Eurobarometer reports and consists of longitudinal and comparative data on immigration, xenophobia, and race, as well as European integration (for a more detailed description, see appendix A1).[33] Eighteen data sets were compiled for statistical testing of attitudinal measures that tap immigration and European integration over time. Bivariate and multivariate correlations were also run and are displayed graphically to show the relationship among the various attitudinal dimensions and national immigration contexts.

My approach to elite analysis follows other work on decision-makers (Putnam 1971; Axelrod 1977; Dalton 2002), and is not new to immigration research, though it has rarely been applied since Gary Freeman's (1979) early comparative work on elites in France and Britain. The primary data on which my elite analysis is based come from interviews and surveys with a sample of members of the European Parliament (MEPs) of the third assembly (1989–94), before the EU was expanded to include Austria, Finland, and Sweden (see appendix A for a full discussion of coding and measurement, and appendix C for survey instrument; see Lahav 1995). They represent twelve countries and nine party groupings (excluding the independents) and embody nearly eighty different national political parties.[34] Each of the 518 MEPs was sent a closed-ended written questionnaire; 168 responded.[35] The analysis was buttressed by in-depth interviews conducted with fifty-four MEPs.[36] The European Parliament offers a rare "test lab" for social scientists – a comparative framework from which to evaluate national, ideological, and transnational affinities as they relate to longitudinal policy developments in Europe (for a full discussion of this testing forum, see appendix A).[37]

To complement and broaden the analysis, discussions with various European elites, ranging from the media to national party politicians and bureaucrats, including the European Commission and ad hoc immigration groups, were conducted over the course of 1992–98. The voices of these European elites can be heard throughout the book, but for obvious reasons they must remain anonymous. They all tell stories of substantial divisions and policy orientations at one "snapshot" in time – as the construction of Europe passed from "project 1992" toward the post-Maastricht era. This snapshot thus represents a more static methodological approach than that provided by the longitudinal mass findings and policy analysis. Together, however, they contribute to a dynamic thesis, which presents an ongoing process of a Europe still in infancy or – at best – after forty-five years, still in its childhood.

I use these attitudinal data to analyze the extent to which states with considerable differences can organize and reconcile their interests in order to forge a common immigration policy. Is there a convergence in thinking? The following chapters attempt to disaggregate the causal factors of immigration attitudes and policy input.

In chapter 3, I offer a comparative attitudinal portrait of public opinion and elite preferences, as they reflect a myriad of competing interests. The story brings to light the ambivalent and paradoxical nature of attitudes surrounding controversial issues. I consider the much-understated role of public opinion in European migration regulation and examine the symmetry between public opinion and elites in an evolving democratic system. The data show a European public and a legislative body that are both rational and global in their thinking yet nationally protective.

Chapter 4 explores these attitudinal patterns in depth by delineating domestic variables, such as national identification, partisan affiliation, and ideological positions related to immigration thinking, which account for important differences in perception of and preferences for immigration policy. Ideological and national sources of attitudes form a basis for understanding (the limitations of) a collective strategy toward immigration policy-making in the EU. While the analysis reveals the persistence of traditional national and partisan/ideological orientations, it suggests that there is some convergence on immigration thinking that is related to the construction of Europe.

Chapter 5 examines this latter, "European" factor by disaggregating the institutional and psychological constraints of regional integration, which emphasizes the distinction between "us" (Europeans) and "them" (foreigners), religion, culture, and identity. The European factor affects immigration policy thinking and generates some attitudinal consensus and norms. These mitigate and, yet, reinvent the role of traditional competing alliances. While it is true that those in favor of immigration are also favorable toward European integration, neither elites nor the masses have fully embraced integration and the free movement of people. Therefore, it is too early to discard the traditional sources of thinking that continue to shape the immigration debate. This observation serves as a reminder that regional alliances still revolve around economic transactions and not the free movement of people.

The book concludes by assessing the prospects for a single immigration policy and the construction of a transnational European immigration regime. In identifying the alliances in and nature of a common immigration policy, the final chapter addresses the debate between intergovernmental and supranational views of cooperation and convergence. While the influence of national norms has been expected to impede regional interests and to be antithetical to regional cooperation, the attitudinal data reinforce the compatibility of these interests, once the liberal framework is abandoned. The book refutes the common argument that public opinion is too diffuse to influence policy, and that more progressive and influential elite, business, legal, or bureaucratic interests are likely to produce more liberal, open outcomes. I show, instead, how broadly the outcomes of restrictive policy in Europe reflect the shifting orientations of public and elite opinion which, on immigration, have tended to head in a restrictive direction.

The data expose a converse relationship between European integration and immigration policy that strikingly contrasts to the unilinear conceptualizations of globalization and regional integration. It reminds us that transnational cooperation or policy regimes – in cases as nationally dear as immigration – while they are slowly developing, continue to be informed by significant traditional interests. The analysis suggests that international immigration regimes may be oriented to protectionism and exclusion rather than the free borders, open markets, and liberal standards that are found in regimes for capital, goods, and services.

NOTES

1. "Europeanization" can refer to a number of slightly different phenomena including: the development of EU-level policies and/or policy networks (e.g., Risse, Cowles, and Caporaso 2001); an increase in positive evaluations of the EU (Niedermayer 1995a); the two-way institutionalization of Europe through norms and formal structures (e.g., Sandholtz and Stone Sweet 1998); top-down influences from the EU level to national systems (e.g., Ladrech 1994); policy-making patterns (e.g., Schmidt 1996; Falkner and Leiber 2003); or very broadly, the sum of all of these notions (e.g., Börzel 1999). I use it here to encompass broadly all of these dynamics and meanings.

2. The term "migrants" to mean the total of emigrants and immigrants is often used interchangeably with immigrants, foreigners, foreign-born, ethnic minorities, and non-nationals. This is a serious problem for survey researchers and demographers, as these categories are defined and measured differently across European countries. For the most part, "immigrants" is a legal term, while "foreign-born" is not. Data analysis should thus be read cautiously. Comparative trends can only be suggestive, as national variations exist.

3. Many of these promises were mixed. See chapter 2 for more detailed discussion of these treaties and conclusions; see also Geddes 2000, Guild and Niessen 1996, and Guild and Harlow 2001 for more comprehensive legal, institutional analyses.

4. Although this simplistic dichotomy of two "ideal types of governance" neglects the wide spectrum of approaches that are available, it follows the notion that EU policy cooperation lies on a continuum ranging from intergovernmentalism to supranationalism (see Stone Sweet and Sandholtz 1998: 8).

5. Theories of neofunctionalism have made two significant contributions to the understanding of integration: an expansive logic of interdependence, and an emphasis on attitudinal change (Taylor 1990: 133; Holland 1994; Deutsch *et al.* 1957; Haas 1961, 1968; Keohane and Nye 1989). Initially, this model does not depend on mass support, but rather on elite will in the economic sector which over time galvanizes public support with its development in other sectors.

6. While Schuck provides a legalistic trajectory of the devaluation of citizenship in liberal polities (1989, 1998), he explicitly rejects Soysal's and Jacobson's "post-national" arguments (1998: 202–205). He also talks about the "reevaluation" of citizenship especially in the United States since the 1990s as a response to public anxieties and other developments (ibid.: 176–206).

7. This use of the term "international regime" follows Steven Krasner's definition, and it refers to either implicit or explicit institutions (1983).

8. On the surface, it appears that intergovernmentalists all agree that national interests drive policy preferences. This consensus masks subtle disagreements between neorealists, who see cooperation to be purely a product of cost–benefit analysis of collective action (Hoffmann 1966), and neoliberal institutionalists, who see institutions such as the EU as "passive structures" which increase bargaining efficiencies by providing a set of transaction cost-reducing rules (Keohane 1984; Moravcsik 1993, 1998). This liberal intergovernmentalism is an example of what Keohane described as "modified structural realism," but it takes more account of domestic politics (1984).

9. This debate often postulates a golden age of state control that may never have occurred (Thomson and Krasner 1989), and sometimes suffers from a monolithic view of the state that omits domestic factors and limits national policy-making, such as self-imposed judicial control on action. According to Joppke, immigration-related "constraints on sovereignty are self-imposed, rather than externally inflicted" (1999: 262).

10. The argument has been made that these officials have, however, been able to gain more domestic legitimacy and leverage from their roles at the international or EU level.

11. Much of the neo-institutional literature focuses on formal institutional evidence to explain behavior and neglects the informal – normative – structures that impute dynamism to the equation. This is somewhat short-sighted, since, according to March and Olsen, rules include not only procedures and organizational forms, but also "beliefs, paradigms, codes, cultures, and knowledge that surround, support, elaborate, and contradict those roles and routines" (1989: 22).

12. It is important to distinguish policy elaboration from implementation (see Lahav 1997b).

13. For more comparative studies on immigration-related issues in Europe, see Brubaker 1989; Hansen and Weil 2001; Favell 1998b; Bleich 2002; Guiraudon 2000b; ECPR 2000; Brochmann and Hammar 1999; Uçarer and Puchala 1997; Messina 2002a.

14. For comprehensive treatment of immigration developments in the EU, see the work of Collinson 1994; Miles and Thränhardt 1995; Papademetriou 1996; Joppke 1998b; Koslowski 2000; Geddes 2000; Guild and Niessen 1996; Lavenex 1999; Guild and Harlow 2001; Groenendijk, Guild, and Minderhoud 2002; Lavenex and Uçarer 2002b.

15. Note that even rationalists would agree that a rational individual becomes interested in and informed about issues only when policy choices are outside an "acceptable" zone. That is, because it is costly to become informed about a policy issue, individuals will make such an investment only when the policy

option under consideration is substantially distant from his/her ideal point (Stimson 1991).

16. On the use of Eurobarometer surveys, and for a critique, see appendix A.

17. As Gabel persuasively argues, the EU, like all democratic institutions, depends on the consent and voluntary compliance of its citizens (legitimacy) but, unlike most nation-states, it lacks a supranational means of enforcement. Consequently, EU authority derives solely from the benign consent of national institutions, and ultimately, EU citizens (1998a: 7).

18. According to Gary Freeman, for example, the disconnect between a diffuse negative public and a more progressive elite may explain liberal outcomes (i.e., unwanted migration), or why immigration continues despite negative public opinion (1995). Fetzer suggests that highly educated and, hence, pro-immigration elites largely dismiss the prejudices of ill-informed publics (2000: 149). Others attribute liberal policy outcomes to the isolation of European elites making immigration policy by circumventing more restrictive national politicians and publics (Guiraudon and Lahav 2000; Guiraudon 2000a; Geddes and Guiraudon 2002).

19. The challenges of measuring factors such as individual differences, social factors, cultural differences, and norms make this type of research difficult. For a good discussion on this topic, see Glynn et al. 1999: 129–133.

20. In their study of elites, Aberbach, Chesney, and Rockman noted that elite attitudes served as important parameters in the behavioral equation: setting limits of the debate; directing inquiry and thought; influencing the interpretation of events; guiding the definition of problems and the response to them (1975: 2). Putnam interprets attitudes of parliamentarians to be synonymous with behaviors: thus, "most of their [parliamentarians'] behavior is not physical behavior at all, but verbal behavior; when we listen to politicians talk about politics and policy, we are in fact watching them behave" (1973: 26–27). He suggests that there is considerable overlap between parliamentarians' verbal behavior in interview situations and elsewhere.

21. These assumptions also overlap with neo-institutional frameworks and keep a balance between state-centric (rational-choice) and behavioral institutionalists who understand policy as a culmination of historically conditioned variables. State-centric institutionalists have shown compelling evidence of the self-interests of states and public officials that create institutional momentum and a capacity to act with relative autonomy. In this view, governments and elites are not neutral arbitrators of interests and values (see Gurr and King 1987). The behavioral corrective to reductionist interpretations of governance as power used by elites considers the important role of popular opinion as a causal factor (see Friedland and Alford 1991: 236–237).

22. In the literature on sociological institutionalism, the "logic of appropriateness" has been used to explain behavior as an outcome of sociocultural contexts. That is, the institutional context provides actors with a logic of appropriateness that effectively bounds the decisions/preferences they can make by way of norms (March and Olsen 1984). The "logic of appropriateness" idea allows us to understand the relationship between the public and elite, because we can view the public as creating (maybe unbeknownst to

themselves) an important type of institution, or system of norms relating to immigration and asylum, simply by having preferences on these issues. Thus policy-makers cannot simply choose from an infinite universe of possible stances on the issue; they are constrained by normative frames (see Checkel 1999). On the application to asylum issues, see Thielemann 2001 and forthcoming.

23. More recently, however, Jacobs and Shapiro argue that changing institutional and political dynamics in the United States since the 1970s raised the personal benefit to politicians of both pursuing policy goals, which decreased their responsiveness to centrist public opinion, and crafting their messages and actions to win over public opinion (2000: 70–71).

24. This perspective is particularly applicable to my comparative study, since it is based on a "most-similar" case selection of countries within a community of democratic political institutions that provide mechanisms for citizens to express their policy preferences. See Przeworski and Teune on "most-similar systems" method (1970).

25. This view does not take into account that elites, as leaders, often aim to transform mass opinion (Burns 1979).

26. This classic assertion can be traced back to Plato and Aristotle. As Hewstone (1986: 17) reminds us, even Machiavelli warned princes to take good note of the public's views: "I conclude, therefore, that when a prince has the goodwill of the people he should not worry about conspiracies; but when the people are hostile and regard him with hatred he should go in fear of everything and everyone. Well-organized states and wise princes have always taken great pains not to exasperate the nobles, and to satisfy the people and keep them content; this is one of the most important tasks a prince must undertake" (1961: 105).

27. Party groups dominate the organization and procedures of the European Parliament. They enjoy first priority in the allocation of posts and finances, choice of the Parliament's leaders, and the setting of the parliamentary agenda.

28. In contrast to the UK, where Thatcher's early shift to the xenophobic right stole the thunder of the British National Front (Kitschelt with McGann 1995; Thränhardt 1997), in the French case the mainstream right paid a heavier electoral toll in attempting to coopt the anti-immigration agenda of the Front national (see Guiraudon 2002b).

29. A 1988/89 report published by the Commission of the European Communities on "Racism, Xenophobia and Intolerance" identified relevant polarizations among the then twelve European Community countries based on a sample of 11,795 individuals (Commission of the European Communities 1989: 4).

30. The Commission issued special Eurobarometer reports in 1993/94 (40), 1997 (47.1), and 2000 (53) specifically to address the themes of racism and xenophobia or social exclusion.

31. According to Hix, for a number of questions concerning the EU agenda, the "variation in the rank ordering of the importance of issues by the left and right is as expected" (1999b: 157). Whereas parties in different European states

tend to have similar views about the role of the state (the left–right question), they are likely to have different views on European integration (Hix and Lord 1997: 26).

32. Based on Lijphart's work, Gabel argues that, "if EU citizens identify their political interests regarding integration solely along national lines, then the introduction of majoritarian democratic institutions may serve to aggravate national political conflicts over EU policy, and to reduce the prospects for compromise in a reformed EU" (1998a: 8). As a result, the "democratic deficit" may be replaced by a crisis in the stability of the EU.

33. The rich body of survey research on mass attitudes was collected biannually by the Inter-university Consortium for Political and Social Research (ICPSR) at the University of Michigan and reported in the European Commission's Eurobarometers series.

34. Paragraph 26 of Part A of the Edinburgh Declaration raised the total number of seats in the European Parliament elected in June 1994 to 567. It gave one new MEP each to Belgium, Greece, and Portugal; four to Spain; and six each to the UK, France, Italy, and the Netherlands. This was done to preserve political harmony by balancing the eighteen new seats given to Germany to reflect the incorporation of the former German Democratic Republic (see Church and Phinnemore 1994: 255). The total of seats in the EP was raised to 626 following the 1995 enlargement to include sixteen for Finland, twenty-one for Austria, and twenty-two for Sweden.

35. The sample group was representative of all countries and parties in the EP. Although in some cases the small size of the cells precluded tests of statistical significance, percentages were suggestive of differences. In addition, the sample size is substantial, considering high rates of absenteeism. In actuality, even the 260 votes required for the approval of a second reading of an amendment in the EP constitutes a two-thirds' majority of members normally present (Tsebelis 1992: 2).

36. The questionnaires as well as the oral interviews were conducted in English, French, or Italian. Interviews varied in length from forty minutes to four hours, and they were taped and coded for content analysis.

37. Since the 1990s, there have been increasing research attempts to theorize about cleavages from studies on the European Parliament. For more extensive work, see Attinà 1990; Bardi 1994; Franklin and Scarrow 1999; Schmitt and Thomassen 1999; Raunio 1997, 2000; Hix 2001a, 2002; Steunenberg and Thomassen 2002.

2 Toward a people's Europe: an institutional analysis of immigration policy in the European Union

Act II, Scene 1: In the spring of 1984, a large protest movement of lorry drivers erupted on the German–French border as a reaction to long queues. The ensuing paralysis of crossings at numerous internal European borders foreshadowed the Schengen Agreement, to pave the way for a gradual suppression of control of persons. Ironically, by the late 1980s, the Schengen group became the symbol of fortress Europe. This irony not only epitomizes the practical nature of freedom of movement, and its vital role in further integration, but it also unveils the proximity between "Europe without frontiers" and "fortress Europe."

(Diary of researcher, June 1997.)

Scene 2: How, finally, can we visualize freedom of movement and freedom of establishment for individuals within the Community, unless we gradually define the elements of a common immigration policy and adopt a comparable, positive attitude to the integration of immigrants already living among us?

(Jacques Delors, president of Commission, 1989: 26.)

The character of immigration and the European movement toward integration together have created a practical need for transnational regulation and standardized policy-making. A major question in considering EU progress on free movement has been: to what extent have European nation-states abdicated state-level and decision-making interests to forge a common immigration policy at the supranational level? This question can be readily answered by examining institutional developments at the ground level.

Whether intergovernmental or supranational in form, the contours of a common immigration policy are shaped by regional integration dynamics. Although the construction of Europe has been arduous and in constant flux, we can identify some important patterns as a measure of immigration cooperation in the EU. Before delving into underlying attitudinal dynamics that explain the path adopted toward integration, I turn in this chapter to the evolving institutional organization (i.e., intergovernmental or supranational) that structures immigration preferences and norms in the EU. The aim of this chapter is thus to outline in broad detail the critical institutional developments relevant to standardizing immigration policy-making. It provides a cursory examination of institutional trends that can be linked to the attitudinal surveys, and defers to a number of authoritative accounts of immigration and asylum policy in the EU (for more detailed accounts, see Geddes 2000; Guild and Harlow 2001; Lavenex 1999).

Using a realist/functionalist framework of analysis, I investigate what institutional attempts to build a common immigration and asylum regime tell us about competing theories of European integration. The chapter assesses the prospects for a collective immigration policy among member-states that not only have different immigration problems, but also have been seeking diverse national and EU policies. To gain any sense of why cooperation may take place, we need to consider the degree to which the integration of immigration and asylum issues may be a product of coinciding national interests, or separate EU pressures.

First, I review longitudinal immigration developments against those related to the construction of Europe. By comparing domestic conditions with EU institutional environments, we can distinguish European exogenous factors from national ones to explain policy outcomes. Second, I examine the level and substance of immigration cooperation. To what extent has cooperation taken place, and what is the policy orientation? Finally, I consider institutional explanations for these outcomes. The prevalence of national or EU factors in driving European immigration policy helps us discriminate between realist (intergovernmental) or neofunctional (supranational) paths to European integration.

The EU framework: widening and deepening

The present structure of the European Union is a culmination of political initiatives by Western European governments, inspired by a common determination to transcend national rivalries that had contributed to the outbreak of World Wars I and II. French foreign minister Robert Schuman's objective in integrating West Germany into Western Europe was to pool European coal and steel industries. This resulted in the 1951 Treaty of Paris, which established the European Coal and Steel Community (ECSC). The six countries (Belgium, France, Germany, Italy, Luxembourg, and the Netherlands) that formed the ECSC incorporated the key constitutional element that is the basis of the EU: they ceded some of their sovereignty to a supranational body. The success of the ECSC in contributing to regional economic growth led to a significantly more comprehensive European Economic Community (EEC) and European Atomic Energy Community (EURATOM), created by the Treaties of Rome in 1957. In 1965, the three treaties and their institutions were merged, leading to the more commonly known "European Communities" (EC).

With Community membership size more than doubling to fifteen member states by the early 1990s (following the addition of Denmark, the UK, and Ireland in 1973; Greece in 1981; Spain and Portugal in 1986; Austria, Finland, and Sweden in 1995), the scope for policy convergence has also gradually expanded. The Community accelerated the pace of its unification. The Single European Act (SEA), ratified in 1987, outlined a more comprehensive strategy for transforming the EC from a customs union into a fully integrated regional market by the end of 1992. It amended the Community's founding treaties to facilitate concrete progress toward European unity through institutional revisions, and strengthened common action in the economic, social, and foreign policy fields. Aiming to complete the internal market, the SEA endorsed the goal of free movement of goods, services, people, and capital, set by the Rome Treaty on establishing the EEC (i.e., the abolition of frontier controls), and it gave a more prominent legislative role to the European Parliament.

The Treaty on European Union (also known as the Maastricht Treaty), signed in 1992 and ratified in November 1993, incorporated the three previous treaties and the SEA, and created the European Union (EU). This Union deepened policy competence in the fields of political, legal-judiciary, economic, and monetary union, sought greater unity in foreign policy and security, and introduced the concept of a "European" citizenship. The Maastricht Treaty further strengthened the role of the European Parliament in Community decisions – an important victory for supranational forces.

Since the 1990s, the European Union has come to enjoy some features of supranationalism, which effectively establish a tier of government above that of the individual member-states. Its purpose has been to work toward "an ever closer union among the peoples of Europe," with law-making powers designed with that objective in mind (Commission of the European Communities 1992b: 7; see also Corbett, Jacobs, and Shackleton 2002 [1992]: 2). The introduction of European citizenship in the Maastricht Treaty serves as an important distinction between the Community and the Union, particularly since citizenship relates both to the democratic legitimacy of the Union, and to the evolution of policies on a "People's Europe" (Church and Phinnemore 1994: 39). The subsequent Treaties of Amsterdam (1997) and Nice (2000), as well as the

Tampere (1999), Laeken (2001), and Seville (2002) Summits, gave more impetus to immigration cooperation, and granted community institutions wider leverage to navigate – albeit not unbridled.

The deepening of Community institutions and policy links to include immigration and asylum has been complicated by efforts to widen EU membership. A large question that looms in the background of enlargement decisions relates to migration issues.[1] The prospect of an additional thirteen member-states, which would increase the EU area by 34 percent, poses many questions about Community solidarity and migration concerns.[2] Clearly, the evolution in the construction of Europe has profound implications for free movement of persons and for national immigration policies.

National immigration patterns in comparative perspective

The longitudinal view: patterns of convergence

Europe's inheritance of a diverse immigrant population has developed over three phases since World War II.[3] The evolution of immigration has been accompanied by changing demographic, structural, and policy needs, and has coincided with a shift in both the geographical origin of flows and the socioeconomic characteristics of migrants. These transformations have met a variety of national policy responses that have fluctuated from *laissez faire* policy in the early postwar years to a complete halt and even deportation by the late 1970s, to zero-immigration appeals by the 1990s.

The immediate postwar period constitutes the first phase in which many Western European countries saw immigration as a demographic and economic springboard for reconstruction and growth after the devastation of the war. A need for reconstruction and modernization led many European countries either to actively recruit foreign workers or to adopt some type of *laissez faire* immigration policy, which involved little or no social planning. A substantial component of this early migration was post-colonial in nature and not subject to legal channels, especially in countries such as Britain, France, and the Netherlands, where agreements with former colonies provided for special rights to former subjects. The sizeable migrant movements in this phase were guided by economic interests and largely escaped the control of political authorities.

The second phase emerged during the early 1970s, when economic and social crises created a new realization that it would be impossible to continue large-scale immigration.[4] Most West European countries were hit by economic recession and were facing growing unemployment and a large foreign population. A demand for the type of labor provided by migrants was declining as expansion of employment ceased and many manufacturing jobs were overshadowed by new production technologies. This phase of immigration was marked by mounting government intervention – especially through measures to halt labor migration and to encourage repatriation.[5]

By the 1980s, most European countries faced economic stagnation and the recognition that migrant workers had become permanent residents (Castles, Booth, and Wallace 1984; Rogers 1985). With critical questions posed by migrant integration and incorporation, the immigration issue had evolved from being primarily an economic and demographic issue into the social and political realm as well. The political dimension of immigration emerged as a growing specter of right-wing anti-immigration movements sent many mainstream parties scurrying to address the issue.[6] The politicization of the immigration issue was particularly discernible through developments in party politics. Before the 1970s, heavy immigration countries had witnessed a convergence of mainstream parties. In order to defuse immigration and race politics, discussions remained largely behind closed doors, and the issue was bureaucratically contained (Freeman 1979; Guiraudon 1997). In the 1980s, however, immigration entered into the rhetoric of electoral campaigns and social movements.

Not all European countries had achieved the same levels of economic development in the postwar period, nor did they experience these phases of immigration uniformly. The traditional north–south divide tended to reinforce differences in immigration developments. The "immigration" countries – primarily in Northern Europe – were profoundly affected by an influx of migrants. In contrast, the Southern countries of Europe (in addition to Ireland and Finland) were more generally referred to as "emigration" countries, with undeveloped immigration infrastructures and traditions.

The distinguishing mark of the third and latest phase of immigration lies in the changing nature of these divisions. By the 1990s the lines between "immigration" and "emigration" were obscured (Salt 1993: 192–196; Koch 1989). This "balancing out" period, as it became known, not only involved the blurring of traditional divisions that had separated the industrialized Northern European countries from the developing Southern ones, but it also entailed the uniform salience of immigration, amid growing unemployment. Although this characterization ignores the distinctive features in Southern European immigration, and how they differ from Northern Europe's experiences of immigration in the early postwar decades, we may speak of a shift in the Southern European immigration "model" that reflected the changing global nature of international migration (see King, Lazaridis, and Tsardanidis 2000 for detailed treatment).

By the 1990s, traditional "sending" countries such as Italy, Greece, Portugal, and Spain, countries that had never experienced large-scale immigration, now joined their EU partners in adding immigration to the political agenda. Now more dominated by sociopolitical and law-and-order considerations, immigration intake was significantly curbed, and the debate became dominated by questions of social integration and immigrant rights, as well as more long-term considerations of the "push–pull" dynamic. Exacerbated by changes in their eastern backyards, most Western European countries focused their immigration energies on border controls and illegal migration.

The political nature of immigration manifested itself in a paradoxical fashion by the turn of the twenty-first century. "New security" issues (i.e., ethnic conflict, terrorism, Islamic fundamentalism, and drug and human smuggling), which supplanted Cold War ideology, became the dark side of globalization that linked migration to crime, smuggling, terrorism, and other policing issues of law and order (Bigo 2001; Koslowski 1998b; Huysmans 2000). But renewed demographic and economic pressures stemming from population decline and aging in the advanced European countries introduced "replacement migration" as a policy option at a time when public resistance had become most visible.[7] These developments have given some credence to France's population expert Jean-Claude Chesnais's apocalyptic warning that, "in the coming years, Western Europe will have to coexist with hostility toward immigrants and a demand for immigration."[8] Despite economic revival, alarm bells have gone off throughout Europe, and have given a political and security spin to the social and demographic nature of immigration issues (Lahav 1992).

Over time, immigration policies, which had long been formulated behind closed doors and with little public attention, emerged as one of the most politicized issues on all Western European agendas. The issue gained salience in the international arena, as well. By 1991, the flurry of diplomatic meetings and conferences devoted to international migration attested to the fact that, in the language of international relations, the issue had gone from "low" to "high politics."[9] As national dynamics have coincided and the areas of EU cooperation have widened, the prospects for immigration cooperation have appeared more pressing and more promising.

Table 2.1 *Foreign populations in EU countries, 1990s*

Country	Total population (thousands)	Foreign population (thousands)	Foreigners as % of total population	EU foreigners as % of total population	Non-EU foreigners as % of total population
Austria	8,040	728.2	9.0	n.a.	n.a.
Belgium	10,143	910	9.0	5.5	3.6
Denmark	5,251	223	4.3	0.9	3.3
Finland	5,117	69	1.4	0.4	1.0
France[a]	56,577	3,597	6.4	2.4	3.9
Germany	81,817	7,173	8.8	2.2	6.6
Greece	10,465	155	1.5	0.4	1.0
Ireland	3,626	117	3.2	2.0[d]	1.2[d]
Italy[b]	54,780	1,095.6	2.0	0.2[d]	1.8[d]
Luxembourg[c]	419	142.8	34.1	27.3[d]	1.0[d]
Netherlands	15,494	726	4.7	1.2	3.5
Portugal	9,921	169	1.7	0.4	1.3
Spain	39,742	499	1.3	0.6	0.7
Sweden	8,837	531	6.0	2.0	4.0
UK	56,652	1,992	3.4	1.4	2.0

Note: OECD and Eurostat data are derived from population registers of foreigners, except for France (census), Portugal and Spain (residence permits), Ireland and the United Kingdom (Labour Force Survey). Figures do not equal total due to the differences in reports.

[a] OECD 1992 (reporting 1990 figures).
[b] OECD 1999 (reporting 1996 figures).
[c] Eurostat 1999b (reporting 1996 figures).
[d] Eurostat 1994 (reporting 1992 figures).

Sources: Data derived from Eurostat 1999b (reporting 1997 figures) unless noted otherwise; OECD 1992, 1999.

A comparative view: patterns of divergence

This longitudinal portrait of common national trends is, however, incomplete. While the various phases of Europe's migration phenomenon provide an evolutionary perspective of the issues that have emerged in all of the European Union countries, they misleadingly overlook the critical discrepancies *among* them which derive from diverse national interests and domestic contexts.

Although immigrants to the EU constitute only 4 percent of a population of 330 million, in countries such as France 11 percent of the population are foreign-born. National variations may be found in the composition and number of immigrants, and in the stage of their immigration process (see table 2.1 and appendices D and E for national demographic breakdowns of different types of migrant groups).

Figures must be read in the context of low rates of naturalization in countries such as Germany and higher ones in France, for example (Baldwin-Edwards and Schain 1994: 2; see appendix D for naturalization figures).[10] These figures also do not include the large numbers of illegal immigrants (an artifact of legal immigration policies) or different types of groups such as ethnic minorities (as in Britain), which are politically salient, and are certainly on many people's minds when they answer survey questions about immigrants. Also, although most migration statistics define an immigrant as "a person who settles for some time in a given country from outside that country," in practice, there are variations which may pertain to a minimum duration for such settlement (Council of Europe 1984: 8). By and large, data come from national censuses, population registers, or frontier controls, and are often not comparable between countries, since they reflect national definitions that vary.[11] These discrepancies have been used to bolster realist arguments about the state-centric nature of migration regulation through administrative formulations of migrant categories.

National policy-making patterns and practices among institutions have been rooted in cultural values and self-images. Beliefs, values, and symbols have weighed heavily on immigration policy-makers. As Miller and Mitchell poignantly noted, for historical reasons, the Swiss have not viewed policies toward aliens as a litmus test for their democratic values in the same manner as have the Germans (1993: 48). Similarly, the ideals of the French Revolution have played a role in formulating citizenship rights in France that has not been replicated in Germany or the United Kingdom. These principles and policy-making styles have determined state action toward immigration as well as in other issue areas.

Immigration in the European Union is a highly diverse phenomenon in terms of the populations involved, their conditions of access to the host country, and legal status there (i.e., refugees, asylum-seekers, labor migrants, family dependants, etc.; see appendix D). Although there is a tendency to conflate economic immigration with asylum issues (especially because of the link between fraudulent asylum-shopping and illegal migration), clearly for many European publics asylum and refugee issues are embedded in diverse emotional histories (Joppke 1997: 263; Lavenex 1999). In Germany, for instance, immigration problems have been typically associated with asylum-seekers, or Eastern European groups, many of whom are ethnic Germans and entitled to German citizenship. They are also linked to Turkish migrant workers (who were previously invited in) and their children born in Germany, many without citizenship. Similarly, in France, major concerns with integration apply to second- and third-generation French-born children of Algerian, Moroccan, and

Tunisian ex-colonial migrant workers, who have French citizenship. As Guiraudon points out, despite any move to harmonize humanitarian-based migration, it is still better to be an Algerian asylum-seeker in the UK than in France or Germany (2001a: 21).

Indeed, each country displays a specific set of attitudes toward the immigration issue – albeit the number of meanings to which the immigration issue is attached varies quite broadly. Not only is this borne out by the evidence in this study which taps into perceptions of immigration issues, and issue linkages,[12] but it is also reinforced by country case studies. Perceptions of immigration problems and the linkage to other policy issues may account for the close association of immigration with asylum and with *Ausländerpolitik* in Germany, or with integration in France. This may explain why in Britain, for example, immigration as an issue faded from electoral significance after the 1979 general election, but "race" issues had continued salience in the early 1980s as a consequence of urban unrest. In Britain and France, the immigration issue may be linked to race, and immigration literature tends to focus on research on the party system and the extreme right, or different models of integration (see Schain 1987, 1988; Weil 1991; Messina 1989; Layton-Henry 1984; Freeman 1979; Husbands 1988; Favell 1998b). In the Scandinavian countries, the issue is more tied to issues of the welfare state (Ryner 2000; Klausen and Tilly 1997; Klausen 1995). Both micro- and macro-level comparative analyses reveal significant nation-state differences on immigration and immigrant politics that emanate from cultural and historical traditions (see LeMay 1989; Hammar 1985b; Layton-Henry 1990; Freeman 1993; Brubaker 1989; Brochmann and Hammar 1999).

For the most part, patterns reflect policies of privileged relations between certain sending and receiving countries, linked by historical, cultural, economic, and/or political affinities (Münz 1996) as well as ex-colonial relations (Messina 1996: 142–144). The geopolitical context of these migration dynamics has left indelible differences in the perception of immigration issues among the Western European countries. Thus, countries such as France, Belgium, and (since the late 1980s) Italy and Spain tend to see demographic pressure from North Africa and the Middle East as a central problem, whereas in Germany, Austria, and Scandinavia, the major concern is about immigration from Eastern Europe.

The general phases of immigration described earlier serve as a reference point by which one can evaluate the position of individual European countries with different political cultures, institutions, socioeconomic and demographic pressures, and immigration experiences (for in-depth examination, see national profiles in appendix E). These differences are particularly relevant in context of changing conditions generated by European integration efforts themselves.

The policy framework: toward harmonization

Since the challenge for the EU is harmonizing national trends, it is useful to consider the substantive discrepancies that are rooted in distinctive immigration experiences. National provisions for immigrants vary widely, and they may be systematically informed by Hammar's comparative schema (1985b). Accordingly, immigration policy may be distinguished along two "separate but inextricably linked" policy components generating four criteria:[13]

I Immigration regulation and alien control, including policy on privileged aliens, family reunification, free movement in the EU:
   (a) "strict" or "liberal" control of the admission and residence of foreign citizens (e.g., entry based on quotas of geographical origin or professional qualifications);
   (b) guarantees of "permanent status," legal security vs. vulnerability to arbitrary expulsion.

II Immigrant policy, including political, social, and economic rights:
   (a) indirect: immigrants' inclusion in the general allocation of benefits, "equal" vs. "discriminatory" distribution;
   (b) direct: special measures on behalf of immigrants, "affirmative action" and the removal of legal discrimination.

Elaborating on this comparative policy framework, the research questions here consider the substantive discrepancies that emerge in these areas of both immigration policy (pertaining to intake) and immigrant policy (related to questions of incorporation). This dichotomy offers a map of the complex institutional and bureaucratic maze that emerges from competing cross-sectoral interests in each arena.

Since this study is premised on the challenge of harmonizing immigration trends fundamentally rooted in idiosyncratic experiences, it is necessary to identify the different areas and national dynamics that are subject to conformity in the EU. Such an analysis provides a link to the views of elites and masses and the national immigration *problematiques* with which they deal. The following policy areas reveal essential national variations that require harmonization under a common immigration policy.[14]

I. Immigration policy: strict or liberal

(A) *Privileged aliens* Each nation has a distinctive history and foreign policy agenda, which have influenced its perspectives on entry of certain non-EU citizen groups. Belgium, for example, accords privileged status to nationals of Monaco, Liechtenstein, Iceland, and Scandinavia, who have an automatic right of residence. Denmark, as a member of the 1954 Nordic Labour Agreements, grants unrestricted travel and employment to nationals of Finland, Norway, Sweden, and Iceland. Germany grants special status to *Aussiedler* or ethnic Germans, and makes special regulations for Polish, Hungarian, US, Austrian, and Swiss nationals.

(B) *Family reunification* The most outstanding areas requiring harmonization continue to be those outlined by a 1992 report of the European Commission on family reunification (V/384/92, 1992c: 40).[15] This includes: the residence qualification period for applying for family reunification; the rights of first- and second-degree relatives in the ascending line; the rights of children who are not dependent or who have reached the age of majority; and the period of validity of the first residence permit and the possibility of obtaining a personal residence permit. The varied definitions regarding suitable accommodation and the meaning of sufficient resources also need to be addressed. The differences between member-states are found less in the general conditions of family reunification policies than in the way in which they are interpreted. The range of family members who can be admitted varies under national regulations (see appendix D). National laws on family reunification may also vary according to types of residence permits (i.e., work permit, "guest-worker," etc.). There are significant differences in the ways member-states' nationals are treated in that, in their own country, such persons come under national legislation pertaining to family members, in terms of both the definition of a family member, and conditions of entry to the national territory and admission to the labor market. Thus, in certain cases, the non-EU family members of a national would appear to be subject to more stringent conditions than the non-EU family members of a national of another member-state residing in the *same* country (Commission to the European Communities 1992c: 40).

(C) *Free movement in the EU* Non-EU nationals, whatever their rights of residence, are not given the right of free movement unless they are family members of EU nationals. This means that national policies on visa requirements determine whether or not an immigrant will be permitted to visit any other EU country.

II. Immigrant policy: inclusive or exclusive

(A) *Rights of residence* Residence permits are required for all non-EU nationals wishing to reside in a member-state. Durations of residence permits vary according to country and purpose of stay.

(B) *Rights of employment* The policy of all member-states is to give priority to EU nationals and other "privileged" aliens. Work permits for third-country migrants are given only when the post cannot otherwise be filled. These are employer-, work-, place-, and time-specific according to member-state. Third-country nationals have no protection in law from discrimination of any description in Community law. They cannot rely on the European Court of Justice for protection against unfair dismissal from employment on grounds of race or from the refusal of particular employers to employ people from ethnic minorities or to limit their employment to low grades. The rights of third-country nationals to associate, to join trade unions, and to obtain standards of health and safety in the workplace, which pertain to EC nationals and EC migrants, are not a concern of any organ of the Community. These provisions depend solely on national legislation (i.e., the UK's Race Relations Act of 1976 forbids race discrimination in a number of social fields [Joint Council for the Welfare of Immigrants 1989: 24]).

(C) *Political rights* Certain states grant the right to vote and stand in local elections by virtue of a period of residence. Some countries grant national enfranchisement to "privileged" aliens (i.e., Irish and Commonwealth citizens in the UK, Brazilians in Portugal [Baldwin-Edwards 1991b: 205]).

(D) *Education* There is little theoretical restriction on access to education, although access to study grants varies by means of foreign students' fees and foreign student admission quotas.

(E) *Citizenship* Citizenship of an EU country guarantees security of residence, voting rights, political and public employment rights, and freedom of movement within the EU. Two entirely different means of citizenship acquisition at birth exist (and a combination of them) and they vary according to national domestic law: *jus sanguinis*, by parental nationality, or *jus soli*, by birthplace. Discrepant citizenship acquisition means that a Turk born in German territory to Turkish parents who may also be born in Germany (which follows *jus sanguinis* principles) has less employment and movement rights than a Turk born in Belgium (who, through *jus soli*, has Belgian citizenship and therefore is an EU national) or a French citizen migrating to Germany. The rules for naturalization or citizenship after birth also vary tremendously in terms of required years of residence, as well as regulations on dual nationality (see appendix D).

(F) *Anti-discrimination* Often interchanged with broader and less controversial concepts such as "social exclusion" or "social inclusion," anti-discrimination legislation is a more loaded and contested term.

Although its more precise association is to the particular integration model in the UK and laws against racial discrimination which have existed in a number of EU countries, it is not solely targeted at migrants, and includes disabled people, elderly people, women, and other minority groups.

Nations differ with respect to rights of residence, employment, family reunification, education, housing, voting, citizenship acquisition, visa requirements, anti-discrimination, and privileged status. Each member-state of the EU has had to deal with asylum and refugee policy, clandestine immigration, and legal immigration. While asylum and refugee policies have been more open to common humanitarian-based and foreign policy concerns, immigration flows have been largely dictated by labor and interior ministries, or national exigencies. Each nation-state has also recognized that immigration involves culturally distinct groups with diverse professional skills. National policies, however, show clear divergence with regard to these groups.

There are obviously pressures on larger regional integration dynamics that stem from disparate national positions on immigration-related issues. The following section evaluates decision-making and institutional responses at the EU level over time.

The evolution of "free movement of persons" in the European Union

The making of European policies on the free movement of persons[16] has been a long and complicated process, marked by a particular set of structures and norms. Decision-making in a unified Europe has broadly vacillated between two traditional approaches: the active involvement of all Community institutions (supranational, functional, political unity or communitarian approach); or direct consultations between the Community's member-states (intergovernmental or national approach). In contrast to the former model, intergovernmentalism assumes no federation and no supranationality, but ongoing interstate bargaining among national governmental organs (i.e., heads of states, ministers, ambassadors) who meet several times a year and reach decisions by unanimous voting. The conflicting trends between the two main decision-making approaches have dominated the evolution of European integration, critically affecting progress on a collective immigration policy.

EU dynamics have notably reflected immigration developments at the national levels, as they have fluctuated in emphasis from economic to social and political considerations. Each stage has been accompanied by institutional wrangling and reforms and by substantive changes in policy.

Although not commonly or methodically studied as part of the "multilevel governance" literature on the EU (see Marks *et al.* 1996; Guiraudon 2000a; Hooghe and Marks 2001), migration policy has evolved as it has been exposed to a multitude of decision-making locations and bodies that have vied for competence and jurisdiction. These include a set of European institutions such as the Commission, Parliament, and Court of Justice as well as a network of experts, national ministries, subnational groups, NGOs, security officials, and ad hoc groups.

Phase 1: economic interests, intergovernmental cooperation, and labor migration

From its genesis through the early 1970s, the first phase of Union activity on immigration was rather limited in scope and, as in national debates, was driven mostly by economic imperatives (e.g., immigration was to be for employment only). The right to freedom of movement was recognized in the three founding treaties of the European Communities: namely the Treaty of Paris, establishing the ECSC in 1951; and the two Treaties of Rome, establishing the EEC and EURATOM in 1957. Because the underlying objectives of the Community Treaties were geared to economic ambitions, these instruments were inherently narrow from the beginning.

First, while the 1957 Treaty founding the EEC established the free movement of workers within the context of economic integration, this did not become a reality until 1968. At this time, the first transitional period stipulated by Article 48 on the free movement of workers and Article 52 on the freedom of establishment for self-employed expired, and EEC Regulation 1612/68 on freedom of movement for workers within the Community was issued (Hovy and Zlotnik 1994: 20).[17] Second, free movement was not originally conceived for persons as citizens, but as workers. Moreover, the Treaty dealt with migration of workers and self-employed citizens of the European member-states only and did not include nationals of a third country (EEC Treaty, Title III, Arts. 48.2, 48.3, and 52). Finally, the economic rationale of the European Communities meant that rights of migrant workers to be accompanied by close relatives would be addressed only later, by secondary law in the form of directives or regulations.[18] Although admissions for non-economic migrants, such as those migrating for family reunification, were theoretically established by the Rome Treaty itself, progress in that direction had been slow because of the different national standards of professional qualifications and training, as well as limitations in definitional criteria.[19]

Throughout the early phases of EU immigration policy-making, the competence of EC institutions thus remained relatively limited, particularly in areas concerning non-EC or third-country nationals. Although the "juridicization" of migration policy through the jurisprudence of courts, constitutional and legal principles, and even international instruments led to the reduction across the board of arbitrary administrative powers, legal protection was geared mostly toward rejected asylum-seekers and certain expelled groups (e.g., family members).[20] States sought to maintain as much sovereignty as possible in matters relating to third-country nationals, and most member-states believed that they were completely free regarding immigration law *vis-à-vis* non-EC nationals (Callovi 1990: 21). As member-states refused to delegate sovereignty over these issues to EC institutions, most of the work concerning cooperation and harmonization took place at the intergovernmental level.

Phase 2: social considerations, limited cooperation, and selective movement

A mood for more rapid European integration marked a new phase of collective activity on immigration during the 1980s. Two trends were notable during this phase: a momentum toward a common immigration policy coincided with more limited rights for migrants. A 1985 Council communication, entitled "Guidelines for a Community Policy on Migration," marked the first time the term "Community" was found alongside "migration policy" (Callovi 1992: 356). The creation of a Passport Union in 1981 reaffirmed a vision of a "people's Europe" with Europeans moving around freely and ultimately developing a European identity, but this remained an abstraction for some time. While the Single European Act signed in 1986 confirmed the four freedoms anchored in the 1957 Rome Treaty (the free movement of goods, persons, services, and capital), it also reaffirmed the primacy of economic objectives. The free circulation of people came *after* that of goods.

Although the adoption of the SEA in 1987 reflected increased efforts to establish a single internal market by the end of 1992, provisions for migration were limited in application (Articles 8a and 8b, SEA).[21] The word "people" was not intended to involve all residents, and so the Treaty legislation was applicable only to EC nationals and their families, and excluded the 12–15 million residents who were non-EC nationals.[22] The anomalous situation of a large migrant community who fell outside EC legal competence led to the creation of what many observers called "two migrant communities" (Joint Council for the Welfare of Immigrants 1989: 5). During this second period, the major obstacle for a common

European immigration policy turned to the future status of "third-country nationals," or those immigrant groups with privileged status and the right of residence in one member-country.

This period was accompanied by two contending institutional impulses: one manifested on the EC level, the other on the intergovernmental one. In the first case, an attempt to "communitarize" immigration put more power in the hands of community institutions, such as the Commission, a momentum that followed the advent of direct elections for the EP in 1979.[23] On the other side, although the Commission inherited legal competence (as arbitrator between two nation-states) to take procedural decisions relating to immigration from non-member states, the General Declaration appended to the SEA required unanimous voting for measures concerning the free movement of persons from non-EC countries. This in effect preserved national boundaries and idiosyncrasies, since in order to differentiate members from non-members border controls needed to remain intact.[24]

More notably, this period witnessed the surge of immigration measures flourishing outside Community structures (Dummett and Niessen 1993: 5). While the first attempt to coordinate national immigration and asylum policies in the European Community was made in October 1986, under the UK presidency and within the context of the SEA, its structure was intergovernmental, and not part of the framework of the European Community.[25] The Ad Hoc Group on Immigration (AHI), created by the interior and justice ministers in 1986, later expanded to formal meetings of member-state immigration ministers on a six-month basis, operating under the coordination of the EU Commission. It set off a flurry of intergovernmental and ad hoc group meetings explicitly for immigration matters. Prior to the ratification of the Maastricht Treaty in 1993, AHI and its working groups held over 100 meetings a year.[26]

While the initial proliferation of these intergovernmental groups reflected essentially national efforts to control immigration through coordinated measures, they also represented the two-speed character of Europe. For example, the 1985 Schengen Agreement was originally signed by only five of the EC countries, France, Germany, and the Benelux countries; the group was believed to serve as a model or, as the European Commission itself termed it, as a "laboratory of what the Twelve would have to implement by 1992" (Pastore 1991: 6). The Agreement aimed at making faster progress in the dismantling of internal frontiers, particularly among the signatory member-states, with gradual harmonization of immigration and security issues as long-term goals. Ultimately the efforts to seriously coordinate free movement prompted more *restrictive* controls over borders. In this sense, the intergovernmental mode of cooperation favored "lowest-common-denominator" interests (i.e., the "laboratory" countries, the original Schengen signatories which were on the fast track, France, Germany, and Benelux).

The evolution of the Schengen Group captures the restrictive implications of coordination for migration. Although commonly understood as an early attempt to tighten up frontiers against immigration, the *raison d'être* of the Schengen Area originated as a reaction to roadblocks set up by truckers who were disgruntled by long waits at intra-EC borders. Migration only later developed as a key issue. The ensuing paralysis of crossings at numerous frontier posts led to quick reactions of Germany and France in signing the Sarrebruck Accord (the precursor of the Schengen Agreement) which provided for the gradual suppression of control of persons at the Franco-German border. Nevertheless, the group was reluctant to let in other members, fearful of allowing entry to those countries that were historically weak on border control. Similarly, not all members had found acceptable the repercussions that membership incurred: open borders and the inheritance of other members' immigration-related problems (e.g., problems of social integration). These conditions, in addition to the growth in the number of asylum-seekers and increasing focus on illegal migration, led to the adoption of more restrictive measures on immigration and asylum (Cruz 1993).

Throughout the 1980s, issues related to the movement of persons exposed the anomalies embedded in the construction of Europe. By 1993, the "free movement of goods, services and capital" prescribed by the SEA was possible, but not freedom of persons. In spite of the idea of creating a single European economy by establishing a common market as defined by the Treaty of Rome, many of the original barriers to the internal market survived for thirty years. Many fundamental issues related to movement were untackled. The EC that was born out of Jean Monnet's functional theory envisaged economic integration as a spillover means toward ultimate political union. In leaving open a number of policy matters that were bound to arise as the Community gradually dismantled its internal border controls, the supranational vision was compromised by the immigration issue.

Although the tensions related to free movement were inescapable by the early 1990s, when the costs of a two-speed Europe began to be felt, any further move toward cooperation was accompanied by more restrictive immigration developments. Starting in 1990, there were repeated calls for "burden-sharing" among the twelve EC states in handling the large numbers of refugees and asylum-seekers concentrating in the territory of a few of the member-states, such as Germany (see appendix D).[27]

The fall of the Berlin Wall and the dramatic events in 1989 were initially met with celebration, which quickly turned to great trepidation about a migration deluge from the east (Lahav 1991, 1992). The subsequent exodus to the west and the use of the asylum system for immigration purposes made nation-states very protectionist (Joppke 1998a). In the context of an imminent "Europe 1992" deadline, asylum issues were placed in a "securitarian frame"[28] (Lavenex 1999; Guiraudon 2003), and the lines between migration and asylum systems were blurred. Asylum issues thus became instrumental in pushing member-states to cooperate in order to avert asylum-shopping and to control migration.

Any move toward harmonizing immigration or asylum policy was marked by renewed efforts to limit applications. In 1990, for example, EC immigration ministers adopted the Dublin Convention Determining the State Responsible for Examining Applications for Asylum Lodged in One of the Member-States of the European Communities. Although Dublin based itself on the Geneva Convention, as its name implied, the aim was to establish the principle that only one EC state should be responsible for determining the validity of an asylum claim.[29] This effort to deter asylum-shopping was fortified by the "safe third country" principle, which attempted to move the burden of asylum-seekers as far away from EU borders as possible[30] and, later, by the Eurodac finger-printing system.[31]

Schengen initiatives further narrowed the possibilities for free movement. The Schengen Group, expanded to include more members, concluded a Supplementary Agreement of June 1990 aimed at removal by 1992 of controls between common frontiers and the correlative strengthening of borders between Schengen members and non-members. The group gained credibility by the expansion of its membership to include Italy, Spain, and Portugal, with Greece becoming a full member in November 1992. The negotiations for the 1990 Supplementary Agreement of the Schengen Convention demonstrated how sensitive these issues were likely to be for EC member-states to resolve jointly, and to implement. Among controversial issues in negotiations were (and remain) the lack of transparency, human rights issues, and the Schengen Information System (SIS), a computer database that served as the backbone of the Schengen Agreement. Although SIS was intended to hold data relating to aliens, asylum-seekers, criminals, firearms, vehicles, and persons under surveillance by a state security agency, this kind of data transmission became controversial on ideological grounds because of data protection safeguards and individual rights.

Although many essential points were left undecided, and the Group was forced to revise its timetable for final implementation several times, the Schengen system made some noteworthy advances toward tightening internal borders. As a consequence of EC and Schengen commitments to strengthen external frontiers, all the Southern European member-states increased coastguard patrols, police checks on third-country nationals, and deportations (Butt Philip 1994: 179–180).[32] The upshot of immigration cooperation was protectionism.

The seeds of restrictive cooperation were sown by 1990. Notably, the Dublin Convention and Schengen Agreements bore the hallmarks of lowest-common-denominator bargaining. They were intergovernmental in structure, were adopted outside the EU communitarian framework, and were subject to national dynamics, which explained why their implementation would be delayed by almost ten years (i.e., Dublin [1997] and Schengen [1995] came into force seven and ten years respectively after they were signed).

Phase 3: political concerns, mounting supranationalism, and restrictive immigration

Immigration entered a third phase in the 1990s, marked by more serious attempts to bring immigration under EU jurisdiction, and to make Union decision-making bodies more central to the debate. EC institutions themselves began to articulate their interest in immigration issues more strongly.[33] In 1993, the European Parliament filed a complaint against the European Commission for failing to ensure the free movement of persons within the Union. The EP became more adamant in demanding that matters relating to "third-country" migrants be brought explicitly within EU competence (Recommendations 47, 56 [1990]).[34] These developments coincided with an overall new spirit inspiring the construction of the European Union.

The Maastricht Treaty or the Treaty on European Union (TEU, ratified in 1993) introduced the concept of European citizenship at the same time as it formally recognized the need for a serious common immigration policy.[35] The outcome of the intergovernmental conference on political union (the Maastricht negotiations) was to make visa policy part of the competence of the EU institutions and to include cooperation at the intergovernmental level on asylum, refugee, and immigration issues in the so-called third pillar of the TEU. Although Title VI, Article K, of the Treaty defined "matters of common interest" as asylum policy, visa policy, immigration policy, third-country nationals, and illegal migration, they were to be dealt with on an intergovernmental basis, leaving goals and implementation strategies to national and administrative interpretation.[36] This meant that migration matters were not necessarily the domain of the

Commission, nor were decisions automatically subject to judicial review by the Court of Justice.[37] The unanimity rule for the Council excluded the democratic and judicial oversight of the Court, the Parliament, and the Commission, which lost its right of initiative, and thus its traditional agenda-setting role.

Although several measures were undertaken at the European level toward the construction of European-wide immigration policies,[38] many provisions were seen to pave the way for more restrictive policies than had already been in place.[39] EU Treaty-based institutions could lead on visa policy, but it was left to individual states, acting separately, to make policy and administrative changes (Butt Philip 1994: 184). Moreover, Maastricht gave credibility to the Schengen "model," as it formally incorporated its intergovernmental agenda. The Maastricht Treaty gave immigration issues more attention, but it did not provide a coherent strategy to overcome the anomalies that had plagued the previous phases. The pillar structure also had the effect of internally dividing community institutions, such as the Commission.[40]

The conflict between national and supranational competences was both preserved and formalized by creating a three-pillar system.[41] Although the Treaty upgraded the role of the European Parliament,[42] a supranational force, it also delegated migration matters largely to justice and home affairs ministers, the third pillar. The communitarian approach was adopted to facilitate free movement of EU citizens within the Union, and to promote equal treatment of these persons. The intergovernmental approach was institutionalized to deal with asylum and immigration from outside the Union, and to be dealt with within the framework of cooperation on justice and home affairs (third pillar).[43] The three-pillar structure established by the Maastricht Treaty left unresolved many contentious points concerning immigration-related issues and the intergovernmental third pillar.

Among these divisive issues were questions regarding the jurisdiction of the European Court of Justice; whether the JHA pillar should be merged into the EC framework (the first pillar); institutional efficiency/democracy; the establishment of a European Information System (EIS); how to establish a common policy against racism and xenophobia; and issues of basic human rights, including the accession to the Council of Europe's Convention on Human Rights (Hix and Niessen 1996). More significantly, although a common visa list was adopted by the Council of Ministers in 1995, the EU was still to deal with the rights of third-country nationals (TCNs) or nationals of non-member states of the Union who had acquired the right to residence in a member-state.

Some of these issues were revisited in the 1997 Amsterdam Treaty, which came into force in May 1999. But many decisions were again shelved for later dates (at least for five years).[44] The inadequacies of decision-making structures and procedures under the third pillar were partially addressed by the Amsterdam Treaty's inclusion of Title IV in the EC Treaty, which shifted issues of asylum, admission, and residence of third-country nationals and immigration from the third to the first pillar. The transfer of the third pillar to the Community pillar under Title IV signified a gradual step toward a supranational immigration policy (for the evolutionary logic of JHA, see Monar 1998, 2000; Monar and Morgan 1994; Stetter 2000; den Boer and Wallace 2000). Nonetheless, it was a partial move again, given that, like the Schengen Agreement when it finally entered force in 1995, Title IV excluded Denmark, Ireland, and the United Kingdom, which reserved the right to not participate in the Council of Ministers' adoption of Title IV (entitled "Visas, Asylum, Immigration, and Other Policies Related to Free Movement of Persons") measures.

The Amsterdam Treaty indeed continued to bear the mark of persistent tension between intergovernmental and supranational control over EU immigration policy. The newly created Title IV seemed to have manifestly increased the level of supranational control over migration issues, but vestiges of intergovernmentalism remained. The European Court of Justice was circumscribed, the Council still retained control over decisions made in the realms of immigration and asylum, and unanimity still pertained to these issues (see Guiraudon 2003, for varying national motivations behind this intergovernmental position). The Treaty allowed for a time period of five years during which the right of initiative would be transferred to the Commission, and during which other important institutional changes were to be made (i.e., resolving issues such as how much input the EP should have).[45] The incorporation of anti-discrimination provisions (Articles 13 and 137)[46] was a victory for pro-integrationist forces, such as the Commission, Parliament, and a slew of pro-migrant NGOs.[47] But, as Geddes concludes, the restrictionist direction of immigration and asylum policy outcomes suggests that lobby groups found it difficult to impact upon decision-making (1999: 185).

Despite the Amsterdam Treaty's objectives to expand competence over third-country nationals, member-state discretion in this domain ensured little progress (Guild 1998; see Kostakopoulou 2000). Since the EC Treaties did not give European institutions a mandate to enact legislation on matters related to non-EC nationals, the treatment of approximately 13 million third-country nationals remains largely outside the EU's scope and within that of Association, Cooperation, and Europe Agreements between the Community and third countries (i.e., the latter two with Central and East European countries, and the former with Turkey and the Maghreb countries).[48] Most of these agreements grant certain rights of residence, working conditions, social security, and access to the labor market, but there have been considerable problems of enforcement (Baldwin-Edwards 1997: 502).

The Tampere Summit in 1999 attempted to respond to Amsterdam's inability to provide for the rights of third-county nationals by making a strong plea for reform. It endorsed the Council of Ministers' newly established (December 1998) High-Level Working Group on Asylum and Immigration (HLWG) and its cross-pillar proposal to end the monopoly of the migration agenda by Interior Ministries (Niessen 1999: 10). The Summit also called for the establishment of "a Common European Asylum System, based on the full and inclusive application of the Geneva Convention" (European Council 1999).[49] Not only did the professed intentions of the Conclusions foreshadow a bold move toward suprana-tionalization, they also implied changes in policy regarding the rights of TCNs for free movement. Such rhetoric did not, however, result in any policy shift, as Tampere failed to make substantive institutional changes that might allow any reform to come about.

The 2000 Treaty of Nice continued to build on the momentum toward supranationalization. It took a significant step in increasing the level of supranational influence over a European immigration and asylum policy when it decided that a large number of issues included under Title IV would be adopted under the co-decision procedure.[50] The adoption of the co-decision procedure, as well as a much more sympathetic stance toward both the rights of refugees and the Europeanization of asylum policy, was a sizeable victory for pro-supranationalization forces. Nonetheless, as with other advances in immigration cooperation, Nice "compensated" for Europeanization by accommodating the more entrenched intergovernmental forces.

By making qualified majority voting (QMV) more difficult, the Nice Treaty institutionalized national interests through lowest-common-denominator bargaining (Garrett and Tsebelis 1996). It added, for example, a new clause (Art. 67, TEC) that made QMV conditional on prior unanimous adoption of Community legislation. According to Lavenex, the decision of the European Council in Nice against QMV in asylum matters confirmed the enduring reluctance of member-states to transfer sovereignty in this area (2001: 865–866).

With the mounting success of extreme-right and populist parties throughout Europe (including those in France, the Netherlands, Germany, Denmark, Austria, Italy, Belgium, and Norway), which played on rising concerns about security and illegal migration in the post-9/11 world, the European Council at Laeken in December 2001 moved to strengthen and hasten common standards on external border controls (European Council 2001). National leaders placed immigration on the forefront of the EU agenda at Seville.[51] Indeed, in their efforts to concretize the Tampere Conclusions and to create a joint immigration and asylum policy for the EU, the Seville Summit in the summer of 2002 was accused of creating a "Fortress Europe." Amid many national contentions, the plan adopted in Seville provided for more resources for border enforcement in front-line nations, and laid the foundation for a common border policy agency and Europe-wide anti-smuggling task forces. It also proposed strategies for working with migrant-sending countries, such as repatriating captured illegal immigrants, improving cooperation, and even denying generous EU economic aid to countries that failed to cooperate (European Council 2002).

A broad summary of the three phases of EU immigration dynamics reveals a pattern of limited cooperation interspersed with selective migration policies. In more general terms, the right of movement of persons across Europe has developed substantially since the creation of the European Community in the postwar period, but is still ridden with disparities and contradictions that are embedded in the construction of Europe. As free movement provisions have evolved, each phase has reinforced different emphases in Union or communitarian policy-making and Community consolidation. Thus, while the first stage essentially emphasized the economic and labor concerns of a common market, the later stages have focused on the integration of people into a European Union. The different orientations reflect deeper attitudes toward community; the more recent strategy is a sign of reopening social contracts embodied in the welfare state regimes of the postwar period (Heisler 1992: 610). The aim of the Maastricht Treaty was to go beyond the economic motivations of the EC, and to create a European Union, integrated socially and politically. This evolution is best reflected by the change in name from the European Community to the European Union. With increasing integration in different arenas, the construction of Europe has transcended its original economic rationale.

As the above discussion underscores, these changes have coincided with institutional developments in the EU. The recasting of the European Parliament – from its inception as a mainly advisory body to an integral decision-making forum – for example, has been said to reflect the institutional strengths of the EU in the construction of a "people's Europe" (Palmer 1983).[52] Decision-making processes have been transformed from having a predominantly informal and behind-the-scenes nature to displaying a more public and political character – epitomized by the creation of the European Parliament's Committee of Civil Liberties and Internal Affairs in 1992,[53] and a commissioner in charge of justice and home affairs in 1999, to deal explicitly with immigration matters. The "deepening" of the EU to include free movement of peoples over time has been marked by gradual institutional cooperation *and* restrictive policy outcomes.

To date, although instruments have gradually expanded the right to free movement to groups other than workers, they have not established completely free movement within the Community. First, the EU has not resolved the status of third-country nationals or nationals of non-member states of the Community who have acquired the right to residence in a member-state. Second, legal admission for categories such as family reunion is contingent upon proof that the persons in question will not become a burden on the host member-state. Third, not only are Community citizens wishing to relocate obliged to present proof of independent economic viability for the whole period of their residence in the host state, they are also subject to considerable local control through the issuance of residence permits (Hovy and Zlotnik 1994: 26). Finally, to the extent states have agreed on accelerated procedures for examining asylum requests, a common definition of a refugee, the Dublin Convention, the Eurodac fingerprinting system, and "safe third country" principles, any EU-wide policies on asylum now coincide with migration control systems. This has not only collapsed the distinct public constituencies for asylum and migration that could preserve migration support, but it has given credence to a "Europe to the rescue" notion – a strategy of policy delegation to the EU level as a way of avoiding domestic adversaries (Guiraudon 2000a; Lahav and Guiraudon 2000). That is, cooperation could undercut even the most liberal national policies for asylum (Joppke 1998a: 122–130).

The lack of progress in these areas stems from the fact that the control of migration is closely linked to national sovereignty. Governments of member-states are finding it difficult to reconcile their sovereign interests and security requirements with the commitment to build an internal market. Consequently, many negotiations regarding the movement and stay of third-country nationals have remained within the framework of intergovernmental cooperation through a variety of ad hoc working groups. In fact, the gap between EU and non-EU citizens widened when the Maastricht Treaty granted formal rights to EU citizens residing in other member-states, such as local voting rights (Guiraudon 2003). On the integration side of the immigration equation especially (i.e., education, acculturation, language, citizenship policies) – regarding issues laden with cultural sensibilities – little Europeanization has taken place, and national self-sufficiency is more evident than any emergent European cooperation.[54]

One trend of this period is clear: the immigration debate has taken on the character of the system that manages it. As the immigration issue passes through the European political system, it runs up against a large bureaucracy (Commission and Council) which it is frantically trying to navigate, and European parliamentarians who are vying to take more control over the decision-making process, as representatives of the "ever closer union among the peoples of Europe." Despite the increased role of European institutions, such as the EP and Commission, and NGO actors, which carry the transnational banner of civil society, the labyrinthine procedures and web of intergovernmental fora ensure that national governments wield heavy influence on policy outcomes. The locus for much EU action on immigration still remains in Brussels, in the interaction between the Commission and NGOs there, in the hidden committees of the Council and ad hoc groups, and in the internal wranglings of ongoing intergovernmental conferences. Many of these locations remain very insulated from public opinion factors, though this is increasingly changing, as the momentum associated with issues of "democratic deficit" prevails.

Despite the incremental Europeanization of migration policy, protectionist states are tenacious; they have simply become better camouflaged. In the first phase of European activity, governments were quite reluctant to remove physical barriers to the movement of persons. Under mounting pressures that ensued from the common market, by the 1980s states began to pursue cooperation in intergovernmental form. While initially they embraced informal mechanisms, eventually they formalized these arrangements in an effort to preserve national sovereignty.[55] By the mid-1990s, the frustrations of intergovernmental cooperation led national governments voluntarily to cede authority to supranational agents (Hooghe and Marks 2001: 22; Stetter 2000). This state-prompted initiative to delegate migration cooperation to the supranational level underscored changing strategies to overcome "negative externalities" resulting from market integration (Stetter 2000: 91; Hix 1999b: 322–323).[56] The abolition of internal border controls meant that member-states were now affected by each other's decisions about refugees, immigration, and policing policies, and thus, to avoid the pitfalls of collective action problems, states had a shared interest in developing a supranational regime (ibid.). Indeed, the intergovernmental reflection group (IGC) that prepared the Amsterdam Treaty criticized the JHA for creating uncertainty and enforcement problems (Hooghe and Marks 2001: 22). The upshot of post-Amsterdam Europeanization has been a "protective Union," offering member-states the opportunity to reinforce their restrictive and security-driven approach to migration control and in fact to gain new forms of power (Kostakopoulou 2000).

At the turn of the twenty-first century, the struggle between regional and national interests affirms a two-way process, by which immigration and asylum issues can preserve both intergovernmental concerns *and* supranational elements. This two-track approach means that any progress toward harmonization of free movement finds its consensus around national protectionism and restrictive cooperation. The practical necessity of dismantling internal frontiers has been inevitably accompanied by more *restrictive* control over borders.

Institutional explanations of cooperation

There is considerable debate in the international relations literature regarding the independent variables used to explain cooperation among EU member-states. From the *realist* and *neorealist* perspectives, the basic institution of the international system is the sovereign state. Cooperation may occur, insofar as states observe common norms that preserve their individual interests (Bull 1977; Waltz 1979), and it may come in the form of intergovernmentalism. Neorealists explain European cooperation as the product of lowest-common-denominator bargaining and strict limits on future transfers of sovereignty.

In contrast, *neofunctional* interpretations of European cooperation have evolved from Jean Monnet's vision of a supranational or federal Europe, and have been more optimistic about long-term policy outcomes. Positing that cooperation in one issue area is a function of integration in another, these theories suggest that once the process of functional organization begins the power of nation-states to act independently is incrementally reduced. The conflict between nationally driven realists and more structural supranationalists focuses on questions of stimuli to integration, and they hinge on the degree to which policy harmonization derives from national convergence.

One institutional camp envisions cooperation as a product of exogenous factors – general institutional biases or historical structural developments, such as the European Union and regional integration itself. These include neofunctionalist theorists (Haas 1958, 1964, 1970; Burley and Mattli 1993) and historical institutionalists, particularly path-dependence theorists (Pierson 1996). Contending scholars envisage policy convergence as resulting from national preferences (especially those of predominant states), induced by common problems faced by member-states (i.e., state-centric, neorealist, or intergovernmental institutionalists such as Moravcsik 1991, 1993, 1995, 1998; Milner 1997). The latter group represents a liberal intergovernmental view that policy convergence is a precondition for cooperation. In contrast, neofunctionalist and path-dependence perspectives consider incremental progress and past decisions taken elsewhere (based on increasing returns) to explain "spillover," "feedback," or "snowball" effects of the system.[57] In this case, cooperation is a precondition for more cooperation. More concretely, intergovernmentalists emphasize actors and interests, while neofunctionalists and historical institutionalists focus on structural and temporal factors themselves to explain cooperation. While the first group focuses on domestic sources of politics, the latter stresses exogenous and supranational forces.

These explanatory factors yield contrasting outcomes. For intergovernmentalists, the transaction costs[58] for unilinear initiatives exceed the benefits of harmonization. Thus, this realist-based perspective understands the prospects for cooperation to be inspired by the increase of bargaining efficiency derived by a set of passive, transaction-cost reducing rules, and yielding lowest-common-denominator results (Moravcsik 1993: 517). In contrast, neofunctionalists and historical institutionalists consider the sunken costs to provide incentives to institutional outcomes that are not controlled by member-states. Thus, according to Paul Pierson, "actors may be in a strong initial position, seek to maximize their interests, and nevertheless carry out institutional and policy reforms that fundamentally transform their own position in ways that are unanticipated and/or undesired" (1996: 126). The intergovernmentalist paradigm posits a playing field of rational-state actors who pursue cooperation to attain common interests and reduce transaction costs, while the neofunctionalist view leaves room for outcomes (sometimes unintended) that stem from institutional momentum and that may not be necessarily compatible with national interests. The results of intergovernmental negotiations never exceed the lowest common denominator of the parties according to intergovernmentalists, whereas for neofunctionalists there can be upgrading of common interests in cooperation. A major contention between the two schools lies in the impetus for cooperation – either nationally or European-driven.

Because of lag effects and other measurement issues, establishing a causal relationship between policy outcomes and policy constraints, such as public opinion or other pressures (for methodological deficiencies, see Freeman 1995: 883), is inherently problematic. While it is difficult to test these theories empirically, the evidence of immigration developments

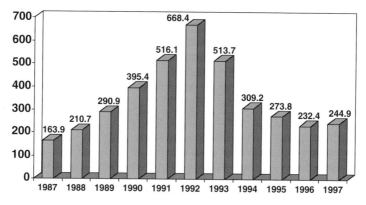

Source: OECD 1998.

Note: The data include the total number of asylum-seekers for those nations that have statistics every year from 1987 to 1997. Asylum figures for Finland and Ireland are excluded. Figures for Austria, Belgium, Denmark, France, Germany, Greece, Italy, Luxembourg, the Netherlands, Portugal, Spain, Sweden, and the United Kingdom are included.

Figure 2.1 Inflows of asylum-seekers into EU countries (thousands)

distinct from European integration dynamics posits an important middle ground, based on the interactive effects of migration regulation and regional integration.

A simple comparison of the sequence of policy events and immigration flows unpacks a commonly held misconception. That is, the increase in immigration numbers did not precede cooperative developments, as may be understood by some claims that large flows engender high centrifugal tendencies among domestic societal groups (see Ugur 1995). This suggests that EU integration itself may explain cooperation more than the increase of immigrant numbers and national reactions to them. Migration and refugee pressures from Eastern Europe led to a significant rise in the number of asylum-seekers only between 1989 and 1993 (see figure 2.1).

By the time the Dublin Convention came into force in 1997, asylum figures had dropped to pre-1989 levels. In fact, one of the lowest points in numbers of entries in Europe is the period 1982–85 (before the SEA was enacted in 1987), with flows comprising mostly family members (see Lu 1999: 4; OECD 1995; Lahav 1997b). Therefore one cannot attribute cooperation to a simple convergence of national interests in the face of geopolitical changes (Lahav and Guiraudon 2000). On the other hand, as the institutional analysis has pointed out, prior to the mid-1980s, most European states appeared uninterested in or even resistant to cooperating on immigration-related matters.[59] The question then is: what happened after the mid-1980s to entice EU member-states to consider immigration cooperation?

Some possible explanations that flow from the longitudinal historical analysis in this chapter revolve around domestic politics or national policy exigencies related to demographic, economic, social, and political considerations, including the growth of extreme-right parties, electoral pressures, the politicization of immigration politics, and other societal pressures (see appendix E; also Schain 1987, 1988; European Parliament 1991d; Kitschelt with McGann 1995; Money 1999; Jackman and Volpert 1996; Schain, Zolberg, and Hossay 2002). They consider state interests, such as the exclusion effects of abstaining from EU coordination. Other explanations look beyond domestic sources of policy and consider EU pressures and developments, particularly in terms of blame-avoidance opportunities or spillover effects. For example, the "externalities" of EU migration policy mean that migration policies are increasingly interdependent with other policy domains (from foreign affairs to welfare policy) and thus their effect on migration flows will be mediated by developments elsewhere (Lavenex and Uçarer 2002; Geddes 2002).

To be sure, the interactive effects of regional integration and migration issues suggest that cooperation is predicated on converging national interests amid a period of rapid regional momentum, which then prompts further cooperation. EU developments themselves can be used as "blame avoidance" strategies (Weaver 1986) by political elites who want either to expand their legitimacy and jurisdiction, or to devolve policy responsibility to the Union's institutions so that they may "blame Brussels for politically unpopular – yet necessary – policies on immigration" (the "Europe to the rescue" syndrome) (Papademetriou 1996: 52; see Messina and Thouez 2002: 120; Guiraudon 2000a). Beyond positive incentives, there are also negative motivations for cooperation. That is, the opportunity costs of abstaining from cooperation may figure prominently in national interests.[60] The exclusion argument flows from a realist paradigm, which poses that once a critical mass of states freely chooses to cooperate and adhere to the rules of a common policy regime, other, more reticent states are disposed to follow, fearing that a failure to do so may jeopardize their ability to realize their individual goals (Moravcsik 1991). The spillover effect is a neofunctionalist correlate that posits the threat to EU developments by failure to harmonize immigration policies. In this scenario, states jump on the bandwagon in the fear that abstaining from collective policy in this sector may jeopardize other policy areas that favor them. Its spillover logic also assumes that public opinion has already been primed as a function of previous integration steps.

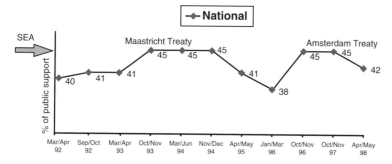

Source (n-size): *Eurobarometer* 37 (14,082); 38 (14,014); 39 (15,136); 40 (15,079); 41 (19,477); 42 (16,677); 43.1 (17,166); 44.2 (65,178); 46 (16,248); 48 (16,186); 49 (16,165).

Q: Which of the following areas of policy do you think should be decided by the national government, and which should be decided (jointly) with the European Community/Union.... Immigration Policy?

Note: SEA: signed in 1986, ratified in 1987; Maastricht: signed in February 1992, ratified in November 1993; Amsterdam: signed in October 1997, implemented in May 1999.

Figure 2.2 Cooperation and public support: competence on immigration

It is fair to say that, once some states agree on a common approach, a momentum may lead to some exclusion *or* spillover effects. The findings here show that public opinion in support of cooperation increased *after* policy was adopted. This is consonant with neofunctionalist assumptions that a function of organizational changes is a gradual shift in popular attitudes. Figure 2.2 illustrates the interactive effects between key EU collective initiatives and public support for further Europeanization of immigration policy. Although there is a limited amount of analysis that one can give figure 2.2 because of sampling error problems and question wording, an incremental pattern can be detected among the aggregated national samples provided by the Eurobarometer surveys. The first statistically significant change takes place from mid-1993 to late 1993 at the height of the Maastricht crisis with public legitimacy, and at the point of ratification. Here the percentage of respondents who want immigration policy to be decided by the national governments increases from 41 percent to 45 percent. Nonetheless, some caution is warranted in interpreting the results because they were yielded with a slightly different question wording: respondents were given the option of having immigration policy decided by national governments or *jointly* with the European Community.

Despite the limited changes in public opinion (and sampling error problems), there is an identifiable trend visible in preferences of immigration delegation. From October 1993 to December 1994, the European public was consistent in its support for immigration policies created by national governments. However, from December 1994 to March 1996, there was a statistically significant downward shift in respondents desiring national control of immigration policies (7 percentage points). This time period follows the enactment of the Maastricht Treaty, and suggests that the Treaty led to more public comfort with EU-dominated immigration policies. The trend was mirrored beginning in late 1996, when the percentage of the public who supported national control over immigration policies spiked back up to pre-Maastricht Treaty levels. But, from late 1997 to mid-1998, there was a directional change toward *less* national control, again. This corresponds to the period after the Amsterdam Treaty, which again created a momentum toward further collective immigration policy. While further inquiry is needed before a causal relationship can be established, these numbers are suggestive of a rough correspondence between public opinion shifts and the inception of EU policies. The data point to an interesting interaction between the enactment of collective action and public support for more cooperation. They support a functional spillover from general EU cooperation to immigration policy.

Still, intergovernmentalists would argue that the realist paradigm continues to guide national interests as EU member-states can – and indeed *do* – opt out or change direction as suits their interests. This is empirically supported by the fact that not all European member-states that supported and participate in single-market policies partake in EU negotiations over migration (the UK, Ireland, and Denmark have opted out of Amsterdam's Title IV, which concerns the harmonization of migration and asylum regulations). The Schengen Agreement offered an "island exclusion" clause to the UK, Ireland, and Denmark in order to facilitate their participation – an "opt-out" which would have permitted them to participate without adopting Schengen's critical requirement, the elimination of external borders. To the extent that the offer was ultimately rejected, it is difficult to talk ex post facto about functional spillover effects. On the contrary, that this "generous offer" was unacceptable speaks to the fears of neofunctionalism (Messina and Thouez 2002: 112). Furthermore, in the sense that Schengen quickly turned its focus away from achieving internal free movement and toward the fortification of external borders, we can surmise that the intergovernmental mode favored the lowest common denominator – or the two big players, France and Germany.

As the empirical evidence shows, while there are structural forces (i.e., regional integration) at work in explaining policy changes, especially with regard to cooperation, a European immigration regime can be understood only in light of the distinct national interests and political pressures that propel each EU member-state along the path of cooperation, collective action, and greater policy harmonization (see Messina and Thouez 2002: 98). On immigration-related questions, each member-state is self-interested, and motivated by its own particular set of policy goals regarding both immigration and European integration. More importantly, even when several or more EU member-states share the same or similar interests and goals, their order of priority differs from one member-state to the next.

Conclusions

This chapter has attempted to link European integration dynamics unfolding against international migration pressures. The longitudinal analysis of policy instruments here draws on the neo-institutional literature to explain how some cultural/national variations may have certain international outcomes (see Thelen and Steinmo 1992). It points to the interactive effects of national migration interests and regional integration as they define the parameters of policy cooperation. The "deepening" or the expansion of policy sectors of the EU to include immigration and asylum policies has generated increasing institutional cooperation among member-states, but restrictive policy outcomes. To the extent that cooperation and spillover have occurred, the free movement of goods and capital has been accompanied by barriers to the free movement of persons.

The scope of European cooperation has expanded to include issues of immigration and asylum. Coordination, however, has been oriented toward the prevention of unwanted migration. Among the most visible developments of such cooperation are the visa policy, readmission agreements, carrier sanctions, buffer zones on the eastern borders, the Eurodac and Schengen Information System databases, the Dublin Convention, and the 'safe third country' principles. The proliferation and diversification of instruments used to restrict immigration in Europe are thought to have fortified the state apparatus in immigration control, leading some commentators to insinuate evolving images of police states or a "fortress Europe" (Bunyan 1991; van Outrive 1990; Pastore 1991).

The analysis reveals that, despite some progress toward harmonization and a common immigration policy, states still resist in many respects. Within the institutional/policy-making process of the EU, national-level interests and decision-making remain crucial. The incorporation of both intergovernmental and supranational approaches into decision-making suggests that states that deal with distinctive immigration problems differently continue to hold on to their own national interests even as the EU matures. Nonetheless, while we can speak to some degree of national convergence, as rational or liberal intergovernmentalists do, we necessarily have to consider historical developments related to regional integration (i.e., historical institutionalism) in order to explain cooperation. Increasing formalization of supranational institutions on migration matters, in the absence of stable flows, is a testament to integration in other areas.

The argument that international forces may drive the evolution of migration policy is compelling. Especially in an institutionally "thick" environment such as the European Union, it is plausible that international institutions and transnational actors have been able to diffuse shared understandings about the treatment of foreigners so as to change and shape the views of domestic state and societal actors, as has been the case in other areas (Finnemore 1993; Wapner 1995).[61] The research so far still suffers from a lack of attention not only to diffusion mechanisms (Guiraudon and Lahav 2000; see Checkel 1998, 1999 for literature reviews that make this point), but to domestic political processes and national norms. Paying attention to immigration norms then is exactly what is needed to assess the validity of the supranational argument.

NOTES

1. It is feared that the removal of legal restrictions on migration would lead to a mass exodus from Eastern to Western Europe, because the former is economically less developed and has a large agricultural sector and industrial production that is still very labor-intensive (Straubhaar and Wolter 1996: 273).
2. These include Bulgaria, Cyprus, the Czech Republic, Estonia, Hungary, Latvia, Lithuania, Malta, Poland, Romania, the Slovak Republic, Slovenia, and Turkey. Most, if not all, accession, association, and cooperation treaties deal with issues related to migration for employment and with equal treatment of immigrants from signatory countries. In many cases, free movement is granted to nationals of new member-states only after a transitional period. To prove their merit, many states both in Central and Eastern Europe (see Vachudová 2000a, 2000b, 2001) and in Southern Europe (Baldwin-Edwards 1997) have adopted treaties and legislation in the area of migration and asylum to conform to the more restrictive EU norms.
3. For a more elaborate overview of these historical developments, see Castles and Miller 1998: ch. 4.
4. For a discerning analysis of this period, see Castles and Kosack 1985 [1973]; Miller 1981.

5. Note, however, after the termination of guest-worker recruitment in 1973 (a process which did not always require legislation since it had not proceeded from legislation in the first place), many countries passed little legislation for a decade, except for some to facilitate return migration (UNECE 1997: 168). Throughout the 1980s and early 1990s, nearly all countries introduced restrictive legislation – in many cases, requiring a few versions or reforms to "get it right."

6. Immigration became a political issue earlier in Britain. Enoch Powell, a member of the Conservative Party, made it one in 1968, and the 1970 election is generally conceded to have been affected by immigration politics (see Freeman 1979).

7. According to the estimates of the United Nations Population Division (2001), in the period 1995–2000, 61 percent of the total growth in developed regions stemmed from migration.

8. For an early discussion of this point, see "In Europe, Immigrants are Needed, Not Wanted" 1990. See also Lahav 1991, 1992.

9. According to Koslowski, the mere fact that foreign ministers rather than labor ministers were discussing migration demonstrated that migration in Europe by this point had moved from the "low politics" of international economic relations to the "high politics" of international security (1998b: 153). See also Favell 1998a: 2; Geddes 2000: 3.

10. For example, the French problem (of integration) is greater than appears from the table if one adds native-born children of Algerians. Consider how the subtleties in terminology affect figures. According to the 1999 French census, there were 4.3 million foreign-born residents (*immigrés*), 1.6 million of whom were naturalized French citizens. The census counted about 3.3 million foreigners (*étrangers*) in France; 2.7 million of these were born outside France, and 500,000 were born as foreigners in France. The variations reflect juridical criteria of nationality (*étrangers*) versus immigration flows (*immigrés*) (INSEE 2000). See also ch. 1, n. 2, p. 21.

11. Even when one source is ostensibly common to a number of countries, critical differences may remain. In 1987, for example, out of a potential 132 pairs of data between European Community countries, there were only 55 possible comparisons: 29 of them showed differences of over 50 percent, and only 10 percent were within a 10 percent margin (see Salt 1993: 188). Such subtleties contribute to the well-known data lags and discrepancies in demographic reporting.

12. In identifying immigration problems and problem areas, elite terminology tends to differ, reflecting cultural and ideological biases. This assumption is substantiated by the data on MEPs. See, for example, the answers to the survey question, "When you think of immigration problems, to which other area do you relate them **first**: (1) social welfare; (2) race relations; (3) unemployment; (4) education; (5) crime; (6) citizenship; (7) drug trafficking; (8) social integration; (9) other (specify)."

13. Ever since Tomas Hammar identified the two interrelated components of immigration policy, the nature of this relationship has eluded immigration scholars. While there has been some work on the two dimensions of

the immigration policy dilemma (Money 1995), a systematic analysis of these separate but inextricable links is still warranted. The nature of the immigration issue in Europe is complicated not only by its national idiosyncrasies, but also by the lack of systematic understanding of *how* its two component parts are interrelated. This confusion has been coupled by overlapping and uncoordinated bureaucratic competence in each domain. In the absence of an immigration ministry *per se*, at any one time, immigration may be the concern of interior, justice, foreign affairs, social affairs, housing, education, sports, and cultural ministries (see appendix E, and Guiraudon 2003 on institutional conflicts).

14. For a methodical breakdown of these policy areas, see Baldwin-Edwards 1991b.

15. Issues of family reunification fall into the gray area of Hammar's typology. After all, it has been argued, foreigners cannot be properly integrated if they are forced to wait for years before their families are allowed to live with them (see Lahav 1997b; Layton-Henry 1990; Money 1998).

16. Note that the meaning of free movement of persons under Community law differs considerably from its context in international human rights conventions. The latter refer to the individual's right to travel freely within countries and to exit and return to one's own country. For the EU, free movement has been seen as the instrument with which to regulate migration and integration of EU nationals moving from one member-state to another (see Niessen 1999: 13).

17. According to Articles 48 and 52, citizens of member-states were granted the right to enter the territory of another for the purpose of accepting or seeking employment or self-employment, or to provide or receive a service (Treaty Establishing the European Economic Community, Title III). Also, EC Regulation 1612/68 states that a worker of one member-state has the right to seek employment in another. The only restriction is that the individual must find employment within a three-month period.

18. Directives are considered binding on national authorities with respect to the aims of the legislation, while leaving choices of methods to national legislators (Böhning 1972: 19; Hovy and Zlotnik 1994: 21). In comparison, regulations are substantially more influential, as they are binding in their entirety. They take direct effect in each member-state, are applicable without the requirement of transformation into municipal law, and cannot be changed (even with regard to wording).

19. In qualified terms, admissions for non-economic migrants have gradually been brought in through Council directives and EEC regulations. In 1964, EEC Regulation 38/64 established the right of workers of a member-state to be joined by family members, irrespective of the latter's citizenship. Family members included not only spouses and children under the age of twenty-one years, but also dependent parents and other descendants of the worker or his spouse (Art. 17.Ib). Admission of family members, however, was subject to the availability of "normal" housing. Regulation 1612/68 of October 15, 1968, reiterated the right of the worker of a member-state to be joined by immediate relatives (defined in similar terms to those used in Regulation

38/64), and again linked it to the availability of normal housing (Art. 10). It also granted family members the right to exercise an economic activity, even if they were not nationals of member-states of the EC (Art. 11). That same year, the Council issued Directive 68/360 on the abolition of restrictions on movement and residence within the Community for workers of member-states and their families.

20. On the juridical and legal constraints on migration policy, see Plender 1986, 1988; Hollifield 1992a; Schuck 1998; Legomsky 1987; Guendelsberger 1988; Neuman 1990; Guiraudon 1997, 1998, 2000a; Guild and Harlow 2001.

21. On June 28, 1990, the Council extended similar rights to students and their immediate family members (Directive 90/366/EEC). Students who were EC nationals were entitled to be joined by their spouses and dependent children, provided they had "sufficient resources to avoid becoming a burden on the social assistance system of the host Member State" (Art. 1). Both the students and their dependants were eligible for residence permits covering the duration of their course of studies, and the dependants were granted the right to take up employment, irrespective of their nationality. Similar rights were also extended to retirees who were citizens of member-states of the EC, and to their immediate relatives of whatever citizenship, provided that the relatives had sufficient resources on which to live and would not become charges to the host state (Directives 90/365/EEC and 90/364/EEC).

22. By 1989, the European Commission estimated that approximately 2 million EC nationals were taking advantage of the free movement of persons provision of the Treaty and had established themselves in a different member-state from that of their nationality. With their families, this migrant community constituted a total of approximately 5 million people.

23. The SEA established a new "cooperation procedure" that compelled the Council to consider parliamentary opinions on proposed legislation in a second reading. The agreement also granted Parliament the right of joint decision-making with respect to the accession of new members and agreements of association and cooperation with non-member countries.

24. Britain, for example, advocated the retention of strong border controls at ports of entry, while Italy, with its long sea and land frontiers, favored after-entry control, which required national identity cards and greater police powers.

25. It was serviced by the General Secretariat of the Council of Ministers, and the European Commission attended meetings as an observer. See Bunyan and Webber 1995.

26. Among these were the TREVI Group (started in 1980), the Coordinators' Group on the Free Movement of Persons or the Rhodes Group (1989), the Horizontal Group on Data Processing and the European Information System (1992), the Customs Mutual Assistance Group (1989), the European Committee to Combat Drugs (1989), the Ad Hoc Committee of Experts for Identity Documents and the Movement of Persons (CAHID, 1991), the Vienna Group (1991), the Berlin Group (1991), and the Budapest Group (1993). The latter three were efforts to replicate Western-based migration

regimes in the east. A number of groups, including TREVI, the Club of Bern (1984), and the STAR group (Standige Arbeitsgruppe Rauschgift, 1984), preceded the formal AHI group, and were based on preexisting security clubs. These groups involved civil servants and police officials dedicated to other policing themes such as drugs or terrorism, but quickly assumed the theme of migration control (Bigo 1996). Many of these international groups coexist alongside the EU, and have varying goals and memberships, sometimes from outside the EU (see Guiraudon 2000a: 254–255). These include the OECD, the Council of Europe (the Committee of Experts on the Legal Aspects of Territorial Asylum, Refugees, and Stateless People, CAHAR), the United Nations (UNHCR and Commission on Crime Prevention), Interpol, Intergovernmental Consultations on Asylum, Refugees and Migration Policies (IGC), the International Organization for Migration (IOM), and the International Labour Organization (ILO). In some cases, the Council Secretariat has been represented, but rarely does the Commission participate.

27. For a cogent discussion on the application of "burden-sharing" norms (i.e., questions about how costs of common initiatives or the provision of public goods are shared between states) to migration and asylum, see Thielemann 2003.

28. Securitization perspectives emphasize the framing of issues, particularly by politicizing them or dramatizing them to "have absolute priority" (Wæver 1996: 106–107). For accounts of EU effects on these issues, and the blurring of external and internal threats, see Anderson and den Boer 1994; Bigo 1996, 2001; Huysmans 1995, 2000.

29. The Convention entered into force on September 1, 1997, for the twelve original signatories, on October 1, 1997, for Austria and Sweden and on January 1, 1998, for Finland. The responsible state is defined as the one which first allowed the asylum-seeker into its territory (i.e., into EC territory), whether by granting a residence permit or visa or by allowing the opportunity for illegal entry. There are some limited exceptions with regard to family applicants (Art. 4).

30. According to this provision, an asylum-seeker is denied access to the refugee-status determination procedure on the grounds that he or she already enjoyed, could or should have requested, and, if qualified, would actually have been granted asylum in another country. In practice, this means that asylum seekers who have traveled through other countries (i.e., in Central and Eastern Europe) before reaching their destination would not have their asylum application examined in the country of their choice and would be expelled to another country. These provisions have been severely criticized by the UNHCR, human rights NGOs, and courts.

31. On December 11, 2000, member-states adopted Council Regulation EC 2725/2000 concerning the establishment of Eurodac for the comparison of fingerprints, in order to foster an effective application of the Dublin Convention (OJ 11.12.2000 L 316).

32. In 1991, the Spanish government imposed on visitors from the Maghreb states a requirement to obtain a visa for entry into Spain. The Italian government instituted an amnesty program to address illegal immigration

problems, and substantially strengthened its efforts to police the Italian maritime frontier. The Portuguese government withdrew the previously automatic right of Brazilians to opt for Portuguese nationality.

33. In preparing for the Maastricht intergovernmental conference in 1991, the Council of Ministers and the European Council invited the Commission in Brussels to draw up a report that could ultimately recommend areas of immigration policy for Community initiatives (Commission to the European Communities 1991a, 1991b).

34. In its drive to actively promote a people's Europe, the EP has been most active in promoting social policies and rights for resident migrants. This goes back to the 1970s and the Vetter Report, which called for rights of political participation for migrants, as well as continuous declarations on anti-racism. In addition to the Evrigenis Report on the "Inquiry into the Rise of Fascism and Racism in Europe" (European Parliament 1985) and the Ford Report on the "Inquiry on Racism and Xenophobia" (European Parliament 1991d), both dealing with immigrant rights and public reactions, the EP also adopted a resolution demanding the incorporation into the EU Treaty of a general clause prohibiting racism and xenophobia, which would include "all individuals within the EU" regardless of citizenship (EP, March 13, 1996). Furthermore, the EP's annual human rights report monitors governmental and non-governmental human rights activities, and is an important instrument for promoting the EU's human rights agenda.

35. The Treaty's preamble speaks of a resolution to mark a new stage in the process of European integration, and to establish a common citizenship (Title I, Article B, Treaty on European Union: Commission of the European Communities 1992b).

36. Articles K1–9 created the third pillar with one full group, GD1 of the K4 committee, dedicated to asylum, visa, and migration. On migration policy, five main Titles have been set out: (1) harmonization of admission policies; (2) common approach to the question of illegal immigration; (3) policy on the migration of labor; (4) situation of third-country nationals; and (5) migration policy in the broad meaning of the term (Article 100(c); Title VI, Article K; Article 2; Article V, Treaty on European Union: Commission of the European Communities 1992b).

37. Article K.2 left these issues outside EU machinery as it noted that "the matters referred to in Article K.1 shall be dealt with in compliance with the European Convention for the Protection of Human Rights and Fundamental Freedoms of 4 November 1950 and the Convention Relating to the Status of Refugees of 28 July 1951 and having regard to the protection afforded by member-states to persons persecuted on political grounds."

38. For example, the Council, in accordance with the new provisions of the Treaty, annexed a list of 129 third countries whose nationals require visas. This list had been in existence since December 1987, when it was mentioned for the first time publicly, after a ministerial meeting of the Ad Hoc Immigration Group in Copenhagen. On April 21, 1994, the European Parliament adopted a report based on the Commission's proposal for a Council regulation on visas. It stated that third-country nationals who do

not require a visa for entry to a member-state should not be on the so-called negative list of the Regulation; COM(94)0684-C3-0012/94; *Migration News Sheet* (Brussels), May 1994: 1.

39. For example, the AHI Group meeting in June 1993 in Copenhagen adopted a resolution, Harmonization of National Policies on Family Reunification, which essentially codified a minimum set of standards already in use, and validated a state's right to allow or deny the admission of foreigners for family reunification. The principles set forth in the resolution apply only to the family reunification of those who are "lawfully resident within the territory of a member-state on a basis which affords them an expectation of permanent or long-term settlement" (Bunyan and Webber 1995: 17). Children are variously defined as persons under the age of sixteen or eighteen, depending on the decision of each member-state. The state has the privilege of denying entry on security grounds, and it reserves the right to grant a work permit or not to family members admitted for family reunification. The resolution grants member-states the right to impose waiting periods before allowing family reunion; the right to impose a primary-purpose test for the admission of spouses and of adopted children; the right to refuse the admission of certain wives and children of polygamous marriages; discretion as to the admission of stepchildren, adopted children, and other family members for "compelling" reasons. States must impose a visa requirement. They also have the right to impose conditions on adequate means of support and the availability of proper accommodation and health insurance before dependants can be admitted.

40. Since 1958, the Commission Directorate General for Employment, Industrial Relations, and Social Affairs (DG V) was the only DG responsible for free movement of labor, and subsequently for matters relating to integration, etc. (since 1958). After 1992, some personnel were transferred to DG XV, the Directorate General for Internal Market and Financial Services, in a unit responsible for "free movement of persons and citizens' rights" (see Guiraudon 2000b). Also, a small taskforce was created within the General Secretariat of the Commission to liaise with the JHA Council. It was only after Amsterdam in 1999 that the post of commissioner in charge of justice and home affairs was established for the first time (first filled by Antonio Vitorino). Andrew Geddes points to conflict within the Commission to illustrate its nature as a network rather than a monolith (1999: 183).

41. This includes: a supranational pillar of the institutions of the European Community, the first pillar; and two parallel intergovernmental pillars for cooperation between the member-states on a common foreign and security policy, the second pillar, and on justice and home affairs, the third pillar.

42. The fact that the Treaty addressed the EP as the first institution was interpreted by some to imply a certain primacy in line with the essential democratic role of parliaments in Western societies, and with the Parliament's claim to represent the people of Europe. Maastricht introduced the right to petition to the EP, or to apply to the ombudsman, who is appointed by the EP. A new article, 138(b), listed five different ways in which the Parliament could share in the EU's legislative process, including assent, conciliation, cooperation,

and consultation, and by inviting the Commission to act. Amendments introduced by the TEU mean that the Commission has to reply and is open to a collective dismissal under Article 144. The EP not only retained its prerogative to dismiss the Commission as a whole, but through Articles 158 and 154, respectively, it now shared in confirming the president and debating the Commission's program (Church and Phinnemore 1994: 257).

43. Intergovernmental cooperation within the third pillar produced numerous non-binding documents, but did not achieve the desired harmonization of asylum and immigration policies (Niessen 1999: 19). In the five years from Maastricht to Amsterdam, the JHA Council agreed on only one joint position, on the common definition of a refugee, and on five legally binding joint actions, regarding school travel for third-country national children, airport transit procedures, a common format for resident permits, burden sharing for displaced persons, and human trafficking (Guiraudon 2000b: 256).

44. The Treaty established a five-year period to deal with: standards on procedures for the issue of long-term visas and residence permits (including those for the purpose of family reunion); conditions of entry and residence; and determination of the rights and conditions under which third-country nationals residing legally in a member-state may reside in another member-state (see Niessen, 1999: 21).

45. The Amsterdam Treaty proclaimed that, from 2004 onward, the Council had the ability to decide upon institutional changes, which would allow for the use of qualified majority voting (QMV) and co-decisional procedures within the EP for immigration and asylum, though the decision to accept such institutional changes has to be unanimous. The Treaty's revision of the EP is seen as a mixed fortune in this regard. It did not go far enough for parliamentarians and commissioners, who have to wait five years for competence and still deal with the unanimity clause, as well as for the European Court of Justice which has been somewhat limited compared with its authority on free movement matters. It may have gone too far for those who are fearful of what may happen after the five years have passed, when limitations placed on the Parliament and Commission can be removed. Only the highest court or tribunal of a member-state can request the Court to give preliminary rulings on issues covered by Title IV (Niessen 1999: 21; Guiraudon 2003).

46. Article 13 envisaged the possibility of the Council, acting unanimously on a proposal from the Commission and after consulting the EP, adopting measures to combat any discrimination based on gender, racial, or ethnic origin, religion or belief, disability, age, or sexual orientation. This clause has been seen as providing an international tool to further the claims of ethnic minorities.

47. Both the Commission (through Article 308) and the EP (through its budgetary power) were able to sponsor anti-racist activities, such as the European Year Against Racism (1997). Also, the NGO–Commission nexus was part of a mutually beneficial relationship to increase the supranational profile of this policy area in the name of civil society. The Commission's Directorate Generals typically finance NGO networks in exchange for expertise and legitimacy (see Geddes 1999; Guiraudon 2001a: 19). There

have been a myriad of NGOs, both Commission-sponsored (e.g., EU Migrants' Forum) and transnational migrant-based, such as the Starting Line Group (SLG), the Churches' Commission for Migrants in Europe (CCME), the European Council for Refugees and Exiles (ECRE), Migration Policy Group (MPG), European Network Against Racism (ENAR), and Immigration Law Practitioners' Association (ILPA), that had a strong presence at the 1996/97 IGC negotiations and/or after. They were seen as instrumental to the incorporation of anti-discrimination and equal treatment legislation, as well as the increased powers given to the EU institutions. However, the nature of national immigration concerns has kept NGOs fragmented and non-effective in alliance formation (for shortcomings, see Geddes 1999: 180; Guiraudon 2001b).

48. This is true despite the 1997 Commission proposal to extend free movement to resident third-country nationals (COM/97/0387 final – CNS 97/0227 [Dec 597PC0387] Proposal for a Council Act establishing the Convention on rules for the admission of third-country nationals to the member-states). For earlier reservations, see the comments made by the ministers responsible for immigration in their report to the European Council meeting in Maastricht in December 1991 (SN 4038/91 WGI 930); and Guild and Niessen 1996.

49. In order to create such a system, the Council proposed "a workable determination of the State responsible for the examination of asylum applications, common standards for a fair and efficient asylum procedure, common minimum conditions of reception of asylum seekers, and the approximation of rule on the recognition and content of the refugee status" (European Council 1999).

50. Title IV, created by the EC Treaty, specifies the decision-making procedures in four areas: measures on crossing of external borders and the abolition of internal borders (Art. 62); measures on asylum, refugees, and displaced persons (Art. 63); measures on immigration policy (Art. 63); and measures on judicial cooperation in civil matters (Art. 65).

51. Tony Blair, José Maria Aznar, and Gerhard Schroeder referred directly to the French and Dutch electoral results in their call for the Seville EU Summit to be dedicated to combating illegal migration (Guiraudon and Schain 2002: 1). Although the Summit dealt with enlargement and some modest institutional reforms, immigration and asylum issues emerged at the forefront of political debate.

52. The idea assumes that the EP is the natural representative of the peoples of Europe, to whom the institutions should ultimately be responsible (see Church and Phinnemore 1994: 255).

53. The choice of name reflected the evolution of emphasis, as it placed immigration within the sociopolitical domain. After the Maastricht Treaty, the formal name of the EP committee became the Committee on Citizens' Freedoms and Rights, Justice and Home Affairs.

54. The success story of anti-discrimination legislation has been attributed more to policy framing and linkage to "social exclusion" (Article 137, Treaty of Amsterdam), which is not solely targeted at migrant groups (Geddes 2000; Guiraudon 2003; Geddes and Guiraudon 2002).

55. National sovereignty is thus preserved because, under intergovernmental arrangements, decisions are taken by unanimity, and governments can veto any measure that threatens a vital national interest. In addition, decisions do not have direct effect in domestic law, unless they are ratified by national parliaments.

56. "Negative externalities" is borrowed from economics and here refers to cases in which "one member-state is affected by regulatory decisions of another (Gatsios and Seabright 1989: 37). According to Lavenex and Uçarer, the notion of externalities may be differentiated according to characteristics of the recipients (i.e., third countries, organizations, policy sectors) and the nature of the external effects (2002a: 8). See also Scharpf (1996) on the tension between "negative integration" (i.e., liberalization of markets) and "positive integration" (process-related market-correcting mechanisms, such as policing or immigration controls). In this paradigm, the procedural exigencies of European decision-making have failed to compensate at the European level for the loss of competence at the national level. This tension creates a precarious scenario for problem-solving, wherein some states may seek the increase of capacity at the European level, while others may attempt to protect their national capacities.

57. The term "spillover" as introduced by Ernst Haas, the founding father of neofunctionalism (1958), posits the view that interstate cooperation in one policy field logically and functionally leads to cooperation in other, related areas. An underlying assumption is that failure to follow the stages of policy integration (from economic to political) jeopardizes system development. "Feedback effects" in path-dependence theories are based on increasing returns, whereby a decision taken at time 0 closes certain policy options for time 1 and sets policies on a particular path (Pierson 2000; Arthur 1994). "Snowball effects" stem from decisions by one country that force others to follow suit; and "spillovers" involve initiatives in other policy areas which may have unintended consequences in the field of migration control, for example.

58. Rational-choice scholars argue that parties enter into contracts with one another when the benefits outweigh the costs of doing so. "Transaction costs" refers to the costs in making and carrying out a market transaction, agreement, or contract between two or more parties. Transaction costs could include obtaining information, locating a bargaining partner, and negotiating and monitoring a contract (Coase 1937, 1960; Stevens 1993).

59. On this point, see Messina and Thouez, who refer to the limited success of some EU countries in challenging, in the European Court of Justice, the European Commission's 1985 decision to compel member-states to give the Commission advance notice of any draft measures they intended to implement regarding third-country nationals living and working within their territory (2002: 98, n. 1; see also Papademetriou 1996: 21).

60. The failure of states to participate early within a common regime may precipitate higher membership costs later, as by then the priorities and rules of the emerging regime have become well established. Thus, while some EU states are wary of intergovernmental agreements on immigration and reluctant to compromise their sovereignty in this policy area, it is often difficult for them

to stand aside and eschew the advantages enjoyed by states that have already acceded to such agreements (see Messina and Thouez 2002: 104).

61. This constructivist approach (Finnemore 1996; Katzenstein 1996; Klotz 1995) is still a matter of controversy in international relations theory (see Checkel 1998 for a review). The constructivist emphasis on the normative framing and practices of ideas and interests lends itself to sociological explanations of immigration and citizenship issues in world politics (see Bigo 1996; Ferguson and Mansbach 1999; Lapid 1996; Kratochwil 1989; Wæver 1995; Koslowski 2000; Soysal 1994).

3   An attitudinal portrait of a people's Europe: a comparative overview of public opinion and elite preferences

Act III, Scene 1: Human nature does not change, but when nations and men accept the same rule and the same institutions to make sure that they are applied, their behavior toward each other changes. This is the process of civilization itself.

(Jean Monnet, "A Ferment of Change" 1962: 211.)

Scene 2: The discussion chamber was reverberating with procedures and rules – not all of which appeared so evident to the deputies. Perhaps over time, these manmade procedures will inculcate a universal mindset about immigration itself. Or, maybe, the difficulty in getting beyond technical issues is a reflection of persistent conflicting norms.

(Diary of researcher, Strasbourg, June 9, 1992.)

According to the official EU mantra, the ultimate aim of the "Community" has been to establish "an ever closer union among the European peoples" (the preamble of the Rome Treaty, the first "constitution" establishing the Community). As with all shared views about Europe, there are many diverse opinions on how to achieve this goal. Nonetheless, its implications, particularly for an immigration regime, are significant. This is because the question of a people's Europe hinges on who those people are, and what to do about the "outsiders" among them.

The basic principle underlying "a people's Europe" relates to the human dimension of the Union – the idea that Community citizenship, irrespective of nationality, bestows the same rights, freedoms, and obligations for all member-state nationals. The concept of European citizenship stresses the universality of human rights throughout the Union. Since June 1984, when the European Council created the working group on a people's Europe, issues of citizenship have addressed representation and electoral questions (i.e., the franchise and voting system for the European Parliament); the rights of permanent residents living in another member-state (i.e., third-country nationals); the rights of the Community's border inhabitants; the equality of legal redress throughout the Community; and common diplomatic provisions in third countries (Holland 1994: 153).

There is much disagreement among scholars about whether and how cooperation on citizenship and immigration may be viable, given the competing national and ideological interests involved. Theorists differ with regard to how institutionalized regional integration affects the average citizen and, conversely, whether the views of elites or masses affect regional integration more generally.[1] As the preceding institutional analysis of immigration policy suggests, there is a great deal of ambivalence regarding the nature of such a common regime. The emphasis on attitudes in this chapter serves to contextualize and illuminate the underlying norms behind these institutional and policy developments.

"Bringing attitudes back in" to integration paradigms: the link between policy and norms

Immigration cooperation and public opinion

The literature on regional integration focuses more on transnational institutions and the economic and political elites who manage cooperation than on normative or attitudinal dynamics.[2] Yet a quintessential barometer of regional cooperation and policy convergence is the set of attitudes and norms that buttresses institutional foundations. Scholars find systematic data in this area wanting.

Researchers of European immigration have been divided with regard to the constraints, particularly of public opinion, on EU policy-makers and on cooperation. There are several reasons for this gulf and for the dearth of information. First, as documented in the previous chapter, immigration policy-making has long taken place behind closed doors, and without public debate (Guiraudon 1997, 2000a). Second, in a global political economy, where human rights and free circulation are "embedded," nation-states have been seen to be limited in regulating migration policy (Hollifield 1992a, 1992b; Sassen 1991, 1996). Based on neoliberal theories of twentieth- century norms, students of globalization have assumed that international regimes or cooperation would be inevitable – regardless of public opinion. Finally, analysts have suggested that there is a disjuncture between public opinion and policy developments (Fetzer 2000; Hansen 2000; Simon and Alexander 1993; Guiraudon 2000a; Beck and Camarota 2002), and that liberal immigration policies have emerged because, among other things, negative public opinion is not factored into elite decision-making or institutional developments (Freeman 1995).

These accounts fail to explain why, as the previous chapter showed, cooperation has been fairly limited up to now. They also neglect to explain how different immigration discourses and public opinion contexts have

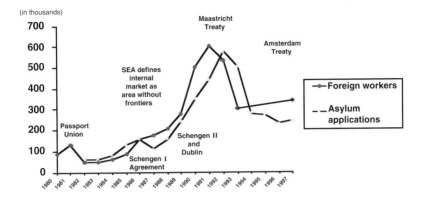

Source: Lu 1999; Eurostat 1999b; Salt 1994, 1996, 2000; UNHCR various years; OECD 1992, 1995, 1999, 2001; Hovy 1993.

Figure 3.1 Cooperative initiatives and immigrant flows

generated more restrictive and protectionist policy responses throughout the EU. More importantly, these liberal paradigms do not consider the possibility that there are more similarities between European elites and publics than previously expected.

The relevance of domestic factors such as public opinion is inferred from a longitudinal analysis of cooperative measures adopted on the immigration front. Figure 3.1 relates the changes in migrant pressures to major cooperative initiatives. It shows that increasing migration flows and asylum applications did not precede policy cooperation, and therefore debunks some commonly held claims that large flows engender policy convergence (Ugur 1995). These findings support the argument made by Baldwin-Edwards and Schain that the immigration issue may be less related to actual changes in migrant flows than to elite and mass reactions to them (1994: 7).

While caution about causal interpretations is warranted given the complexity of variables (see Kessler and Freeman 2002), figure 3.1 reveals that a number of important EU cooperative initiatives (e.g., SEA, Schengen I and II) preceded the large inflows of the early 1990s.[3] In this chart, there is no apparent relationship between the ebbs and flows of migration and policy coordination. Figure 3.1 suggests that cooperation may reflect domestic societal pressures (i.e., the feeling that there are "too many" foreigners) rather than the actual number of immigrants. It makes the role of public opinion and elite preferences more critical to any analysis of convergence and cooperation than inflow numbers alone.

Realist vs. neofunctional views of attitudes

In lieu of immigrant flows to explain cooperation, this chapter considers public and elite reactions. If we cannot infer a causal relationship between immigrant flows and the sequence of cooperative policy acts adopted, we are still left with the question of what happened after 1985 to spur even the most limited steps toward immigration cooperation in Europe. These answers provide the key to understanding not only the present climate of integration, but also what is likely to develop into the future.

This empirical puzzle may be addressed through the prism of evolving norms, notably, by linking attitudes to institutional frameworks of cooperation. The theoretical paradigms of integration posed in the previous institutional analysis are useful. The role of attitudes may be distinguished based on models of *intergovernmentalism* or *neofunctionalism*.

The intergovernmental perspective of cooperation does not put much emphasis on public opinion, and understands European integration as an elite affair (Moravcsik 1991). It is premised on a realist notion that elites usually ignore their public's preferences altogether or educate the public to support their policies.[4] This view led to Karl Deutsch's pessimistic account of regional integration in the 1950s, when he concluded that the future of Europe would be as a collection of nation-states, not as a supranational entity. He proposed that "bolder steps toward substantially greater European unity would have to be 'sold to' mass opinion by the sustained and concerted efforts of leaders and elites" (1967: 251). In more contemporary terms, an intergovernmental view of immigration cooperation would posit that domestic elites as a group act to protect the interests of a national public who are unyielding to outside competence on matters as nationally sensitive as immigration.

In contrast, for neofunctionalist or historical institutionalists, attitudinal change is not a prerequisite for, but a consequence of, integration in economic sectors or previous cooperation. Although this paradigm focuses on the development of a social-psychological community and views ties of mutual affection, identity, and loyalty as the building blocks of integration (see Hewstone 1986: 11; Lindberg and Scheingold 1970: 6–7), there has been a conceptual evolution in emphasis. For early proponents of the neofunctionalist view, the most important attitudinal measure was not at the level of mass support, but among political elites (Haas 1968: 17). This perspective changed in the late 1970s, when empirical evidence began to suggest a shift in values and attitudes among young citizens of Europe, supporting an emergence of a supranational identity (Inglehart 1970a, 1970b, 1971, 1977, 1990a, 1990c). These citizens proved themselves capable of evolving integrationist attitudes in ways that historical institutionalists had previously expected from elites alone. Although the role of public opinion began to be taken more seriously when mass attitudes appeared more positively inclined to integration, the value imputed to it by behavioralists remains questionable in light of the low popular support for the Maastricht Treaty (Eichenberg and Dalton 1993). Notwithstanding the questionable role of public opinion, neofunctional interpretations of popular attitudes are more optimistic about long-term cooperation than intergovernmentalist ones.[5]

This debate requires some assessment of attitudinal formation, though, as noted in the institutional analysis, the interactive effects of policy and norms are difficult to disentangle in terms of a causal relationship. Theorizing about the prerequisite of convergence for cooperation versus spillover effects remains problematic (see institutionalist paradigms discussed in chapter 2). Although this realist/functional controversy is difficult to resolve on the basis of attitudes alone, the distance between elites who make policy and the masses or constituents may tell us a little bit more about the nature and direction of immigration cooperation in Europe.

The policy–attitude connection

Public opinion studies offer some general wisdom on this topic, though they are equally conflicted on the *leading–lagging* question regarding whether the masses are passive or active, leading or following policy decisions (see Putnam 1983; Page and Shapiro 1983; Risse-Kappen 1991; Stimson 1991; Zaller 1992; Stimson, Mackuen, and Erikson 1995; Carrubba 2001; Gabel and Palmer 1995). According to the "leading" hypothesis, public opinion in Europe is ahead of the decisions taken (Hallstein 1972; Gabel 1998a; Carrubba 2001), and consequently serves as a constraint on policy-makers.[6] In contrast, "trickle-down" or "permissive-consensus" theories understand public opinion to be lagging – reflecting or following elite decisions (Key 1961; Lindberg and Scheingold 1970; Zaller 1992; Franklin, Marsh, and McLaren 1994; Wessels 1995b). To the extent that beliefs are a learning process, individuals may acquire some attitudes from elites who provide a "package" of interconnected policy positions (Feldman 1988). The *leading–lagging* debate neglects a third alternative, which comes in the form of *public–policy congruence*. This latter perspective emanates from Page and Shapiro's extensive research on American public opinion surveys and policies, which found a high degree of congruence (defined as consistency between opinion and policy and whether changes in policy

and changes in opinion occurred at the same time) between public preferences and policies (1982, 1983, 1992).

The public–elite connection

At the core of these theoretical discussions on the policy–attitude
connection is the controversy regarding *which* attitudes are meaningful
for understanding change. Thus, for many classical students of public
opinion, mass attitudes appeared relatively unstable (Converse 1964,
1970, 1974; Converse and Dupeux 1962), unorganized or unsophis-
ticated (Sears 1969), uninformed and random (Zaller 1992), lacking
in "political attitudes" (Hennessy 1970: 463), ideology, or knowledge
(Lippman 1955; Sears 1969), or, at worst, leading to bad policy
decisions (Key 1961: 557).[7] This thinking spawned an extensive literature
proposing that attitudinal research should concentrate on elites, who are
ideologically sophisticated (Converse 1964), influential (Merritt 1967),
and politically active (Sears 1969). The view that elites have considerable influence over individual attitudes has been applied to immigration
scholarship (Freeman 1995; McLaren 2001). According to Freeman,
public opinion has been mitigated by the lack of information, the lagging
effects of immigration, a constrained debate, and skewed discourse
generated by consensus management of the issue in liberal democracies
(1995).

The contending view has been much more optimistic about the value
imputed to the "common man" (Lippmann 1922; Lane 1962), more
recently suggesting that the public is rational (Page and Shapiro 1992;
Yankelovich 1991; Dalton 2002), even when uninformed (Gabel 1998a,
1998b; Eichenberg and Dalton 1993; Dalton and Eichenberg 1998;
Anderson 1998). Thus, while V. O. Key might have argued that public
opinion was actually elite opinion, Robert Lane would find that political
ideologies were formed by a complex set of circumstances, which shape
the opinions of common men, as they do those of the elite. One does not
stem from the other. This complex portrait has led to a more intricate
understanding of the interaction between mass and elite opinion, whereby
some mass opinion has been seen to have more influence on elite decisions
than others.[8] In the context of the EU, electoral connections and national
referenda make public opinion a more important constraint on policy-
makers than initially expected (Gabel 1998a; Carrubba 2001).

Contemporary scholars have not resolved the debate, but there is a
broad consensus that the consolidation and stability of democratic systems depend on the relationship between elites and publics. This Western
notion that the legitimacy of governments rests on the consent of the

governed represents a Rousseauian "will of the people" perspective that the decisions of political actors should coincide with their constituents' views (Hewstone 1986; Oskamp 1977). This view is particularly relevant to the European Union system because of "democratic deficit" concerns (the relationship gap between the institutions and people), and because in the absence of supranational means of enforcement (i.e., similar to those that may exist in nation-states) EU authority ultimately stems from the voluntary compliance of citizens (Gabel 1998a: 7).

Hence, there appears ample reason to warrant the study of attitudes in the EU. Public influence in constraining institutional change is inescapable when considering the popular backlash of the French referendum, the Danish and Norwegian vetoes, and the entire Maastricht ratification crisis. It explains why it took more than two years from the time the Treaty was agreed upon in Maastricht (in December 1991) until it was ratified (November 1, 1993). This ratification crisis, echoed again in Ireland's second referendum standoff on the Nice Treaty, showed that any "permissive consensus" that may have inspired European integration in the past could no longer be relied upon.

To be sure, the role of the public has evolved, and is indicative of the institutional aspirations of community development. Thus, while the Rome Treaty initially provided for a parliamentary role that was limited (but reflective of the Community's fledgling experience), Monnet believed that, before effective democratization could be introduced, the Community had to prove itself worthy of supranational authority (Holland 1994: 144).[9] The nominal change from European Assembly to European Parliament in 1962 marked a substantive shift in this direction, as did the first direct elections, held in 1979. These developments reflect the legislature's burgeoning role in European decision-making processes, and they capture the growing relationship between elites and publics.

This chapter assumes that both elite attitudes and mass opinions are worthy of study, because they are critical to the immigration debate in terms of discourse, policy parameters, and outcomes. It does not set out to prove one model of attitudinal influence over another. Members of the European Parliament (MEPs) formulate policy that will have large ramifications for the EU, and the individual countries that are a part of that Union. We can therefore understand the importance of studying their positions, as representing a cross-section of elite attitudes. The value of the European publics, whether they constrain the behavior of elites or resemble them, is largely in their reflection of particular junctures or "snapshots" in time.[10] The congruence or distance between the two groups offers a statement about the structure and nature of immigration policy-making in the EU. This attempt to avoid the "chicken-and-egg" dance associated with the policy–attitude link allows us to assess the functionalist thesis more directly by testing whether a broad consensus (and shift in loyalty) has occurred on issues of migration and asylum. We can thus weigh evolving norms against the shifting context of institutional and policy developments.

Disaggregating immigration attitudes

In mapping attitudes and behaviors, it is important to note the differences between how people think about issues and what they know about them. Social psychologists provide important insights into the relationship between the three components of attitudes (affective, cognitive, and evaluative). For example, if an individual believes that the aim of the Community is to eradicate unemployment from Europe, then his/her judgment may be very negative, given the current European economic trends. On the other hand, if one believes that the Community was founded to increase trade between member-states, then a more positive overall evaluation may be expected to form (Hewstone 1986: 52). In this sense, an effort needs to be made to relate what people think about issues to what they know. Various data have been used to explore the relationship between cognitive mobilization and feelings about European integration (Inglehart, 1970a, 1971, 1990a; Feld and Wildgen 1976; Gabel 1998a), and they have been supported by findings on American public opinion (Zaller 1992).[11] Framing this relationship more broadly, Daniel Yankelovich provides a useful account of judgment, which inherently presumes that knowledge may be linked to attitudes (1991). According to Yankelovich, once people move beyond the abstract dimensions of their opinions and come to consider the concrete consequences of their views, they may formulate judgments that appear more predictable and stable.

Leading migration scholars recognize the importance of knowledge as a basis for predicting attitudes and policy preferences. In an influential migration study, presented in 1993 and published by the *International Migration Review* (1995), Gary Freeman explained "why the immigration intake is too large in democracies." Identifying the constraints in the immigration debate that account for larger-than-optimal annual intakes – more liberal than public opinion calls for – Freeman concluded that the public had little knowledge about immigration flows and policies. In arguing that immigration issues are debated in a manner that distorts the information available, he averred,

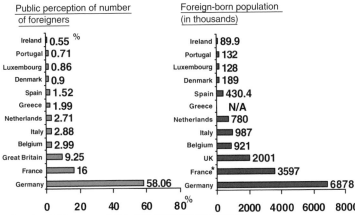

*France's stock data were unavailable for 1993; 1990 figures are reported here.

Source (n-size): *Eurobarometer* 39,1993 (15,136); OECD 1999 (reporting 1993 figures).

Q: *Which country of the European Community has the most immigrants and/or political asylum-seekers?*

Figure 3.2 Perception vs. reality: which nation has the greatest foreign-born population?

Citizens in democracies tend to be rationally ignorant of many issues because the incentives to become informed fail to override the costs of obtaining information. (1995: 883)

According to Freeman, the diffuse costs of migration on an uninformed public work in favor of advocates of expansion, who reap the concentrated benefits – hence the disconnect between elite and public preferences. While this observation is partially accurate, especially in cases related to organized interests that Freeman talks about, the findings in my study paint a more complex attitudinal portrait.

Although it is difficult to assess the existence of a "rational public,"[12] the data do not support the notion of an ignorant public.[13] In fact, it may appear that publics are more sophisticated or aware than initially believed. A comparison of the public's perception (among an aggregated European sample) of where most immigrants and political asylum-seekers resided and the number of foreign-born people in each nation in 1993 shows a high correlation (see figures 3.2 and 3.3).[14] A remarkable 93 percent of the variability in the public's perception of where most immigrants and political asylum-seekers reside is explained by the actual foreign-born population.

When Europeans were asked to identify which country had the largest concentration of immigrants and asylum-seekers, approximately 58 percent reported Germany, 16 percent identified France, and over

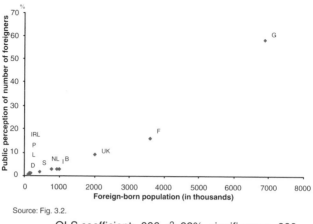

Source: Fig. 3.2.

OLS coefficient: .006, r^2: 93%, significance: .000

Figure 3.3 Public perception vs. actual foreign-born population, by country

9 percent identified Britain. These estimates roughly correspond to the actual size order of the foreign-born population in each country.

Although members of the mass public do not qualify as experts, the data do prove them to be more knowledgeable than Freeman suggests. As a whole, they offer sensible responses that are reflective of the world around them.

These same data can be looked at in another light. One might conclude from the data above that only those respondents who said Germany had the most immigrants and political asylum-seekers were correct while all other respondents were wrong. Indeed, had they been experts on the immigration issue, these respondents would have all said Germany. However, there is some order to mass assessments of immigrant numbers, in the sense that the majority of respondents thought Germany was the largest receiver nation, followed by the second-largest group, who thought France had the largest number of resident migrants. These estimates mirrored the actual numbers for the British case, and the others as well. Immigrant numbers yield evidence of a public able to make informed assessments of immigration demographics in their country context. We may infer that attitudes toward immigrants are neither random nor biased in some systematic direction, but based on informed views.

These sentiments do not necessarily, however, translate into rational or consistent policy preferences. According to Freeman, for example, "it might appear that immigration is one of those highly salient and emotive issues about which voters would feel strongly and with respect to which

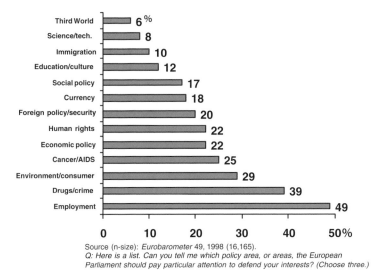

Source (n-size): *Eurobarometer* 49, 1998 (16,165).
Q: *Here is a list. Can you tell me which policy area, or areas, the European Parliament should pay particular attention to defend your interests? (Choose three.)*

Figure 3.4 Public policy priorities for the European Parliament

they would develop well-informed opinions" (1995: 883). Although publics are more informed than migration scholars have assumed, there are multiple aspects to their immigration concerns.

Freeman's commentary on public opinion requires another qualification, which may clarify some otherwise anomalous aspects of public opinion data. It calls attention to an important distinction between *politicization* (intensity) and issue *salience* (attachment). While immigration issues may be politically charged, their salience in the minds of ordinary citizens may be uneven.[15] For example, when asked to assess critical policy areas to be addressed by the European Parliament, European publics are far more concerned with issues such as AIDS, drugs, crime, and employment. In contrast, other highly publicized and inflammatory issues such as immigration, culture, education, and Third World poverty seem to bother publics little (see figure 3.4).

We know that immigration is an issue that can spark controversial debates, engender ambivalence, polarize the public, and/or threaten the capacity of the EU to govern. So why would the public seem to rank immigration so low on the EP agenda?

A partial explanation may be that publics prefer to see national, rather than EU, competence over immigration, as the question in figure 3.4 poses. This phenomenon is examined more extensively in chapter 5 by considering the dynamics and polarizations generated by European integration – especially as they affect immigration attitudes. Related to this explanation is the more general criticism about the dubious linkage between public opinion and the EP as the latter is perceived to be politically marginal. To neutralize this point, one may consider the replication of these proclivities when Europeans were asked about priorities for the European Union (see Eurobarometer 45.1, 1996).

Another explanation that merits consideration relates to the distinction between personal (private) and political (public) concerns. In this scenario, we may compare the immigration issue in Europe to the abortion issue in the United States. When Americans were asked to identify the most important problem facing their country, only 1 percent said abortion (Gallup/*USA Today*, 1997).[16] Yet many more feel passionately about this issue. Neither immigration nor abortion is relevant to the vast majority of people in their day-to-day lives. Instead, issues relating to the economy and security are a much more daily concern. Although issues such as abortion and immigration can spark public debate and challenge the governing order, they do not necessarily rank high as salient issues.[17]

More can be learned about these anomalies by disentangling the effects of personal concerns from public or societal considerations. These distinctions may be understood by the different motivations underlying people's assessments. People tend to separate their personal concerns from broader judgments about social issues and politics. That is, while attitudinal motivations may be driven by personal self-interest – the classic pocket-book voting model (Kinder, Adams, and Gronke 1989), sociotropic motivations or national/societal concerns often dominate policy preferences.[18] These are conditions that extend beyond people's immediate situation (Kinder and Kiewiet 1981; Citrin, Reingold, and Green 1990; see ch. 5 for a fuller discussion). Applied to the immigration context, opposition or support for immigration may be linked more to perceptions of general societal conditions than to personal effects.

Immigration preferences may be informed by these models (used in different contexts, such as voting) of attitude constraints.[19] They include *symbolic politics* (long-standing abstract predispositions such as ideology, political beliefs, racial prejudice), *self-interest* (the "pocket-book" hypothesis), and *sociotropic* (conditions of the nation at large) motivations (see Sears *et al.* 1980; Sears and Citrin 1982; Kinder and Kiewiet 1981; Kinder, Adams, and Gronke 1989; Kinder and Sears 1981; Kinder and Sanders 1996; Bobo 1983). Each of these models may explain the tractability and nature of immigration concerns by distinguishing the bases of these attitudes – external realities (both personal and public) or internal values.[20] The value of these models lies in their power to reconcile an informed but detached public body. More powerfully, these distinctions allow us to resituate our discussion of immigration attitudes

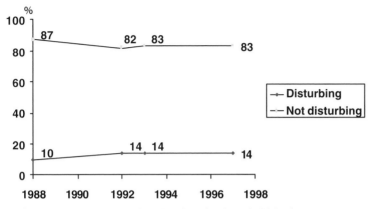

Source (n-size): *Eurobarometer* 30 (11,791); 37 (14,082); 39 (15,136); 48 (16,186).
Q: *Do you personally find the presence of people of another nationality disturbing in your daily life?*

Figure 3.5 Attitudes toward the presence of people of other nations, 1988–1997

by overcoming the tendency to label all oppositional attitudes as racist or xenophobic.

The lines between private and public concerns are captured in longitudinal analyses of general attitudes toward people of other nations. For example, in surveys conducted from 1988 to 1997, fewer than 15 percent of Europeans ever said that the presence of people of other nations was disturbing *on a personal basis* (figure 3.5).

Consistently, over 80 percent of Europeans said that the presence of people of other nations was not personally disturbing. Again, this suggests that the salience of the immigration issue in the daily lives of Europeans may be small relative to its politicization.[21] Self-interest does not seem to be a factor in their responses. Evaluations of the data would be incomplete without an understanding of Europeans' symbolic or sociotropic motivations – their abstract beliefs or concerns about general societal conditions.

Despite national variations, we know that there is some unease with immigrants among Europeans (see figure 3.6). In 1993, a majority of Europeans (54 percent) said immigrants were, in some way that is left open to each respondent's interpretation, a big problem. Only 36 percent said they were not a big problem. Feelings of tolerance coexist with the belief that immigrants are a big problem for host countries.

A notable nation-based variation in the assessment that "immigration is a big problem" (illustrated in figure 3.7) is revealing. Despite an overall consensus about the problematic nature of the immigration issue, the

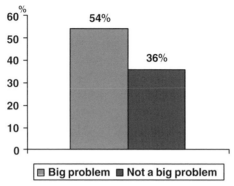

Source (n-size): *Eurobarometer* 39, 1993 (15,136).
Note: Figures do not add to 100 percent because don't knows are excluded.
Q: Do you think that immigrants and/or political asylum seekers are a big problem for (name of country), or are they not a big problem?

Figure 3.6 Views on immigrants and asylum-seekers as a problem

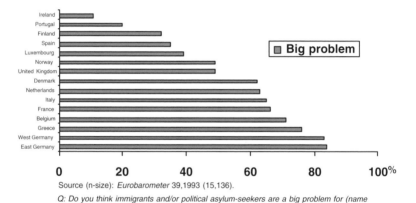

Source (n-size): *Eurobarometer* 39,1993 (15,136).
Q: Do you think immigrants and/or political asylum-seekers are a big problem for (name of country), or are they not a big problem?

Figure 3.7 Views on immigrants and asylum-seekers as a problem, by country

public opinion findings indicate that the sentiment that immigrants were a big problem was most pronounced in Germany, Belgium, and France – countries with substantial immigrant populations (see figure 3.7). In contrast, significantly fewer than 50 percent of respondents in Luxembourg, Spain, Finland, Portugal, and Ireland felt this way. The latter were countries with significantly smaller non-EU populations.

These national variations are suggestive of public sensitivity not only to general domestic environments (sociotropic concerns) even when they are not *personally* disturbed, but also to immigration demographics, reinforcing the notion that publics are informed. These findings serve to further clarify the discrepancies between politicization and issue attachment (salience).

Nonetheless, there is a kernel of truth in Freeman's account of the public–elite chasm when it comes to issue salience. Overall, elites tend to be more troubled by immigration issues, and rank them higher on the political agenda than their publics. Although in many countries national debates over immigration have been heated and have had political impact, according to the Eurobarometer study of public opinion, "by and large, Europeans do not see immigration as a problem of the first order; in most countries we find it at the bottom of the list or in the last place but one" (see figure 3.4).[22] In direct contrast, nearly all of the elites interviewed in the MEP sample identified immigration as among the first four problems facing Europe in the 1990s.[23] Other urgent areas of concern included unemployment, economic convergence in the EU, and questions relating to Eastern Europe[24] and to the "institutional future of the EP."[25]

Both the elite and public opinion samples concur that "unemployment" is a predominant common concern. However, while unemployment tends to be a latent factor in accounting for public support of extreme-right, anti-immigrant movements (Kitschelt with McGann 1995; Husbands 1981; Mayer and Perrineau 1989; Betz 1993; Jackman and Volpert 1996; Lewis-Beck and Mitchell 1993), only 11 percent of MEPs linked immigration to unemployment. Thus, although unemployment is an important issue to both publics and elites, it appears to be both an independent and a dependent variable of immigration-attitude formation.[26] Concerns with unemployment seem to be linked to immigration more among the publics than in the mindset of elites. But immigration is less important than unemployment to publics, whereas elites are equally attached to both issues. Notwithstanding, while people's assessments of immigration are tied to unemployment considerations, their attitudes are based on more national (sociotropic) considerations than personal ones (see chapter 5).

The sense that immigration is important to elites is further illuminated in the closed-ended surveys themselves. The dichotomy between public and private interests used to discern some of the attitudinal contradictions among publics is applicable to elite thinking. The questionnaire specifically identified four value perspectives, which ran the gamut of sociotropic (public) to self-interest (private) considerations: the importance of immigration to (1) the European Union; (2) the country; (3) the party group; (4) to the individual (MEP). On the basis of these four criteria combined, an index was constructed to determine the overall level of importance the immigration issue held in the minds of MEPs.

Two striking findings emerged. First, it is clear that for a large majority of members, the immigration issue was very significant. The combined index of importance resulted in a cumulative score of 64 percent of MEPs who identified immigration as important or very important in all four categories.

Second, this view became relatively most prevalent when placed in the European context. While the degrees of unanimity differed slightly, it is noteworthy that, as the immigration issue involves more players, more MEPs claimed that it was important. This sentiment grows as the focus broadens from the personal (69 percent) or country (70 percent) levels to the European Union (82 percent). These findings reinforce the distinction, noted above, between personal and political considerations of immigration problems. Moreover, the greater importance attributed to immigration at the European level than at the personal or national level may indicate that immigration issues seem to be more serious when they are perceived as a compounded problem, that is, affecting more member-states. That 82 percent of MEPs reported immigration as an important issue for the EU demands further inquiry as to the prospects for common policy-making. It also suggests that immigration, far from being motivated by self-interest projections, may indeed be driven by broader societal conditions – sociotropic effects.

Not only did MEPs agree that immigration was important, they also largely perceived immigration problems to be growing over time. Figure 3.8 shows that MEPs understood the immigration issue to be more problematic today than ever before. An overwhelming 84 percent of MEPs endorsed this view. Only 15 percent said the immigration problem was the same today as it was in the past. No one believed it was less of a problem today.

This is consistent with the trend that Rita Simon (1985) found in public thinking. Her study of magazines over the past century in the United States indicated that people look back to prior waves of immigration with more positive feelings than they have toward present waves. One may consider the possibility that any given generation looking back is either not currently threatened by that wave, or simply looking back at its grandparents. A plethora of literature on anti-foreigner sentiment in Europe prior to World War II confirms this cyclical dynamic (Wihtol de Wenden 1987; Layton-Henry 1992). A shift in sources of immigration challenges societal order as events change faster than beliefs, values, and symbols. Many elites interviewed support Tomas Hammar's suggestion that "changes mean that many of the new minority groups are more highly

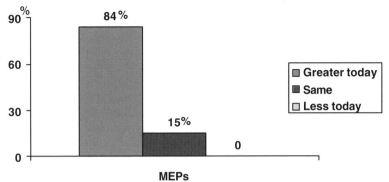

Source (n-size): 1992 survey of members of the European Parliament (167).
Q: Are the problems of immigration in Europe . . . greater today than in the past, about the same today as in the past or lesser today than in the past?
Note: Total does not equal 100 percent because of "don't knows."

Figure 3.8 Perceptions of immigration problems over time

visible, more different in culture and tradition from indigenous European populations than the so-called 'traditional' immigrant groups of the past" (1985b: 6). Since "traditional" groups seem to change over time, it is difficult to identify whether there is a tendency to romanticize the past, or whether new types and numbers of immigrants make problems seem particularly intractable. Are old immigration problems superseded today by new ones, have they been resolved, or were they non-existent in the minds of these politicians?

Past experiences may correspond to future expectations. MEPs may be willing to extend their backward assessments into forward-looking policy judgments. More empirical research is needed to determine whether there is a difference in future outlook between forgetful romanticists and realists who see today's problems as unparalleled.[27] The latter group may feel that immigration problems are insurmountable and therefore have a more pessimistic outlook. Conversely, romanticists tend to be inherently more idealistic. In immigration debates, this may be reinforced by immigration folklore. As Gary Freeman notes, the most common response to any criticism of immigration is that the same old arguments were used when the critic's forefathers arrived; as they were false then, they must be false today (1993: 5). Those romanticists who believe that present problems are greater because yesterday's immigration problems now appear manageable should generate some minimal confidence and optimism about the future.

In fact, this study reveals that a majority (60 percent) of MEPs were pessimistic or very pessimistic about the future resolution of immigration problems. Although there were optimists among this group, not one MEP was "very optimistic" about the resolution of immigration problems. Uncertainty about the future (and pessimism) may follow feelings that immigration problems are important, and have worsened over time. This brings to light the critical nature of immigration for a Europe under construction. It reminds us that, under conditions of uncertainty, attitudes tend to be distrustful of, or negatively oriented to, change. This will be further explored in chapter 5.

In tracing the linkage between attitudes and policy, we need to consider the cognitive, affective, and evaluative components of attitudes – what people know, feel, and value about immigration. As this study shows, like elites, the public knows more than we think they do when it comes to the emotionally charged immigration issue. They also feel that the issue is important, but place its value in societal and global perspective. As we move forward, a story will unfold that helps to reveal the greatest obstacles toward forming a comprehensive, supranational immigration policy. At the same time, an attitudinal study of policy preferences will help to reinforce the notion that the public has an approach toward this issue that is informed and systematic, if not always certain, and therefore important. The following discussion provides a general overview of attitudes toward immigration by breaking down the issue areas according to Hammar's conceptual framework – immigration and immigrant policies.

Attitudes toward immigration and immigrants

To understand public and elite opinion surrounding controversial issues, analysts need to examine a variety of data. A greater understanding of the general views of the European public and MEPs on immigration and immigrants can be achieved by analyzing data that pertain to both general intake orientations and specific immigrant or integration preferences.

Intake

Despite the tempered – even possibly ambivalent – response of Europeans to immigration, the European publics exhibit their resistance to increased numbers of immigrants very clearly. As shown in figure 3.9, a plurality of Europeans surveyed in 1992 and 1993 said that there were too many non-EU residents in their country.

And while in 1988 less than one-third (30 percent) said there were too many foreigners in their country, by 1997 this had increased to 41 percent (figure 3.10). Although the data points are not strictly comparable, they

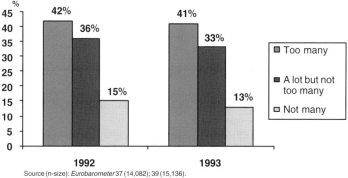

Source (n-size): *Eurobarometer* 37 (14,082); 39 (15,136).
Q: Generally speaking, how do you feel about people living in (name of country) who are not nationals of the European Community countries...are there too many, a lot but not too many or not many?

Figure 3.9 Perceptions of non-EU nationals

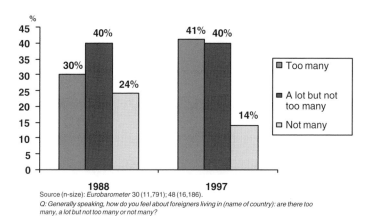

Source (n-size): *Eurobarometer* 30 (11,791); 48 (16,186).
Q: Generally speaking, how do you feel about foreigners living in (name of country): are there too many, a lot but not too many or not many?

Figure 3.10 Perceptions of all foreigners

are suggestive of a slight bias against non-EU nationals, as distinct from foreigners in general.

In comparison, MEPs' resistance to increasing numbers of immigrants was less clear but still evident.[28] With the same time points, we can generalize that MEPs make broad distinctions between EC/EU immigration and immigration in general. Figure 3.11 shows that a plurality of MEPs (40 percent) said in 1992 that an increased level of immigration from the European Community would be a good thing. Only 5 percent desired a decreased level of immigration from the EC.

From figure 3.11, we know that MEPs were just as likely to say that immigration in general should be decreased as to say it should be

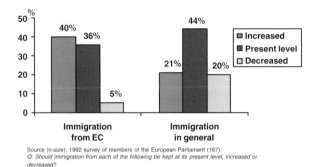

Source (n-size): 1992 survey of members of the European Parliament (167).
Q: Should immigration from each of the following be kept at its present level, increased or decreased?

Figure 3.11 MEP attitudes toward level of immigration

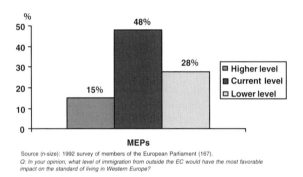

Source (n-size): 1992 survey of members of the European Parliament (167).
Q: In your opinion, what level of immigration from outside the EC would have the most favorable impact on the standard of living in Western Europe?

Figure 3.12 Immigration level and the standard of living

increased (20 percent vs. 21 percent respectively). Most MEPs seemed comfortable with the current level of immigration. But further probing paints a different picture.

MEPs tend to have a negative outlook on the implications of increased immigration as shown in figures 3.12 and 3.13. When these elites were asked what level of immigration would have the most favorable impact on the standard of living in Western Europe, almost twice as many MEPs said lower than current levels (28 percent) as said higher than current levels (15 percent). Figure 3.13 exhibits a more striking finding. MEPs were nearly three times more likely to say a lower level of immigration as compared to a higher one would have a more positive impact on the social fabric of Western Europe (31 percent vs. 11 percent).

These variations in attitudes must be interpreted in the context of specific immigrant group preferences. A look at the opinions Europeans

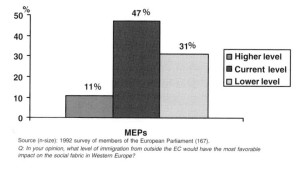

Source (n-size): 1992 survey of members of the European Parliament (167).
Q: In your opinion, what level of immigration from outside the EC would have the most favorable impact on the social fabric in Western Europe?

Figure 3.13 Immigration level and the social fabric

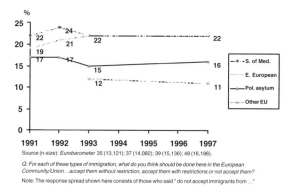

Source (n-size): Eurobarometer 35 (13,121); 37 (14,082); 39 (15,136); 48 (16,186).

Q: For each of these types of immigration, what do you think should be done here in the European Community/Union...accept them without restriction, accept them with restrictions or not accept them?
Note: The response spread shown here consists of those who said " do not accept immigrants from ..."

Figure 3.14 Public opposition to migrant groups over time

and MEPs hold toward specific types of immigrants is instructive about the perceived threats associated with increased immigration.

Most and least preferred immigrant groups   From 1991 to 1997, Eurobarometer surveys asked Europeans whether or not certain groups should be accepted as immigrants. Figure 3.14 shows that, while fewer than 25 percent of Europeans believe any of the identified groups should not be accepted into their nation, there is a statistically significant difference in the levels of group rejection. Europeans were most likely to say that immigrants from south of the Mediterranean and Eastern Europe should *not* be accepted. When asked in 1993 and 1997, Europeans were least likely to say that members of other EU nations should not be accepted.

In 1988, Europeans were asked to rate groups of people on a scale from one to ten, with one being least favorable and ten being most

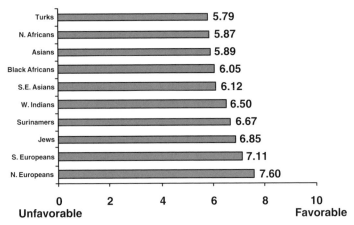

Source (n-size): *Eurobarometer 30*, 1998 (15,136).

Q: I would like to get your feelings, favorable or unfavorable, about the groups on this list.

Figure 3.15 Mean ratings of affinities toward various migrant groups

favorable. They ranked South Europeans and North Europeans highest (mean ratings of 7.1 and 7.6 respectively). Ranked lowest were Asians, North Africans, and Turks (mean ratings of 5.9, 5.9, and 5.8 respectively). These rankings can be seen in figure 3.15.

It should be noted that all groups were rated favorably (above a ranking of 5) by a statistically significant margin, according to a one-sample T-test. However, some groups were more highly preferred by respondents. With national variations that will be analyzed later, across the board and over time, public opinion preferred European migrants to those from south of the Mediterranean (mostly developing countries).[29] These data indicate a slight bias among Europeans toward immigrants who are like themselves and against immigrants who are least like themselves. When Europeans indicate that immigrants are a problem, they may be resistant to the potential destabilization of their national and cultural identity. Or, as has been shown in the US case, cultural opposition to certain newcomers may derive from threats to national values such as individual rights or entrepreneurship (Citrin, Reingold, and Green 1990). These conclusions are not surprising, given that cultural affinity (Thrändhardt and Miles 1995; McLaren 2001; Espenshade Calhoun 1993), like cultural threat (see Zolberg 1981, 1999; Zolberg and Long 1999; Fetzer 2000), has been shown to affect immigrant preferences.

Among MEPs, there exists a similar bias, as shown in figure 3.16. One-quarter to one-third of MEPs favored decreased levels of immigration by groups that were least like themselves. They were least favorable toward decreasing the level of immigration for groups of people that were

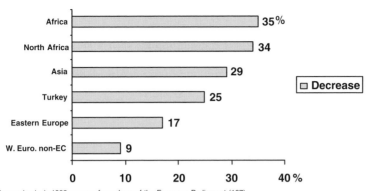

Source (n-size): 1992 survey of members of the European Parliament (167).
Q: Should immigration from each of the following be kept at its present level, increased or decreased?
Note: The response spread shown here consists of those who preferred to decrease the levels of immigration from the following areas.

Figure 3.16 MEP opposition to migrant groups

most like themselves (Eastern Europeans and Western Europeans from outside the European Community as well as immigrants from within the European Community). MEPs, like the European public, are less accepting of groups that least reflect the national and cultural identity of their nations.

Elites in general preferred the more economically competitive, yet culturally more similar Eastern European immigrants to those from developing countries. These affinities may reflect functional or realistic ideas of future European developments, especially regarding enlargement (see appendix F for Eastern European profiles). Thus, one member of the European Parliament's Civil Rights Committee reported that no specific rules were yet created in his committee except for "the obvious":

We have only just started discussing it [rules regarding immigration]. Obviously, it will be much more simple for East Europeans than for North Africans. That is about the only distinction. They [East Europeans] will be more welcome to people than North Africans, or Asians for that matter, because they are Europeans and the Community will one day include all those countries. (interview no. 198; London, April 16, 1992: 3).

These projections have become an increasing reality, given that over ten East European countries have had their applications considered as part of the enlargement proceedings which have paved the way for EU membership.[30]

Although the elite data reinforce those of public opinion, it is difficult to identify with certainty the bases of these preferences, whether they are racial, religious, occupational, or cultural considerations, because they crosscut. Some cross-tabulations, however, are telling. MEPs' priorities,

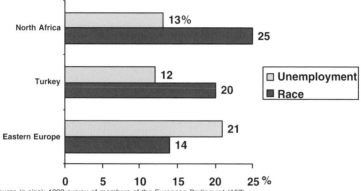

Source (n-size): 1992 survey of members of the European Parliament (167).
Q: Should immigration from each of the following be kept at its present level, increased, or decreased?
Q: When you think of immigration problems, to which area do you relate them?

Note: Figures exclude those who link immigration to other problem areas and therefore do not equal 100 percent. The table should be read as follows: of those who preferred decreased immigration from Eastern Europe, 14 percent said that immigration problems were linked to race; 21 percent reported that immigration problems were related to unemployment. Response spread for first question reflects those who preferred decreased levels; for second question, response spread consists of top two answers, race and unemployment.

Figure 3.17 MEP rejection of migrant groups, linked to race and unemployment concerns

for example, vary with the individual issues that concern them (i.e., unemployment, race). Of MEPs who associated immigration with race problems, many felt that immigrants from the developed countries of North Africa and Africa should be decreased (44 percent and 41 percent respectively).[31] In contrast, those that favored decreased immigration from Eastern Europe were slightly more preoccupied with unemployment than those who preferred decreased levels from North Africa (21 percent vs. 13 percent). The converse was true for considerations of race relations (see figure 3.17).

MEPs who were concerned with unemployment were most likely to seek a reduction of migrants from Eastern Europe. One socialist MEP, for example, described the gravity of East European influxes:

The fear of immigration from Eastern [European] countries, even though it is very low, can virtually be explosive because it is different from immigration [already existing] in Europe – which is from North Africa. People from Eastern Europe, unlike those from North Africa, will compete for normal jobs with the Europeans . . . There should be less in terms of racial problems because it's more or less the same. But there is more competitiveness in the market. So, economically, immigration from the East is worst. In terms of integration, or religion, or ethnic groups, it's much easier. (interview no. 515; Brussels, May 6, 1992)

Table 3.1 *EU and non-EU foreign populations in EU countries, 1990s*

Country	Foreign population (thousands)	Foreigners as % of total population	EU foreigners (thousands)	EU foreigners as % of foreign population	Non-EU foreigners (thousands)	Non-EU foreigners as % of foreign population
Austria	728.2	9.0	n.a.	n.a.	n.a.	n.a.
Belgium	910	9.0	555	61%	355	39%
Denmark	223	4.3	47	21%	176	79%
Finland	69	1.4	18	26%	55	74%
France[a]	3,597	6.4	1,322	37%	2,275	63%
Germany	7,173	8.8	1,811	25%	5,362	75%
Greece	155	1.5	44	28%	111	72%
Ireland	117	3.2	73[d]	63%[d]	44[d]	37%[d]
Italy	1,095.6[c]	2.0[c]	111[d]	10%[d]	984[d]	90%[d]
Luxembourg[b]	142.8	34.1	115[d]	80%[d]	28[d]	20%[d]
Netherlands	726	4.7	192	26%	534	74%
Portugal	169	1.7	42	25%	127	75%
Spain	499	1.3	235	47%	264	53%
Sweden	531	6.0	179	34%	352	66%
UK	1,992	3.4	818	41%	1,174	59%

[a] OECD 1992 (reporting 1990 figures).
[b] Eurostat 1999b (reporting 1996 figures).
[c] OECD 1998 (reporting 1996 figures).
[d] Eurostat 1994 (reporting 1992 figures).
Sources: Eurostat 1999b; OECD 1999.

In contrast, the more an MEP was concerned with race, the more likely he/she was to want to see a reduction in migration from the Third World. As the following chapter of country breakdowns reveals, these concerns are determined more by numbers and geopolitical considerations than by the nature of threat.

One thing is clear: preferences of immigrant groups are based on some concrete conditions. In addition to patent racist or xenophobic explanations, it may be fruitful to reevaluate the objective component of public attitudes, and consider the proportions of EU versus non-EU foreigners per total population (see table 3.1). Immigrant opposition may be relative to size of out-groups.

With the exceptions of Belgium and Luxembourg (which are EU centers) and Ireland, the relative size of non-EU foreigners per foreign population is significantly larger than the proportion of EU foreigners.[32] In most EU countries, non-EU populations account for two-thirds of the foreign population.

It is difficult to tell if attitudes are least favorable to visible non-EU migrants because of unabashed xenophobia. But in the context of the

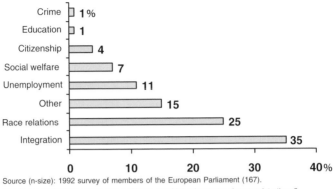

Source (n-size): 1992 survey of members of the European Parliament (167).
Q: When you think of immigration problems, to which other areas do you relate them?

Figure 3.18 Immigration problems and issue linkages among MEPs

most current breakdowns of immigrant group figures, there is no clear evidence that Europeans reject non-EU immigrants in a xenophobic fashion. A comparison between people's attitudes toward EU and non-EU populations further reveals only a limited degree of preference for EU migrants – over time – with most individuals seemingly not making a distinction (McLaren 2001: 85). According to the Eurobarometer data in 1993 and 1997, most EU citizens wanted to restrict all types of migration in some way (i.e., "accept, but with restrictions"). It is plausible that numbers speak more of discerning distinctions between non-EU and EU foreigners than of xenophobia itself.[33]

Immigrant and integration policies

Many Europeans find immigrants threatening in some way. Although MEPs were also threatened by the prospect of increasing immigration, they appear less resistant to integrating current immigrants. When MEPs were asked to indicate which issue areas they are most likely to identify with immigration problems, they revealed an understanding of integration as the foremost challenge in the immigration debate. As figure 3.18 shows, over one-third of MEPs (35 percent) said that integration was the issue most related to the immigration problem. Interestingly, one-quarter associated immigration predominantly to race relations. All other issues, including unemployment, social welfare, citizenship, education, and crime, had significantly fewer mentions by MEPs (see figure 3.18).

The emphasis on integration and race relations as most related to immigration problems and the inextricable linkage between these

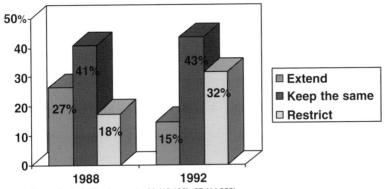

Source (n-size): *Eurobarometer* 30 (15,136); 37 (14,082).

Q: *Talking about these people living in (name of country) who are neither (nationality) nor citizens of the European Community, do you think we should extend their rights, restrict their rights or leave things as they are?*

Figure 3.19 Public views on the rights of non-EU immigrants, 1988 and 1992

concerns indicate a body of legislators who know well where the greatest difficulties in the immigration debate lie.

Although the data show some agreement on immigration policy as it relates to intake, this consensus breaks down with regard to issues of integration. Public opinion findings not only show support for a restrictive immigrant policy, but also shed light on some important distinctions between elites and masses with regard to the nature of immigrant policy. Figure 3.19 shows that a small and declining number of Europeans wish to extend rights to non-EU immigrants. Only 27 percent preferred to extend rights to non-EU immigrants in 1988. This declined to 15 percent in 1992. By 1992, the European public was 14 percent more likely to say that the rights of non-EU immigrants should be restricted than it was in 1988.

Although MEPs were asked about the rights of immigrants as a whole while the European public was asked about immigrants from outside the European Community/Union, the data remain telling.

Figure 3.20 underscores that MEPs were dramatically more likely than the European public to prefer extending the rights of immigrants. Over three-fourths of MEPs believed that immigrant rights should be extended. Less than one-fourth of MEPs said that the rights should be kept the same or restricted. Some of the discordance between mass and elite attitudes may be explained by the different question wording provided to the two samples as well as distinct schemata held by the

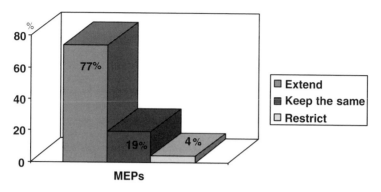

Source (n-size): 1992 survey of members of the European Parliament (167).

Q: What should be done about the rights of immigrants?

Figure 3.20 MEP views on the rights of immigrants

two audiences. For example, MEPs and the European public may define "rights" in dissimilar ways, a term which has been classically understood as a trilogy of civil, social, and political rights (Marshall 1963).[34] The pronounced difference in attitudes, however, cannot be so easily explained away.

There seems to be a much stronger impulse toward immigrant integration among MEPs than among the general European public. This marks an important divergence in the opinions of MEPs as compared to the opinions of the European public. Decision-makers are not unaware of public opinion, however. When asked about voting and other political rights for immigrants, MEPs emphatically underlined the distinction between their personal convictions and those they contend the public wanted to hear. One French socialist talked about the difference:

You are not asking me how I am going to win votes; you are asking me what I think. It's not the same thing – it is true that often there is a Realpolitik and we, the Socialists, say: here is what we would like. But there is public opinion. There are two things. First, to know what are our beliefs and, after, if we are prepared to delay some things due to the fact that it is not the right time for the public. (interview no. 310; Strasbourg, May 11, 1992)

In thinking about immigrant policy, public opinion counts:

I believe an immigrant who has come here and works should have all the rights of the citizen, and he must vote. But, as you can see, we could not give him the right to vote. We could not go that far because we know public opinion. (ibid.)

Though these commentaries underscore the differences between publics and elites that Freeman described, they give more credence to the impact of public opinion in conditioning the debate.

If V. O. Key's theory on elites guiding mass opinion is correct, we can expect that the public will be influenced by the governing elite in favor of extending immigrant rights. If the public is not so easily swayed by elites, then the extension of immigrant rights may be a point of enormous contention that will result in some political upheaval. Given some of the accounts of European elites, we may expect that this may be slow in coming. So far, the prevalent attitude toward liberal immigrant policies is counterintuitive to (and may ultimately be circumscribed by) the fact that few politicians in Europe have been able to mobilize votes by being favorable to immigrants (Messina 1990).

Although much has been written about "immigration thresholds," how immigrant group size translates into immigrant exclusion remains tenuous and ambiguous (see next chapter for fuller treatment).[35] Both the interviews and questionnaires confirmed the public opinion data regarding the impact of immigrant numbers. However, the relationship between size of immigrant group and rejection of foreigners is complex. On the one hand, as the Eurobarometer study suggested, there is a pattern of negative attitudes toward immigrants, which rises according to the size of immigrant population.[36] This also follows accounts of electoral behavior; extreme-right parties such as the French Front national tend to do best in areas of high immigrant concentration (Mayer and Perrineau 1989; Schain 1987, 1999; Mayer 1999; Perrineau 1985, 1997).

On the other hand, as the Eurobarometer 30 report revealed, relationships between the number of immigrants and attitudes appear only on national averages (correlation rate = .82), not in individual answers (Commission of the European Communities 1989: 64). The relationship between immigrant numbers and rejection of foreigners does *not* indicate that people with more exposure to, and familiarity with, immigrants are less favorable to them. In fact, at an individual level, the Eurobarometer study found that people who live in neighborhoods or work within contexts where there is a wider range of different people are neither more nor less inclined than the rest of the population to have a hostile attitude to "other" people. The report suggested that attitudes may be more symbolic and subjective than concrete and objective.[37]

These contradictory findings stem either from ecological fallacies of attitudinal research, or from the potency of symbolic and sociotropic motivations (in this case, concerns about general conditions, such as European integration) over competitive self-interest, *per se*.[38] More specific to the European case, it also supports Dominique Schnapper's

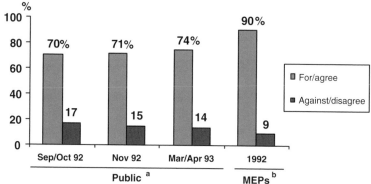

Source (n-size): *Eurobarometer* 38 (14,014); 38.1 (13,024); 39 (15,136); 1992 survey of MEPs (167).
Notes: Figures do not add to 100 percent because don't knows are excluded.
a. The public was asked, "The governments of EC member-states should work toward common rules in matters of political asylum, refugees and immigration…for or against?"
b. MEPs were asked, "How strongly do you agree or disagree that there should be a common immigration policy for members of the EC?," where "for" represents those who "agree" and "strongly agree" and "against" represents those who "disagree" and "strongly disagree."

Figure 3.21 Public and MEP attitudes regarding a common immigration/asylum policy

argument that "it is less the objective difficulties of integrating migrants – even if they do exist" – that explain the passion of the European debates on immigrants than the crisis of the nation-state itself (1994: 138). While numbers matter, it may be only in the context of other threats (i.e., community integration) that they fully make sense (Lahav 2002). The subtle but underlying sentiment of protecting the historical essence of one's homeland becomes more apparent when one looks at how much sovereignty the European public is willing to release to a supranational governing agency.

The politicization of immigration in the European Union

There is considerable accord in Europe on vague and idealistic policy goals, such as European integration and common immigration rules. However, this consensus dissipates on the particulars. On a general level, European publics and MEPs were in very strong agreement with the notion that EU member-states should follow common rules in matters of immigration. Figure 3.21 shows that, in 1992 and 1993 (after the signing of Maastricht and before its ratification), upwards of 70 percent of the European public supported such common rules.

Similarly, the figure shows that over half of MEPs (56 percent) agreed or agreed strongly in a common immigration policy. Only 9 percent of MEPs either disagreed or disagreed strongly with such an approach.

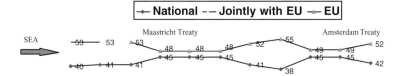

Mar/Apr 92 Sept/Oct92 Mar/Apr93 Oct/Nov 93 Mar/June 94 Nov/Dec 94 Apr/May 95 Jan/Mar 96 Oct/Nov 96 Oct/Nov 97 Apr/May 98
Source (n-size): *Eurobarometer* 37 (14,082); 38 (14,014); 39 (15,136); 40 (15,079); 41
(19,477); 42 (16,677); 43.1 (17,166); 44.2 (65,178); 46 (16,248); 48 (16,186); 49 (16,165).
Note: Break in data denotes change in response categories from "jointly with EU" to "EU."
SEA: signed in 1986, ratified in 1987; Maastricht: signed in Feb. 1992, ratified in
Nov. 1993; Amsterdam: signed in Oct. 1997; implemented in May 1999.
Q: *Which of the following areas of policy do you think should be decided by the national*
government, and which should be decided (jointly) with the European Community/Union...
immigration policy?

Figure 3.22 Key EU policy milestones and public opinion regarding immigration control

As global and pan-European thinkers, it is not surprising that MEPs overwhelmingly favored a common immigration policy for EU members. These sentiments need to be qualified, however.

First, it is important to delve deeper into what those "common rules" really mean. As the next chapter shows, this is an area of great variance. For example, while 70 percent of MEPs wished to speed up integration efforts, each party group had different motivations for and conceptions of a united Europe.[39] Members on the mainstream right tended to focus on a united Europe based on charity. Those on the left talked about a common Europe based on solidarity. As one Greek conservative MEP described:

Both the Socialists and the European People's Party consider it necessary and also imperative for the Community to formulate its common immigration policy. Now, how this common immigration policy could be formulated nobody knows exactly. (interview no. 468; Strasbourg, May 15, 1992)

Finally, these trends must be analyzed against longitudinal fluctuations that revolve around important policy output. Thus, it is noteworthy that support for common rules tends to follow major EU initiatives (e.g., the Maastricht Treaty agreement at the end of 1991). The trends illustrated in figure 3.22 complement those revealed in figure 2.2 and reflect these policy developments.

As figure 3.22 suggests, attitudes toward immigration policy tend to fluctuate with developments in the EU (see previous chapter). Europeans are more receptive to EU authority over immigration matters after closer cooperation has already taken hold in other sectors.

There are other interesting nuances when regulation is considered. Although MEPs unanimously favored a common immigration policy, they diverge on principles of implementation. MEPs were vague and divided on the technical matters of immigration policy. They did not uniformly identify the largest obstacles facing the Schengen Group.

Two significant findings emerged from questions probing the status of Schengen. Interestingly, over 10 percent of respondents felt strongly enough about this issue to go beyond the "closed" question and to offer spontaneous elaboration to their criticisms. Equally striking was the number (16 percent) of blank responses. This may be best explained by the finding (clarified during the interviews) that many MEPs in 1992–93 were not familiar with the Schengen Group at all. This Group, which until recently sat outside EU auspices and public supervision, is representative of the secretive and non-public administrative culture of immigration decision-making. Formal debate in a public forum is relatively new, and this accounts for the lack of familiarity with the substantive issues and developments at both the mass and elite level. Despite Amsterdam's adoption of the "Protocol integrating the Schengen *acquis* in the framework of the European Union," even officials of the ministries of interior and justice (the third pillar) seemed to be unclear about the content, with its 3,000 pages of documents (see Guiraudon 2000a: 265).

When it comes to policy resolution, MEPs seemed to have somewhat vague notions, rather than well-formulated ideas. This may stem from the politically defused nature of immigration issues in a Europe where such interests have been traditionally defined by bureaucrats and civil servants (Freeman 1979). Issue resolution may be replicated at the transnational decision-making level. The numerous extraparliamentary and intergovernmental bodies that are currently involved in EU immigration policy elaboration represent the trend toward this type of "behind closed doors" administrative policy-making. The Schengen Group and other such non-public bodies discussed in the last chapter have exerted a great deal of influence over the European Commission and individual governments, at the expense of pubic debate and publicly elected officials such as MEPs. That MEPs were largely unaware of Schengen or its challenges as late as the 1990s is therefore not surprising.

A less clear story emerges when respondents were asked to choose between a "common immigration policy" that is made by their nation-state and an immigration policy that is dictated by the EU. Figure 3.22 shows that the European public is polarized over whether the EU should make immigration policy over their national governments. A majority

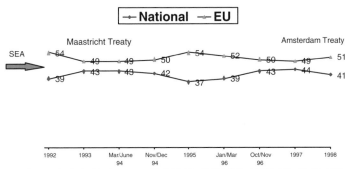

Source (n-size): *Eurobarometer* 38 (14,014); 40 (15,079); 41 (19,477); 42 (16,677); 43.1 (17,166); 44.2 (65,178); 46 (16,248); 48 (16,186); 49 (16,165).

Note: In 1992, the response categories read "national" or "jointly with EU."

Q: *Which of the following areas of policy do you think should be decided by the national government, and which should be decided (jointly) with the European Community/Union...policy on political asylum?*

Figure 3.23 Key EU policy milestones and public opinion regarding control over political asylum

(about 50 percent) believe that authority on immigration issues should lie with the European Union. As figure 3.23 reveals, the same holds true for policy relating to political asylum-seekers – though overall in recent years, publics are slightly more favorable to national competence over immigration than over asylum policy.

Approximately 50 percent of publics are willing to delegate asylum policy to EU institutions, but a large group (between 39 and 41 percent) would give national governments power to undercut EU governing authority on this issue.

This pattern is more exaggerated but roughly replicated among MEPs. Indeed, in figure 3.24, a majority of MEPs (71 percent) believed that authority on immigration issues should lie with the European Community in some form. However, a combined 57 percent of MEPs would give national governments power to undercut EC governing authority on this issue. Thirty-one percent of MEPs believed that national governments should have the option to veto EC policy on immigration, rendering it meaningless. Over a quarter (26 percent) believed that national governments alone should have jurisdiction over immigration policy.

In the same year, this trend was echoed by the European public when it was asked about competence over immigrants' status (i.e., integration issues). In 1988, a majority of respondents said they would prefer some role for the national government in defining the status of non-EU

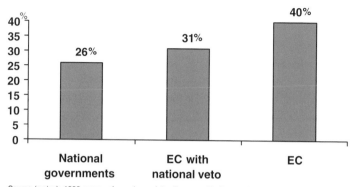

Source (n-size): 1992 survey of members of the European Parliament (167).
Note: "National governments" includes MEPs saying "national governments acting independently" and "national governments, through prior consultation with other EC governments."
Q: Who should be responsible for regulating immigration policy?

Figure 3.24 MEP preferences on immigration competence

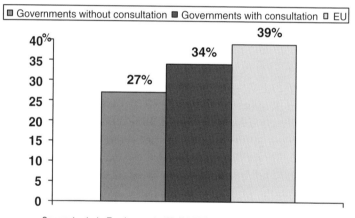

Source (n-size): Eurobarometer 30 (11,791).

Q: Talking about these people living in (country) who are neither (nationality) nor citizens of the European Community, which of these ways would you define their status?

Figure 3.25 Public preferences on competence over immigrant status

immigrants (61 percent). Twenty-seven percent of these respondents believed that the national governments should act alone in this capacity. Slightly more respondents (34 percent) said that governments ought to make these decisions but in consultation with other nations. In contrast, 39 percent of the European public was willing to give this decision-making power to the European Union. In sum, most Europeans in 1988 felt that

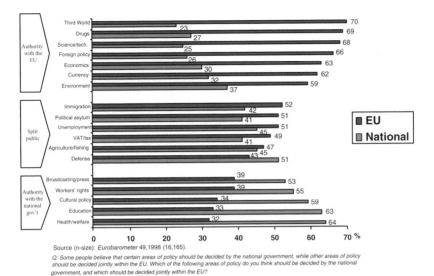

Source (n-size): *Eurobarometer 49,1998 (16,165).*

Q: *Some people believe that certain areas of policy should be decided by the national government, while other areas of policy should be decided jointly within the EU. Which of the following areas of policy do you think should be decided by the national government, and which should be decided jointly within the EU?*

Figure 3.26 Public preferences on policy competence across issue areas

the national government should have jurisdiction over the EU in dictating the status of non-EU immigrants.

These figures show that Europeans are polarized over whether the EU should make immigration and asylum policy over their national governments. The attitudes of both the European public and the MEPs forewarn of the great struggles to come as a unified Europe undertakes to resolve the immigration issue. The split opinions on where immigration authority should lie present a thorny challenge for policy-making. Placed in the EU context, immigration generates substantial polarization. A look at where Europeans believe authority should lie across policy areas brings to light some interesting findings that help to illuminate how challenging immigration cooperation is likely to be.

These contradictions are particularly evident in immigration and asylum policies. Consider the areas over which Europeans are comfortable to delegate responsibility. For example, figure 3.26 shows that in the areas of drugs, foreign policy, science and technology, economics, the Third World, currency, and the environment, Europeans are willing to have the EU make policy. These are issues that are clearly international in flavor or issues that can be more effectively addressed by a supranational authority without compromising national culture and identity. But in the areas of political asylum, cultural policy, VAT/tax, education, agriculture/fishing, unemployment, immigration, workers' rights, broadcasting/press, health/welfare, and defense, Europeans are either split or unwilling to cede power to the EU.

A close look at these policy areas reveals some interesting trends. Europeans view policy areas that most contribute to the unique national experience of each country – cultural policy, education, broadcasting/press – as clearly in the realm of national authority. They are unwilling to abdicate national sovereignty to the EU where it may threaten their national culture and identity. The more international issues on which Europeans are willing to cede control to the EU also reflect broader societal concerns and are less personally threatening than issues such as education, workers' rights, and welfare, over which publics want to see national control.

These two sentiments – a willingness to have a supranational entity take over certain issue areas for more effective policy-making, but a resistance toward this trend when it disrupts the national culture and identity – clash with respect to the immigration issue. Earlier data have shown that Europeans have a slight bias against immigrants and political asylum-seekers who have cultures and identities very distinct from theirs. However, add to this the clear need for a supranational approach toward these issues, and one is faced with a conundrum. Should the European public succumb to the threat of losing their unique cultures and identities for a viable European Union to exist or should the potential of this supranational force be dismissed for the preservation of national identity? Clearly, this issue will not be easily resolved. Hence, there exists ambivalence on where immigration authority should lie. The European public is about equally split on allowing authority on the immigration issue to lie within national government or with the EU. As discussed earlier, they also have multiple dimensions (e.g., self-interest, sociotropic, symbolic) motivating their considerations.

The theories of public judgment put forward by Daniel Yankelovich are helpful in understanding public and elite opinion on the debate over where authority should lie in immigration policy. Yankelovich proposed that "the quality of public opinion be considered good when the public accepts responsibility for the consequences of its views and poor when the public, for whatever reason, is unprepared to do so . . . When the people's views flip-flop the moment the possible consequences of their opinions are raised, this is a sure sign of poor quality" (1991: 24–26). As an example of poor-quality public opinion, Yankelovich analyzed survey data on Americans' attitudes toward protectionism. At first, Americans were in strong support of protectionist legislation that was thought to save American jobs. For example, an NBC News/*Wall Street Journal* poll had 51 percent of Americans favoring "greater limits on goods imported into the United States." However, once they were presented with the possible consequences of protectionism (restrictions on the variety and choice of products, higher prices, and poorer quality), the support for greater limits on imports dropped from a 51 percent majority to a 19 percent minority. Americans had not given this issue thorough consideration before they were surveyed (Yankelovich 1991: 24–26). Therefore, public opinion seemed unstable and easily manipulated.

From the analysis above, we learn that public opinion, as well as the opinions of MEPs, can undergo dramatic change when the consequences of their issue stances are discussed more concretely. Therefore, we may conclude that the public and MEPs have only slowly considered and taken full responsibility for these consequences. They have not, to paraphrase Yankelovich, come to complete "public judgment." Thus, while 70 percent or more of the public during the early 1990s consistently agreed that there should be common rules in matters of political asylum, refugees, and immigration (figure 3.21), this same public is evenly split when they are asked if immigration or political asylum policy should be dictated by national governments or the EU (figures 3.22–3.23). Similarly, 90 percent of MEPs agreed that there should be a common immigration policy (figure 3.21), yet a majority of these same MEPs (57 percent), like the publics (61 percent) in figure 3.25, said that authority should lie with national governments or that, at least, the national governments should have a veto power over immigration regulation (figure 3.24) – rendering a common EU immigration policy futile.

Conclusions

In view of the summary evidence outlined in this chapter, we need to reconsider the image of a public uninformed about immigration matters and irrelevant to elite decision-making. Despite the ambivalent sentiments of public opinion, there is an objective and systematic attachment to immigration issues that exposes a fairly sophisticated European public (see figures 3.2–3.3). Attitudinal patterns are suggestive of public sensitivity not only to domestic environments (societal concerns) even when they are not personally disturbed, but also to immigration demographics, reinforcing the notion that perceptions have some context (see figure 3.7). The distinctions between personal and societal considerations as well as between politicization and issue salience help unravel all sorts of paradoxes and inconsistencies that we find in exploring immigration attitudes. They merit further exploration.

Even more surprisingly, the comparative analysis of public and MEP attitudes reveals a broad collective correspondence. The two groups – with exceptions in some areas of immigration (e.g., salience, immigrant integration, common principles) – are not poles apart: elites may be less knowledgeable (e.g., about Schengen and other regulation processes) than expected, and equally negative toward immigrant intake.

Overall, there is some consensus among both the elites and the public opinion samples on the general and abstract dimension of the immigration issue. As this chapter underscores, they agree that the immigration problem is greater today than ever before; that it is one of the most controversial issues on the political agenda; that they want it controlled. They are highly pessimistic about its future resolution. Although public opinion was preoccupied with issues other than immigration (figure 3.4), over 50 percent of Europeans reported immigrants to be a big problem for their countries (figure 3.6); nearly all the elites interviewed in our sample identified immigration among the first four problems facing Europe in the 1990s. Further, over 80 percent of those surveyed indicated that it was very important in the context of European integration. Most Europeans find immigrants threatening in some way or another.

Nonetheless, this agreement hides the fact that there are significant divisions regarding how policy-makers might manage and European publics might respond to the more concrete dimension of the issue. MEPs and publics in fact disagree on all types of immigrant policies and migrant group preferences (figures 3.14–3.17). They differ in the definitions of the problem, in their preferences for immigration levels and immigrant groups, and on the structure and content of a common immigration policy (figures 3.22–3.26). They also fundamentally diverge with regard to issues of immigrant rights (figures 3.19–3.20).

Although the data show some agreement on immigration policy as it relates to intake, there is a pronounced divergence of opinion between the European public and MEPs on components of immigration policy that relate to integration. These distinctions tap into the classification scheme outlined by Hammar (1985b). They give credence to the two-dimensional space occupied by the immigration issue, whereby policy on intake or control is marked by consensus, while immigrant policy is characterized by more dissonance and partisan competition (Money 1995). This dichotomy represents the normative template of the mixed policy developments noted in the previous chapter.

To understand emerging institutions and norms surrounding contro-versial issues, analysts need to take a look at a variety of data. The seeming inconsistency of institutional developments in EU immigration initiatives described in the previous chapter, for example, has important underpinnings in attitudes. Although public and elite opinion may seem random or contradictory at first, there is often an underlying story to be told. This narrative brings to light the complex and ambivalent nature of human beings when confronted with weighty issues. The story behind the European public and MEP attitudes toward immigration as it plays out in the EU is no exception. This is an issue that takes on new importance as the European Union struggles to build a political union or federation that facilitates the free movement of people along with the free movement of goods. Europeans exhibit interest in market freedoms, but reticence about the consequences for national control over immigration borders.

As we look toward the future, the issues that will intervene and hamper the progress of the EU most are those that must transcend the nation-state for an adequately strong international agency to exist, but threaten to disturb a nation's identity and culture. Like immigration and political asylum, these issues divide the European public into two nearly equal camps: those who wish for EU authority and those who wish for national authority. According to Yankelovich's theory, once the public and MEPs have taken positions on the immigration issue that take full responsibility for any consequences, they will have made the decision to circumscribe the EU as a supranational body or to risk losing their nation's unique identity. For now, Europeans and their elected representatives will continue to grapple with the issue, wishing to have it both ways and being easily swayed from one position to the next.

Much evolution is yet to come for public and elite opinion on the immigration debate. It is likely that, as the EU moves forward and continues to take an increasingly important role in the European policy, all will have to come to "public judgment" on the immigration issue. With it, we may expect the emergence of a coherent public voice, or as Yankelovich describes it, "a genuine *vox populi.*" In the meantime, we can only explore the direction of these attitudes. We are thus compelled to examine the nature and bases of attitudinal differences.

NOTES

1. For a detailed overview, see Hewstone 1986: 9–22; Niedermayer and Sinnott 1995b.
2. "Bringing attitudes back in" implies that public opinion is rediscovered, and raises the question of whether it was ever considered. For a cogent intellectual history of the role of public opinion in integration theory, see Sinnott 1995.
3. There does seem to be a peak around the time of the Maastricht Treaty agreement in late 1991, but this is difficult to interpret, because ratification took place in 1993, by which time numbers had decreased substantially.

4. This view has also been adopted recently to argue more positive outcomes of the mass–elite relationship (see Carrubba 2001 for a compelling overview of this connection). For example, some argue that a "permissive consensus" between elites and masses (positively predisposed to integration) existed until 1992 because the issues surrounding European policy were technical in nature and had minimal direct impact upon Europeans (Lindberg and Scheingold 1970; Inglehart 1971; Carrubba 2001). Other theoretical accounts include the cue-taking thesis which assumes that weakly held preferences facilitate elite persuasion of public opinion (see Zaller 1992). Finally, Stimson's policy-mood argument claims that a disinterested public exists because political elites have been hewing "close enough" to public preferences (1991).

5. In "A Ferment of Change," Jean Monnet, the father of this supranational vision, argued that the problems in Europe required radical changes in the way people thought, and that the step-by-step adoption of common rules would ultimately create a "silent revolution in men's minds" (1962). However, some early works have contradicted these unilinear functionalist accounts of a shift of support from national to supranational identities. According to Shepherd (1975), for example, support will remain driven by utilitarian or economic considerations, and will be limited to that domain. Despite support for Community membership, nationalists will thus not necessarily transfer that to support for unification as a whole.

6. In the United States, James Stimson, Michael Mackuen, and Robert Erikson (1995) have made a compelling case for the impact of public opinion by looking at the effectiveness of public mood in driving governmental activism. This phenomenon has been corroborated by findings that politicians respond rationally to a public's rationally motivated preferences, even when the public is uninterested and uninvolved (Carrubba 2001; Gabel and Palmer 1995).

7. This roughly correlates to Pierre Bourdieu's bold claim that "L'opinion publique n'existe pas" (1973).

8. Ippolito, Walker, and Kolson (1976) describe three models of mass–elite interaction: direct influence by elites of the masses (i.e., through sanctions); group influence of activists (through organizations such as political parties and interest groups); and elite deference because their opinion mirrors public opinion.

9. As Jean Monnet reflected on his original plan, he reiterated that the task of the Community would be to ensure that, each in its limited field, the new institutions would be thoroughly democratic (Monnet 1978: 367; see Holland 1994: 144). To this end, the first direct European Parliament elections took place in 1979 and the European Commission commissioned the Eurobarometer biannual reports on public opinion data as "a barometer . . . to measure the atmospheric pressure . . . and to some extent forecast public attitudes with regard to Community activities, particularly in the areas of most interest to the public" (*Eurobarometer* 1, 1974: 1). The fact that these social surveys continue lends testament to the importance of public opinion in European decision-making processes.

10. This shares Inglehart's (1970b) view that the value of aggregate public opinion is in its longitudinal study over time.

11. The broad term "cognitive mobilization" encompasses education, media exposure, factual knowledge, etc. Zaller's study of public opinion in the United States suggests that the greater a person's cognitive engagement with an issue, the more likely he/she is to receive political messages concerning it (1992: 42). Thus, variation in public opinion may be found despite similar messages, due to differences in citizens' levels of political awareness.

12. This term follows Page and Shapiro's (1982) definition, and is used here to mean a stable public opinion which is seen to fluctuate predictably with policy changes. It deviates from its more common instrumental usage, which implies a means–ends relationship based on data available to the individual. From this standpoint, the rational individual will employ rules of evidence and inference, while the irrational one will employ other means to reach conclusions (Jervis 1976: 119). In this sense, the term "rational public" may be misleading, as it would be difficult to impute rationality to an abstract and variegated public.

13. We can infer from the lack of ignorance that people have put sufficient investment into becoming informed and, thus, may be less rational, in Freeman's terms.

14. In efforts to standardize public opinion and migration figures, the data on foreign-born population were based on 1993 data on stocks. Note also that the terms "immigrants," "foreigners," "non-nationals," "out-groups," and "minorities" are also technically different, though they are often perceived equivalently. The literature and data are not consistent with regard to terminology, and therefore slight national variations are to be expected. Not all immigrants are "foreign-born," for example. Many are naturalized, such as in France, but are still thought of as immigrants, and vice versa, such as in Germany, where some foreign-born are not considered immigrants. In general, "immigrants" refers to a legal category and therefore excludes millions of naturalized foreigners. Since various names are used interchangeably, and are not necessarily reflective of technical public knowledge, I remain true to source, unless otherwise noted.

15. Politicization is reflected not only by the pervasiveness of the issue in electoral platforms, party politics, and the extraordinary rise of xenophobic movements, but also by public unease with immigrants.

16. The findings are based on a Gallup/CNN/*USA Today* poll of telephone interviews with 1,014 adults in August 1997. The question, "What do you think is the most important problem facing this country today?" produced the following top four responses: crime/violence, 20 percent; drugs, 15 percent; unemployment/jobs, 12 percent; education, 11 percent. Multiple responses were accepted.

17. While this is consistent with Gimpel and Edwards's account of American public opinion on immigration – namely that immigration is not a salient or decisive issue for voters (attachment) – it deviates in its assessment of politicization (intensity) and extent of partisan and ideological consensus (see Gimpel and Edwards 1999: 41–45).

18. Although self-interest may sometimes have a role in sociotropic interpretations, in the classical economic voting sense, self-interest models speak to the maximization of personal well-being (see Downs 1957).

19. The application of such models in various forms has increasingly come into academic vogue among scholars of immigration and prejudice (see Fetzer 2000; Gibson 2002; McLaren 2002; Espenshade and Calhoun 1993; Citrin, Reingold, and Green 1990; Quillian 1995), but it has yet to be systematically tested in the EU context.

20. Thus, for example, people who place a high priority on immigration because their fundamental cultural values are at stake may not find incremental actions by European governments as satisfying as those who are disturbed by large societal changes in their environment. Self-interest and sociotropic origins of attitudes emphasize external attitudinal processes, suggesting that citizens react to concrete problems in their environment, whereas symbolic models focus on mechanisms or values that exist within people (for a cogent application to environmental issues, see Rohrschneider 1988). Symbolic politics may be triggered in this case, for example, by instinctual threats to symbols attached to national sovereignty or identity.

21. This speaks to the differences between issue intensity and attachment (see appendix A for methodological issues on this point).

22. Based on the survey question, "In your opinion, which of the problems that seem to face us nowadays is the most important? And which of these is the least important?" (*Eurobarometer* 30, 1989: 4).

23. To overcome the question-order bias of the survey questionnaire, which inherently forced respondents to focus on immigration, the oral interviews were conducted weeks after the questionnaire, and began by first surveying ideas on random issues (see appendix A for fuller discussion of methodological issues of measurement).

24. Interview no. 198 (London, April 16, 1992); interview no. 123 (London, April 24, 1992); interview no. 15 (Brussels, May 6, 1992).

25. Interview no. 198 (London, April 16, 1992).

26. The 1997 public opinion study found that immigrants are most welcome when they have an economically useful function. Forty-three percent of respondents said that "legally established immigrants from outside the EU should be sent back to their country of origin" if they were unemployed. Views on minorities and immigrants, however, were ambivalent. Approximately 63 percent of respondents said "the presence of people from these minority groups increases unemployment" and 68 percent claimed that minorities do jobs nobody else wants to do (*Eurobarometer* 47.1, Spring 1997).

27. The literature on voting may be valuable, as it is divided on whether voters base their preferences on retrospective or prospective evaluations (see Fiorina 1981; Miller and Wattenberg 1985; Mackuen, Erikson, and Stimson 1992). See Citrin *et al.* for the application of a "pessimism hypothesis" to explain attitudes toward immigration (1997: 860–861).

28. Note that in standardizing questions for comparative analysis, one needs to consider the different wording of questions posed to elite and masses. Thus, while in the latter case it may be appropriate to gauge attitudes toward

immigrant numbers by "too many" (i.e., projecting on numbers), a corresponding question to decision-makers involves policy-related dimensions that come in the form of "increase," "decrease," etc. This reflects an effort to avoid treating elites as "bricklayers" (or laypeople; see Brown 1969), and to engage them on policy-based attitudes. On the terminology and measurement of "immigrants," see n. 2, p. 21.

29. Data in 1993 and 1997 revealed that more respondents would sanction EC/EU citizens to migrate with no restrictions to their countries than would allow migrants from south of the Mediterranean the same treatment. Conversely, fewer respondents would reject EC/EU migrants outright than were willing to reject migrants from south of the Mediterranean in both years of the Eurobarometer surveys (nos. 39 and 48). See also McLaren 2001: 85.

30. The Helsinki Conference of the European Council on the Enlargement Process (December 10–11, 1999) included thirteen applicant countries: Bulgaria, Cyprus, the Czech Republic, Estonia, Hungary, Latvia, Lithuania, Malta, Poland, Romania, the Slovak Republic, Slovenia, and Turkey. The Seville Summit and the ratification of the Nice Treaty by the last country (Ireland) have essentially opened up the way for the expansion of the EU. With the exception of Bulgaria, Romania, and Turkey, all ten countries are scheduled to be admitted by May 2004.

31. Only 12 percent of those who linked immigration to racial relations felt that immigration from Eastern Europe should be decreased. This is based on those who claimed that, when they think of immigration problems, they relate them to race relations first, in the survey questionnaire.

32. Analysis must factor in the fact that, since free movement rights have been implemented, most countries do not keep statistics on the flow of EU nationals in member-countries, though these figures may be deduced indirectly from data on stocks (see Koslowski 1994 on intra-EU migration dynamics).

33. I refer here to Bernd Baumgartl and Adrian Favell's definition of xenophobia as "the dread of 'foreigners' as a group, whether defined legally as 'immigrants,' or by their strangeness as a visible group . . . taken as a classic device of self-definition as part of an 'in-group' in opposition to an 'out-group' " (1995: 379). For an early methodological approach to the study of immigration and racism, see Bogardus 1928.

34. Generally speaking, civil rights include freedom of movement, freedom of religion, freedom from torture, and the right to privacy; political rights include the rights of association, to vote, and to stand for elections, and freedom of speech; and social rights include the right to equality, education, and health care. In liberal democracies, citizenship rights have also included economic rights such as the right to private property and freedom to work or trade and to provide or receive services (Rawls 1971; Walzer 1983).

35. The "threshold of tolerance" notion is similar to the contact thesis, which largely stems from the work of Gordon Allport (1979 [1954]). It relates receptivity to the distribution of immigrants in one's neighborhood or region and to how many and what kind of personal contacts one has with newcomers. While there has been some evidence that casual contact with immigrants promotes

xenophobia and direct contact generates tolerance, there is much controversy on how to measure the two. Attitudinal research has consistently yielded contradictory results over ecological and contextual factors of immigrant rejection, and theoretical advancements have remained inconclusive. For a rigorous comparative attempt to empirically sort through this puzzle, see Money 1999; Fetzer 2000. See also Lubbers, Gijsberts, and Scheepers 2002 for a multilevel approach to disentangling extreme-right support.

36. This is based on the correlation between percentage of "answers stating 'too many' others" (in terms of nationality, race, religion, culture, and social class) and percentage of "non-EEC nationals in relation to population of country" (n = 12), *Eurobarometer* 30, p. 45.

37. If this is true, then Allport's distinction between casual and true acquaintance may be relevant. Perrineau's study of support for the anti-immigrant Front national found a correlation between immigrant numbers existed less in *communes* (city precincts) than in much larger *départements*. His explanation, that xenophobia forms "more from fantasy than from the actual perception of objective" or around "the stranger with whom one doesn't live but whom one senses at the city limits," follows the casual contact thesis (1985: 29; see also Fetzer 2000 for a fuller discussion).

38. Ecological fallacies involve the use of aggregate data to predict individual level behavior (see King 1997).

39. On party group positions, see Pridham and Pridham 1981: 11. See also Gabel and Hix 2002.

4   Immigration politics and the new Europe: organizing competing interests

> Act IV, Scene 1: We think that when vital interests are contradictory, it is the national interests which have the edge over all the others. In other words, we have a preferential philosophy. That is to say that we think that social life is made in concentric circles: the family, the city, the profession, etc., and that we have to look after ourselves first. There is a saying in the Front national, "I love my daughters more than my nieces, my nieces more than my cousins, my cousins more than my neighbors." And I add happily that does not mean that I detest my neighbors, it means that I love them less than my daughters. Our adversaries say, "You are xenophobic; you do not want anyone but the French." No, it is not true. But, we do think that there are hierarchies of affinity and tolerance.
>
> (Jean-Marie Le Pen in interview with researcher, Strasbourg, June 10, 1992.)

Immigration policy typifies issues caught between national and supranational domains. On the one hand, defining citizenship and deciding who should enter a country are a state's prime tasks, symbolizing national sovereignty and control. On the other hand, citizenship of a member-state now confers economic and social rights exercisable throughout the EU, and has consequently brought immigration policy under transnational regulation. As the EU attempts to integrate and manage these competing demands, attitudes toward immigration are swayed by country-specific and partisan/ideological interests. The findings here show that, even when several EU member-states share the same or similar interests and goals (i.e., European integration, controlled immigration), given domestic exigencies, their order of priority differs from one member-state to the next.

This chapter provides an attitudinal portrait of the factors that underlie the structural developments of the immigration debate as it evolves within the European Union. It probes domestic constraints – variables such as national identification, partisan affiliation, ideological positions related to immigration thinking – as a basis for understanding a collective immigration policy (or lack thereof). It is easy to detect the impact of multilevel interests in the European Parliament, given the diversity of

MEPs who, besides holding distinct national loyalties, represent different party affinities, political cultures, and immigration experiences. These differences result in attitude clusters that reflect certain discrepancies and patterns in policy thinking.

Primarily based on data derived from the study on members of the European Parliament (MEPs), elites who represent partisan-ideological, national, and transnational interests, this chapter assesses factors that account for differences in perception of immigration preferences.[1] In addition, I refer to comparative evidence from national public opinion surveys, collected by the European Commission's Eurobarometer series (see appendix A). Together, this normative and cognitive component of immigration represents the policy *input* dimension of immigration regulation. It allows us to identify the divisions in the European migration debate, to delineate how interests may be organized in a transnational community, and, hence, to evaluate prospects for regional integration.

National sources of attitudes

In an evolving Europe of increasing interdependence, national interests *are* significant. This is not surprising; after all, migrants do not move to Europe – they move to a physical land, a city or a village in a European country (Hammar 1985b). National attitudinal patterns underscore the multidimensionality of the immigration issue as it confronts the European Union. As discussed in chapter 2, immigration in Europe is a highly diverse phenomenon in terms of the populations involved and their conditions of access to rights in the host country. National experiences that include the degree of national heterogeneity or cultural diversity, rate of immigrant arrival, religious differences, and integration concerns invariably affect attitudes toward immigrants. According to Zolberg, an "ethnically undiversified nation with a dominant religion and which as a consequence of its insularity has experienced little immigration in the recent past may have a lower threshold of tolerance than a more heterogeneous one" (1981: 16).[2] The geopolitical context of national migration dynamics has left enduring differences in the perception of immigration issues and immigrant groups among the EU countries. While immigrants are often conceptualized as one uniform group, a harmonized EU immigration policy makes the particularities more relevant. These distinctions are based on immigrant origins, as well as cultural, religious, ethnic, and professional factors.

First, there is the division that has stood in the way of a truly unified Europe: namely, that which distinguishes advanced industrialized Northern Europe from traditionally less advanced Southern Europe. Second,

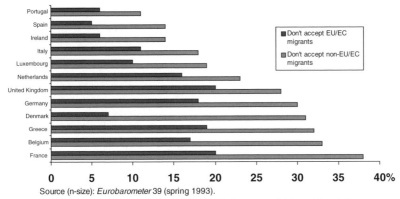

Source (n-size): *Eurobarometer* 39 (spring 1993).

Q: "If people from different countries south of the Mediterranean wish to work here in the European Community?"

Q: "And what about people coming from other countries of the European Community who wish to settle in (our country)?"

Figure 4.1 Public attitudes toward EC/EU and non-EC/EU migrants, by country

there is the group of West Europeans from countries such as Switzerland and Norway who are not members of the EU but who are equally developed economically and industrially. Third, there is the more recent exodus of peoples from the liberated countries of Eastern Europe, which are scheduled to join the EU in the future. Finally, there is the migratory pressure by the influx of mostly unskilled migrants and asylum-seekers from developing (often ex-colonial) nations. Generally speaking, reference to "immigration problems" is tantamount to referring to this fourth group. As illustrated in the previous chapter, these distinctions are translated into preferences toward different groups (see difference in mean ratings toward various immigrant groups in chapter 3).

As the previous chapter revealed, public opinion over time (1988, 1993, 1997) preferred European migrants to those from south of the Mediterranean, mostly developing countries. Although these distinctions exist across the board, national variations exist and may be analyzed (see figure 4.1).

In 1993, more respondents would reject outright migrants from south of the Mediterranean to work in their countries than would reject those from the EC/EU. Citizens from Spain, Portugal, and Ireland were the most likely to allow European citizens to migrate to their countries with no restrictions and even to extend to migrants from south of the Mediterranean the same treatment. These differences are worthy of further exploration.

Table 4.1 *MEP rankings of least desirable immigrant groups, by country*

Immigrant region	B	DK	F	FRG	G	IRL	I	L	N	P	S	UK
EU	3	X	6	5	X	X	X	X	X	2	4	X
Eastern Europe	2	2	5	1	3	3	5	X	3	X	5	4
Non-EU Western Europe	4	2	6	4	X	3	4	X	4	3	3	5
Turkey	**1**	2	4	3	**1**	X	3	**1**	2	3	4	3
North Africa	**1**	2	2	3	2	2	**1**	**1**	**1**	**1**	2	**1**
Africa	**1**	**1**	**1**	2	2	**1**	**1**	**1**	2	**1**	2	2
Asia	2	**1**	3	3	4	**1**	2	**1**	2	**1**	**1**	4

X represents no ranking provided; bold-faced represents first choice of least desirable immigrant group. Columns may have more than one number in bold, as a result of tie percentage.
Key: B = Belgium; DK = Denmark; F = France; FRG = Germany; G = Greece; IRL = Ireland; I = Italy; L = Luxembourg; N = Netherlands; P = Portugal; S = Spain; UK = United Kingdom.
Source (n-size): 1992 survey of members of European Parliament (167).

National patterns of preference regarding specific immigrant groups may also be seen in table 4.1, which presents MEP rankings of immigrant groups from least desirable (score of 1) to most desirable (score of 6), according to national averages. With the exceptions of Greek and British MEPs, each country ranked immigrants from North Africa, Africa, and Asia among the top three least desirable groups. Nonetheless, the preferential order of these three groups varies, indicating that national preferences do exist. The most prominent examples were the Greek and German MEPs for whom the least desirable groups were Turkish migrants and East Europeans respectively. In each case, these groups represent countries with the most proximate political impact. Further, migrant group preferences are often related to definitions of immigration problems and issue linkages. As noted in chapter 3, those MEPs who are concerned with unemployment are most likely to seek a reduction of migrants from Eastern Europe, while those who are preoccupied with race focus on migrants from the Third World (see figure 3.17).

Interestingly, however, these concerns were more influenced by immigrant numbers than the nature of threat, as one can conclude from dispositions toward East European migrant groups. East European influxes were deemed most threatening to countries such as Germany, Belgium, and Denmark, more recently affected by asylum-seekers from the east. They were less receptive than Southern countries such as Greece, Portugal, and Spain, where people tend to be most competitive with East European workers whose wages are low and skills are relatively high.

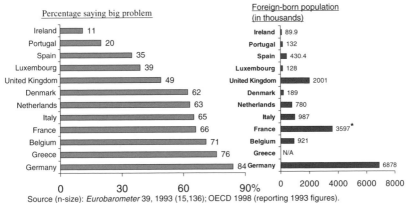

Source (n-size): *Eurobarometer* 39, 1993 (15,136); OECD 1998 (reporting 1993 figures).
*France's stock data was unavailable for 1993 so 1990 figures are reported here.
Q: *Do you think immigrants and/or political asylum-seekers are a big problem for (name of country), or are they not a big problem?*

Figure 4.2 Views on immigrants and asylum-seekers as a problem vs. numbers of foreigners, by country

The major country-specific factors that shape thinking on immigration are immigrant numbers, public opinion, and national levels of socio-economic development (see appendices A, E–F; see pp. 33 and 59, n. 10, for more information on terminology). These factors appear to be collinear with each other. Thus, one can argue that there are broad and comprehensive differences in the assessment of immigrants and immigration policy between countries. Those countries which are economically more developed, more geographically central, (predominantly) traditional immigration societies, and with higher immigrant concentrations are easily distinguishable from the others. To some degree, this portrait coincides with the North–South discrepancies that have long characterized Europe. To the extent that countries are still in distinct phases of the immigration cycle, and experience different numbers of immigrants, country effects may be profound.

The degree to which Europeans reported immigrants and asylum-seekers to be a problem seemed to be explained largely by the numbers of resident foreigners (see figure 4.2).[3] Figure 4.3 reveals the relationship between the number of foreigners and the perception of immigration problems per country. Forty percent of the variability in the notion that immigrants are a big problem is explained by the amount of foreign-born population. Nonetheless, the ordinary least-squares (OLS) coefficient shows a weak substantive significance, and a scan of the scatterplot reveals that this relationship may be largely driven by three outliers (Great Britain, France, and Germany).[4] A similar regression between

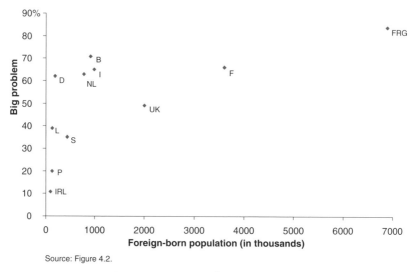

Source: Figure 4.2.

OLS coefficient: .007, r^2: 40%, significance: .036

Figure 4.3 Scatterplot of public opinion on immigrants as a problem by number of foreigners

those saying that immigrants are a big problem and the *percentage* of total foreigners yielded statistically insignificant values (p = .91; OLS = .111; r^2 = .00).

A more nuanced understanding of demographic figures is necessary in order to understand why the immigration problem is perceived as greater in some countries than in others. Indeed, the use of abstract numbers (whether in absolute figures or relative percentages) to explain measures of attitude formation, though common, inhibits a deeper understanding of the real nature of immigration attitudes. That is, as figure 4.4 illustrates, it is not the numbers of foreign-born that affect attitudes as much as the concentrations of certain *types* of foreigners. The ambiguous relationship between numbers and attitudes is further illuminated by the findings on proportions of various immigrant-specific groups. Interestingly, a regression between the percentage of the European public who believe immigrants are a big problem (across nation) by percentage of EU foreigners was statistically insignificant (p = .65; OLS = .511; r^2 = .02). However, a regression between this same dependent variable and the proportion of non-EU foreigners per nation revealed a statistically significant relationship (see figures 4.4 and 4.5).

The scatterplot in figure 4.5 captures this relationship graphically. In fact, 52 percent of the variability in the European public's perception that

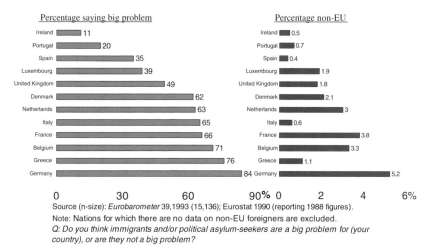

Source (n-size): *Eurobarometer* 39,1993 (15,136); Eurostat 1990 (reporting 1988 figures).
Note: Nations for which there are no data on non-EU foreigners are excluded.
Q: Do you think immigrants and/or political asylum-seekers are a big problem for (your country), or are they not a big problem?

Figure 4.4 Views on immigrants as a problem vs. proportion of non-EU foreigners, by country

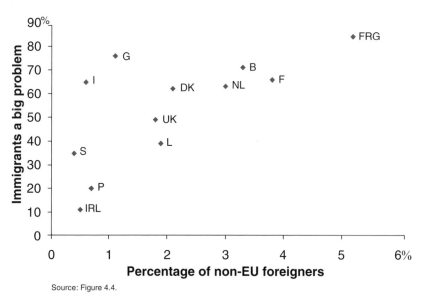

Source: Figure 4.4.

OLS coefficient: 9.9, r^2 : 52%, significance: .005

Figure 4.5 Scatterplot of views on immigrants as a problem by proportion of non-EU foreigners, by country

Table 4.2 *Tolerance thresholds relative to foreign population, 1992–1993*

	Percentage of non-EU foreigners/population	Percentage of EU foreigners/population	Percentage of total foreigners/population
Immigrants are a big problem	9.9[1] .52[2] (.005)[3]	−.511 .02 (.65)	.111 .00 (.91)
Too many foreigners	4.99 .30 (.051)	−.455 .035 (.540)	−.078 .001 (.911)
Nation most hostile to immigrants	5.44 .49 (.011)	−.151 .007 (.792)	.140 .008 (.785)

[1] OLS coefficient.
[2] r^2 value.
[3] Significance.
Source: *Eurobarometer* 37, 1992 (14,082), and 39, 1993 (15,136).

immigrants are a big problem by nation is explained by the percentage of non-EU foreigners per nation. As the percentage of non-EU foreigners resident in a country increases by 1 percent, those saying immigration is a big problem increases, on average by 9.9 percent. This is significant at the .005 level. The fact that such a relationship does not exist for a regression where the independent variable is EU foreigners rather than non-EU foreigners points to the greater resistance Europeans have toward accepting immigrants least like themselves.

These patterns are repeated when publics are asked about perceptions of the number of immigrants, or about which nations are most hostile (see table 4.2). Table 4.2 reinforces the importance of non-EU foreigners in driving attitudes about immigration. A statistically significant relationship emerged, for example, between those saying there are "too many immigrants" and the percentage of non-EU foreigners. As table 4.2 reveals, for every increase of 1 percent in the number of non-EU foreigners per nation, there is on average a 4.99 percent increase in the propensity of that nation's public to believe there are too many immigrants. A similar regression run with the total number of foreigners per nation or the total number of EU foreigners per nation shows a much weaker correlation. These trends support the thesis that immigrants are more of a concern when they are non-EU populations.

Further, a statistically significant relationship exists between those nations that Europeans label as most hostile to immigrants and the level

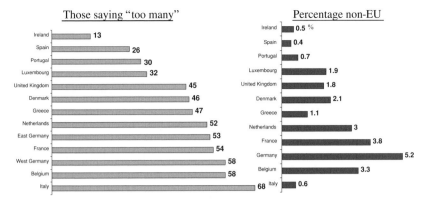

Source (n-size): *Eurobarometer 37*, 1992 (14,082); Eurostat 1990 (reporting 1988 figures).

Q: *Generally speaking, how do you feel about people living in (name of country) who are not nationals of the European Community countries...are there too many, a lot but not too many or not many?*

Figure 4.6 Perceptions vs. size of non-EU foreign populations

of non-EU foreigners in those countries. A 1 percent increase in the number of non-EU foreigners in any given country results in an average increase of 5.44 percent likelihood that Europeans believe a nation is hostile to immigrants. In both cases, the percentage of EU immigrants did not yield statistically significant results in predicting these two perceptions. This corroborates McLaren's findings (2001) that EU migrants generate consensus and are therefore not good indicators of variations in attitudes. The percentage of non-EU foreigners is considerably more important in determining attitudes toward immigration than levels of EU foreigners.

These relationships can be further studied with the help of figures and scatterplots 4.6–4.12. In 1992, the perception that there were "too many" immigrants was greatest in Germany, France, and Belgium, countries with high concentrations of non-EU populations (see figures 4.6 and 4.7). Immigrant rejection seems to be associated with proportions of non-EU immigrants found in each country. The exception of countries such as Italy may reflect not only the changing nature of the immigration/emigration divide, but also the sentiment that immigration is "too much" when specifically related to non-EU populations. Consider the differences between country perceptions toward all foreigners and those toward non-EU residents, illustrated in figures 4.8 and 4.9, respectively.

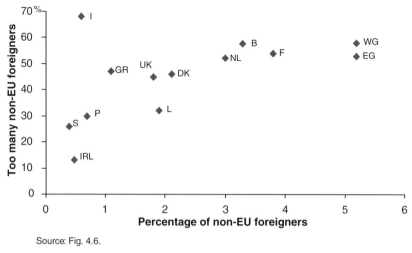

Source: Fig. 4.6.

OLS coefficient: 4.91, r^2: 30%, significance: .05

Figure 4.7 Scatterplot of perceptions, by size of non-EU foreign populations

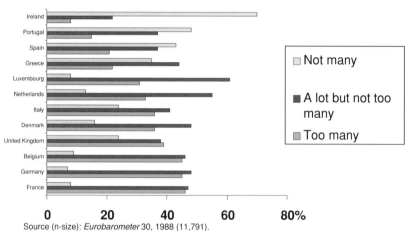

Source (n-size): *Eurobarometer* 30, 1988 (11,791).
Q: Generally speaking, how do you feel about foreigners living in (name of country): are there too many, a lot but not too many or not many?

Figure 4.8 Perceptions of all foreigners, by country

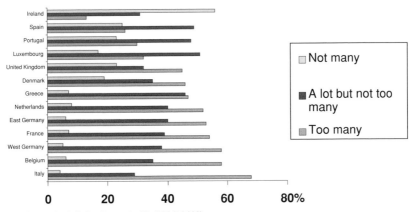

Source (n-size): *Eurobarometer* 37, 1992 (14,082).
Q: *Generally speaking, how do you feel about people living in (name of country) who are not nationals of the European Community countries...are there too many, a lot but not too many or not many?*

Figure 4.9 Perceptions of non-EU foreigners, by country

The case of Italy notably reveals that views are more differentiated than appears at first sight. Italian respondents tend to be more resistant to non-EU immigrants than to foreign residents in general. Most importantly, this seeming anomaly, as well as the Italian distortions shown in figures 4.5 and 4.7, underscores the critical need to factor in illegal migration. In Italy, official figures greatly underestimate actual numbers of non-EU nationals. The lack of integration structures for reception of immigrants, compounded by visible press coverage, means that perception corresponds to reality far closer than might otherwise appear because Italians are responding to immigrant numbers that are higher than officially recorded.

Even when European publics were asked to identify EU countries which appear to be hostile to immigrants, a notable association is made with countries that have large non-EU concentrations residing on their territories (see figures 4.10 and 4.11). These various measures of immigrant thresholds suggest that the numbers of non-EU migrants figure largely in public perception.

Similar survey data on attitudes of members of the European Parliament, who represent national and partisan interests, corroborate the Eurobarometer findings on public opinion, that there is a relationship between the number of immigrants and public attitudes toward immigration (correlation rate = .82).[5] Table 4.3 provides a snapshot of the variables that may be construed to impact immigrant preferences.

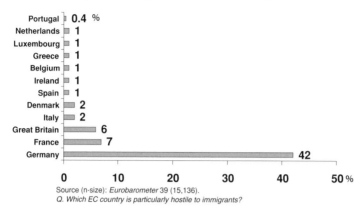

Source (n-size): *Eurobarometer* 39 (15,136).
Q. Which EC country is particularly hostile to immigrants?

Figure 4.10 Public perceptions of which nation is most hostile to immigrants

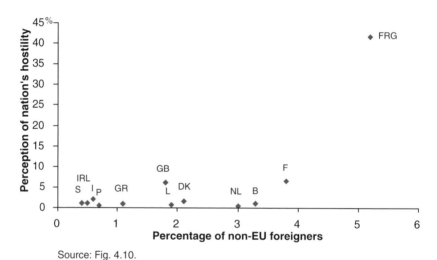

Source: Fig. 4.10.

OLS coefficient: 5.44, r^2: 49%, significance: .011

Figure 4.11 Perceptions of xenophobia across the EU, by size of non-EU populations, by country

Although the European public is more likely than elites to say there are "too many immigrants,"[6] mass and elite data underscore the relationship between demographics and acceptance/rejection of immigrant flows (see table 4.3). The scatterplot in figure 4.12 reinforces the associations shown in the previous figures, illustrating that as early as 1988 public opinion regarding immigrants was strongly related to non-EU proportions of foreigners. As in 1992, public opinion in Germany, France, and Belgium

Table 4.3 *Foreign percentages, public opinion, and MEP preferences to "decrease" immigrant levels, 1989–1992*

Country	Foreign population as % of total population	Non-EU foreigners as % of total population	% of public saying "too many" immigrants[a]	% of MEPs who prefer decreased immigration[b]
Belgium	9.1%	3.8%	44%	33%
Denmark	3.1%	1.8%	36%	67%
France	6.4%	3.9%	45%	37%
Germany[c]	8.2%	5.3%	47%	35%
Great Britain	3.3%	2.2%	45%	10%
Greece	0.7%	0.6%	19%	43%
Ireland	NA	0.6%	7%	17%
Italy	1.4%	0.7%	35%	23%
Luxembourg	27.5%	1.0%	30%	0%
Netherlands	4.6%	2.7%	30%	23%
Portugal	0.9%	0.5%	14%	0%
Spain	0.9%	0.3%	17%	11%

[a] As measured by *Eurobarometer*'s public opinion survey reporting percentage of answers stating that there are "too many" immigrants.
[b] Percentage of MEPs preferring a decreased level of immigration.
[c] West Germany.
Sources: OECD 1992; *Documents Observateur* 1989; Commission of the European Communities 1989; survey of members of the European Parliament (1992).

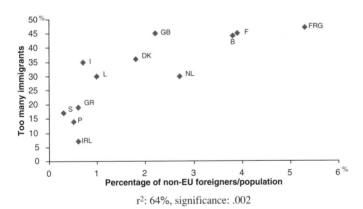

r[2]: 64%, significance: .002

Source: Commission of the European Communities 1989: 45; see also *Documents Observateur* 1989.

Q: Generally speaking, how do you feel about the number of people of another nationality living in our country...are there too many, a lot but not too many or not many?

Figure 4.12 Attitudes toward immigrants by proportion of non-EU foreigners

felt that there were "too many non-EU foreigners" resident in their countries. The contrast between countries with a substantial number of non-EU foreigners and those with fewer foreign residents underlines the fact that immigrant presence has a considerable psychological impact.

Elite positions closely resonated with these findings. Belgian (33 percent), German (35 percent), and French (37 percent) MEPs claimed that immigration in general should be decreased. All of these countries exceeded the EU average (24 percent) preferring a reduction of immigration. MEPs who were more likely to prefer decreased immigration tended to represent countries with larger non-EU foreign populations. MEPs from Greece (43 percent), Denmark (67 percent), and the United Kingdom (10 percent) were again exceptions in this context, and are therefore worthy of some comment. Interestingly, these countries commonly straddle the geographic and cultural boundaries between the EU and its external borders.[7] Thus, the irregularities are interesting for what they say about how national perceptions are shaped.

The exceptions of countries such as Greece, Denmark, the United Kingdom, and to some degree Italy (see table 4.3) may suggest that the blurring of lines between the traditional immigration and emigration countries of Europe is occurring at the attitudinal level. These cases also underscore another trend noted by Baldwin-Edwards and Schain: the feeling that there are too many immigrants may be strong even in many countries with small immigrant populations, while expressed tolerance may be found in some countries where the proportion of immigrants is relatively high (1994: 6). In explaining these inconsistencies, it is useful to consider the conclusion of the 1997 Eurobarometer report (no. 47.1). The anxieties expressed by a number of respondents seem to result not so much from the actual presence of minority groups as from the perception as to the ability of the host country to accommodate them. These discrepancies suggest that an analysis of sources of mass attitudes may benefit more from an examination of political processes than from an examination of demographic trends. Since approximately 82 percent of the elites surveyed reported immigration to be an important issue, the data reveal that the significance attached to immigration is not necessarily related to numbers alone. The following analysis considers the political dimension of immigration preferences.

Partisan/ideological sources of attitudes

National patterns in immigration thinking hide considerable party and political dynamics, and obfuscate the impact of traditional ideological

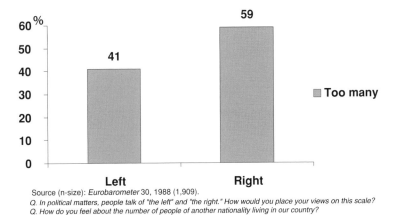

Source (n-size): *Eurobarometer* 30, 1988 (1,909).
Q. In political matters, people talk of "the left" and "the right." How would you place your views on this scale?
Q. How do you feel about the number of people of another nationality living in our country?

Figure 4.13 Immigrant thresholds, by ideology

sources in structuring political attitudes toward immigration (see Lahav 1997a). As figure 4.13 illustrates, there is a clear polarization between Europeans of the ideological right and those on the left with regard to preferences of immigrant levels. Attitudes toward immigrants are distinguishable along ideological lines, and, consequently, according to party lines.

The general assumption is that party and ideology are inextricably linked. In most nations, partisanship and ideological orientation exist side by side and tend to have reinforcing effects (Huber 1989; Dalton 2002: 28; Inglehart 1979: 353; Inglehart and Sidjanski 1976; Fishel 1972). My data corroborate the thesis that there is not only a theoretical but also an empirical relationship between elite membership in a party group and ideological self-placement. The survey in this study asked MEPs to place themselves on an ideological scale from 1 to 9 (left to right). As table 4.4 reaffirms, there is a positive correlation between parties and left–right ideological placement.

An MEP's party affiliation is indicative of where he/she stands ideologically. Both party and self-placement measurements reinforce the presence of the left–right construct in differentiating elite attitudes. Recognizing the relationship between partisan affiliation and ideological positions, we can probe issue attitude differences between party groups along a left–right continuum.

The role of political parties in defining debates is particularly important for the European Union since parties serve as the basis for transcending national lines and, hence, European integration (Attinà 1990).[8] The European Parliament is the major institution in which this goal is pursued,

Table 4.4 *Ideological dimension in the ordering of parties, MEPs (mean self-placement according to party groups in EP)*

European party	Self-placement on 9-point ideological scale	N
EP	4.23	167
DR (Technical Group of the European Right)	7.83	6
RDE (European Democratic Alliance)	5.67	6
PPE (European People's Party)	5.46	46
LDR (Liberal, Democratic and Reformist)	4.59	17
SOC (Socialists)	3.05	56
GUE (United European Left)	3.11	9
CG (Left Unity)	2.00	1
Greens	2.50	8
ARC (Rainbow)	3.33	3
NI (Independent)	7.00	1
No answer		14

$N = 167$; gamma $= .79$ p $< .001$; lambda $= .32$ p $<. 0000$.

Note: Mean self-placement of each party is measured by a scale of 1 (left) to 9 (right), and based on the question "On the ideological spectrum, where do you place yourself from left to right?"

as representatives are grouped in broad, cross-national political families (see appendix A for comprehensive overview). The existence of cohesive party-group positions in the European Parliament would indicate that ideology (a consistent system of beliefs and values) is guiding the choices of policy-makers, and that MEPs may be transcending their particular national visions. More than a measure of European integration, the European party system presents a comparative framework for identifying party interests and political cleavages on diverse issues. Transnational cooperation provides a standpoint from which to evaluate party elites cross-nationally and to identify some common trends regarding representation throughout the EU (Pridham and Pridham 1981; Henig 1979; Attinà 1990; Bardi 1994; Hix and Lord 1997; Thomassen and Schmitt 1999; Katz and Wessels 1999).

Elite trends follow public opinion findings. European voters report that the left–right scale is not very important to them, but continue to self-position themselves along that scale, indicating that it is more important to them than they claim (Dalton 2002 [1988]). Political elites also tend to devalue the role of traditional partisan ideological sources in structuring political attitudes, but their positions on immigration may be distinguished by party identification. Their accounts of ideological constraints tend to support the more general literature described in chapter 1, which argues that the left–right tool of analysis is declining in significance. MEPs devalue the relevance of the ideological construct, particularly on immigration. They claim that such a construct is anachronistic and inadequate in structuring their positions and attitudes on the immigration issue. According to one MEP interviewed:

There is no question of difference between the right and left because the class struggle has finished. The immigration question cannot be understood in terms of right or left. It is a new question. Absolutely new. It's not a plastic ideological scheme. (interview no. 339; Strasbourg, May 13, 1992)

Another MEP summarized an oft-mentioned theme:

I think that the bottom line is [that], ideological lines have been blurred by the immigration issue, and no longer provide a yardstick or even a direction for the parties themselves. Everybody is coping with the problem. (interview no. 44; Strasbourg, May 12, 1992)

Although MEPs believed that the left–right organizing framework is not applicable to the immigration issue, or that it is exaggerated, the data suggest an opposing scenario. A common conviction that "everybody is coping with the problem," described by the MEP above, portrays a consensus which hides the fact that there are significant divisions on policy preferences; or *how* policy-makers choose to "cope with the problem." Elites disagree on all types of policy and migrant group preferences. They differ with regard to their definitions of the problems; their preferences for immigration levels and immigrant groups; and the structure and content of a common immigration policy. Many of these differences stem from variations in ideological conceptions.

Party group polarizations emerge in important areas of immigration, such as immigration policy and immigrant preferences. Figures 4.14, 4.15, and 4.16 provide evidence of party and ideological orientations in distinguishing MEP ideas on appropriate levels of immigration. A unilinear direction of response emerged regarding preferences for both increasing and decreasing levels of immigration.

As figures 4.14 and 4.15 illustrate, MEPs from parties of the left (i.e., communists, socialists) were less likely to advocate decreases in levels of immigration; MEPs of the right (conservatives, Christian democrats, radical right) tended to be more supportive of such decreases. The small sample size precludes the use of most tests of statistical significance. However, percentages are suggestive of partisan differences.

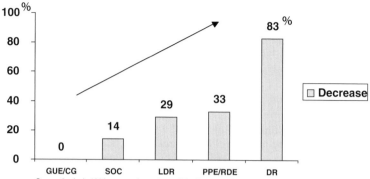

Source (n-size): 1992 survey of members of the European Parliament (167).
Q: Should immigration in general be kept at its present level, increased or decreased?
Note: Left to right: GUE/CG = Communists; SOC = Socialists; LDR = Liberal Democrats;
PPE/RDE = Christian Democrats and Conservatives; DR = Radical Right (see table 4.4
for full acronym and ideological self-placement). EP average for decrease = 30.5%. Total
data yield gamma = .58, p<.01.

Figure 4.14 Immigration should be decreased, by party group

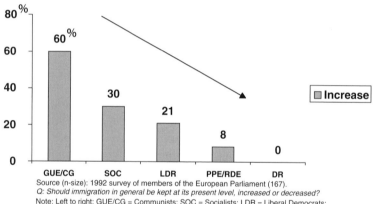

Source (n-size): 1992 survey of members of the European Parliament (167).
Q: Should immigration in general be kept at its present level, increased or decreased?
Note: Left to right: GUE/CG = Communists; SOC = Socialists; LDR = Liberal Democrats;
PPE/RDE = Christian Democrats and Conservatives; DR = Radical Right (see table 4.4
for full acronyms and ideological self-placement). EP average for increase = 24%. Total
data yield gamma = .58, p<.01

Figure 4.15 Immigration should be increased, by party group

This unilinear ordering was reinforced when elites were asked to talk about specific immigrant groups. Figure 4.16 and table 4.5 present the percentages of MEPs who indicated they would like to see the respective immigrant groups "increased." With the exception of the Liberal Democrats, who lack ideological homogeneity and fluctuate between center-right and center-left, a left–right ordering informs immigrant

Table 4.5 *Distribution of MEP support for migrant groups, by party group*

Party	EP average	Left GUE/CG	SOC	LDR	PPE/RDE	Right DR	gamma/ significance
Immigrant origin							
EU	50%	67%	54%	50%	51%	0%	.26/p > .05
E. Europe	43%	70%	54%	39%	30%	0%	.49/p < .01
Non-EU W. Europe	26%	33%	39%	0%	23%	0%	.44/p < .02
Turkey	15%	20%	15%	31%	4%	0%	.47/p < .01
North Africa	50%	50%	22%	31%	8%	0%	.56/p < .01
Africa	40%	40%	20%	31%	8%	0%	.58/p < .001
Asia	30%	30%	16%	23%	6%	0%	.58/p < .001

Note: Left to right: GUE/CG = Communists; SOC = Socialists; LDR = Liberal Democrats; PPE/RDE = Christian Democrats and Conservatives; DR = Radical Right (see table 4.4 for full acronyms and ideological self-placement).
Source (n-size): Those responding "increase" in 1992 survey of members of European Parliament (167). Green and Rainbow party groups omitted.
Q: Should immigration in general be kept at its present level, increased or decreased?

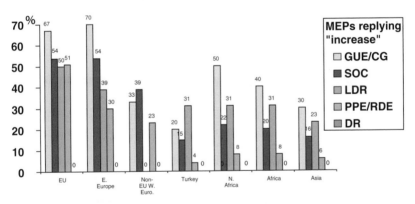

Source (n-size): 1992 survey of members of the European Parliament (167).
Q: Should immigration in general be kept at its present level, increased or decreased?
Note: Left to right: GUE/CG = Communists; SOC = Socialists; LDR = Liberal Democrats; PPE/RDE = Christian Democrats and Conservatives; DR = Radical Right (see table 4.4 for full acronyms and ideological self-placement). No members of the DR group wanted immigration of any ethnic group to be increased.

Figure 4.16 MEP "increase" preferences for immigrant groups, by party group

Table 4.6 *Mean ideological self-placement ratings for MEPs on immigration level and immigrant group preferences*

Immigrant origin	Increased	Decreased
EU	4.25	5.25
Eastern Europe	3.88	4.96
Non-EU Western Europe	3.96	4.93
Turkey	3.44	5.10
North Africa	3.40	5.26
Africa	3.35	5.16
Asia	3.50	5.33
In general	3.47	5.24

Note: Means of ideological self-placement, based on a scale of 1–9, where 1 refers to the extreme left, and 9 represents the extreme right.
Source (n-size): 1992 survey of members of European Parliament (167).

group preferences.[9] This left–right ordering on immigration more generally has appeared to become clearer over time, as has been recently confirmed in Hix's study of MEP roll-call votes (2001a). Beyond verifying that immigration/asylum issues correlate with left–right positions, the roll-call findings substantiate an emerging trend I detected in the 1990s. That is, even the Liberal Democrats more often than not tend to side with the Socialists and other leftist parties against those of the right when it comes to immigration-related policies (ibid.: 680–683).

The presence of the left–right ideological continuum in ordering MEP preferences toward certain immigrant groups is further confirmed by means data. The table of means, table 4.6, shows that on a scale from 1 to 9, where 1 represents the extreme left and 9 represents the extreme right, there is a left preference toward "increasing" and right one toward "decreasing" immigration levels. Again, these differences fluctuate according to origin of immigrant group.

Tables 4.5 and 4.6 point to two interesting dynamics. First, despite the slightly wavering position of the Liberals (who inherently tend to be more individualist), there is a clear pattern of attitudes regarding immigrant preference which is sensitive to the left–right component of parties. From party groups that represent the ideological left to those of the right, MEP acceptance of immigration levels decreases. These noticeable preference orders exist for all immigrant groups.

A second trend emerged from a vertical scan of the data (see table 4.5). That is, among all parties (with the exception of the Radical Right group), there is a more positive attitude toward EU and East European migrant groups than toward other groups. Interestingly, MEPs are more supportive of East European immigrant populations than they are of West Europeans from non-EU countries (i.e., at the time, including Austria, Switzerland, and the Nordic countries). Since the responses regarding non-EU West European migrants were also unfavorable,[10] it is difficult to say if distinctions are based on political, cultural, race, ethnic, or professional considerations. Most likely, it either varies with each specific group, or it is a product of these factors reinforcing each other (i.e., professional distinctions often coincide with cultural ones).

These findings substantiate McLaren's (2001) hypothesis that the left–right ideological construct informs immigrant preferences, although they throw into question an important claim put forward about the distinctions that elites make between internal (EU) and external (non-EU) migrants. Accordingly, the left–right cues that elites use to shape public opinion on external migration preferences are not applicable to issue areas in which elite consensus exists, such as on internal migration. In this formulation, it is likely that left–right self-placement will matter only in determining attitudes toward non-EC migrants (ibid.: 93). This is because elites in many European countries have tended to divide across parties on external migration, providing divisive cues, and have been most supportive with regard to migration from within the EU. The data presented above clearly deviate from these assertions. My findings on MEPs refute the claims that ideology does not inform internal migration preferences, and that elites are in consensus about EU migrants though, in relative terms, they are more favorable to EU migrants than to others. According to the MEP data, the left–right construct is a powerful predictor of immigrant preferences across the board.

The left–right construct also orders more substantive policy preferences. The findings provide evidence of substantial ideological differences in policy positions. They support the argument that politicians deduce policy solutions from their conceptual frameworks (Aberbach, Putnam, and Rockman 1981: 92). As table 4.7 and figure 4.17 reveal, a left–right party continuum informs policy choices.

Partisans of the left are more likely to endeavor to amend social inequalities and to extend immigrant rights, to delegate authority about immigration regulation to EU institutions, and to be open to increased immigration than their colleagues on the right. In addition, they are more likely than their counterparts on the right to promote more immigrant

Table 4.7 *Policy preferences by party group*

Party	Total EP%	Greens	GUE/CG	SOC	LDR	PPE/RDE	DR	Gamma/ significance
Attitude response	(N)							
Common immigration policy[a]	84% (149)	84%	100%	90%	94%	96%	50%	.06/p > .05
Regulation entirely by EU[b]	41% (66)	75%	70%	42%	35%	37%	0%	−.31/p < .02
Extend immigrant rights[c]	77% (122)	100%	90%	97%	60%	62%	0%	.78/p < .001

Note: Left to right: GUE/CG = Communists; SOC = Socialists; LDR = Liberal Democrats; PPE/RDE = Christian Democrats and Conservatives; DR = Radical Right (see table 4.4 for full acronyms and ideological self-placement). The ARC Rainbow Group and Independent group have been excluded from the tabulated data.
[a]Based on those who somewhat and strongly agreed that there should be a common immigration policy for EU members (Q8).
[b]Based on those who reported that the EU institutions, through majority vote, should be entirely responsible for regulating immigration policy (Q9).
[c]Based on those who reported that the rights of immigrants should be extended (Q12).
Source (n-size): 1992 survey of members of European Parliament (167).

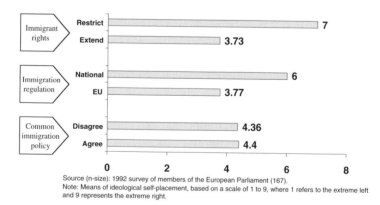

Source (n-size): 1992 survey of members of the European Parliament (167).
Note: Means of ideological self-placement, based on a scale of 1 to 9, where 1 refers to the extreme left and 9 represents the extreme right.

Figure 4.17 Mean ideological self-placement ratings for MEPs on policy preferences

rights (e.g., voting), and educational and economic assistance to countries of immigrant origin (Lahav 1997a).

It may be true that the ideological lines between the left and right regarding immigration are more symbolic than objective. Their reported demise, however, may be more anecdotal and fashionable than substantive. In Europe, parties and ideology have remained significant at the level of political discourse and debate. They continue to shape the dialogue on immigration intake, and educate the public about various policy dilemmas and goals. Ideological rhetoric continues to provide powerful cues for communication among MEPs. The legacy of these images, among other political reasons, figured in the reluctance of the British Conservatives to join the Liberal group in the EP, despite the fact that, as some have argued, they were considered to be ideologically closer to them than to the Christian Democrats (interview no. 123, August 25, 1993).

The ideological patterns on immigration support the general findings on MEPs, which report that EP parties are more cohesive than many people would have expected (Attinà, 1990; Hix and Lord 1997; Raunio 1997; Bardi 2002); indeed they may be "more cohesive than the major American parties" (Hix 2001b: 4–5). Interestingly, according to the more recent findings, the main explanatory factor of MEP defection from his/her legislative party is the ideological position of the national party delegation *vis-à-vis* their party group (Hix 2002, 2001b: 20, 2001a: 666). This warrants an examination of the connection between national and ideological interests.

National and party sources of attitudes: intricate links in the EU

The reported demise of ideological relevance to immigration preferences in contrast to the empirical evidence prompts us to consider why partisan/ideological distinctions have been so elusive. The seeming contradictions between national and transnational or partisan/ideological attitudinal patterns compel us to examine the interplay of both, and how together these sources structure attitudes toward immigration. An in-depth analysis of four of the largest countries (France, Germany, Italy, and the UK) of the EU (in terms of population and numerical representation) offers a parsimonious test of these patterns. It suggests that, while partisanship/ideology shapes the attitudes of MEPs toward immigration, those attitudes are significantly conditioned by national party traditions and national experiences with immigration.

Country portraits provide a "snapshot" of the differences parties make with regard to immigration thinking in each European member-state. The

Table 4.8 *Mean ideological self-placement of MEPs, by party group and country*

Party	Greens	Communists (GUE)	Socialists (SOC)	Liberals (LDR)	Christian Democrats/Right (PPE/RDE)	Radical Right (DR)
Country						
UK	NR	NR	2.69	NR	5.73	NR
France	4.00	NR	2.38	5.00	6.17	9.00
Germany	1.67	NR	3.25	4.00	6.00	7.00
Italy	2.00	3.14	3.63	6.00	3.83	NR
		NR = nonrelevant				

Notes: Based on a nine-point scale, and the question asked of MEPs, "On the ideological spectrum, where do you place yourself from left to right (1 = left; 9 = right)?"
Source (n-size): 1992 survey of members of European Parliament (92).

four countries capture the major cultural distinctions that affect immigration thinking in Europe: the North–South divide; immigration versus emigration experiences; and the presence or absence of a colonial tradition. They also represent countries with different levels of immigration, from Italy with a relatively low concentration of foreign residents, to France and Germany with substantially higher numbers (see figure 4.2 and table 4.3).

The four nation profiles corroborate other studies, which profess "the cross-national traveling capacity of left–right scales" (Huber 1989: 601). However, it cautions against the assumption that elites with the same ideological self-placement will respond similarly to issues across countries. A sense of attitudinal distance is needed to capture the complexity of ideological positions within different systems and countries (see table 4.8). This requires an understanding of how ideological differences are filtered through the political cultures of particular EU countries.

As table 4.8 demonstrates – e.g., Greens in France position themselves to the right of the Socialists; and Italian Christian Democrats are left of the Liberals – party identification and self-identification must be interpreted in country context.

Interviews with European elites underscored the recognition that left and right are relative and dynamic terms which may fluctuate according to country and issue. As one Danish MEP commented:

Differences between left–right parties are very small . . . Maybe only in countries like France and Germany that differs. But not with a country of 5 million, with distance of 300 miles, all the same religion, same culture, same education. There is no need for differences. (interview no. 48; Strasbourg, June 13, 1992: 3–4)

A Greek Communist also noted national sensibilities:

Left and right exist but it is a question of priority. I mean, in France, it is much more important, so even the left and right will have to take into account the experiences of France. It is not so important to Greeks. (interview no. 37; Brussels, May 30, 1992: 2)

In immigration matters specifically, national immigrant contexts may be relevant. One MEP succinctly addressed this correlation:

When left and right crosscut, you need to look at numbers or the masses of migrants. For example, France. The problem is so heavy in France that all forces are displaced a bit. (ibid.: 4)

Discussions with national and European elites illuminate intraparty and contextual ideological differences. As noted earlier in this chapter, they also indicate that national experiences with immigration mitigate traditional ideological orientations.

MEPs from the same party groups may differ on their attitudes toward immigration. These differences often reflect deeper party traditions and political cultures. Parties with the same name may adopt slightly different ideologies. Parties with similar ideological placement in their countries may belong to the same party family in the European Parliament and yet be ideologically distant. The British Labour Party, for example, has traditionally been radically more left-wing than the German Social Democratic Party. Partisans nevertheless sit together in a formal united front at the European Parliament. Furthermore, if an issue is highly salient for a particular domestic party and an MEP is torn between the positions of his/her EP party group and the domestic party, the MEP is likely to align with the national party against the EP party group (Hix 2001a: 666). This means that, as immigration salience varies across the fifteen EU member states, party cohesion may be compromised. Finally, internal differences within party groups may reflect national party experiences of governing and party roles ("government–opposition dynamics") in immigration debates. They may also be related to party experiences with what E. E. Schattschneider called the "scope of conflict."[11] Thus, in an effort to expand their power base, parties will be motivated to consider how victory or defeat on the immigration issue will affect their long-term prospects. Controlling the scope of conflict may "take the form of restricting or expanding it" (Schattschneider 1975: 8). To the extent that electoral systems (Perlmutter 1995) and local politics (Schain 1987; Body-Gendrot and Schain 1992) shape party dynamics, one may expect different levels of polarization depending on a country's political system. These factors suggest that ideological and party patterns of the left and right must be considered in country-specific contexts. Attitudes toward immigration policy are strongly conditioned by national party traditions, experiences with immigration, roles in government/opposition, and party policy profiles.

Policy styles vary from party to party, and often cut across traditional left–right positions. This may explain why the data often point to common fault lines between the Socialist group and DR extreme-right group on one side and conservative and centrist parties on the other. While the former two groups differ substantially in their appeals, they tend to resemble each other in mobilizing certain segments of the working class,[12] and most importantly in "party policy style" (active vs. reactive).[13] In contrast to the traditional view of competition that parties offer different policies to the electorate on the same issue(s), an alternative view poses that parties may compete selectively, emphasizing the importance of different issues or issue stands.[14] Parties may stress particular issues because they work in their favor and, in some sense, they "own" them.[15] Thus, once electors decide which issue is salient, the question of which party to support generally follows automatically. In this way, it is particularly interesting to note party differences with regard to immigration. The efficacy of political parties in "creating" an environment that is accepting of certain types of immigration and, at times, unaccepting of others has been corroborated by migration scholars (McLaren 2001; Hoskin 1991). Although some migration scholars place more emphasis on ideological components of party differences, ideological proximity is not the basis of all patterns of policy preferences.[16] As Butler and Stokes (1969) concluded in their classical electoral studies, if this model were true, no one who most preferred the party farthest to the left should have his next choice party farthest right or vice versa.[17] This trend has continued to astound observers of the French political scene, as the strengthening of the extreme right comes after periods of relative success for center-left parties (Harris 1990: 165; see also Harris 1994).

In countries with larger foreign concentrations, such as France and Germany, party dynamics are instructive. Attitudinal data on MEPs reveal that elites from parties of the left differ markedly from their competitors on the right, who tend to accentuate the severity of their country's immigration problems compared to those of other European countries (see table 4.9). Although this dynamic fluctuates from country to country, the tendency toward interparty disagreement is constant. This phenomenon underscores the Eurobarometer's warning that, although attitudes are related to size of foreign populations, hostility toward immigrants does not necessarily grow in proportion to numbers. Rather, political debate about immigrant presence tends to become more heated when immigrant size is, and/or is perceived as, large.[18]

Table 4.9 *MEPs reporting that their country has more immigration problems than other EC countries, by country*

Country	N	Affirmative response: N (%)	Greens	GUE/CG	SOC	LDR	PPE/RDE	DR
EP average	161	30 (19%)	8%	6%	37%	11%	32%	4%
France	22	9 (41%)	17% (1/6)	–	14% (1/7)	100% (1/1)	83% (5/6)	50% (1/2)
Germany	21	12 (57%)	0% (0/3)	–	44% (4/9)	100% (3/3)	100% (2/2)	100% (3/3)
Italy	25	2 (8%)	0% (0/2)	0% (0/7)	13% (1/8)	0% (0/1)	17% (1/6)	–
United Kingdom	24	1 (4%)	–	–	7% (1/14)	–	0 % (0/10)	–

Note: The table should be read as follows. There were 24 members from the UK in the sample. 1 of the 24 (or 4%) answered in the affirmative. Socialists constituted 14 of all the UK members in the sample. 1 of the 14 (or 7%) responded in the affirmative. There were 10 members of the PPE party in the UK. 0 or 0% of them answered positively.
Left to right: GUE/CG = Communists; SOC = Socialists; LDR = Liberal Democrats; PPE/RDE = Christian Democrats and Conservatives; DR = Radical Right (see table 4.4 for full acronyms and ideological self-placement).
Source (n-size): 1992 survey of members of European Parliament (167).

The majority of Socialist MEPs (with the exception of the British) tended to take similar positions regarding their comparative country positions. They were proportionately less inclined than their opponents on the right to perceive their immigration problems as acute. The patterns in this response spread revealed that, in countries where immigrant numbers were high, MEPs tended to disagree about the extent to which immigration problems were greater than those experienced by other European countries. This corroborates the previous hypothesis that the politicization of immigration debates relates to the phase of the immigration cycle in particular countries. The case could be made that Italy exhibits less polarization because, unlike France or Germany, it is closer to the beginning of the immigration cycle, having transformed itself from an emigration to an immigration country (see chapter 2).

While discernible political divisions (along a left–right continuum) are evident in areas of problem resolution, party group cohesion varies in each country (see table 4.10). For example, a plurality of MEPs in each of the four countries preferred the extension of immigrant rights (voting, associational activity, etc.). While party groups do not exhibit the

Table 4.10 *MEPs reporting that immigrant rights should be extended, by country and party group*

Country	N	Affirmative response: N (%)	Greens	GUE/ CG	SOC	LDR	PPE/ RDE	DR
EP average	160	123 (77%)	100%	90%	97%	60%	62%	0%
France	23	16 (70%)	100% (6/6)	–	100% (8/8)	100% (1/1)	17% (1/6)	0% (0/2)
Germany	19	12 (63%)	100% (3/3)	–	100% (8/8)	0% (0/3)	0% (0/3)	0% (0/3)
Italy	25	20 (80%)	100% (2/2)	86% (6/7)	88% (7/8)	0% (0/1)	83% (5/6)	–
United Kingdom	24	18 (75%)	–	–	93% (13/14)	–	50% (5/10)	–

Note: For method of reading table, see note in table 4.9.
Left to right: GUE/CG = Communists; SOC = Socialists; LDR = Liberal Democrats; PPE/RDE = Christian Democrats and Conservatives; DR = Radical Right (see table 4.4 for full acronyms and ideological self-placement).
Source (n-size): 1992 survey of members of European Parliament (167).

same levels of cohesion in each country, they are equally polarized. The dynamics between parties of the left and those of the right remain the same (see table 4.10). Attitudinal distance is similar as the parties of the left prefer change, while those on the right are more likely to want to maintain the status quo. The former thus support the extension of immigrant rights, while the latter are less likely to do so. Italy is an exception as MEPs across parties tend to resemble each other. This tendency for party convergence in Italy again reinforces the trend noted in the previous section: each country is at a different phase of the immigration issue, and this affects the nature of party dynamics. Party polarizations are clear on immigrant rights, except in Italy.

The theory that political debate tends to increase with a growth of immigrant presence is empirically confirmed by the elite data (see table 4.11). The perception that national public debate over immigration was very divisive was prevalent in Germany (90 percent) and France (70 percent). In the UK (13 percent) and Italy (32 percent), where immigrant figures are lower, MEPs reported fewer divisions. There are significant country differences regarding national public debates. MEPs positions tend to reflect their national perspectives rather than their party families in the EP.

Table 4.11 *MEPs reporting that national public debate on immigration is very divisive, by country and party group*

Country	N	Affirmative response: N (%)	Greens	GUE/ CG	SOC	LDR	PPE/ RDE	DR
EP average	162	32 (52%)	54%	40%	36%	35%	17%	71%
France	23	16 (70%)	50% (3/6)	–	75% (6/8)	100% (1/1)	67% (4/6)	100% (2/2)
Germany	20	18 (90%)	100% (3/3)	–	100% (9/9)	100% (3/3)	50% (1/2)	67% (2/3)
Italy	25	8 (32%)	0% (0/2)	57% (4/7)	25% (2/8)	100% (1/1)	17% (1/6)	–
United Kingdom	24	3 (13%)	–	–	15% (2/13)	–	9% (1/11)	–

Note: For method of reading table, see note in table 4.9.
Left to right: GUE/CG = Communists; SOC = Socialists; LDR = Liberal Democrats; PPE/RDE = Christian Democrats and Conservatives; DR = Radical Right (see table 4.4 for full acronyms and ideological self-placement).
Source (n-size): 1992 survey of members of European Parliament (167).

The four nation profiles above confirm the phenomenon found in public opinion findings (that political debate increases with the size of immigrant populations – particularly non-EU nationals). They also suggest that the politicization of immigration debates may relate to the phase of the immigration cycle. These findings support Huber and Inglehart's study (1995) of expert assessments and shed light on the uneven power of xenophobia to divide parties of the left from those of the right in France, Belgium, and Germany, but not in other countries.[19] The primary conclusion to be drawn from these different sampled populations is that the left–right scheme is conditioned by national contexts (Huber and Inglehart 1995; Hix 2001a: 677; Knutsen 1998; McLaren 2001; Laver and Hunt 1992).

To the extent that party debates reflect national experiences, the phase of immigration experience becomes crucial.[20] MEPs from traditional immigration countries such as the United Kingdom and France are less likely to identify immigration issues as being more problematic today because they have been on the agenda for a long time (see table 4.11). The immigration issue that has been on the national agenda in the UK since the 1960s, and in France since the 1970s, in some ways resembles the one confronting Italy and other more recent countries of immigration

Table 4.12 *MEPs reporting that immigration problems are greater today than in the past, by country and party group*

Country	N	Affirmative response: N (%)	Greens	GUE/ CG	SOC	LDR	PPE/ RDE	DR
EP average	165	140 (85%)	54%	100%	75%	100%	96%	86%
France	23	14 (61%)	33% (2/6)	–	38% (3/8)	100% (1/1)	100% (6/6)	100% (2/2)
Germany	22	20 (91%)	67% (2/3)	–	100% (9/9)	100% (3/3)	100% (3/3)	100% (3/3)
Italy	24	23 (96%)	50% (1/2)	100% (7/7)	100% (8/8)	100% (1/1)	100% (5/5)	–
United Kingdom	25	17 (68%)	–	–	50% (7/14)	–	91% (10/11)	–

Note: N may not equal 100% because the ARC Rainbow Group and Independent Group have been excluded from the tabulated data.
For method of reading the table, see note in table 4.9.
Left to right: GUE/CG = Communists; SOC = Socialists; LDR = Liberal Democrats; PPE/RDE = Christian Democrats and Conservatives; DR = Radical Right (see table 4.4 for full acronyms and ideological self-placement).
Source (n-size): 1992 survey of members of European Parliament (167).

today. During the early stages, there was a large cross-party consensus in each country in an attempt to defuse the issue. However, as the immigration debate inevitably became politicized, parties have increasingly struggled to differentiate themselves and break the mainstream consensus.[21] This pattern is also identifiable in the European Parliament. MEPs from traditional immigration countries are more likely to be divided on immigration, regardless of party affiliation (see tables 4.9–4.12). The evidence suggests that varying sizes of foreign concentrations and different phases of immigration cycles among EU countries may account for some diversity in response spreads as they also condition party dynamics.

In some cases, the traditional immigration countries may be differentiated from the newer immigration regimes (i.e., the Southern countries) in terms of party-system convergence or divergence. In the former, party groups tend to be more polarized, while in the latter party distinctions remain more blurred (see Lahav 1995: ch. 7).

The four nation profiles suggest a complex dynamic between country and party patterns regarding the magnitude ascribed to immigration problems (see table 4.12). Consensus within the Socialist group

(75 percent) on the question of whether immigration problems had worsened was lower than for all other party groups (with the exception of the Greens with 54 percent), and lower than the EP average of 85 percent. Socialists in Britain and France were even less inclined to report this sentiment. The lack of interparty accord in these countries tends to support the argument that the evolutionary phase of immigration has implications for party consensus (see also Messina 1996). Moreover, Germany (91 percent of MEPs) and Italy (96 percent) displayed remarkable cross-party consensus regarding the nature of problems today. This included the Socialist MEPs. The data here show that party patterns must be interpreted within country-specific contexts, which include each nation's phase of the immigration issue, and traditional party consensus in general.

These attitudinal disparities may have been overlooked given the finding that a vast majority of elites (85 percent of MEPs surveyed) reported that immigration problems were greater today than in the past and that the immigration issue was important (82 percent). National patterns provide a sense of change in immigration politics that has substantial implications for the immigration issue at the European Union level. That is, among consensus about the nature of the immigration problem, there is a distinct tendency emerging in the former-emigration countries of the Southern EU. Italian (96 percent), Portuguese (100 percent), and Greek (100 percent) MEPs exceeded the European average (85 percent) in responding that immigration problems were greater than in the past. This heightened perception among elites from traditional emigration countries with relatively smaller immigrant concentrations reflects a globalization or a "Europeanization" of the immigration issue in a transnational community. If Gary Freeman was correct in suggesting that the effects of migration and their recognition tend to lag, the transition from emigration to immigration societies was being felt by the 1990s (Freeman 1995, 1993).

The changing structure of immigration regimes appears to be recognized by German and Italian MEPs. Table 4.12 shows that they almost unanimously agreed that immigration problems are greater today than in the past. This underscores Freeman's finding that "people develop more accurate impressions of the consequences of immigration and immigrants over time, as migration is repeated year after year, or as the migrants settle in their new countries" (1993: 5). The findings here confirm that Italian elites are adjusting to their new status as an immigration country. Italians across the political spectrum described the unique nature of their immigration history:

The starting point is, perhaps, the particular situation of Italy. Our country was, up to ten years ago, an emigration country, not an immigration country. Unlike Germany, Belgium, France, the United Kingdom, and America too, north and south, up to the 1970s we were an emigrant country. Now we have discovered the problems . . . of rich countries. (interview no. 7; Brussels, May 15, 1992: 1)

Italy is a latecomer in terms of immigration. (interview no. 51; Brussels, April 14, 1992: 2)

Similarly, Germans are dealing with changing patterns as they have discovered that the "guest worker" programs are not temporary after all. It is no coincidence that German politicians have for the first time in the postwar era formulated an "immigration policy" in the 1990s. As discussed earlier, the salience of immigration issues appears to fluctuate with changes in numbers.

Conclusions

Ideological and national sources of attitudes form a basis for understanding issues surrounding the development of a common immigration policy in the European Union. An in-depth exploration of attitudinal patterns reveals that domestic constraints, such as partisan affiliation, ideological position, and national identification, may account for important differences in immigration preferences that may impede transnational policymaking. At the most general level, the country variable is discriminating, particularly on questions which ask people to assess the immigration issue (its salience and importance). National cultural factors give rise to beliefs and attitudes that are more conceptual and abstract. But country patterns are weaker on the more specific and detail-oriented issues such as the nature of immigration issues, principles of immigration regulation, and sources of political divisions. Empirically, ideology of party is a better predictor than national or cultural values regarding substantive policy. The left–right construct has an organizing power among parties in the European Parliament regarding preferences of migrant groups and policy, particularly with regard to technical matters such as immigration authority and immigrant rights.

The analysis of MEP attitudes provides a revised image to the premature obituary of ideological constraints that has been described by "new politics" scholars and by this group of elites themselves. There is a contradiction between what MEPs say about political polarizations regarding immigration and what, in fact, is advanced by the empirical data. The elite sample reinforced the tendency among public opinion not only to devalue the role of traditional sources in structuring their thinking, but also to embrace positions on immigration that may be distinguished by party identification. This seeming contradiction between the survey data and what individual MEPs recounted in interviews underscores the importance of employing the two types of methods used in studying elite attitudes.[22] It also requires further analysis to resolve these confusions. More specifically, why are partisan/ideological distinctions so elusive?

In assessing the relative strength of national and partisan factors, the link between the two becomes particularly relevant in explaining overlap and consensus. As the four-country party analysis in this chapter revealed, attitudes toward immigration are based on an intricate relationship between partisan/ideological and national factors. They support the thesis that party group dynamics in the EU are conditioned by national traditions.[23] Attitudes toward immigration and immigration policy must be understood against the background of such factors as national experience with immigration, party roles in governing, and traditional party ideological distances. Equally striking is the finding that Europeans clearly draw on the immigration experience of other EU countries, a phenomenon which reflects the "Europeanization" of the immigration issue in an interdependent community.

Heightened sensitivities on the immigration front, even on the part of the less experienced countries, may indicate that the lines between MEP attitudes from traditional immigration countries and emigration countries are narrowing. Global structural changes mitigate traditional attitudinal polarizations, and mobilize some consensus in immigration thinking. Given traditional policy experiences and long-standing national interests, how do we account for these attitudinal changes?

Such a convergence may be an outcome of international learning (Weil and Crowley 1994),[24] a reluctant recognition of policy limitations at the national level (Butt Philip 1994), a narrowing in the range of treatment of populations (Heisler 1992), or the threat of European integration to the nation-state (Schnapper 1994). In this attitudinal analysis, global considerations may not only be a product of the interactive nature of the European Parliament itself, but may also reflect the fact that European publics read newspapers, watch television, and follow elections in other countries. All of these changes may account for the elusiveness of traditional national and partisan/ideological dynamics, and they undermine the role of loose party groups in organizing the immigration debate in a transnational polity. But, in arguing that partisanship/ideology continues to order preferences, one must not discount the fluidity of party positions as they incorporate new issues. Parties are adjusting to new conditions, particularly ones that result from globalization and European integration. There are many ambiguities, which stem from the fact that, in an increasingly complex European landscape, several interests must be reconciled.

While the analysis here reveals the persistence of traditional national and partisan/ideological orientations, it suggests that there is some convergence on immigration thinking (i.e., on immigration intakes, regulation) that is related to the construction of Europe. Chapter 5 will explore the basis of this convergence by placing these factors in the EU context. In this way, we may evaluate prospects for a collective immigration regime.

NOTES

1. The data on elites are derived from interviews and surveys with a sample of 167 members of the European Parliament, representing twelve countries and ten party groups (see chapter 1, and Lahav 1997a, 1995).
2. This measure has been also operationalized statistically by Money (1999).
3. The relationship between perceptions and numbers can be analyzed only broadly, as comparisons should use care in linking attitudes toward "immigrants" or "non-nationals" to the size of "foreign-born" populations, which are often loosely interchanged.
4. The OLS coefficient relates the direction and strength of the variability in the dependent variable described by the independent variable.
5. This is based on the correlation between "percentage of answers stating 'too many' others" (in terms of nationality, race, religion, culture, and social class) and "percentage of non-EEC nationals in relation to population of country" (n = 12), *Eurobarometer* 30, 1989. Migration figures are reported for 1990. In order to standardize the timeframe of the MEP (1992) and public opinion (1988/89) findings with the demographic picture, table 4.3 and the following regressions employ figures reported for 1990, the mid-point. They thus differ from current estimates, reported in tables 2.1 and 3.1, and appendices D and E, though changes in national patterns have remained the same.
6. According to the Eurobarometer findings, one in three Europeans believes that there are "too many" people of another nationality or race in his country (30: 42). According to the MEP sample, the number of immigrants does not necessarily need adjustment: 51 percent of MEPs claimed that immigration in general should be kept at the present level.
7. In her explanations of the Danish outlier with regard to opposition to open borders, McLaren suggests that it is not so much that Danes would like to close borders to Europeans as that they worry about border policing standards in keeping other immigrants out (2001: 86–87). Niedermayer (1995a) points to Britain's imperial legacy and Denmark's ties to other Nordic countries as explanations for resistance to integration more generally.
8. The Maastricht Treaty explicitly underscored the role of political parties for this purpose, by incorporating Article 138a: "Political parties at the European level are important as a factor for integration within the Union. They will contribute to forming a European awareness and to expressing the political will of the citizens of the Union."

9. The Liberal Democratic and Reformist group is marked by a basic split between parties of Southern Europe which are right-wing in economic matters but possess a historic left-wing character in their anti-clericalism, and those of Northern Europe which can be considered as progressive non-socialists. The term "democratic" was incorporated in the title of the party group as an attempt to give some common meeting point. The group largely rejects state intervention and dirigisme in economic affairs, believing in the values of market forces, individualism, and free enterprise. Its tenets of individual freedom and the principle of diversity are a limiting factor when it comes to group cohesion.

10. Since the survey was conducted in 1992, prior to the accession of Austria, Finland, and Sweden to the EU, respondents may or may not have included these countries as "non-EU Western Europe."

11. See the early but applicable work in the US context, Schattschneider 1975 [1960].

12. Consider the success of the French Front national in the 2002 presidential elections among the working class and old leftist bastions in the north of France. Le Pen was considered the most popular candidate of the working class (24 percent of the blue-collar vote) and made his greatest gains among the unemployed (Guiraudon 2002b: 10). Given's (forthcoming) sociological anatomy of the European extreme right reveals that the typical voter is young or prime-age male blue-collar worker – an optimal candidate for the left. See also Money 1999 on how the political right sought to win votes in constituencies of the left with a high proportion of immigrants.

13. According to Thränhardt (1997: 188), an anti-immigration position, though threatening to broach extreme-right territory, is a "reliable weapon of last resort for conservative parties pitted against social democrats, particularly in relatively quiet times when issues are needed."

14. According to Budge and Farlie, for example, the British Conservatives could never appear more committed to social reforms than the Labour Party. The best Conservative strategy is to divert attention from the need for social reforms to the need for law and order, on which Labour could not credibly propose a firmer line than the traditional party of order. See Budge and Farlie 1983: 260.

15. For a good discussion of theories of issue ownership, see Petrocik 1996. Since many issues will never be emphasized by particular parties, certain areas of resulting space will be out of bounds to some parties and effectively owned by others. The immigration issue is a relevant example, for it does not lure the individualist Liberal group as it does the more statist, Socialist party.

16. According to McLaren (2001), for example, EU elites cue the public to accept internal immigration while leaving support for external immigration to be decided on the left–right continuum. This logic derives from Zaller's contention that if the messages coming from all political parties and political elites are supportive of a particular policy (in the case at hand, EU immigration), then cognitively aware individuals will incorporate these preferences; if the messages are conflicting along partisan lines (i.e., non-EU migrants),

then the individual's own partisan values will influence preferences (Zaller 1990, 1991, 1992).

17. They noted that, among British Labour supporters in 1963, a third preferred the Conservatives to the Liberals as a second choice, and among Conservatives, more than a quarter preferred Labour to the Liberals; see Butler and Stokes 1969: 327.

18. See findings of *Eurobarometer* 30, 1988/89: 45, 64. They give some support to Money's "conjunctural" argument that opposition to immigration which becomes politically important is triggered by the presence of an immigrant community in conjunction with economic recession (1999: 56–60).

19. In this study, experts were asked about various issues that were important in distinguishing left–right positions. The "xenophobia" category referred to parties of which the following expressions were used: "religious/ethnic chauvinism, racism, xenophobic, anti-semitic, anti-emancipation, primordial appeals, white, black, intolerance, minority rights, nationalism, immigration, asylum, migration, exclusion of foreigners" (Huber and Inglehart 1995: table 1).

20. In her efforts to distinguish attitudes toward internal and external migration, McLaren suggests that the length of immigration experience may account for different rates of acceptance. Thus, mainstream politicians have not had much opportunity to debate the issue of internal migration because it is not perceived as a problem (i.e., there has not been an influx into Germany of Greeks as there has been of Turks) (2001: 93).

21. In emphasizing the importance of partisanship in dealing with immigration and racism, Messina (1989) has shown how parties in Britain tried to articulate distinct liberal or restrictive positions in order to capture their electorate. Thus, although bipartisan consensus on race-related issues prevailed in the UK from 1964 to 1975, by 1979 the Conservative and Labour Parties were thrown back onto their core constituencies and political ideologies, and this led to policy divergence on race-related issues. This "race" consensus broke down as a result of electoral pressures and other systemic influences and change (i.e., the breakup of the Conservative and Labour Parties' postwar "Butskellite" or Keynesian welfare state settlement).

22. For other fruitful methods (i.e., "vanilla") using party election manifesto data, see Gabel and Huber 2000.

23. This conforms with evidence from studies of European elections, which found that voters treat European elections as surrogate national elections, and in many cases as a way of sending political messages to the main parties in "second-order" national elections (Reif and Schmitt 1980; Reif 1984, 1997; Eijk, Franklin, and Marsh 1996). These findings are also consonant with Hix's conclusions that the main factors behind voting in the EP are the policy positions of national parties (2002).

24. For more on learning, see Rose 1991; Olsen and Peters 1996.

5   The "European factor": institutional and psychological constraints on immigration attitudes

Act V, Scene 1: In his affluent home in the suburbs of London, one of the most pro-European Tories of the European Parliament reflected on the contentious fate of Europe. "Let's just take a bird's eye view of the political landscape of Europe, when it comes to reaction to the EC. The Maastricht Treaty in the last few months has triggered a nationalist response in most of the member-states – not all, but most of them. That backlash has to do with a perception of the national identity – that the national culture is being threatened by things foreign. It is often not more specific than that. There is this feeling of minority cultures being swamped by something terrible. And this something terrible is linked to Europe, because the feeling is that all of a sudden there is too much Europe happening."

(Diary of researcher, based on interview no. 44, London, April 22, 1992.)

Although traditional partisan/ideological and national interests continue to inform issue attitudes in Europe, the elusive organization of political cleavages in the immigration debate compels us to examine the changing "playing field." While the analysis in chapter 4 underscored the relevance of domestic constraints on immigration thinking, it suggests that there is some attitudinal convergence that may be related to regional integration. The emergence and consolidation of some type of transnational Europe merit consideration for their effects on policy motives and preferences. How are competing interests organized in a transnational framework, and how does "the European factor" – the construction of Europe – contribute to attitudinal patterns?

The continent that has pioneered the nation-state and nationalism has also been the first to formally develop transnationalism. In the 1950s, neofunctional theory, as set out by Ernst Haas (1958: 16), described the process of political integration as one that would prompt actors in distinct national settings to shift their loyalties, expectations, and political activities toward a new center, the institutions of which would demand jurisdiction over the preexisting national states. Accordingly, the end result of political integration would be a new political community superimposed over the preexisting ones.

149

At its current phase of development, the European Union can be best viewed as a "set of complex overlapping networks" in which the supranational system seeks to find compromise and to upgrade common interests, "which under favorable conditions lead to the pooling of sovereignty" (Keohane and Hoffmann 1990: 277).[1] According to even more optimistic "multilevel governance" accounts of Europe, decision-making competences are shared by actors at different levels, and thus the independent role of European-level actors themselves may help to explain policy-making in certain arenas (Hooghe and Marks 2001; Marks 1993; Marks, Hooghe, and Blank 1996; Scharpf 1988, 1996; Schmitter 1996).

As we have seen, ideas on how Europe should be structured vary from highly centralized to polycentric visions of Europe – from more supranational visions to more intergovernmental images. Levels of support also waver. The more one believes in Europe (pan-Europeanism), the more the question "which Europe?" emerges (Hall 1992: 7). But this question comes after the fact because, as Keohane and Hoffmann argue, Europe already has an institutional core which is the EC (1990: 278). Clearly, the nature of European integration has a critical impact on how political conflicts are organized, and must therefore be examined for how it defines issue publics, and the "Euro demos."[2]

The primary division in the European equation lies between the supporters of this new order – the pan-Europeanists – and those who embrace a more traditional national order. The battle over the nature and speed of the European integration process may be understood as a single dimension on which actors are located on issues ranging from "more integration" to "less integration" (Hix 2001a: 664–665).[3] The predominant attitudinal polarization on European integration is thus, broadly, between those who identify with a more diverse entity called Europe, and those whose memory of and outlook on history are more nation-specific. These divergent philosophies stem partially from the fact that industrialization and colonial expansion unfolded in different parts of Europe and spread in distinctive directions. They also reflect deep ideological undercurrents. Attitudes toward Europe clearly cut across countries and parties, and these affect other priorities, related to immigration. But how?

In this chapter, I propose that the political construction of Europe affects thinking on immigration and mobilizes some new alliances. The "European factor," as I refer to it, considers that *institutional* and *psychological* constraints associated with community-building may straddle traditional lines of political contestation, and help explain the oft-noted tendency of immigration politics to create "strange bedfellows" coalitions (see Zolberg 2000). Psychological factors involve boundary identification, and emphasize the distinction between "us" (Europeans) and "them" (foreigners) in terms of religion, culture, and identity. These distinctions also have an institutional dimension. Institutional constraints include conflicts inside and outside the EU project, such as supranational versus intergovernmental forces; parties of the left and parties of the right; those who have more to gain versus those who have more to lose from both immigration and European integration. In this way, the European factor may generate some norms that cut across traditional competing alliances or fault lines examined in chapter 4. This chapter argues that European institution-building and the promotion of a "European demos" with a common European identity reinforce and reinvent traditional polarizations. By galvanizing consensus, the processes of community identity and polity formation in an evolving European landscape mitigate traditional sources of attitudes toward immigration and immigrants, and in turn promote a common immigration regime.

First, I introduce the "European factor" by delineating its institutional and psychological components. Second, I investigate how the European factor affects immigration attitudes both conceptually and empirically. Finally, I explore the effects of the European factor on traditional lines of battle, and on the drawing of new fault lines. Factoring Europe into the equation allows us to reconcile a growing consensus and solidarity among Europeans with exclusionary outcomes for out-groups.

Europe as a factor in immigration cooperation

As new institutions have been seen to liberate citizens from old ties or to undermine national authority in Europe, they have been said to provide important sources of thinking about elite and mass behavior (Inglehart 1990a, 1990b; Dalton 2002; Caporaso 1996, 2000; Hooghe and Marks 1999, 2001; Risse-Kappen 1996). An international/national or pro-integration/anti-integration cleavage has become increasingly relevant to understanding the polarization of elite and public opinion in the EU (Inglehart 1970a, 1990a, 1990c; Lahav 1997a; Hix and Lord 1997; Lahav and Bafumi 2001; Noury 2002; Carrubba 2001; Hix 1999b, 2002; Hooghe and Marks 1999, 2001). The development of the EU has been shown to affect national voting choices, party platforms, national agendas, and even prospects for cooperation among member-states.

Indeed, empirical data have supported the thesis that European integration may create an "issue public," for whom knowing the position on European integration provides additional knowledge about other policy preferences.[4] They suggest that the "integration vs. independence" dimension is relevant beyond the political space of the European Union itself (Schmitt and Thomassen 2002: 30). Since this dichotomy may structure political conflicts and give meaning to political controversies over specific policies, it is important to delineate the sources that inspire these positions, and how they structure attitudes toward immigration. Assuming that European integration affects the agendas of national and European politics, as has been extensively documented (Eichenberg and Dalton 1993; Hix and Lord 1997; Carrubba 2001; Noury 2002; Marks, Hooghe, and Blank 1996), how does the integrationist continuum capture immigration politics?

The drive toward a common Europe affects traditional attitudes in two ways. Institution-building and -consolidation require power shifts to support the process. Their psychological counterpart contributes to the emergence and consolidation of the Community. In promoting consensus, both processes have the potential to rearrange traditional alignments. How do these dynamics affect the prospects for and nature of immigration cooperation?

Institutional constraints: national vs. supranational conflicts

As chapter 2 extensively described, the construction of Europe presents all sorts of institutional struggles among a diverse array of interlocutors over how much Europe – more or less – and how the EU should be organized – intergovernmentally or supranationally. Furthermore, given its transversal character, immigration issues inevitably invoke cross-sectoral conflicts (i.e., ministries of labor, social affairs, internal affairs, justice), with domestic actors "venue-shopping" at the EU level in order to get more power or clout at home (see Guiraudon 2003). In this complex setting, institutional conflicts over European authority materialize among domestic institutions (i.e., parties, government, bureaucracies, courts) and EU institutions (Council, Commission, Parliament, party groups) as well as between the two levels of actors.

Political contestation over European integration has not been captured so neatly by traditional party or national dynamics. EU scholars have provided some evidence that the left–right party yardstick is weaker than the national divide in predicting attitudes related to European integration (Hix and Lord 1997; Hix 1999b; Thomassen and Schmitt 1999; Wessels 1995a). National variations have been found along an integrationist continuum, distinguishing between large and small countries, and old and new members (Feld and Wildgen 1976; Deheneffe 1986; Eichenberg and Dalton 1993; Niedermayer 1995a; Hix 1999b; Ray 1999: 293), bringing into question the nature of political competition.

Nonetheless, while much of the left–right party literature has been challenged by new ordinal schemes that have promised to better organize issues related to globalization and protectionism, and which I discuss below, the relevance of parties to the EU dialogue cannot be underestimated. Partisan conflict is still suggestive of some EU preferences (Hooghe, Marks, and Wilson 2002; Wessels 1995a: 130–134; Marks and Steenbergen 2002; Hix and Lord 1997; Hix 2001a; Gabel and Anderson 2002; Gabel and Hix 2002). It is true that party positions on Europe cannot be charted on a broad left–right scale in a unilinear fashion. But their organizational power can be captured on an inverted U-curve, so that extreme-left parties and extreme-right parties unite in Euroskepticism, and parties in the major party families (social democratic, Christian democratic, liberal, and conservative) are more supportive of European integration (Hooghe, Marks and Wilson 2002; Noury 2002; Carrubba 2001; Taggart 1998).[5] More generally, parties at the political extremes take the most skeptical positions on European integration, and on any type of supranational Europe (Taggart 1998), though countermovements to European integration involve mainstream parties as well (Hooghe, Marks, and Wilson 2001, 2002; Marks, Wilson, and Ray 2002: 590–591), further corroborated by the evidence here.

Broadly speaking, the European factor elicits patterns of contestation that affect and may even supplant more traditional cleavages. Beyond traditional ideological and intranational institutional conflicts over policy preferences, power struggles are evident *internally*, within and among EU institutions, such as the European Commission, the Council, and the Parliament, and *externally*, through national, intergovernmental, and ad hoc institutions, which seek to retain domestic sovereignty.

Institution-building and -consolidation in a new transnational community tend to mask traditional antagonisms within the EU because they rely on consensus and power shifts for support. In Europe, these institutional struggles may contribute to strategic collaboration, giving an impression that ideological factors are not operative. The "new institutional" literature has cogently identified the importance of structural differences in partisan behavior.[6] This tendency is particularly evident in the European Parliament, which in the third assembly (the timeframe of my survey) required 260 votes for a second reading.

The European Parliament has been engaged in a fierce power struggle with the European Commission and Council (Tsebelis 1994, 1996; Moser 1996; Steunenberg 1994). External opposition to the authority of the EP has diverted potential internal opposition. One MEP explains this dynamic:

We can find within the European Parliament the consensus of options against the Council and the Commission. Our goal in the European Parliament is first of all to formulate an opinion with a significant majority, so the Council and Commission will bring the Parliament in, and that can be done only if we have a big majority . . . It seems to be possible on major issues to find a compromise between Socialists, Christian Democrats, and Liberals. It means that, when there is an external pressure, the differences decline. (interview no. 12; Brussels, May 5, 1992: 4)

The interviews revealed that MEPs are extremely sensitive to these external threats. According to one Dutch MEP:

If we simply had our national views echoed in the European Parliament, we wouldn't have any power. That means we have to combine our national points of view, make compromises, and form integrated opinions to have majorities in the European Parliament. If you do not have these significant majorities, you can't influence, for example, the European Commission or the Council. So, in our Group . . . we just talk and talk as long as we can find a general consensus. I think that, in about 80 percent of the cases, we find a general consensus, as we normally have rather significant majorities in the European Parliament to influence the European Council and the Commission. It is just for survival that you have to do this. (ibid.)

It is apparent that institutional factors play a large role in affecting MEP attitudes toward issues such as immigration. One Belgian Socialist captures this:

There is a tendency for the European MPs to have a broader view of a lot of issues, but that's institutional. (interview no. 271; Brussels, May 6, 1992)

Clearly, these types of institutional struggles mitigate traditional lines of competition, and must therefore be examined for the new cleavages that may replace them.

The impact of institutional membership on party cohesion, especially in displacing traditional contestation, has been noted by a number of EP scholars (Thomassen and Schmitt 1999; Katz 1999: 33–40; Bardi 2002: 302–304). There is ample evidence suggesting that issues related to European integration may be marked more by institutional allegiances than by party lines. According to Thomassen and Schmitt, "the closer issues come to the constitutional framework of the Union, to its institutional makeup, the more the EP will tend to move to a non-party, or institutional mode, rather than an interparty mode" (1999: 138). This view has its foundation in Haas's early neofunctional thesis (1958) that institution-building creates a shift in beliefs, and involves arguments that those who work in certain European institutions may be socialized into a European outlook more than others (Spinelli 1966; Laffan 1996; see Scully 1999, 2002).

Since the early days of the European Coal and Steel Community, there has been an interparty desire to influence both executives – the High Authority (now the Commission) and the Council of Ministers – to follow the Assembly's resolutions (Haas 1958: 411). In the European Parliament today, when the Socialists (the second-largest group) want to make significant impact on legislation, they link up not necessarily with the rest of the left, but with the largest group, the Christian Democrats or PPE (for a similar account of the 1990s, see Gallagher, Laver, and Mair 1992: 279). Since these two groups control the majority of the seats, they effectively control the European Parliament between them.[7] These trends concur with what has been found in the American legislature. Students of American politics have been able to explain patternless shifts of party policy cohesion and polarization as a function of both the institutional and external environments of Congress (Serra *et al.* 1993: 7; see also Cover, Pinney, and Serra 1997).

In the EU, opposition to supranational institution-building comes in nationalist form, and is evident among EU institutions as well as between the EU institutions and external actors. One German Socialist explained this opposition:

The enemy is not in the house; the enemy is sitting in Brussels [the Commission], and it is the Council. Because there are twelve [now fifteen] national governments, every minister is coming out of the room, and discussing with his [own] press, with the German press, French press, with his press about the items and about the aims he achieved for his people in his country and not for Europe . . . they are the real nationalists. (interview no. 167; Strasbourg, May 14, 1992: 1)

Similar national tendencies involve extra-EU institutional conflicts or national institutions which seek to retain domestic sovereignty. Many European Parliamentarians underscored these sentiments:

I'm being the spokesman now for the average politician in a national parliament. The average politician in a national parliament says, "I don't like this European business because it takes the cheese off my slice of bread in the morning." National politicians are concerned that, if the Community becomes too important, their jobs lose a lot of their fun . . . so the juicy bit will be dealt with in Brussels politically, and they're left with the scraps. (interview no. 44; Strasbourg, May 12, 1992: 3)

Indeed, "the struggle over European integration" is about how to manage "multiple-level governance" among frequently rival units (Hooghe and Marks, 1999, 2001; Marks, Hooghe, and Blank 1996; see also Scharpf 1999). In this sense, institutional conflicts may include the relevant actors found in Brussels, in certain national ministries and central agencies, and at the subnational level. Shared competences have been formally promoted by the incorporation of the "subsidiarity" principle into the Maastricht Treaty, which deferred to national and local actors all policy decisions that could better be achieved "as closely as possible to the citizen" (Article A).[8] However, maintaining a delicate balance between EU and member-state authorities has been cumbersome, given the legal ambiguity ascribed to the term and, as a result, subsidiarity has generated more contention among a constellation of forces.

Such institutional rivalries over competence are endemic to immigration politics. They are exacerbated because migration issues have been increasingly caught between domestic and international mandates more generally. That is, states are forced to deal with competing obligations, on the one hand, to liberal markets and rights-based principles enshrined in international law versus, on the other, national interests and fundamental state prerogatives to determine who shall enter their territory – the ultimate embodiment of sovereignty (Lahav 1997b; Soysal 1994; Jacobson 1996). These tensions bring to life the conflict between international law, which may or may not sanction the state, and constitutional law and national policies which vary, especially as they affect outcomes.

European activity on immigration reinforces the traditional conflict between supranational institutions and intergovernmental ones, or "joint-decision traps" between European and national regulation.[9] Immigration and citizenship policy is manifest on the European level, under EU regulation, and is at the same time susceptible to country dynamics. As immigration and asylum policies are increasingly showing characteristics of a multilevel governance regime (Guiraudon 2000a: 257; Hooghe and Marks 2001: 22–23), they make institutional constraints more pertinent to this analysis.

In a broad sense, EU institutional antagonisms involve not only competing "policy venues"[10] and actors, but conflicts over symbolic and substantive visions of how Europe should be organized. A commitment to consolidating the power of the European Union institutions includes overcoming the tendencies toward intergovernmentalism. As I noted in chapter 2, this is particularly evident in the case of migration, a topic engaging a plethora of ad hoc organizations which have been largely non-transparent in their administrative decision-making structure (and for which the Schengen "lab" serves as a model). The Maastricht Treaty, like subsequent treaties, proposed to shift this balance back to EU institutions such as the European Parliament, rendering MEPs more influential in the debate on immigration policy. The 1997 reflection group on the Amsterdam Treaty specifically noted the inadequacies of the intergovernmental approach in migration and asylum, and moved to transfer the bulk

of immigration policy from the third to the first pillar. Although EU institutions have been gradually incorporated in the decision-making process
since Amsterdam, to date, the form of EU cooperation on migration and
asylum still favors intergovernmental bargains over supranational institutional actors. Clearly, the nature and outcome of these institutional
conflicts influence the prospects for a common immigration policy in the
EU. And vice versa – the ability of the EU to construct and uphold those
common policies such as immigration affects the institutional structure of
the EU, and determines the extent to which the EU can operate as a fully
supranational enterprise. It is precisely in areas such as the second and
third pillars (foreign policy, security, justice) or "high politics" arenas
that member-states are most reluctant to forego national traditions,
interests, and sovereignty. These are also at the core of external security
that prompted the European Union in its original conception (Dalton
and Eichenberg 1998: 268). To the extent that the 2002 European
Convention is poised to create a constitution for the people of Europe
and make the institutional direction of the EU more evident, the consequences will become more certain.[11] For now, EU dynamics are notable
for transforming traditional attitudes and alliances into coalescence.

Psychological constraints: "us" vs. "them"

The second component of European integration that influences attitudes
is related to psychological processes that buttress the emergence and
consolidation of new forces in Europe. The classical literature in
sociology and political behavior offers insight into the impact of
community-building and -consolidation on immigration attitudes (see
Lahav 2002; for the connection between nationhood conceptions and
immigration/citizenship policies, see Brubaker 1992).[12] Easton describes
a sense of community as a "we-feeling among a group of people – they
are a political entity that works together and will likely share a common
political fate and destiny" (1965: 332). Deutsch explicitly referred to
integration as the "attainment within a territory of a sense of community
and of institutions and practices strong enough . . . to invoke mutual
sympathies and loyalty, a we-feeling, and trust" (Deutsch *et al.* 1957:
5, 36).

Erikson contends that communities have a specific territory in the
world as a whole, not only in the sense that they occupy a defined region
of geographical space, but also in the sense that they take over a particular
niche in what might be called cultural space and develop their own
"ethos" or "way" within that compass. Both of these dimensions of group
space, the geographical and the cultural, set the community apart as a

special place and provide an important point of reference for its members (Erikson 1966: 11; Pastore 1992). The relationship between territory and cultural or national identity has been particularly pronounced in Europe, where nationalism and nation-states have flourished (Tilly 1990, 1994; Gillespie 1996).[13] Both European integration efforts and migration necessitate a renegotiation of this traditional relationship.

We may infer from these notions that "Europeanness," the identification with a larger community, is a culturally significant mobilizing force (see Sinnott 1995: 12–14). It is particularly relevant to thinking on the immigration issue, as "Europeanness" is defined in an *in*clusive manner, including all Europeans, and inherently *ex*cluding foreigners. In interviews, MEPs frequently attributed unanimity in the European Parliament to "European" culture. Respondents often mentioned common religion, shared visions, and the legal entity of the common market as elements of this culture.

It is possible to evaluate the development of national identity and identity crises by focusing on policies and attitudes toward *non*-members. Instrumental to the European nation-building process is the "construction of the alien" (Cassell 1993: 3–4; Kaschuba 1993; Armstrong 1982). Consider the classical theories of communities as boundary-maintaining (Erikson 1966: 10; Deutsch *et al.* 1957; Deutsch 1981).[14] This function is roughly tantamount to Talcott Parsons's "pattern-maintenance" process – the maintenance of order and predictability in society against external and domestic threats (1951).[15]

According to Erikson, "one of the surest ways to confirm an identity, for communities as well as for individuals, is to find some way of measuring what one is *not*" (1966: 11). Anderson described the "imagined community" of the nation as creating primary social identities through which prejudices against outsiders are formed (1991). Indeed, the problem of immigration in the European Union has more to do with defining members outside the EU (i.e., "third-national" status) than with movement within the EU.

This thesis is supported by the distribution of immigrant group preferences, noted in chapters 3 and 4. That is, European publics and elites consider immigrants from North Africa, Turkey, and Asia least favorable as groups compared to migrants from other EU and European countries, and are most likely to say that immigrants from south of the Mediterranean should not be accepted (see figure 4.1 and table 4.1). Further, the relationship between those who would reject certain immigrants and the numbers of *non-EU foreigners* in their nation is statistically significant, while such a correlation does not exist for rejection of immigrants and the numbers of *EU* or *total foreigners* (see table 4.2).

Some scholars attribute these bivariate patterns of immigrant group preferences to elite opinion leadership.[16] According to McLaren (2001), for example, because elites are more contentious about non-EU migrants than they are about internal migration, they provide important ideological cues that polarize the publics. This thesis is tenuous for several reasons. First, as the evidence in chapter 3 demonstrated, elites are ideologically divided about EU migrants as well as non-EU migrants. Second, it is plausible that external migration is simply an issue on which ideological positions play a more discriminating role, not because of elites, but simply because the issue of external migration differs from that of internal migration in a number of ways that are relevant to the left–right distinction. The manners in which non-EU migration differs from internal EU migration include the very critical notion of what it is to be a "European." The "elite opinion leadership" argument neglects to consider the case that it may be this distinction – "Europeanness" – that causes a rift between the public stance on external immigration and that on internal EU immigration, and not simply elite cues.

Given the inconsequential change in public support for EU migrants between the years 1993 and 1997, a period of enormous supranational activity (McLaren 2001: 85–86), these migrant distinctions are not necessarily a product of EU diffusion or socialization.[17] According to *Eurobarometer* reports 39 and 48 (Spring 1993 and Autumn 1997, respectively), public opinion toward EU migrants, which is more favorable than that toward non-EU migrants, has remained relatively stable over the four-year period; and in most cases there have been slight drops in support for accepting EU migrants with no restrictions. I therefore expect that these affinities and preferences may have less to do with the legal entity of the common market and conditions created by regional integration on the EU front (see chapter 2) than with cultural and religious distinctions.

The construction of Europe and European identity has faltered on religion, a factor that can be traced back to ancient history – from the Crusades to the aftermath of the Thirty Years War – when the principle of conformity to the prince's religion was generalized throughout the German Empire (Zolberg 1983: 234). A historical logic imputed to religion is pervasive in conceptualizations of European identity. One Socialist reported: "It's the same as what made a European identity during medieval times – always – it's religion" (interview no. 172; Brussels, May 6, 1992: 8). A Belgian MEP further mentions "the old background of Christianity mixed with the French Revolution" (interview no. 271; Brussels, May 6, 1992: 3). The European factor exposes the lingering notion of a greater Europe based on "Christendom." The surprising renaissance of this term in contemporary discourse reflects the symbolic durability of ties between the Roman church and efforts to unite Europe. It underscores the vital role that cross-national religious bonds have long played in facilitating integration (Deutsch *et al.* 1957; Haas 1958; Nelsen, Guth, and Fraser 2001).[18]

The construction of Europe tends to bolster convergence by highlighting religious differences between in-groups and out-groups. According to one MEP,

An influx of Islamic people into what is conceived as a Christian Democratic Europe obviously produces tensions. You could go back and refight the wars. (interview no. 134; London, April 22, 1992: 4)

In defining "Europeanness," religion intrinsically serves to demarcate insiders from outsiders. One Greek Communist even referred to a religious history in conjuring images of a European tradition:

Our religion is Orthodox Christian, an orthodox religion, which is very traditional, very old. It is the oldest part of Christianity. And, as Greece was occupied for four or five centuries by the Ottoman Empire which was a Muslim one, the opposition of Christian Orthodox to Muslim in our tradition is very strong. (interview no. 461; Strasbourg, May 13, 1992: 3)

We may have expected that the schism between the Greek and Latin churches would render Orthodox believers less enthusiastic about an EU dominated by Roman Catholic countries, and more sensitive to older religious divisions within Europe. This is somewhat neutralized by the fact that, like the Latin church, the Orthodox church also has universal goals, and thus consistently favors European integration. European community-building promotes solidarity by defusing long-standing religious fractures.

Explaining cultural markers, one MEP posed a symbolic analogy between Europe and a secular religious state:

We must do the same as the Jews did in Israel, when they declared that any Jew presenting himself at the borders of Israel has a right to come, whatever his motivations. And I personally hold that every European who comes to another country of Europe has the same right as a Jew to Israel. He is the European to Europe. That's where the line is for me. Extra Europeans no; inner Europeans, yes. (interview no. 63; Strasbourg, May 11, 1992: 3–4)

According to researchers at the European University Institute in Florence, this type of cultural logic explains why, although Turkey is a member of NATO, it is not a member of the EU.[19] MEPs acknowledge this paradox as they describe the Turkish request to become an EU member:

Leaving aside the cost because they [Turkey] are very backwards . . . [it is] Christendom, the area where Christians roughly were during the Middle Ages . . . We
all [identified with] the Church, whether we [went] or we didn't. But Turkey is
an Islamic country – it is entirely different. We have Sundays as our days of rest.
Turks have Islamic practices. The real problem is that the differences between
Christendom and Islam are quite big. (interview no. 123; London, April 24,
1992: 5)

A French Senator explains, "It can be dressed up as an economic
argument, but one gets the feeling that they just don't think of it as
Europe, because it is an Islamic country" (interview no. 310; Strasbourg, May 11, 1992: 4).[20] As countries such as Turkey and Malta
are being considered candidates in the EU enlargement process, these
cultural concerns have become more politically charged, especially when
immigration projections are raised (on the Turkish case, see Teitelbaum
and Martin 2003). The contrasts between the Islamic world and the
Christian world are not only relevant to European identity but they
cultivate a type of solidarity, which leads to all types of exclusionist
policies.

The prominent cultural divisions between the European and non-
European worlds or Christianity and Islam go beyond the rubric of
religion, and center on secular democracy. One MEP implied that,
beyond religious differences, there were also the antagonisms of opposing
"systems":

The big problem is that you can take people with the same religion as being of the
same culture. But if you are taking people from a Muslim system, for example,
it's so different and people hate it. And then you have a confrontation between
these two systems. (interview no. 15; Brussels, May 6, 1992: 3)

Responses to the Salman Rushdie affair in the United Kingdom or to
the French row over the asserted rights of Muslim girls to wear the
veil in public schools reflect the sentiment that Muslims do not fit
the pluralist, multicultural, or "European" ideas so easily. Indeed, a
common European interpretation of fundamentalist Islam is a revolt
against modernity (that is, against Europe) – a "countermodernism,"
as suggested by Jan Pieterse in his treatise on "Fictions of Europe"
(1991: 5). In the European Union, religion serves more as a marker of
cultural boundaries than as a testimony of persuasion and beliefs. The
presence of religious out-groups tends to be magnified by the construction
of Europe, which strives for universalization and community-building
among Europeans.

The links between religion and the conceptualization of Europe are
evident in immigration thinking, and are empirically explored later in this

chapter. They inform all types of inclusionary and exclusionary preferences. As one Italian Socialist explains:

You see, in Italy, you don't have any repulsion at all from the people in front of
the Filipinos. You know why: because they're Catholic. They do what we do. On
Sundays, they go to church. (interview no. 395; Strasbourg, May 11, 1992: 3)

Although religion has often been the defining factor in many nascent
right-wing movements in Europe, it has become salient in communities,
which search for identity during times of change. Thus, religion may
be evoked as a rallying force either for nationalism or for Europeanism.
Interviews with European policy-makers and bureaucrats revealed that
arguments for restrictive immigration policy were based upon the idea
of protecting the unique nature of European culture. These attitudes
centered on the threat from *non*-European and *non*-Christian religious
values.

Reactions against the psychological processes of forging a European
identity provide insight regarding polarizations in Europe. These, in turn,
affect attitudes toward immigration. The abolition of internal borders
(which are some of the most obvious symbols of national communities) has contributed to a collective sense of identity crisis, marked
by the growth of nationalist and xenophobic movements. As one MEP
explained:

First, we have the development of the European Community. People are rather
for Europe, but, and this is very interesting, they start to be afraid for the nations.
Will the power of the nation change? Are we going to have a dominant Europe?
(interview no. 329; Strasbourg, May 13, 1992: 4)

Further, as one Spanish Socialist spelled out:

It is very easy to talk about Europe. Many times, when it comes down to national
interests, we are all the same nationalists. I'm not talking about Hitler or Le Pen
and so on. I mean just a nationalist feeling that we have to protect our own nation
against certain laws which the Community will make and so on . . . and so I think
we are all alike on that . . . it depends on how close you touch the very core of it.
(interview no. 387; Strasbourg, May 14, 1992: 2)

Clearly, the construction of Europe generates resistance, and this is not
limited to extreme-right or peripheral groups, as some scholars have
argued (Taggart 1998), but implicates large moderate parties as well
(Marks, Wilson, and Ray 2002: 590; Hooghe, Marks, and Wilson 2001).

One of the bases of cross-party and cross-national agreement in
immigration thinking may be inspired by more general issues and fears
related to Europe, rather than by strict numbers or specific national

experiences. This may explain why public opinion findings suggest that many people hold a negative view on the presence of immigrants – as an expression of frustration in other areas, such as unemployment, insecurity, poverty, drug abuse, and corruption (*Eurobarometer* 30, 1989: 70). The construction of Europe and its psychological impact on immigration attitudes is a factor worthy of analysis.

European integration is clearly linked to the case of immigration. Both phenomena require a restructuring of boundaries. The creation of a supranational community requires physical and psychological adjustments. The period of change heightens insecurity and activates a search for common symbols of attachment and for a collective identity. Immigration touches the nerve of this dynamic. An influx of immigrants tends to be visible, and thus the newcomers are often the focus of concerns arising from difficulties in coping with change (Heisler 1992: 610). The rapidity of the process of change in the modern world is reflected by events such as European integration or immigration. As Geoff Harris captures in his study on *The Dark Side of Europe*, both may inspire many to hope for a "better world" (1994). Yet, they may lead to a great sense of insecurity and bewilderment among those who fear that these changes will be in some way costly in economic terms or in terms of their self-esteem as citizens of a particular place or country (ibid.: 161–192). These people would be what the school of "modernization crisis" identifies as the "losers of modernization," such as those suffering or facing unemployment or economic marginalization (Lipset 1990 [1960]; Inglehart 1997). Several benchmark studies have suggested that the rise of militant religious fundamentalism and xenophobic movements in advanced liberal democracies represents a reaction against rapid cultural changes that seem to be eroding some of the most basic values and customs of the more traditional and less secure groups in these countries (Inglehart 1997: 251; Barber 1992). This phenomenon has been most commonly used to interpret the growth of extreme-right movements in Europe since the 1980s (Minkenberg 1994; von Beyme 1988; Betz 1993, 1994; Taggart 1998; Gibson 2002; Kitschelt with McGann 1995) but manifests itself more diffusely.

For Heisler, reopening the social contracts of the democratic welfare states established in the postwar settlement in order to accommodate immigrants requires "cognitive and institutional adjustments" that need time (1992: 610). At least one MEP articulated this goal:

One of the great challenges of the work in the EP is precisely to break down psychological barriers. One does that not immediately, but first by breaking down the physical and legal ones, and then by addressing psychological ones indirectly. (interview no. 44; Strasbourg, May 12, 1992: 1)

As is true for national regimes, the challenges posed by immigration dynamics and European integration relate to redistribution, and the renegotiation of resources. Whether or not migration is a (re)distributive issue that fits into the classical Lowi model is debatable.[21] While Gimpel and Edwards (1999: 307) find that American congressional politics on immigration since the late 1970s have increasingly become a partisan issue because of the redistributive costs of related programs (i.e., refugee assistance), Hammar suggests that immigration eludes political parties precisely because it uncharacteristically divides the economic pie between citizens and non-citizens rather than among voters (1985b: 280). There is limited evidence in this study suggesting that those who feel deprived of their part of the pie feel most threatened by non-EU migrants, but the jury is still out as to the cultural or economic motivation behind such a threat.

Regardless of distributive effects, there is ample evidence based on T. H. Marshall's (1965: 93) argument linking welfare states to community-building. The literature on migration and the welfare state suggests that, historically and presently, threats to the welfare state focus on its central features – national identity, homogeneity, or solidarity (Baldwin 1990; Guiraudon 2002a: 133; Bommes and Geddes 2000). As Freeman (1986) and others have noted (see Lieberman 2002; Leibfried and Pierson 2000: 279), the principles of the welfare state presuppose the existence of non-members in order to rally against free-market mechanisms and for community-building. In this scenario, an associated condition of porous geographical borders is more exclusive entry to the welfare state.

The drive toward a common Europe demands institutional restructuring and psychological consonance which intrinsically affect attitudes toward foreigners. The twin processes of institution-building and psychological conformity rely on a reservoir of what David Easton called "utilitarian" (personal assessments or economic or political interests directed to specific authorities, institutions, policies) and "affective" (diffuse allegiance and attachment, based on ideological or non-material evaluations) support (1965, 1975).[22] The differentiating effects of each dimension of public opinion on European policy output have sparked a renewed interest in Easton's work among students of the EU. Aided by longitudinal data sets provided by the Eurobarometer, these scholars have looked to this public support model as an empirical template for measuring attitudes toward European integration and, by extension, to various policy issues (Gabel 1998; Niedermayer and Westle 1995).[23] They enhance my contention that institutional and attitudinal transformations related to Europe fundamentally shape attitudes which impinge on immigration concerns. The question that then concerns us is what attitudinal manifestations we might expect to observe in the link between European integration and immigration.

The "European factor" and immigration attitudes: the empirical connection

The movement toward a common European identity with strong supra-national institutions generates reactions that influence immigration thinking. These can be found both *inside* (or among) the European institutions, such as the Parliament, Commission, and Council, and *outside*, often expressed through support for nationalism or a drive toward intergovernmentalism. Even within the European institutions, it is legit-imate to participate in the Union process and take a restrictionist line about future development (Pridham and Pridham 1981: 16). Margaret Thatcher's speech at the College of Europe in Bruges in October 1988 was a ground-breaking effort to present an alternative to the ideal of political union. The evidence in my study supports other systematic correctives to the view that European elites are necessarily pro-integrationist (Franklin and Scarrow 1999).[24]

In the European Parliament, although there is a tendency to support integration of the European Union, some MEPs want *less* and *slower* integration than others (see table 5.1).[25] Table 5.1 depicts national and party differences toward European integration that are expressed within European institutions themselves. Together with figure 5.1 on MEP attitudes toward immigration, table 5.1 shows that some of the more substantial polarizations were located along national and partisan lines, both of which reinforced positions on European integration and immigration. A relationship exists between those MEPs who were more anti-Europe and those who held more negative attitudes toward immigration.

Two regressions illustrate this relationship more clearly. Table 5.2 shows the correlations between independent variables such as party and country affiliations and dependent variables, positions on Europe and on immigration. Regressing MEPs' party allegiance and a dichotomous variable for their country of origin across their position on EU unification (speed up, present speed, or slow down) yields a statistically significant relationship for party and country. Table 5.2 reveals that both coefficients are in the direction one would expect. An ordinary least-squares (OLS) analysis was conducted here, but order probit coefficients yield similar results. Moving from a more right-leaning party leftwards, we can see that MEPs' positions on unification grow more favorable. Further, as

Table 5.1 *MEP attitudes toward Europe, by country and party group*

	Speed up EU	Present speed	Slow down EU	Total N
EP total	70%	22%	9%	164
Country				
Benelux	73%	15%	12%	26
Denmark	**50%**	**25%**	25%	4
France	65%	26%	9%	23
Germany	**52%**	**24%**	24%	21
Greece	**87%**	13%	0%	8
Ireland	83%	17%	0%	6
Italy	**92%**	8%	0%	25
Portugal	**86%**	14%	0%	7
Spain	79%	16%	5%	19
UK	**44%**	**48%**	8%	25
Party group				
Greens	**85%**	0%	15%	13
GUE/CG	**90%**	10%	0%	10
SOC	68%	27%	5%	60
LDR	82%	12%	6%	17
PPE/RDE	70%	26%	4%	53
DR	**0%**	33%	**67%**	6

Note: Party group figures do not include the ARC Rainbow Group and the Independents. Figures do not equal 100% due to rounding.
Bold type indicates percentages that are 15% over or under EP average.
GUE/CG = Communists; SOC = Socialists; LDR = Liberals Democrats; PPE/RDE = Christian Democrats and Conservatives; DR = Radical Right (see table 4.4 for full acronyms and ideological self-placement).

we consider countries with more than the average number of non-EU citizens (2.03 percent) rather than those with fewer than this average, MEPs are approximately 20 percent more likely to indicate a desire for slowing European integration.

The second regression employs these same independent variables regressed across MEP positions on immigration levels (increase, present level, decrease). This is also presented in table 5.2. The results can be interpreted similarly, with only slight differences. For example, the party variable tends to have more substantive and stronger statistical significance when applied to MEPs' positions on immigration levels than to European integration.

The country variable reveals a weaker but statistically significant relationship (with $p \leq .05$, we can be 95 percent certain of this result), and a similar substantive significance (as indicated by the OLS coefficient,

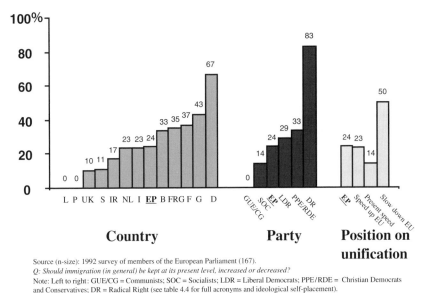

Figure 5.1 MEP views on decreasing immigration, by country, party group, and position on European unification

and where order probit yields similar results).[26] As a whole, it is clear that a MEP's partisan/ideological stand and country are crucial to understanding his/her position on European integration and the immigration debate.

Beyond extrapolations that we can make about the confluence of European integration and immigration preferences, a chi-squared goodness-of-fit test shows the relationship between the two dependent variables in the preceding regressions (positions on European unification and immigration levels). Table 5.3 shows a statistically significant relationship between integration and immigration levels preferred by MEPs.

MEPs who wish for slower integration are more likely also to desire decreased levels of immigration. Conversely, those who wish for more rapid European integration are more favorable toward increased immigration levels. Seventy-nine percent of MEPs who were satisfied with the current rate of European integration were also comfortable with the present level of immigration.

Table 5.4 shows that these patterns are replicated among the European public. As the European public became more unfavorable toward EU membership, those saying there were too many non-nationals in

Table 5.2 *Relationships between party and country across positions on European integration and levels of immigration*

	Position on EU unification	Position on level of immigration
Party	$-.06^a$	$-.161$
	$(.05)^b$	$(.00)$
Dichotomous variable for country[c]	$-.238$	$-.215$
	$(.01)$	$(.05)$

Notes: Excludes Austria, Finland, and Sweden, which were not represented in the MEP sample.
[a]OLS coefficient.
[b]Significance.
[c]Dummy variables were used to capture country effects. Based on a dichotomous variable coding for the number of non-EU citizens in the country of origin, where 0 is coded for those countries where non-EU populations are greater than the EU average (2.03%) and 1 is for those countries where non-EU populations are less than the average.

Table 5.3 *MEP positions on EU integration and levels of immigration*

	Level of immigration		
EU integration	Increase	Present level	Decrease
Speed up	30	47	23
	30%	47%	23%
Continue at present rate	2	23	4
	7%	79%	14%
Slow down	3	3	6
	25%	25%	50%

Note: Pearson chi-square $= 15.961$, df $= 4$, significance $= .003$. Excludes Austria, Finland, and Sweden, which were not represented in the MEP sample.
Source (n-size): 1992 survey of members of European Parliament (167).

their country increased (approximately 60 percent, from 27 percent to 43 percent). Those who viewed the EU negatively were almost 75 percent more likely to have unfavorable assessments about immigrant numbers (403 respondents said there were "too many" non-nationals) than favorable ones (227 respondents reported that there were "not many").

The issue of European integration serves to distinguish not only the far right from its political competitors, but also the unequivocally immigration restrictionist MEPs from the others. Party analysis revealed

Table 5.4 *Public opinion on EU membership and immigration levels*

	Number of non-nationals in country		
EU membership	Too many	A lot but not too many	Not many
Good thing	2,048	3,424	2,016
	27%	46%	27%
Not good or bad	875	788	477
	41%	37%	22%
Bad thing	403	310	227
	43%	33%	24%

Source: *Eurobarometer* 30, 1989.
Note: Pearson chi-square $= 208.4605$, df $= 4$, significance $=. 000$.

that the differences between extreme-right politicians and others relate not only to their views on immigration, but also to their position on a common Europe as well. Although the theme of European integration has been underdeveloped by extreme-right parties (see Messina 2002b) the Euroskeptic dimension of anti-immigration parties has been implied by those researching the extreme right (Betz 1994; Betz and Immerfall 1998; Fieschi, Sheilds, and Woods 1996; Hainsworth 1992; Kitschelt with McGann 1995; Karapin 1998). This trend was also evident in the country analysis, as MEPs from the northern, more developed countries of the EU (i.e., the UK, Denmark, Germany, and France) who expressed a less favorable view toward European integration also exhibited more restrictionist attitudes toward immigration and immigrant rights. With the exception of Denmark, these countries not only constitute the dominant players of the European Union project, but they have substantial immigrant concentrations. On average, over a thirteen-year period, 90 percent of non-EU foreigners live in three of those countries, France, Germany, and Britain (Abadan-Unat 1992).

Some explanatory power can be derived from analysis of overt racism. The 1997 Eurobarometer survey allows us to measure resistance to migrants and minorities more directly among publics – by looking at xenophobic attitudes – than among elites, for whom researchers use policy dimensions as proxies.[27] While expressions of racism are not synonymous with anti-immigration sentiment, it may be one measure of intolerance and protectionism (see appendix B on comparing different measures of attitudes). Data analysis reveals striking similarities with national patterns of elite attitudes when we consider the relationship between the number of non-EU migrants residing in each country and levels of

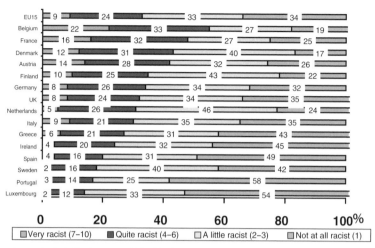

Source (n-size): *Eurobarometer* 47.1, 1997 (16,154).

Q: Some people feel they are not at all racist. Others feel they are very racist. Would you look at this card and give me the number that shows your own feelings about this? If you feel you are not at all racist, you give a score of 1. If you feel you are very racist, you give a score of 10. The scores between 1 and 10 allow you to say how close to either side you are.

Figure 5.2 Degree of expressed racism, by country

self-declared racism. Figure 5.2 shows that public opinion roughly mirrored country patterns found among the elite sample in table 5.1.

Country patterns revealed that Belgium, France, Austria, and Germany exceed the EU average (33 percent) in reporting that they were either "very racist" or "quite racist." Countries with the lowest number of declared "very racist" respondents included Spain, Ireland, Portugal, Luxembourg, and Sweden. These patterns reinforce the divide between countries where non-EU populations are greater than the EU average (over 2.03 percent) and those where non-EU populations are fewer (see appendix A for operationalization). Again, the Danish exception reemphasizes the point made in chapter 4 about not inferring too much from stark numbers, and placing more weight on the perception of political processes and other national concerns regarding these numbers.[28] The role of larger political processes and the reactions that they galvanize are important considerations, and may be drawn out by considering the link with attitudes toward European integration.

More importantly, these manifestations of discrimination divide countries where support for EU integration has been continuously higher from those whose public opinion has been less supportive of integration (see figure 5.3).

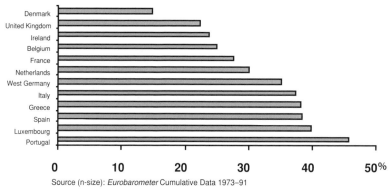

Source (n-size): *Eurobarometer* Cumulative Data 1973–91

Percentage responding completely for European unification to the question "In general, are you for or against further efforts being made to unify Western Europe?"

Figure 5.3 Public support for further European integration, by country

As figure 5.3 reveals, during the period 1973–91, the percentages of those reporting that they were "completely for European unification" were highest in Portugal, Luxembourg, Spain, and Greece. Taken together with the MEP findings, these patterns imply that xenophobia and protectionism come in many versions – including immigrant rejection and anti-European integration. As one British Conservative explained, the protectionist impulse is not limited to non-EU nationals alone:

If I took you to my own district constituency, . . . you hardly see a black person . . . [it is] a totally white agricultural area, and if I stood up and made a speech saying "really I think it is actually better for humanity if we all start mixing up and having our share in here," they would be very unhappy with me indeed. It's the fear of the unknown. It is not just black men they resent. If I actually stood up and said I think we ought to import half a million Frenchmen here, they would be equally angry. And Germans. We are British. We don't want the other people. It's the fear of the unknown, that they are slightly different to us. The French eat frog legs! (interview no. 123; London, April 24, 1992: 6–7)

This humorous account exposes an indiscriminate and sweeping sense of exclusion that marks sentiments both toward "Europe" and toward immigration.

Political preferences and positions on Europe clearly inform public opinion on outsiders. Figure 5.4 reveals that those who declared they had racist feelings presented some common characteristics, either ideologically or with regard to their position on the European Union. As figure 5.4 shows, those who declared themselves to be on the right of the political spectrum, as well as those who were opposed to their country's

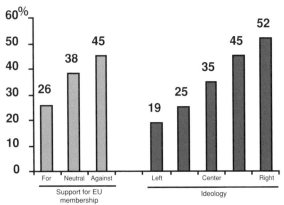

Source (n-size): *Eurobarometer* 47.1, 1997 (16,154).
Note: The data refer to those respondents who labeled themselves 4 to 10 on a
10-point racism scale, where 1 is "Not at all racist," 2–3 are "A little racist," 4–6
are "Quite racist," and 7–10 are "Very racist." Similarly, ideology was measured on
a 10-point scale and collapsed into five categories.

Figure 5.4 Self-declared racism, by support for EU membership and
ideology

membership of the European Union, were also more likely to express
racist feelings.

These trends substantiate more controversial assertions of party effects
on European integration. Hooghe, Marks, and Wilson's data bear signs of
a traditional/authoritarian/nationalist dimension of politics, which powerfully structures variations among party positions on European integration
(2002). Wessels's analysis of party support for European integration
suggests that supporters of nationalist parties in France, Germany,
Italy, and the Netherlands are less positive about integration than their
respective populations as a whole (1995a: 132). To the extent that
European integration limits or undermines national culture, community,
or sovereignty, political parties that defend these values are likely to be
strongly opposed. On the basis of party inferences, it is safe to conclude
that opposition to European integration appears to grow from the same
roots as disposition against immigration (Hooghe, Marks, and Wilson
2001: 23).

These findings resonate with my analysis of public opinion regarding
immigration in Europe, and they are consistent with studies of specific
subsets of the European publics. Analysis of European youth support
for European integration revealed that the position on immigration is
among the most robust indicators of EU support – stronger than those of
demographic, social capital, or other issue indices (see Nelsen and Guth
2001).[29] As expressions of xenophobic attitudes increase more generally,

Table 5.5 *Public opinion on immigration competence, by views on immigrant rights*

	Regulation authority			
	National governments	Governments after consultation	EU institutions	Total
Immigrant rights				
Should be improved	18%	32%	50%	100%
Should be maintained	28%	36%	36%	100%
Should be restricted	38%	30%	32%	100%
Total	27%	34%	39%	100%

N = 11,796; excludes "no reply."
Q: "Talking about these people living in (name of country) who are neither (nationality) nor citizens of the European Community, do you think we should extend their rights, restrict their rights or leave things as they are?"
Q: "Talking about these people living in (name of country), in which of these ways would you prefer to define their status: government of each member-state decide; government of member-state should consult each other before any action in order to legislate nationally in a similar fashion; the institutions of the European Community decide?"
Source: *Eurobarometer* 30, 1989.

popular support for European integration has been shown to decrease (see De Master and Le Roy 2000). These patterns are durable and generalizable, as they have been documented earlier in the construction of Europe, and across more diverse samples of the European population. The *Eurobarometer* 30 report on racism and xenophobia, for example, noted that opinion on the presence of immigrants in Europe is closely linked to opinion expressed with regard to the building of Europe and vice versa (Commission of the European Communities 1989). According to the report, the more one is inclined to have faith in the building of Europe to ensure the future, the more one tends to see immigrants as a potentially positive factor.[30] Public opinion also reveals that commitment to the European Union plays a major part in whom people would like to see in charge on immigration matters. The more one supports Europe, the more one tends to opt for Union competence in this regard (*Eurobarometer* 30, 1989: 86). Finally, opinion on where authority should lie also varies according to one's opinion regarding the status of immigrants, and whether one wishes to see a more or less favorable policy in their regard (see tables 5.5 and 5.6).

Half of those respondents who wanted to see immigrant rights improved were prepared to delegate immigration authority to EU institutions in some form. They were nearly three times more likely to do so than to maintain national authority (18 percent).

Table 5.6 *MEP attitudes on immigration competence, by views on immigrant rights*

	Regulation authority			
	National government	Governments after consultation	EU institutions[a]	Total
Immigrant rights				
Extend rights	3%	18%	79%	100%
Leave rights	13%	38%	49%	100%
Restrict rights	50%	50%	0%	100%
EP total	6%	22%	72%	100%

N = 167; includes those who said EU institutions with national governments having veto and EU institutions.

Q: "What should be done about the rights of immigrants . . . extend their rights, leave things as they are, or restrict their rights?"

[a]"EU institutions" refers to the combined percentage of respondents who preferred EU institutions, with national veto options, as well as EU institutions through majority vote.

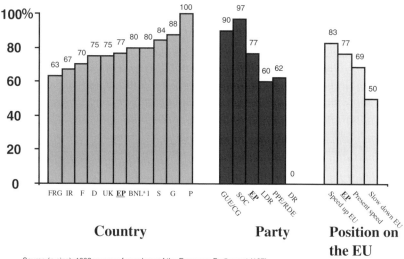

Source (n-size): 1992 survey of members of the European Parliament (167).
Note: Left to right: GUE/CG = Communists; SOC = Socialists; LDR = Liberal Democrats; PPE/RDE = Christian Democrats and Conservatives; DR = Radical Right (see table 4.4 for full acronyms and ideological self-placement).

[a]BNL is the average of Belgium, Netherlands, and Luxembourg; commonly referred to as Benelux.
Q: What should be done about the rights of immigrants?

Figure 5.5 MEP views on extending immigrant rights, by country, party group, and position on European integration

This tendency was not just replicated, but strikingly more pronounced, among the elite sample (table 5.6). Among the MEP sample, 79 percent of those who wished to extend immigrant rights favored EU institutions compared to 3 percent who preferred strict national control. Fifty percent who wanted to restrict immigrant rights preferred national control compared to none who accepted EU authority.[31]

Those who support immigrant rights are much more likely to support Europe and European institutions. There is substantial consensus among MEPs that immigrant rights should be extended, more than in the general population; support of this proposition is related to support for European institutions (see figure 5.5), as well as ideological and country affiliation.

The interrelationship between immigration attitudes and position on the European Union is unmistakable. Broadly speaking, it may also be argued that the more one supports Europe and European institutions, the more supportive one is of general immigrant rights.[32] Attitudes can be distinguished not only along the left–right continuum and by country identification, but also according to position on European unification. These findings are consonant with other evidence from public opinion (Gabel and Anderson 2002), MEP roll-call votes (Hix 2001b), and experts' evaluations of national political parties on a series of issues in the EU (see Ray 1999), including immigration and asylum (Hooghe, Marks, and Wilson 2002). Once European integration is disaggregated into its component policies, explicable patterns of support and opposition emerge, giving credence to "new politics" cleavages and the conventional left–right dimension. The main point is that several dimensions may be at work in categorizing political positions (i.e., national affiliations, EU position, ideological positions, new politics cleavage) and, as other scholars of the EU system have shown, these positions vary with the issue concerning the EU agenda (Hix 1999b: 158; Hix 2001a; Hix and Lord 1997: 25; Marks and Steenbergen 2002; Hooghe, Marks, and Wilson 2002).

My empirical findings reveal that those who support European integration are more likely to prefer a common immigration policy for the EU, and to accept immigration levels and immigrant rights, than those who oppose European integration. Pro-European attitudes, however, are not tantamount to pro-immigration. In fact, Gabel and Anderson's citizen models of EU political space indicate that, in certain policy areas, respondents who are pro-integration tend to be more pro-protection, suggesting that support for building a stronger supranational authority is also commensurate with a "fortress Europe" character (2002: 907). If one recalls that the European Coal and Steel Community and the customs union were early attempts to regulate areas of conflict between states, and to improve the effectiveness of governments in these sectors by coordinating policies, then the program for a common immigration policy engenders an image of controversial and restrictive character (see figure 5.1).

Moreover, pan-Europeanism and nationalism may resemble each other as they promote a spirit of collectivity with common goals, and harbor similar images in their search for defining common symbols. There is ample evidence, stemming from Hoffmann's early insight, that there is a fine line between the legitimacy of the nation-state and that of a supranational entity (1966; Sinnott 1995; Martinotti and Stefanizzi 1995).[33]

Eurocentrists and nationalists alike grapple with similar questions: "Who am I?," "Who am I not?" Like all questions of identity, they are a prelude to differentiation which, in turn, entails the drawing of some kind of line between things like and things unlike. Nonetheless, the point of departure for each group is the level of cultural homogeneity that is envisaged for community- or nation-building. In the answers to these questions is where the fundamental differences between the extreme right and other parties lie on European integration and immigration. The leader of the French Front national captured these concepts best when he proclaimed that "we have a preferential philosophy . . . [of] concentric circles: the family, the city, the profession . . . a hierarchy of affinity and tolerance . . . [and] when vital interests are contradictory, it is the national interests which have the edge over all the others" (interview no. 289; Strasbourg, June 10, 1992). Those on the extreme right and nationalists in general are protectionist with regard both to the nation-state and to immigration; they seek cultural homogeneity, which is threatened by the construction of Europe. They differ from their pan-Europeanist counterparts whose criteria for exclusion are less narrow, but nevertheless restrictive.[34]

An analogous version of a pan-Europeanist preference order of immigrants groups may typically sound like this:

For Europeans, absolutely no limitation – that is their right. But for the others, we are simply not an area of immigration. I would make a difference, yes, for all those who belong to Europe, all the Europeans. Yes, they should have the right to vote, and not for the non-Europeans. (interview no. 63; Strasbourg, May 11, 1992: 4)

As suggested above, the majority of MEPs are pro-Europe, and in favor of *qualified* immigration (they are not necessarily *pro-immigration*), meaning they prefer qualified immigrant rights, and specific types of immigrants – European. In this sense, levels of affinities described by the extreme rightist Le Pen may be more commonplace and relevant than many Europeans care to believe. They can be expected to become more pronounced as the construction of Europe continues to develop. The general point is that European integration is a good indicator of receptivity to foreigners – and vice versa. For this reason, it is fruitful to examine the role of the "European factor" in political cleavages and how it creates an EU political space.

Religion, the European factor, and immigration attitudes: more empirical findings

The empirical relationship between immigration sentiment and attitudes toward the EU point to an interesting discrepancy remaining in Europe that derives from religious traditions. Although there is a paucity of systematic data on the role of religion in European politics today, its impact on political behavior is demonstrably not negligible (Nelsen, Guth, and Fraser 2001; Broughton and Donovan 1999; Lijphart 1979; Lipset and Rokkan 1967).

Several aspects of the religious variable, ranging from intensity or devotion to denomination (see Wessels 1995a: 116), have been analyzed to shed light on attitudinal differences and their implications for the EU and immigration politics. Thus, in the first case, the more religiously devout – regardless of denomination – are expected to be more traditional and more resistant to change, exemplified by both immigration and the EU (Rogers and Shoemaker 1971: 31–32).[35] An alternative hypothesis is that the vitality of economic and social conditions that have separated Protestant and Catholic traditions continue to divide European publics into one camp of universalist Catholics and a group of more nationalist Protestants.[36] In terms of EU history, it is worth recalling that the European project was led by Christian Democratic leaders of the postwar period, backed by the Vatican and national Catholic hierarchies all tied to a supranational vision of Europe.

My effort to unpack the "European factor" for the purposes of determining its effect on immigration attitudes puts the spotlight on patterns derived from religious differences between Catholics and Protestants. It is noteworthy that MEPs from the more predominantly Protestant countries of the United Kingdom, Denmark, and Germany are less enthusiastic about a Europe that is often tied to a concept of "Christendom." One Danish MEP succinctly emphasized:

It's a very big problem with culture. You have a Catholic system in the South and you have a Protestant system here. We have such different cultures, so you cannot make a rule and say, "From this day, we are in Europe." Because a thousand years ago, they started with a culture, and you cannot change it with a paper. (interview no. 15; Brussels, May 6, 1992)

Religious and other cultural differences, such as those derived from the North–South or Catholic–Protestant divide *within* Europe, may reinforce protectionism from outside influence and a reluctance to support European integration. Interestingly, although all parties in the EP incorporate religious symbolism (e.g., the PPE the European People's Party, or Christian Democrats), no party group has been able to find a European symbol such as the DR (the far right) managed to deftly introduce with a Celtic cross.[37] The United Kingdom, Denmark, and Germany fall substantially below the EP average in pursuit of an accelerated EU (see table 5.1). So too does the extreme-right DR group. These countries and this party group are also least likely to defer immigration regulation to EU institutions.

Although the functions of religion have diminished since Max Weber wrote his seminal treatise on the emergence of Calvinist Protestantism and the rise of capitalism (1958), its role in advanced EU countries should not be underestimated. As one Scottish MEP proclaimed: "The role of the Church is terribly important – I mean even to non-believers like me!" (interview no. 32; Brussels, May 5, 1992: 2). The findings in this study concur with Inglehart's empirical conclusions that, while religious differences between Catholics and Protestants have become smaller, aggregate results from longitudinal surveys reflect cultural patterns that originally arose around the religious factor (1990a: 61; Inglehart and Baker 2000). They also concur with other characterizations of religious traditions as faltering between internationalist and pro-EU visions and more nationalist and Euroskeptical positions (Nelsen, Guth, and Fraser 2001; Nelsen and Guth 2001).

Public opinion data confirm the surprising durability of religion as a determining factor. Figure 5.6 illustrates that Protestants (73 percent) and other religions (75 percent) are least likely to say they are for European unification. Catholics (89 percent) and Orthodox (92 percent) are the most likely to say they are for unification, with secular respondents in the middle (80 percent).

While all groups support European integration, Protestants from Northern and Central Europe may be slightly more resistant to unification than other groups not only because of historical images of Christendom, an exclusive type of Europe, but because of perceived threats of an EU that includes traditional emigration nations with weaker economies.[38] Catholics and Orthodox (often from these emigration nations) are somewhat more enthusiastic about the prospect of European integration, which could produce stronger economic powers and social standardization. Religious out-groups or "others" may be as resistant to unification as Protestants because they have minority status. In fact, a

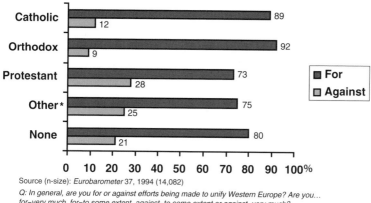

Source (n-size): *Eurobarometer* 37, 1994 (14,082)

*Q: In general, are you for or against efforts being made to unify Western Europe? Are you...
for–very much, for–to some extent, against–to some extent or against–very much?*

* Other includes primarily Jewish, Buddhist, Muslim, and Hindu.

Figure 5.6 Public opinion on European unification, by religion

supranational European entity may seem overbearing and more antagonistic to Jewish, Buddhist, Muslim, and Hindu populations. This may help to explain the variation of attitudes in support for unification, which is – on the whole – enormously strong, considering that over 70 percent of respondents are in agreement about European integration.

These trends are also suggestive of the confluence between attitudes toward immigration and European integration that has been discovered by students of religion and politics (Nelsen and Guth 2001). With the exception of religious minority groups, the tendency to endorse Europe parallels support for immigrants. A view of public opinion on immigrant rights, broken down by religion, is very telling. Of the five religious categories illustrated in figure 5.7, Protestants were the most likely to want to restrict the rights of non-EU immigrants, with nearly one-third (32 percent) expressing this preference. Approximately one-fifth of Catholics, Orthodox, or those with no religious affiliation preferred the restriction of rights for non-EU nationals (17 percent, 20 percent, and 19 percent respectively). The groups that were least likely to wish for such restrictions fell into the "other" category (primarily Jewish, Buddhist, Muslim, and Hindu).

Protestants appear to be threatened by the prospect of increasing current non-EU nationals. Therefore, they are looking to limit the rights of this group. Contrary to theories of marginality, which postulate that the experience of being marginalized breeds sympathy with such groups (see Fetzer 2000: 5–12), it is also true that out-groups may be averse to granting new rights or promoting further immigration because of

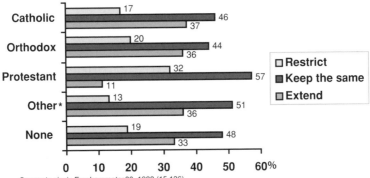

Source (n-size): *Eurobarometer* 30, 1988 (15,136).
Q: *Talking about these people living in (name of country) who are neither (nationality) nor citizens of the European Community, do you think we should extend their rights, restrict their rights or leave things as they are?*

* Other includes primarily Jewish, Buddhist, Muslim, and Hindu.

Figure 5.7 Public opinion on the rights of non-EU immigrants, by religion

fear of competition from the newcomers. According to Allport, victims of discrimination can develop greater hostility toward other out-groups (1979: 153–161). Clearly, these theoretical disputes remain empirically unresolved. Muslims, Jews, Hindus, and Buddhists are the least likely to want to curb the rights of non-EU immigrants, possibly because many of them were at one time or another non-EU migrants coming to EU nations – a case in which Fetzer's "marginality hypothesis" may hold true (2000).[39] These findings are also reinforced by those illustrated in figure 5.5. While caution must be used in attributing to religion what are national characteristics,[40] countries with predominantly Protestant populations are less likely to support the extension of immigrant rights. They are also slightly less favorable toward European integration.

New fault lines? 'New politics'?

Whereas immigration issues have eluded conventional tools of political analysis, it seems that there is far greater polarization on immigration, generated by the "European factor." Students of European integration have recently embraced this variable in their research agendas (Hooghe, Marks, and Wilson 2002; Marks and Steenbergen 2002; Hix and Lord 1997; Hix 1999b; Nelson and Guth 2001), though a lot more systematic work on policy implications is still wanting. As we saw in chapter 3 (figure 3.26), immigration and political asylum are among the six issues on which the public is most evenly split with regard to EU versus national authority preferences. All six issue areas – immigration, political asylum,

VAT/tax, unemployment, agriculture/fishing, and defense – are also the most contentious issues in Europe today. This is reflected by their prominence on political agendas.

Table 5.7 reinforces the findings in chapter 3 regarding the multiple concerns that influence these types of attitudinal patterns. Again, though several factors determine attitudes toward immigration (e.g., integration, income, religion), we may get better purchase on the nature of political competition by cross-sectional analysis. In contrast to more instrumental or utilitarian-driven evaluations, when it comes to issues like immigration, which touch the core of identity, cultural proxies of affective considerations, such as religiosity and European integration, are more robust indicators of attitudes toward immigrants for the majority of the population than are more utilitarian considerations, such as family income.

Table 5.7 provides a breakdown of immigration attitudes according to cognitive mobilization, and relates them to concerns about European integration, family income, and religion, and demographic/ideological control variables. The cognitive mobilization index is constructed from responses to questions about education levels and reporting of tendencies to discuss political matters in one's daily life.[41] Each column represents a regression equation, according to cognitive mobilization groupings, from least (1) to most (5) cognitively mobilized.

The table reveals that, across the majority of information groups, respondents are not motivated by family income, but rather by affective attitudes toward European integration, religion, or other cultural values. Among the 6 percent of the most cognitively mobilized Europeans, attitudes toward immigration are significantly related to income but not to other factors. With the exception of the second least cognitively mobilized (regression 2), all the others were influenced by one or the other affective measures. The most cognitively mobilized may be said to behave as rational self-interested or utilitarian thinkers in the sense that, as their income increases, they become more favorable toward immigration. Assuming that high levels of education are correlated with high cognitive mobilization and high income levels, it can be argued that the most cognitively mobilized are most enlightened with regard to immigration, and least likely to bear the direct costs of immigration. There are of course certain anomalies that still need to be explained (i.e., the convergence of the most informed and least informed with regard to religion). More broadly, however, this table gives credence to the ability of European integration or religion to distinguish patterns of opposition on questions of immigration over traditional socioeconomic factors.

These patterns are noteworthy as they not only elucidate the limitations of traditional cleavages in discriminating attitudinal alliances, but

Table 5.7 *Affective vs. utilitarian motivations for attitudes toward immigration, by cognitive mobilization*

	Relationship with attitudes toward immigration by cognitive mobilization[a]					
Regression of cognitive mobilization and immigration attitudes	(1) Low	(2) Medium-low	(3) Medium	(4) Medium-high	(5) High	Total
% of cognitive mobilization	19%	28%	29%	19%	6%	100%
Integration attitude[b]	*	*	*	*	NS	*
Family income	NS	*	NS	NS	*	*
Religiosity[c]	NS	*	*	*	NS	*

* Statistically significant below the .05 level. NS: Not significant.

[a] Ordered probit regression includes the following control variables: nation-specific dummies, materialism, sex, age, ideology, and ideological intensity. The question on immigration (Q. 169) is derived from *Eurobarometer* 30, "Generally speaking how do you feel about the number of people of another nationality living in our country: too many, a lot but not too many, or not many?"

[b] Factor score for integration attitudes is derived from principal components analysis of three affective variables (v520, v523, v524) in *Eurobarometer* 30 (1988), n = 11,791. See appendix A for question wording.

[c] Religiosity variable refers to *Eurobarometer* 30 Q. 561, "Whether or not you follow religious practices, would you say that you are religious, not religious, or an atheist?"

also resonate with other evidence of "new politics" as a source for structuring political controversy (Inglehart 1990a; Dalton 2002 [1988]; Kitschelt 1989; Franklin 1992; Müller-Rommel 1989; Rohrschneider 1990, 1993; Hooghe, Marks, and Wilson 2002). Since the 1980s, a variety of labels has been employed to describe the weakening of established societal cleavages and the emergence of new ones that have been associated with "new politics." These dimensions include postmaterialism/materialism (Inglehart 1990a, 1990b), new politics/old politics (Franklin 1992; Müller-Rommel 1989; Dalton 2002 [1988]), and left-libertarian/authoritarian (Kitschelt 1994, 1995; Flanagan and Lee 2003; see also Hooghe, Marks, and Wilson's [2002] GAL/TAN version), and may be fruitfully applied to immigration policy in the EU. Scholars of the extreme right have aptly incorporated a "new politics" dimension into their understanding of the "new right" – understood as a reaction against the emergence of postmaterialist values (Minkenberg 1992, 1994; Ignazi 1992; Veugelers 2000; Betz 1990, 1993, 1994; Betz and Immerfall 1998). To elucidate the extreme-right phenomenon further, Taggart developed the concept of post-materialism by distinguishing between the "new politics" of the left (e.g., the Greens) and the "new populism" of the radical right (1995). In all of these assessments, the "new right" or "new populist" movements represent a backlash against a fundamental change in culture and values that does not get captured by old cleavages of class and partisan lines. European integration itself provides peripheral parties with a "touchstone of domestic dissent" against alienation from the establishment or the system (Taggart 1998: 384).

Inglehart's postmodernization theory (1977, 1990a, 1997) posits that a new dimension of political conflict has become increasingly salient, as a shift in values has occurred from traditional economic or ideological issues to cultural and quality-of-life concerns; this is also referred to as a shift from "material" to "postmaterial" values (see appendix A for methodological critique).[42] This new dimension is considered distinct from the classical left–right cleavage, as political conflict is no longer dominated by socioeconomic issues alone. It is schematic of a political axis that pits postmaterialists – who are forward-looking in their worldview, change-oriented, favorable to the rights of all types of minorities and alternative causes – on one side against materialists – who are culturally conservative, protectionist, security-conscious, and anti-change – on the other. These divisions often coincide with age and education, as younger and more educated groups are expected to be far more permissive and tolerant than older and less educated cohorts (Espenshade and Calhoun 1993: 208; Citrin, Reingold, and Green 1990: 1134; Sullivan, Piereson, and Marcus 1982). This synopsis offers few

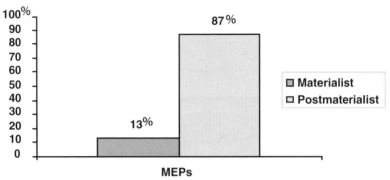

Source (n-size): 1992 survey of members of the European Parliament (45).

Note: Based on the cross-tabulation of two questions: one asking MEPs whether they "think that the movement towards European unification should be speeded up, slowed down, or continue at present speed" and the other asking MEPs to indicate their priorities which reflect "materialist/postmaterialist" values (based on Inglehart's materialism/postmaterialism index; see Inglehart 1990c). Those who only mentioned one of materialist or postmaterialist themes are not included in the figure.

Figure 5.8 MEP position on acceleration of European unification, by materialist index

surprises to immigration researchers, since several previous studies have demonstrated that increased education powerfully decreases reported opposition to foreigners (Hoskin 1991: 147; Hernes and Knudsen 1992; Fetzer 2000: 148–149; Espenshade and Calhoun 1993; Citrin, Reingold, and Green 1990). According to Inglehart, postwar generations tend to seek more "postmaterialist" or qualitative values over the more materialist ones (1977). Such values also coincide with an emphasis on internationalism and European integration, and are manifested by a shift from national to European loyalties.[43]

Longitudinal public opinion data indeed support this "postmaterialist" or "postmodern" versus materialist/fundamentalist cleavage dimension posed by several students of Europe (see Knutsen 1989a, 1989b, 1995a, 1995b; Kitschelt 1994, 1995; Inglehart 1990a, 1990b, 1997). My elite data also support this pattern (figure 5.8). Although the MEP sample is somewhat biased because elites in general tend to be more educated (96 percent of this study's elites went beyond high school or vocational education), their attitudes on European integration were somewhat distinguishable by the materialist/postmaterialist index.[44]

MEP attitudes toward Europe are clearly informed by their value orientations. The more materialist-oriented one is, the less likely it is that one will be favorable to European integration and to attitudes that are associated with Europeanism. Given that attitudes toward the European

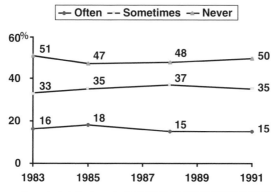

Source (n-size): *Eurobarometer* 19 (9,305); 24 (11,329); 30 (11,354); 36 (13,550).

Q: Do you ever think of yourself not only as (nationality) citizen but also as a citizen of Europe?

Figure 5.9 Self-identification as European citizen, 1983–1991

Union and immigration are based on the same impulse, we may consider attitudes toward community as a proxy for immigration sentiment.

According to postmodernization theses, intergenerational shifts or "culture shift" (Inglehart 1990a) spur support for European integration. Diffusion theory gives some credence to this process, as it suggests that institutions articulate shared norms, and thereby mediate between international structures and domestic change (Checkel 1999; see also Kurzer 2001: 13–17 for a helpful review of the adaptation to European standards through the diffusion of norms). Diffusion arguments differ from Inglehart's postmodernization claims in that they assume that processes of intrasocietal diffusion, not cohort replacement, are responsible for developing awareness of, and support for, the EU. Consequently, diffusion processes can go either way. As Wessels, shows they may be more favorable or less favorable to the EU (see Wessels 1995a: 106).

While it is true that intergenerational shifts or diffusion processes that are expected to occur make it possible that more people will relate to a European identity as European integration proceeds, it is equally likely that resistance to Europe could prevail, and that national protectionism may inform immigration policy. Consider the affective dimension of European support, measured by the evolution of self-identity and citizenship.[45]

As figure 5.9 reveals, public conceptions of European identity are evenly split between national and European affinities in the pre-Maastricht period, when few cooperative initiatives on immigration and

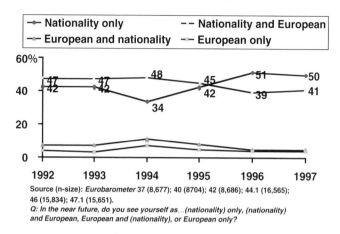

Source (n-size): *Eurobarometer* 37 (8,677); 40 (8704); 42 (8,686); 44.1 (16,565); 46 (15,834); 47.1 (15,651).
Q: In the near future, do you see yourself as…(nationality) only, (nationality) and European, European and (nationality), or European only?

Figure 5.10 Europeans' self-conception of citizenship, 1992–1997

citizenship took place. From 1983 to 1991, about half of Europeans said they never regarded themselves as citizens of Europe; half sometimes or often identified themselves as both nationals of their countries and Europeans. Whereas this time period is marked by consistency, the interval between 1992 and 1997 is witness to shifts in public opinion (see figure 5.10).

After 1995, a period marked by growing cooperative initiatives and even support for them (see chapters 2 and 3), the European public begins to emphasize a "nationality only" self-conception at the expense of "nationality and European." This move toward national affinity may be a response to an increasingly prevalent EU. As it takes shape from the theoretical to the practical, Europeans may be more likely to feel that their national identity and culture are being threatened.

While figure 5.10 reveals a persistent polarization of identification with Europe, figure 5.11 shows public shifts toward national identity. Since these trends coincide with the aftermath of Maastricht, they may be interpreted as a backlash against the construction of Europe – though there are some contentions that this may have been presaged on the eve of the treaty signing (see Niedermayer 1995a; Everts and Sinnott 1995: 435). Similar conclusions are supported by diffusion theorists, who claim that, when structural factors become less important to the formation of attitudes toward the EU, political factors become more persistent and divisive. In this line of thinking, the decline in support for the EU since 1991 is a product of diffusion processes – a combination of increased "Communitarian" competence and penetration, and

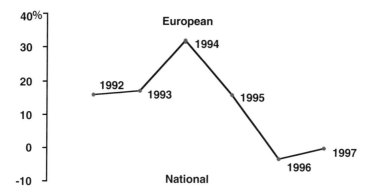

The above values were calculated using public opinion response categories according to specifications in the *Eurobarometer* 50 report as follows: (European only + European and nationality + nationality and European) – Nationality only = European identity.

Figure 5.11 European vs. national identity (net difference)

growing politicization of support for the European Union (Wessels 1995a: 135–136).[46]

On the whole, identity with Europe seems to peak immediately after EU initiatives, and falter toward national protectionism following cooperation. These alternating cycles of "Europeanization" and "nationalization" of public opinion, as Niedermayer (1995a: 57–65) calls them, resonate with general observations of other researchers (Everts and Sinnott 1995). This does not contradict the fact that, as documented in chapters 2 and 3, cooperation prompts more positive views of integration. It merely reflects the dynamic momentum of community-building and reaction to European integration. Figure 5.11 is suggestive of the fluctuations in national/European identification over time. Showing in graphic form the distribution of respondents identifying with Europe or nation, its purpose is strictly illustrative.

Taking into account the coding method (used in the *Eurobarometer* 50 report), the percentage of those feeling European takes a dramatic upturn in 1994. However, it decreases back to pre-1994 levels in 1995. Feeling European then declines to its lowest point in 1996. After Amsterdam in 1997, it begins to make a directional move back toward a sense of Europeanism. These trends need to be further studied with regard to generational and policy shifts over time.

Although Inglehart's postmodernization schema is generally helpful in understanding thinking on conflicts such as immigration and European

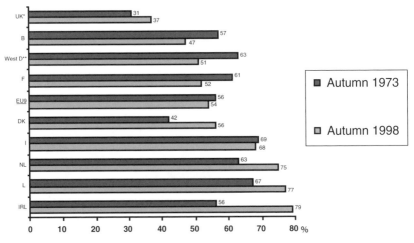

Q. *Generally speaking, do you think membership in the common market/European Union is a good thing, a bad thing or neither good nor bad?*

Figure 5.12 Percentage saying EU membership is "a good thing," 1973 and 1998

integration (where we often find "strange bedfellows"), it is important to underscore his own precautions. That is, the direction of these trends largely depends on who the winners and losers are over time. Time-series analysis shows that the winners and losers may change – at least by people's own perceptions.

Figure 5.12 reveals that support for EU membership has dwindled among the longest-standing members and largest countries over time. This is somewhat surprising, given our prior understanding of differences between large and small countries, and between old and new members. As previous studies have shown, new entrants tend to lag behind in terms of their support for institutional integration (Feld and Wildgen 1976: 49; Holland 1994: 150; Hewstone 1986: 25–29; Deheneffe 1986: 28–33; Eichenberg and Dalton 1993: 517–520; Hix 1999b: 141).[47] However, the distribution of national attitudes over time may confirm Feld and Wildgen's prediction that the dichotomy between new members and older ones will be less important than the dichotomy between *les grandes* and *les petites* (1976). According to their early findings, larger countries are expected to show much less stability in opinion given changing levels of Community performance.[48] Utilitarian measures of support for Europe over time give some credence to these predictions.

As figure 5.12 illustrates, France, Germany, and Belgium (all founding signatories of the Treaty of Rome) have decreased their support for membership between 1973 and 1998. In those twenty-five years, the idea that membership is "a good thing" has become less obvious to the people of these prominent EU members.

In gauging attitudinal change and the implications for the future of European immigration policy-making, we must consider how conditions of uncertainty factor into the "new politics" postmodernization equation. As noted in chapter 3, much of the optimism or pessimism toward immigration resolution in Europe is derived from a general sense of trust and security.[49] According to Inglehart's (1977) extrapolation of social psychology (i.e., Maslow's [1954] hierarchy of human needs), stable and secure postwar generations are free to seek more "postmaterialist" or qualitative values (e.g., identity issues, community-building) over more materialist ones.[50] Under conditions of uncertainty – in which Europeans find themselves at the start of the twenty-first century – the impulse to be open or protectionist is dependent on a sense of well-being and security. In this respect, the data still reveal important national differences.

According to Eurobarometer trends, subjective well-being and trust on a national level (as distinct from individual level) give rise to cross-cultural variation, on which a wide range of orientations are structured (Inglehart 1997: 86). This is particularly relevant to immigration issues in the EU. Societies marked by high levels of life satisfaction (which are also considered high on postmaterial indices, in Inglehart's terms, as they have a .68 correlation) tend to be markedly more tolerant than are those characterized by low levels of satisfaction or materialist values. Inglehart's findings reveal that these factors are closely related to the extent that publics "reject out-groups" – saying that they would not like to have foreigners as neighbors (significant at the .001 level). Societies with relatively high levels of subjective well-being rank relatively low on intolerance of outgroups (ibid.: 89). Security is conducive to tolerance. Conversely, insecurity promotes xenophobia. According to Inglehart,

The narrower one's survival is, the more likely one is to fear that strangers are threatening. This is especially true if the strangers speak a foreign language or hold different values and therefore seem incomprehensible and unpredictable. (ibid. 89–90)

This thesis is supported by the data presented below, as well as by studies on threat.

The literature on threat has exposed an explicit link between different aspects of threat and xenophobia, derived from psychological foundations. It has found that threat increases ethnocentrism, in-group

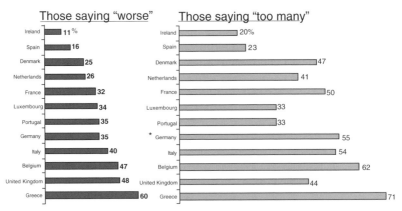

Figure 5.13 Attitudes toward foreigners and national employment
expectations

solidarity, and xenophobia (Levine and Campbell 1972; Seago 1947;
Huddy 2001; Tajfel and Turner 1979; Brown 1995). Threat promotes
intolerance and a willingness to forego basic civil liberties (Feldman 1988;
Marcus *et al*. 1995; Feldman and Stenner 1997; Gibson 1995), and leads
to closed-mindedness (Rokeach 1960). Heightened risk appraisal and
insecurity lead to increased vilification, support for policies that restrict
the rights of out-groups, and increasing willingness to compromise civil
liberties, personal freedoms, and democratic values in general (Huddy
et al. 2003 forthcoming; Davis and Silver forthcoming; Gibson 1996;
Sniderman *et al*. 1996). The research sheds some light on subjective and
objective conditions of threat as they affect attitudinal dynamics,[51] and
thus gives more weight to the distinctions elicited by different attitudinal motivations discussed in chapter 3 – the sociotropic, self-interest,
and symbolic models. Whether perceived or real, threats to the economy,
physical safety, culture, status, and way of life have triggered varied attitudinal reactions and behaviors. These conclusions provided by political
psychologists and students of political behavior offer some evidence of
the varying effects of threat on attitudes that is helpful in thinking about
immigration (see Lahav 2002 for an overview).[52]

The data analysis presented in figure 5.13 on employment insecurities supports these theses. They replicate the findings of researchers
in the US case, mainly that those who have more pessimistic assessments
of the current and future state of the economy are less receptive to

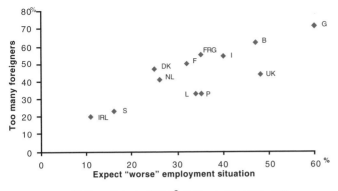

OLS coefficient: .918, r² : 65%, significance: .001

Note: Those saying "too many" foreigners in East and West Germany were averaged and regressed against respondents saying "worse" employment situation from united Germany.

Figure 5.14 Scatterplot of attitudes toward foreigners and national employment expectations

immigration than those who are more optimistic (Espenshade and Hempstead 1996).[53] Generally, as people in EU countries grow increasingly pessimistic about their nation's future employment prospects, they also become more likely to believe there are too many foreigners residing among them.

Regression analysis confirms the existence of a relationship between these variables. The scatterplot in figure 5.14 helps to illuminate the links between measures of national economic insecurity and immigrant rejection. As expectations for a worsened employment situation increase by 1 percent, respondents are nearly 1 percent more likely to believe that there are too many foreigners in their nation. This is statistically significant at the .001 level. Two-thirds of the variability in those responding that there are too many foreigners is accounted for by the underlying insecurities (measured here by future employment expectations).[54]

However, the 1997 Eurobarometer finding that there was no significant correlation between *being* unemployed and degree of racist or xenophobic feelings expressed is worthy of mention (47.1, Spring 1997). In fact, while nearly one-third of respondents had themselves been unemployed at one stage during the last five years, the report found that nearly half of those interviewed worked in a company that had been affected by unemployment at some stage during that period. A regression of the unemployment rate across those saying "too many" non-EU nationals (by country) yields a statistically insignificant result (.84). Predicting attitudes toward minorities more generally was also not statistically significant (.58).[55]

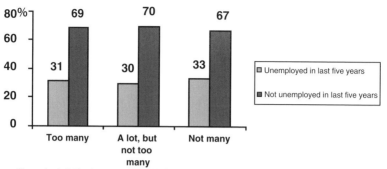

Source (n-size): *Eurobarometer* 47.1, 1997 (16,154).
Q: *Again, speaking generally about people from minority groups in terms of race, religion and culture, do you think there are not many, a lot but not too many or too many?*
Q: *If you think back over the last five years, could you please tell me for each of these situations whether it applies to you, or not? During the last five years I have been unemployed once or more.*

Figure 5.15 Personal unemployment and attitudes toward minorities

These regressions, together with figure 5.15, suggest that knowing the unemployment status of respondents does not yield any information about his/her predisposition toward immigrants. The fear of losing one's job in a declining national labor market (as appraised on societal conditions) appears to be a much more important factor than unemployment itself. This is not surprising, given what we know about the Weimar German experience and the failure of the SPD to win the support of the middle classes against the NSDAP's genocidal undertaking.[56] That is, support for Hitler and the Nazi Party's platform came not from the disenfranchised poor who had lost their jobs, but from the frightened lower middle classes and petite bourgeoisie who were observing the collapse of capitalism above (see Allen 1984: 41–51; Gibson 2002: 69).

As noted in previous chapters, people's assessments of immigration are tied to economic insecurity.[57] Figures 5.13–5.15 combined replicate what was found in other areas of immigration attitudes. Attitudes toward immigration may be based more on national (sociotropic) conditions than on personal threats. The findings are consonant with the argument that immigrant fears may be driven by symbolic or sociotropic motivations – their abstract concerns about general conditions. They also concur with the trends noted in the American case, that personal economic circumstances figure less prominently in public opposition to immigration than do beliefs about the national economy (Citrin *et al.* 1997) or other considerations of group or collective threat (Quillian 1995). A sizeable immigrant population or a large out-group is perceived to be a threat to the group advantages of dominant in-groups when the economic situation of the host country is precarious (Blalock 1967; Bobo 1983; Money 1999; Quillian 1995), but these dynamics may work less through realistic conflict over resources than through psychological states that produce animosity toward out-groups (Oliver and Mendelberg 2000: 587). There is a cultural or "identity-based" component to perceptions of threat that fuels hostility to immigration (Gibson 2002; McLaren 2002).

Although economic threat has demonstratively evoked different attitudinal responses than have cultural or physical threats (Feldman and Stenner 1997; Gibson 2002), the multiple dimensions of threat are inextricably linked. There are other measures of well-being and insecurity that affect attitudes toward immigrants and minorities. Expressions of well-being may also be measured by feelings of life satisfaction, trust, and attitudes toward democratic functioning.[58] These are linked not only to each other (e.g., unemployment, economic performance), but also to attitudes toward immigrants. For example, there is some relationship between national gross domestic product (GDP) and feelings that there were "too many" non-EU immigrants (p = .07, r^2 = .28 percent). The independent variables analyzed here (trust in the EU and satisfaction with democracy in the EU) prove to be multicollinear. Therefore, they can be thought of as measuring the same underlying attitude. Each shows a strong relationship with those saying too many non-EU immigrants (OLS coefficient = .96, p = .006, r^2 = .55 for satisfaction; OLS coefficient = .84, p = .024, r^2 = .41 for trust; see *Eurobarometer* 48, October–November 1997).

Although according to the 1997 Eurobarometer findings, 82 percent of interviewees agreed that democracy was the best political system, wide national variations emerged as to how satisfied they were with the functioning of their country's institutions and political establishment. Nearly half of those who declared themselves as quite or very racist were dissatisfied with the political working of their country. Dissatisfaction with the authorities needs to be seen in conjunction with unemployment, insecurity, corruption, and racism. Since these variations are distinguished by national or cultural distinctions, they support the findings regarding the relevance of these factors in shaping attitudes, discussed in the previous chapter.

The confluence of changes posed by immigration and European integration means that uncertainty will prevail, and that these types of cultural differences on trust and security may remain particularly relevant. Furthermore, the insecurities brought about by both immigration and European integration are linked to solutions they promote. As one Italian MEP summarizes:

All people are afraid of the future and, when they are afraid, they want to close themselves. If you are afraid, you close yourself. If you are not afraid, you are open. (interview no. 351; Strasbourg, May 15, 1992: 3)

Attitudes toward immigration underscore the inevitable conflict between changes aggravated by the EU and those prompted by what one MEP calls "the fear of the other, the different, the unknown" (interview no. 329; Strasbourg, May 13, 1992: 5).[59]

Reaction to postmodern politics has always existed, but the findings here deviate from postmodernization conclusions regarding its strength and viability to eclipse mainstream trends or traditional fault lines. Thus, while there is some evidence to support the claim that "new right" groups reinforce the postmodern politics cleavage, pitting postmaterialists against materialists, we need to remain more tentative about the conclusion that "they do not represent the wave of the future" (Inglehart 1997: 251). Whether postmaterialists will prevail remains questionable, in light of continued rapid transition, spurred by both cultural changes of immigration and European integration, as well as by new renditions of physical insecurity that come in the aftershock of September 11. By Inglehart's own admission, "the rise of a sense of security among mass publics . . . can be undermined by economic decline or rapid change" (ibid.: 246).

The question remains how much traditional parties, such as the left or right, can appeal either to the economically and psychologically marginal segments or to those promoting more individualist and secularist interests. Although it is true that parties tied to the classic programs have been faring poorly in Western countries, the findings in this study reveal that they are far from obsolete. On the contrary, they remain quite durable and adaptable to new issues.

Conclusions

Institutional and psychological processes in an evolving Europe have generated some attitudinal consensus and norms, questioning the role of traditional competing alliances. Transnational interests tend to confound traditional partisan/ideological and national alliances. Nonetheless, the evidence in this chapter suggests that these phenomena are not mutually exclusive. The data reveal that the European factor reinforces and reinvents traditional polarizations, as it offers a new framework for the immigration debate and alliance formations. The evolution of the European Union (even if the supranational vision prevails) does not preclude the possibility of a consolidation of ideological and national convictions to order policy thinking. In fact, the findings underscore the subtle influence of these interests. The particular positions of extreme-right parties should not underplay the importance of the ideological continuum that we find with respect to immigration thinking. The persistent politicization of the immigration issue on the EU platform – as reinforced by public and elite attitudes – is symptomatic of the vitality of ideological and national sources in shaping the immigration debate.

At the same time, it is important to underscore the significance of the EU system as it channels traditional affinities. There can be no doubt that the European factor – the institutional and psychological adjustments associated with European integration – recasts traditional interests. Despite the evidence revealed in chapter 4 that national and ideological constraints to European integration are well embedded in migration thinking, there is abundant evidence supporting the emergence of a supranational tendency. This coalescence lends some optimism to a collective immigration policy over the coming years. European integration has altered traditional thinking about territory and identity, making it easier to construct common immigration and asylum policies.

Early neofunctionalist scholars like Ernst Haas projected that, as beliefs and aspirations of groups undergo change due to the necessity of working in a transnational institutional framework, values and doctrine can be expected to merge, uniting groups across former frontiers. Haas even suggested that these are likely to produce, in effect, an advent of a "new nationalism" (Haas 1958: 14). The impetus toward a common Europe and its countervailing movements, such as nationalism or intergovernmentalism, ironically all tread similar ground, which may explain why the dominant attitude toward immigration may be restrictionist and protectionist, wherever immigration and asylum policies ultimately land on the continuum. The degree of attitudinal convergence toward restrictive immigration gives some credence to forecasts that the capacity to live with diversity is the compelling question of the twenty-first century.[60] One might argue that Huntington's projection that the "clash of civilizations" will be more fundamental than differences among political ideologies evokes a repugnant justification for repressing immigrant minorities. Indeed, these arguments are a bit of a stretch given the objectivity of European attitudes unveiled in chapter 3, but the emphasis on cultural factors and their effects on public attitudes toward immigration cannot be discounted (Putnam 1993; Huntington 1996, 2000; Zolberg 1981; Zolberg and Long 1999; McLaren 2002; Espenshade and Calhoun 1993).[61] In view of the evidence presented in this chapter, we may be somewhat cautious of how European integration affects traditional alliances, and what the construction of Europe means for immigrants.

Contemplating "ways to reduce nativism," Joel Fetzer suggests that as the sense of being French or German or Spanish gives way to the feeling of being European, and as the EU expands to include much of Eastern Europe, the kind of prejudice that once pitted natives against immigrants is bound to decline (2000: 153). This prescription is not so obvious, and is somewhat at odds with the entire story as it is unfolding. As this chapter shows, there is a bivariate relationship between integrationists and tolerance toward immigrants, and conversely between Euroskeptics and immigrant opposition. To the extent that values of internationalism and protectionism are consistent, the development of a supranational Europe is a testament to the erosion of barriers between citizens and non-citizens or between natives and foreigners, as many students of immigration have contended (Soysal 1994; Jacobson 1996). But this argument cannot be carried to its logical extreme, because it discounts the turning point, whereby Europeanization triggers its own reaction. In fact, the analysis in this chapter reveals that exclusionary politics take place in the name of community construction, and under the blue and yellow flag of Europe.

The trajectory of public and elite opinion regarding European integration uncovered here is consistent with much of the social psychological research on threat and intolerance. The data reveal that threats to national communities and identity accompany general immigrant rejection. Clearly, this logic may be extended to the construction of Europe with its transformative institutional and psychological effects. The recreation of boundaries heightens in-group solidarity by increasing bias against out-groups. In this case, we may expect patterns of opposition to crystallize less along economic lines and more around cultural affinities. Indeed, the data on immigration have substantiated what other researchers have found in Europe in general: that is, a growing level of European penetration can also polarize society further.

NOTES

1. This synthesis of neofunctionalist and intergovernmental perspectives on European integration is consonant with my findings on European migration policy (for theoretical overview, see Sinnott 1995: 23–24).
2. It is commonly agreed that at present a "European demos" is sketchy at best, and relies on the development of a European-wide "democratic praxis" (Habermas 1995; Hix 1999b: 187; see also Koslowski 2000).
3. This construct has stimulated extensive empirical analysis of the EU, as the dimension has been used to locate actors' propensity to approve of particular policy proposals or positions on the EU's institutional framework or competence. The framework has been formalized in rational choice models of EU decision-making (see Tsebelis 1994; Garrett and Tsebelis 1996).
4. Issue publics or issue voters are those whose choices can better be predicted when information about issue positions is added to knowledge of other traditional dimensions, such as partisanship (Carmines and Stimson 1980). Issue voting can be directional or proximate (see Rabinowitz and Macdonald 1989; Macdonald, Listhaug, and Rabinowitz 1991).

5. Such an internationalist/isolationist cleavage has been replicated in political debates about issues of globalization in the United States as well, where the most liberal and most conservative Americans tend to share protectionist views (see Lahav and Bafumi 2001).

6. For studies in American politics and other arenas, see Shepsle and Weingast 1987a, 1987b; March and Olsen 1989; Allison and Halperin 1972; Huntington 1968.

7. For some co-decision votes, an overall majority of the total numbers of the Parliament is required (314 votes of the total 626, which is just over 50 percent) by the Treaties. In this case, the PPE's easiest way of winning is to link up with the Socialists. Clearly, they can do so only if the question is not about the typical left–right argument or, if it is, then both parties have to markedly compromise their views in order to be in the majority. On some issues, the Liberals (the third-largest group) have been able to swing the vote, choosing between the big two parties (Liberal MEP, personal communication with author, November 17, 2002).

8. The principle of subsidiarity stipulates that "the Union shall only act to carry out those tasks which may be undertaken more effectively in common than by the Member States acting separately, in particular those whose action requires action by the Union because their dimension of effects extends beyond national frontiers" (Commission of the European Communities 1992b: Art. 3B). The broad idea is traced back to medieval political thought and has been used over time by various groups (e.g., Dutch Calvinists, Catholic Church) to defend the rights of vulnerable groups against repression from above by rules on the distribution of power. See Miall 1993: 56; Church and Phinnemore 1994: 68–69.

9. This term has its origin in Scharpf 1988. It has been applied to immigration research by Patrick Ireland (1995).

10. Since policy actors seek policy venues where the balance of forces is tipped in their favor (Guiraudon 2000a: 252), political strategies vary according to the rules that guide each political arena (Immergut 1992).

11. The European Convention was inaugurated in early 2002 to initiate a debate on the future shape of the European Union. It is charged with producing the blueprint for a treaty establishing a constitution for Europe and addressing issues such as the division of competences between EU institutions and member-states, and the status of the European Charter of Fundamental Rights. The Convention delivered its first draft of a treaty at the end of October 2002, and this draft has served as the basis for discussions leading to a final report in June 2003.

12. Brubaker argues that different models of citizenship and thus different tendencies for exclusion and inclusion can be historically traced to national models.

13. This is the case despite large migrations and many conquests of European states, and is in stark contrast to the United States, for example, where migration created the celebrated melting pot of diverse cultures and ethnic groups from which arose the non-territory-specific "e pluribus unum" (Gillespie 1996). Note that these differences predate the modern nation-state. Other sources of community bonding (e.g., dynasty and tradition,

hereditary rights, acquisition by marriage or conquest, and religion) preceded the emergence of nations and nationalism (Fulbrook 1993: 4).

14. For political scientist Karl Deutsch, the coordination and integration of activities, attitudes, and adaptive learning so as to bring about the creation of new structures of organization and patterns of behavior constitute one of the most fundamental and universal functions of states and communities (see Deutsch 1981).

15. Whether communities are "imagined" (Anderson 1991: 6–7) or not, they are inherently exclusive in performing "boundary work," or what Lamont refers to as the process by which people differentiate themselves from others (2000). Their exclusive membership criteria even recently have been shown as a viable alternative to explicit coercion in maintaining the order necessary for the stability of democratic regimes (Kook 2002).

16. The central assumption is that elites have considerable influence over public opinion (see Zaller 1992), based for example on cognitive mobilization, ideology, and education.

17. This is based on those who answered "accept without restriction" to the question, "And what about people coming from other countries of the European Community/European Union who wish to settle in (our country)?"

18. Although Deutsch did not explicitly talk about European integration, he did argue that religious affiliation promoted national unification in Great Britain, and later in former American colonies. Many scholars have noted the influence of Catholic thinking on the founders of the EC in the 1950s – i.e., devout Catholics such as Adenauer, Schuman, and De Gasperi (see Nelsen, Guth, and Fraser 2001 for an original overview).

19. See Welsh and Neumann 1991, quoted in *Research Review* (summer), no. 5 (Florence: European University Institute), 1993.

20. The cultural rationale for these sentiments was most publicly reiterated in November 2002 by Valéry Giscard d'Estaing, the former French president in charge of overseeing the drafting of an EU constitution, when he emphatically declared in an interview with *Le Monde* that Turkey was simply "not a European country" (Giscard d'Estaing 2002).

21. Theodore Lowi's (1964) classical typology of public policy in the United States distinguished distributive, redistributive, and regulatory forms, and has been applied to immigration politics in both the American and European settings (see Freeman 1995; Gimpel and Edwards 1999).

22. According to Easton's model, utilitarian support is based on individual cost–benefit perceptions, and is less stable than affective support, which is diffusely socialized over time. Both kinds of support, however, are linked in the sense that affective support derives from accumulated positive utilitarian evaluations of governance (Easton 1975: 445).

23. The Eurobarometer public opinion polls have provided EU scholars with limited but consistent questions that tap into Easton's distinct support dimensions. Besides those questions that are posed occasionally or others that deal with EU versus national competences, four questions regularly included are: (1) "In general, are you for or against efforts being made to unify Western Europe . . . very much for, to some extent for, to some extent against, very

much against?"; (2) "Do you ever think of yourself not only as a [nationality] citizen but also as a citizen of Europe . . . often, sometimes, never?"; (3) "Generally speaking, do you think that [your country's] membership of the EC is . . . a good thing, neither good nor bad, a bad thing?"; (4) "Taking everything into consideration, would you say that [your country] has on balance benefited or not from being a member of the EC . . . benefited, don't know, not benefited?" Although there is some debate about how to classify these indicators (see Niedermayer 1995a), broadly speaking, we can say that the first two questions elicit affective evaluations, while the latter two tap into utilitarian appraisals.

24. In their comparative study on MEPs and national MPs, Franklin and Scarrow show that MEPs are barely more pro-European than their counterparts in national governments or parliaments, and certainly much less than has been casually suggested (1999: 52). They argue that this similarity is indicative of the health of European democracy.

25. According to Scully (2002), MEP positions on this issue may be swayed by various national party influences.

26. The coefficient of determination (commonly known as r^2) for both multivariate regressions (party and country) is not shown in table 5.2 as in other figures, because they are not measuring continuous variables. This parameter is low for each regression because the dependent variable (i.e., position on EU, $r^2 = .06$; position on immigration levels, $r^2 = .18$) is discrete ordinal rather than continuous.

27. Clearly, measures of self-declared racism are not as obtainable among elite samples as among publics. See methodological logic of comparing elite and public opinion in chapter 3. The first is usually measured on a policy dimension, while the latter is on more normative questions.

28. I point again to the impact of national experiences such as immigration rates, religious differences, integration concerns, and levels of national and cultural heterogeneity.

29. The study was based on a sample of respondents aged fifteen to twenty-four in *Eurobarometer* 47.2 (Spring 1997).

30. Attitudes toward European integration in the Eurobarometer are based on the choice of either: (a) If the countries of Europe were really to unite one day, it would be the end of our national, historical, and cultural identities, and our national economic interest would be sacrificed; or (b) The only way of defending our national, historical, and cultural identities and our national economic interest in the face of the superpowers is really to unite Europe (*Eurobarometer* 30, 1989: 71).

31. Although minimum value can be imputed to the last row, since so few MEPs opted to restrict rights (a total of six), the chi-squared test still showed statistical significance in the direction I discuss.

32. A caveat is made with regards to attitudes of some minority out-groups (e.g., Protestants; see pp. 179–180).

33. For Hoffmann, the success of the European project requires a national consciousness that is not too strong but not too weak. That nation-state obsolescence is conditional upon "integrated units which are themselves integrated political communities" may be interpreted to mean that

nation-state and European loyalty are contingent on similar levels of cohesion and community bonding (1966: 904–905).

34. They also differ from other Euroskeptics (e.g., some partisans of the Greens, Radical Left, and the Union for a Europe of Nations [UEN]) and other regionalist parties which are more critical of economic aspects and accountability issues (see Hooghe, Marks, and Wilson 2002; Gabel and Anderson 2002). According to Taggart and Szczerbiak (2002), Euroskeptic parties may be divided into two broad groups: (1) "hard" or those who oppose the EU on principle and endorse withdrawal; and (2) "soft," who are concerned about the trajectory of certain policy areas, particularly as they affect their country's national interests. While the former are disproportionately represented by extreme-right parties, the latter group has been more electorally successful, diffuse, and numerous (ibid.). This distinction allows us to understand the opposition of Greens to the European project (e.g., disempowerment of public interest groups, competition, etc.) and yet their support of immigration (Hooghe, Marks, and Wilson 2002: 984).

35. For an American counterexample, see Fetzer (2000: 45), who argues that religious involvement may increase sympathy for immigrants regardless of one's religious identification, because religious ideals promote pro-immigrant altruism.

36. Wessels reminds us that a universal church is a Catholic concept, whereas the process of nation-building led to the Protestant Reformation and to the creation of national churches, proof that Catholicism may be more strongly related to internationalization than is Protestantism (1995a: 116).

37. The notion of Christian Europe matters to Christian Democrats as it does to Socialists. However, while the Socialists conjure images of Christian solidarity, Christian Democrats talk about Christian Europe. According to one PPE member, "The PPE is basically a Christian Democratic group, with a view of Western Europe or the building of the EU very much as Christendom" (interview no. 134; London, April 22, 1992: 7). The notion of a Christian Europe matters to Christian Democrats. This was the major obstacle to uniting the British Conservative Party with the PPE party group before 1992.

38. One may also invoke Inglehart's argument about the historical differences between a large, hierarchical, centralized Roman Catholic Church and the relatively decentralized, locally controlled Protestant churches (Inglehart and Baker 2000: 35). These differences may be used to argue that a Catholic Europe engenders a loss of local control, which increases perceived threat and decreases interpersonal trust among Protestants and other more diffused religious groups.

39. According to Fetzer, marginality theory predicts that belonging to a religious minority (e.g., being Protestant in a predominantly Catholic country; Catholic in a predominantly Protestant country; Jewish, nonreligious, or another religion in a predominantly Christian country), being a racial or ethnic minority, being unemployed, poor, or female, or having a recent immigrant heritage should all reduce opposition to immigrants and immigration (2000: 21).

40. According to Inglehart, however, the transmission of religious traditions today is through national institutions. Hence, it is fair to say that the predominant religious tradition of any given society shapes a national political culture. Regardless of religious affiliation, we can talk about national religious values that can be subscribed to by a wide national cross-section of a population (see Inglehart and Baker 2000: 36–37).

41. The literature on cognitive mobilization tends to interchangeably refer to this as opinion leadership. The opinion leadership index constructed by Inglehart (1970a) for analyzing cognitive mobilization in the Eurobarometer public opinion studies is derived from combining responses to two questions: "When you get together with friends, would you say you discuss political matters frequently, occasionally, or never?" and "When you, yourself, hold a strong opinion, do you ever find yourself persuading your friends, relatives, or fellow workers? If so, does this happen often, from time to time, or rarely?" The assumption is that opinion leaders pay more attention to the mass media and all forms of political information, and communicate more frequently with each other (see Wessels 1995b: 142; see ICPSR 1980 for construction of opinion leadership index). In *Eurobarometer* 30, the index for this was referred to as "cognitive mobilization" (v723) and includes question 1 (Q.122) and Q.536, which refers to age at which respondent finished school.

42. While Inglehart's work is of seminal value and cannot be easily dismissed, it has generated a number of important critiques that need to be reckoned with (see appendix A for shortcomings). In two recent *American Political Science Review* articles, political scientists have argued that the results of Inglehart's scale are a measurement artifact and are invalid (see Clarke *et al.* 1999; and Davis and Davenport 1999).

43. In a study of secondary school students in four European countries, Inglehart concluded that "Europeanness" tends to be associated with a broader internationalism (1970b). See also Inglehart 1990a. Similarly, in a study of American attitudes, Espenshade and Hempstead found a link between "isolationists" and those who desire lower levels of immigration (1996: 553).

44. According to my data set, 55 percent of the MEP sample were "postmaterialists," 10 percent were "materialists," and 35 percent were "mixed." These figures were derived according to Inglehart's materialism/postmaterialism index. Respondents were divided according to preferences for (1) materialist themes: first and/or second choice on maintaining order and fighting rising prices; (2) postmaterialism: first and/or second choice on increasing participation and guaranteeing freedom of expression; and (3) mixed: one postmaterialist answer and one materialist one. A substantial number of MEPs are of a younger generation of European elites: 43 percent of those surveyed were under forty-nine years of age.

45. In interpreting these trends, one notes that to a large degree the real cleavage in mass opinion relates not to national vs. European conceptions of identity, but rather to those who identify exclusively with their nation and those perceiving themselves as attached to both their nation and Europe. These proclivities confirm our more recently established understanding of multiple identities and the non-exclusivity of terms (see Risse 2002; Duchesne and Frognier 1995).

46. According to Wessels, for example, where EU membership is politicized by political parties as in Denmark and Greece, it polarizes society (1995a: 135). Everts and Sinnott conclude from their country analyses that the source of declining support (e.g., in Britain) was the politicization of the EU and that, in the British case, "the danger was *unlearning*" (1995: 434; italics added).

47. Although the differences in support between original members and those joining later seemingly hold true for countries of the first expansion, this thesis has been largely discredited by the southern enlargement. The closing of this gap has made the "length of membership" argument more tenuous. Alternative suggestions have posed that: (a) levels of public support for European integration plateau (particularly among original member-states; and (b) political, cultural, and historical characteristics of member-states may better explain cross-national differences in EU orientations (Niedermayer 1995a: 62–67).

48. They note that, for the big countries, the Community is a way to create a larger stage, and they are free to leave (as France and the UK have threatened to do early on) if it is not profitable. In contrast, for the smaller countries, the Community is a forum of national survival, and so its performance counts for less (Feld and Wildgen 1976: 64–66).

49. For a pertinent argument on the issue of trust and attitudes toward the European Union, see Niedermayer's review of trust and sense of community (1995b).

50. In his influential work on political culture, Inglehart introduced the contributions of social psychology to the analysis of political behavior (1977, 1990a, 1997). Based on Maslow's hierarchy of human needs, he posited scarcity and socialization hypotheses to argue that people's political preferences derive from their most pressing needs at a formative stage of their life cycle. In this pyramidal structure, needs range from more quantitative-based goals such as food, shelter, and protection, to more qualitative ones, culminating in self-actualization and belonging. Translated into political space, where an individual sits on the hierarchy during formative times determines where he/she stands on a variety of issues, and this is applicable to countries on aggregate.

51. One of the critical research questions in the area of threat is the degree to which perceived personal risk is based on actual risk factors. Most of the evidence in crime research indicates that personal experience plays a large role in shaping risk estimates (Tyler 1984), though some evidence also suggests that the perceived risk of physical threat has little to do with the actual likelihood of victimization (Stafford and Galle 1984).

52. On this point, I am grateful to Leonie Huddy, Stanley Feldman, and Chuck Taber, and for the generous support of the National Science Foundation for the inclusion of a battery of immigration questions in the survey on American public opinion. See Huddy, Feldman, Taber, and Lahav, "The Dynamic, Multi-Faceted Effects of Threat on US Domestic and Foreign Policy Attitudes: Public Response to the September 11 Terrorist Attacks" (National Science Foundation, Grant SES-0201650, 2001).

53. The variables tapping into economic health were found to be less significant, however, to how Americans evaluate immigration levels than other determinants such as isolationist outlooks (Espenshade and Hempstead

1996: 533). In the EU context, they may be equated with pro-integrationist attitudes.

54. I compare with caution because the survey questions on employment prospects and immigrants are not available in the same surveys. Using the most proximate time periods for questions tapping into each, the current analysis is thus able to interpolate immigrant sentiment only over time. I infer that immigrant sentiment is relatively stable from the earlier analyses of *Eurobarometer* 30 (1988/89) and 37 (1992) (see ch. 3), and from my key findings here that these attitudes largely depend on numbers (which during this timeframe have in fact remained relatively stable). It is true that unemployment has been on the rise in Europe, and reached a peak in 1997, and thus it is possible that these findings are spurious. Although the literature consistently supports these connections, without actual identical data over time, we are unable to capture the interactive dynamics of these variables.

55. Again, while wording of survey questions is not perfectly comparable, we can deduce from these weak relationships that unemployment is at best indirectly related to immigrant opposition.

56. It also supports the immigration literature that argues that there is no relationship between extreme-right voting and unemployment over either time or space. For attitudinal analysis, the problem is that unemployment is a priority issue for all voters, and slightly less for those who vote Front national (see Perrineau 1997). There also appears to be no relationship over political space (Mayer 1999; see also Mayer and Perrineau 1992).

57. These may take various forms besides unemployment (e.g., crime, housing shortages, falling educational standards, rising taxation, welfare abusers; see Gibson 2002: 69–70). In accounting for the roots of nativism in the United States, France, and Germany, Fetzer empirically tests several forms of objective and perceived economic self-interest (including classical utilitarian, "labor market," or "use of services," and relative deprivation variants of economic threat) as well as sociotropic motivations. He finds that, education aside, economic threat appears to have few common causes in all three nations (2000: 133).

58. For a complementary point in the American case, see Sullivan, Piereson, and Marcus 1982. According to Lubbers, Gijsberts, and Scheepers (2002), dissatisfaction with democracy, immigrant numbers, and public opinion on immigration largely accounts for cross-national differences in support of extreme right-wing parties in Europe.

59. This same Communist MEP was concerned about the widespread effects: "I have always wondered if everybody is afraid of the immigrant because he is the other, the different, and the different is always a little worrying . . . always . . . We are a little narcissistic, but because we are afraid. Because maybe the different knows things that you do not know."

60. See Hall 1992: 8. Huntington has also claimed that the "fault lines between civilizations will be the battle lines of the future" (1993: 22).

61. Although Huntington's theory is most readily applicable to relations between states, he also noted that within a given state: "Differences in culture and religion create differences over policy issues ranging from human rights to immigration" (1993: 29).

6 Conclusions: the construction of a European immigration regime?

> Closing Act: The fate of a congressman from Youngstown [Ohio] depends on decisions taken in Brussels or Tokyo. The tradeoff for price stability in Hamburg may be unemployment in Harlem. In such predicaments, governments and politicians must choose some mix of two broad strategies: one nationalist, one internationalist. They may try to regain control over their own destiny by reerecting barriers. Or they may seek instead to cooperate in an effort to manage politically.
>
> Robert Putnam and Nicholas Bayne, in *Hanging Together* (1987: 3)

If the preceding analysis on immigration norms has proved anything, it is that efforts to create a common regime in Europe may take several forms. Nationalist and internationalist impulses within the European Union may be more compatible than traditional assumptions about cooperation have suggested. Too often, the policy discourse on globalization or European integration ignores the restrictive nature of cooperation that allows nations to remain protectionist – especially with regard to issues that are emblematic of their national sovereignty and identity. Perceptive immigration scholars have noted the trend toward restrictivism since the 1990s, yet the momentum toward Europeanization belies this phenomenon, and therefore the general point bears repeating. Increasingly, progress in European integration is accompanied by a reinvention of borders that can be understood only by examining the norms and attitudes that underpin immigration policy.

Do attitudes make a difference?

The overarching question driving the inquiry of this book is how liberal states in a global order can manage the movement of people across national frontiers, while surrendering borders for the movement of goods and capital. This is not merely an academic riddle, but one of critical practical significance for the European Union, whose *raison d'être* is the dismantling of barriers to the four factors of production – trade, capital, service, and labor – the so-called four freedoms. In the absence of a common immigration policy or the free movement of persons, the EU cannot operate as a fully supranational entity. To what extent, then, can heterogeneous European states overcome competing ideological, national, cultural, and religious interests for the sake of a viable collective immigration and asylum policy?

Scholars of immigration have been hotly contesting the nature of immigration control in light of globalization demands. Their lively debate has been generally polarized around the resilience or decline of the nation-state in governing immigration. They have been helped by insights from the European Union "playing field," where nationalist impulses have met interdependence and globalization. The endemic tension between national and supranational approaches has led to divergent assumptions about the prospects for immigration cooperation. Clearly, the state-centric perspectives of (neo)realists, though receptive to intergovernmental types of policy-making, were much less optimistic about the compelling power of cooperation than the advocates of neofunctionalism, with their expansive logic of supranationalism. In its cursory form, then, supranational cooperation on immigration has been associated with sovereignty erosion and open borders, intergovernmentalism with national power and protectionism.

Immigration policy at the EU level has seemingly reconciled both approaches to decision-making. The coexistence of both intergovernmental and supranational institutions, consecrated by the Maastricht Treaty and other agreements since, represents one of the most original approaches to policy-making in an increasingly global world. The EU has organized value preferences and reconciled interests in such a way as to incorporate national tendencies *and* supranational influences. It ensures open markets and regulated migration. More importantly, it reminds us that one of the tenets of liberal trade theories applies more to the movement of economic actors than to that of individuals.

There are several reasons why these two-way dynamics have been overlooked. First, European integration has been viewed in a bifurcated manner. This is, proponents of supranational cooperation have been wedded to liberal principles, while intergovernmentalists and realists are in the skeptic camp. Second, "new politics" or "new security" issues of the post-Cold War period – immigration, ethnic conflict, terrorism, identity politics – have not been adequately figured into the changing political space prompted by the European Union itself (Gabel and Anderson 2002; Hooghe, Marks, and Wilson, 2001). Finally, the significant role and impact of public opinion in driving EU dynamics have been largely undermined by theorists of European integration and immigration alike.

My attitudinal approach has attempted to moderate these theoretical proclivities by offering an empirical corrective to the portrait of Europeanization – corroborated by immigration researchers – as a chiefly economic, liberal, or elite affair. Until recently, students of the EU have largely neglected mass attitudes, focusing instead on institutions and the economic and political elites who direct political cooperation (for some early exceptions, see Mathew 1980; Hewstone, 1986; Feld and Wildgen 1976; Shepherd 1975; Slater 1983).[1] For the most part, theorists of European integration, even when they acknowledge public opinion factors, tend to focus on economic factors (Duch and Taylor 1997; Gabel 1998a; Gabel and Whitten 1997; Gabel and Palmer 1995). Inasmuch as regional integration has been seen to promote cooperation, a liberalization of the factors of production has been expected.

These biases have also been held by immigration analysts as a general rule. The large body of work on citizenship and nationality has made valuable contributions to our understanding of national dynamics (Aleinikoff and Klusmeyer 2000; Feldblum 1999; Favell 1997, 1998a; Weil 1996; Brubaker 1992), but their state-centric approaches have tended to downplay the impact of the EU on immigration. There have been some promising attempts among those studying right-wing populism to consider the weight of globalization and European integration on domestic politics (see Swank and Betz 2002; Messina 2002b; Taggart 1995, 1998). But generally, because these movements and actors are studied as isolated phenomena related to xenophobia and racism, there is a tendency to overlook the broader – more taboo – public opposition toward immigrants. Some attempts to place these manifestations within larger party systems have provided an important hint as to more diffuse anti-immigrant sentiment on the political agenda (Freeman 1979; Schain 1987, 1988; Messina 1989; Money 1999), but for the most part immigration norms have been deduced from behavioral or policy output.

Political economic approaches to immigration have also allowed important systematic strides within the migration research field (Hollifield 1992a; Freeman 1995, 2002: 82; Kessler 1997; Money 1999; Stalker 2000), though there has been a tendency to underestimate the impact of diffuse public opinion. Whether adopting spatial analyses of immigration politics or cost–benefit equations of policy preferences, these "rational" approaches have imputed a liberal or expansive character to immigration. An influential body of immigration scholarship has found that exogenous constraints, from either elites (McLaren 2001) or international structures, have set the debate's parameters, which are oriented to liberal immigration policy outcomes (Hollifield 1992a; Freeman 1995). They have been bolstered by arguments that public constituencies have been circumvented by traditionally insulated decision-making (Guiraudon 1997; Tichenor 2002) or, among other things, by the lack of information available to publics on immigration (Freeman 1995). Even those who have espoused more attitudinal perspectives have accepted as a foregone conclusion that there is a large mismatch between official immigration policy and mass public opinion (Fetzer 2000: 148; Freeman 1995; Hansen 2000; Betts 1988; Beck and Camarota 2002) – notably with higher-educated elites being more pro-immigration than their jingoistic, uninformed, and volatile publics. Given these parameters, does public opinion matter?

This book's analysis gives ample reason to believe that it does. First, the momentum toward democratic institutions, incarnated by the growing role of the European Parliament and changing framework for EU policy-making, mounting citizen protests, and the looming impact of refer-endum politics, provides an important entry point for mass effects on European (Gabel 1998a; Dalton and Eichenberg 1998) and immigration reforms.[2] Regardless of cognitive sophistication about the EU, national experiences trigger public responses to European integration that vary across policy domains (Dalton and Eichenberg 1998; Gabel and Palmer 1995) and over time (Shepherd 1975; Anderson 1998). Second, my data build on other studies on diverse population subsamples, such as youth, national publics, policy experts, or party platforms (Ray, 1999; Hooghe, Marks, and Wilson 2002; Nelsen et al. 2001; Gabel and Anderson 2002). They are suggestive of the impact of new mobilization patterns as they condition electoral politics and interest group pressures. Spurred by more contemporary concerns, "new politics" and "new security" issues (such as immigration) influence and are structured by European integration, and provide evidence of variegated and non-random attitudes which can be systematically explained (Inglehart 1990a; Rohrschneider 1990; Hooghe, Marks, and Wilson 2002). Finally, these observations return us to the early work of Stanley Hoffmann (1966), revisited by more recent scholars. They suggest that the triumph or failure of integration is "contingent to a remarkable extent on developments in political culture and public opinion" (Sinnott 1995: 19). These developments of course vary from issue to issue. Jean-Marie Le Pen is a continual reminder of the import of public opinion and consent, and the power of ideas when it comes to issues related to immigration (Favell 1998b: 250). The dramatic breakthrough of extreme-right parties throughout Europe – ranging from Denmark and the Netherlands in the north to France and Italy further south – underscores the growing public discontent and the viability of populist agendas to penetrate democratic systems. Though these parties tend to manipulate fears that national opinion is being undermined by Brussels, they skillfully carry the banner across Europe, and ironically get maximal exposure at the EU level.[3]

It is difficult to reconcile the conclusions of immigration and EU scholars with the empirical developments I observe. Liberal accounts of European cooperation fail to explain the limited and piecemeal nature of immigration policy at the European level. They also underestimate the extent to which different immigration discourses and public opinion contexts are generating more restrictive and protectionist policy responses throughout the EU. More importantly, these liberal paradigms do not consider the possibility that, as this study shows, there are far more similarities between European elites and publics than previously expected. Indeed, more recent evidence systematically comparing decision-makers and general publics across policy dimensions (see Commission of the European Communities 1996) has also confirmed what was earlier only inconclusively implied. That is, while national patterns vary, elites and general publics embrace similar priorities and are driven by fears that converge considerably (see ibid. ch. 3; Feld and Wildgen 1976: ch. 3).

A broad "collective correspondence" exists between the masses and MEPs, who represent a diverse group of national, party, and European leaders.[4] Although there are some notable disagreements (e.g., on immigrant integration, issue salience, collective goals), the distance between the two groups is far narrower than presumed. Elites are less knowledgeable about immigration regulation, publics are more sophisticated, and both are equally negative toward immigrant intake. These findings offer redeeming signs for "democratic deficit" matters, and revive the credibility of the median voter model, whereby parties and politicians may seek to maximize support by locating themselves at the center of opinion (Freeman 2002: 79). Though they close the contended gap between opinion and policy, they have more tepid implications for the nature of immigration cooperation in the EU.

The institutional fence-straddling between supranational and intergovernmental approaches to Europe is rather logical once public opinion and elite attitudes are figured into the equation. The two approaches are reconcilable, because public and elites are consistent in ways rarely acknowledged. Europeanization is compatible with growing national-level influence over migration policy. In general, restrictive cooperation is the likely outcome, driven not only for reasons to do with its effectiveness as a policy output but also, more importantly, by the powerful policy input of emergent consensual attitudes on restrictive policies among elites and publics alike. The evidence in this book shows how broadly the outcomes on restrictive policy throughout Europe reflect the shifting orientations of public and elites on immigration during recent decades. They have tended to head in a restrictive direction.

These trends provide the key to unraveling the working questions I posed at the onset of my study. What would drive states to cooperate on migration? Would cooperation be organized along intergovernmental or supranational bases, and what outcome (liberal or restrictive) might we expect? In chapter 2, I examined institutional dynamics and found that, despite limited supranational developments in EU immigration, there are important national variations that linger and that inform the nature of policy cooperation. In order to better understand how policies change, and particularly how they may converge, I considered what drives these national interests and how they might be manipulated in such a way as to foster immigration coordination among the fifteen European member-states. My longitudinal analysis of cooperative immigration measures revealed that increasing migration flows and asylum applications did not precede important EU cooperative initiatives (e.g., SEA, Schengen). It therefore debunks some commonly held claims that large flows engender policy convergence (Ugur 1995).

In the absence of immigrant flows to explain policy cooperation, in chapter 3, I turned to immigration norms more broadly. In the process, I uncovered these policy ambiguities by illuminating some of the paradoxes that have confounded immigration researchers. I found that opinion is ambivalent, and thus policy, regardless of its contradictory appearance, reflects this thinking in two minds. Europeans are more informed than previously detected in the literature, but their policy preferences vary from racist motivations to self-interest concerns and societal consider-ations. On the whole, publics see immigration as an issue growing in importance, though its politicization is greater than its salience (personal issue attachment) in the everyday lives of Europeans. Public opinion, like that of elites, is more favorable toward EU migrants than non-EU (mostly Third World) migrants, though not exclusively for racist reasons. The distinctions between personal and societal considerations help unravel all sorts of paradoxes and inconsistencies we find in exploring immigration attitudes. Once untangled, the pieces of the immigration puzzle become more orderly, and the value of public opinion more crucial. Despite the ambivalent sentiments of public opinion, there is a coherent and systematic attachment to immigration issues that is predictable. Hence European publics are a meaningful component of the immigration debate.

Given the finding that public opinion is neither random nor capricious, the sources of attitudinal thinking become more critical to our analysis.

In chapter 4, I explored the nature of the "issue public" in an enlarged Union by considering traditional national interests as well as the classical left–right ideological yardstick that typically divides issue publics. These attitudinal sources offer us a view on how competing interests may be reconciled in a larger political playing field. On the one hand, I found that the traditional lines of contestation are more ubiquitous than commonly proclaimed, given that they continue to differentiate immigration preferences. On the other hand, there is a convergence of thinking that coincides with the so-called strange-bedfellows coalitions, and that accounts for the elusive nature of immigration attitudes. As I spelled out in chapter 5, European integration reinvents traditional alliances. But it also provides new opportunities for thinking about migration control.

The greatest obstacles toward forming a common supranational immigration regime are that: (1) within the institutional and policy-making process of the EU, state-level interests and decision-making are still crucial; (2) both mass publics and European elites continue to exhibit dramatically different and important national perspectives on immigration and EU issues; (3) despite the extent to which immigration cuts across traditional cleavages, the left–right ideological and partisanship distinctions structure immigration attitudes, and speak to some redistributive conflict; (4) immigration touches on and exacerbates a number of key contentious issues regarding European integration, especially those of identity (religious, cultural, national, ethnic) and national sovereignty; and (5) European integration reinvents traditional polarizations.

Given these constraints, one might ask what propels immigration cooperation at all. The institutional analysis of immigration developments in chapter 2 revealed that any limited steps toward a common immigration policy since 1985 are less a function of increasing flows of non-EU migrants, and more a result of the momentum associated with integration in other policy areas. The emergence of EU cooperative agreements on immigration does not appear to follow the ebb and flow of immigrant numbers. This is not so much a reflection of uninformed publics, a popular thesis I discounted in chapter 3, as a result of public concerns with other political processes. The "elite opinion leadership" and "permissive consensus" explanations are also not adequate, given the elite–mass "collective correspondence" discovered in the empirical analyses presented in chapters 4 and 5. Since this study does not profess to resolve the elite–mass causal debate, it is sufficient to evoke the "logic of appropriateness" argument to say that public opinion is important in that it sets down the norms, or the "rules of the game," by which elites must structure their discourse (see March and Olsen 1984; Powell and

Dimaggio 1991; Checkel 2001; see also Thielemann 2001 and forthcoming for application to European asylum policy).

Nowhere do I argue that public opinion is the decisive factor in carrying the European project on immigration forward. The value of mass attitudes, then, is in their capability of being politicized by elites who can then bring them to bear on issues such as immigration or European integration, and convert them to the public policy agenda. Much of the focus remains on elites and on structures and processes, at both the international and national levels. More can be learned from a comparative analysis of how publics are mobilized and immigration is politicized. As Schmitter (1992) and others (i.e., Wessels 1995b, Sinnott 1995: 24) have aptly noted in revisiting theories of European integration, the importance of politicization is one of the key factors that will determine the future development of the Euro-polity.

These assumptions lead us to consider the patterns of political contestation. What is the nature of political space with regard to a European immigration policy? Gabel persuasively returns us to these types of elementary questions, as he reminds us that, without cleavages, no systematic assessment of public opinion is possible or warranted. If attitudes were unstructured or simply a reflection of a select group of elites, any explanatory attempts would prove impossible or futile (1998a: 115). Societal cleavages are the bedrock of any political system, and consequently need to be reexamined within a Europe of changing boundaries. In light of the politicized nature of immigration in the EU, it behooves us to take stock of the bases on which mass opinion is diffusely formulated.

Though the evidence here puts more credence on publics, the ambivalence uncovered thus far indicates that the range of policy options remains polarized. The data give us some assurance that Europeans understand the import of ceding control to a supranational entity, despite the trepidations and insecurities about the consequences. Assuming that societal evaluations or general conditions inform immigration preferences, what happens with regard to European immigration cooperation will largely depend on how the European Union fares. To the extent that the European Convention, designing the institutional future of the EU, makes the direction of the Union more evident, the consequences will be more certain. Since it appears that public support for immigration cooperation follows general policy developments in the EU, we may envisage a more decisive issue public to emerge. Therefore, we can expect that as the implications of the EU for societal conditions become clearer, public opinion will become less ambivalent about immigration and more relevant to both policy-makers and researchers alike.

Organizing immigration interests in the European Union: from competition to cooperation

Throughout this book, I have attempted to gauge the prospects for the first modern international migration regime of its kind. In this search, I have pondered how competing migration interests may be reconciled and organized in an emergent EU system. In his timeless account of traditional party politics, E. E. Schattschneider said, "What happens in politics depends on the way in which people are divided into factions, parties, groups, classes, et cetera" (1975: 60). Conflicts divide people and unite them at the same time, and the processes that prompt each reflect the times. What can developments on the immigration front tell us about an integrated Europe at the turn of the twenty-first century? Does the construction of Europe offer a new framework for organizing the immigration debate, and for structuring policy attitudes and alliance formations that can inspire cooperation?

National, ideological, and EU cleavages

The success of a supranational Europe fundamentally rests on its capacity to transcend parochial national interests that may impede cooperation or consensus-building. As we have seen in chapters 2 and 3, issues such as immigration, like defense, touch the core of national identity and security, and are therefore particularly vulnerable to national sensitivities. These are of course exacerbated in the context of regional integration. Under these conditions, the traces of intergovernmental decision-making and lowest-common-denominator bargaining that prevail among member-states in matters of immigration and asylum are rather unsurprising. Placed against Dalton and Eichenberg's (1998) reformulation of Hoffmann's (1966) thesis, support for policy integration is expected to be greater for "low politics" issues such as welfare policies, tariff policies, and technical areas, and more resistant to "high politics" areas which affect national security or identity. Given that immigration matters have transcended their traditional status of "low" questions of domestic public policy to become "high" issues of international politics as many scholars have conceded (Koslowski 1998b; Geddes 2000; Favell 1998a), we may expect this "paradox" to apply as much to immigration concerns as it does to foreign policy and security, the original impetuses for European cooperation (Dalton and Eichenberg 1998: 268). Nonetheless, the institutional analysis of immigration evolution in chapter 2 uncovered a complex maze of immigration policy-making at the EU level, more favorable to cooperation than might have been expected of narrowly defined statist interests. These institutional intricacies would appear irreconcilable and irrational, if not for the findings illuminated by the attitudinal data. Chapter 3 focused on the ambivalent yet stable underlying attitudes to explain policy outcomes.

The empirical evidence in chapters 4 and 5 disaggregated the critical sources inspiring these norms. National factors clearly influence immigration thinking in the EU. The attitudinal data in this study reveal comprehensive differences in their assessment of immigration and policy preferences between people from countries that are economically more developed, more geographically central, predominantly traditional immigration societies, with higher immigrant concentrations, and the others. To some degree, this portrait coincides with the North–South discrepancies which have long plagued Europe, and the cultural impact of which apparently remains. To the extent that European countries are *still* at different phases of the immigration cycle, and experience different numbers of immigrants, national effects may be profound.

Notwithstanding national barriers, the analysis in chapter 4 delivered a note of optimism for the forces of a supranational Europe, transcending national alignments and building coalitions that may be found in any political system. The evidence supports renewed conviction among contemporary scholars about the resilience of ideological commitments and the ability of political parties more generally to absorb and respond to new issues (see Knutsen 1998; Marks, Wilson, and Ray 2002; Hix 2001a; Laver and Hunt 1992; Marks and Steenbergen 2002; Gabel and Hix 2002; Kreppel and Tseblis 1999; Tsebelis and Garrett 2000; Macdonald, Listhaug, and Rabinowitz 1991). To put the spotlight back on ideological and party positions as informing the European immigration debate, the data are suggestive of broad ideological patterns that distinguish European elites and publics alike on issues related to immigrant preferences, control, and even integration policies. Despite the classical "doom and gloom" predictions about ideology, partisan/ideological differences in migration policy continue to be relevant. Partisans on the left are more likely than those on the right to support increased immigration levels and to want to remedy social inequalities and extend immigrant rights. They are also more likely to delegate authority over immigration to EU institutions.

These findings are at loggerheads with the notion that ideology no longer has a role in postmodern societies, and vindicate immigration specialists who have long tried to make sense of the elusive immigration issue through party politics (Schain 1988, 1999; Messina 1985, 1989). The evidence in this study indicates that it is too early to dismiss traditional sources, such as partisan/ideological politics, that continue to shape the immigration agenda in the European Union. For scholars of EU integration, it gives credibility to neofunctionalist visions of transnational party affinities organizing an emerging European system. Nearly five decades after the formation of the EP system, party affiliation and ideological orientation inform migration policy preferences.

This thesis has been largely underestimated due to the tendency to equate evidence of convergence with the demise of traditional affiliations to inform policy thinking. This logic lacks historical perspective and denies the processes of alliance formations in an evolving political system, where traditional values serve as a broad organizing device to map interests. In this context, the existence of the European Parliament creates an incentive for policy coordination between parties sharing similar platforms in different countries. This is consonant with the vision of the original framers of the Treaty of Rome, who created a parliament with members whose common interests would emanate from partisan/ideological affinities. Signs that these polarizations exist give credibility to the EP, and the development of the European system.

Admittedly, however, if we stopped here the portrait would not include the issues noted by Hix and others that are colored by national, cultural, or European interests. Indeed, when one controls for ideological variables, as I did in chapter 4, national factors related to immigration account for important differences in perception and preferences of immigration policy. More interestingly, the link between national and ideological factors not only appears to undercut the institutional organization of the EU: this effect also provides ammunition to those who have lost faith in ideology. The impact of national sources of attitudes on ideology has resulted in cross-national parties that do not always follow traditional ideological distinctions. For this reason, it is still important to consider party patterns at the EU level in country-specific contexts.

As far as the nature of party debates reflects national experiences, the phase of immigration experiences becomes crucial. The traditional post-World War II immigration countries may be differentiated from the newer immigration regimes (i.e., the Southern countries) in terms of party system convergence or divergence. In the former, party groups tend to be more polarized while, in the latter, party distinctions become blurred. Chapter 4 reasoned that the longer immigration remains on the political agenda, the more politicized it becomes, as parties scramble to differentiate themselves from each other. My analysis provides evidence that varying sizes of immigrant concentrations and different phases of immigration cycles among EU countries may account for some diversity in attitudes and policy preferences, which also conditions party dynamics.

When parties converge, one must consider national situations, particularly immigrant numbers.

Immigration issues may place political parties in unfamiliar waters, since "the issue is not the usual one of how to divide the economic pie between the voters, but instead how to divide it between the citizens and non-citizens" (Hammar 1985b: 280). My data unearth striking distinctions between attitudes toward fellow EU citizens and those toward non-EU foreigners. The immigration issue may resemble others, such as crime and poverty – issues that Robert Putnam proposed do not involve competing interests among social groups, but rather common problems facing the community (1973: 112–113). Furthermore, immigration policy has a great deal in common with other political issues affecting a country's international relations or security in general. Crosscultural research shows that, as immigration policy becomes linked to security, publics coalesce around a common national interest, which favors more restrictive immigration policy (Hammar 1985b; Bartram 1998). As the aftermath of the September 11 terrorist attacks shows, immigration may be fundamentally embedded in the security dynamic, an impetus for community consolidation and exclusion. Political psychologists have shown in other contexts that threats to community and identity impact attitudes toward "out-groups," as they promote solidarity (Tajfel and Turner 1979; Brewer 1979; Brown 1995; Huddy 2001; Huddy et al. 2002). These types of threats coincide with general immigrant intolerance and rejection. All of these dimensions of the immigration issue may explain why political parties mysteriously agree to act concertedly in the "national interest" – or in the European Union case, the "transnational interest."

Institutional and psychological factors related to the construction of Europe reinforce and mitigate traditional sources of policy thinking related to immigration, and compel us to say something about the more general nature of conflict in Europe at the turn of the twenty-first century. The "European factor," as I described in chapter 5, both crystallizes and transforms traditional alliances. On the one hand, it provides a rallying force to obtain national interests collectively. On the other hand, it relies on traditional party and ideological ties as organizing tools in an enlarged forum. The European factor reinvents traditional affinities by placing them in a broader perspective that fosters some degree of consensus-building.

The attitudinal overview in chapter 3 discovered some optimism about the prospects of a European immigration regime, motivated by common norms. Although terminology, contexts, and policy prescriptions tend to vary, elites and publics are in consensus about the nature of immigration. They agree that immigration problems are greater today than ever before, and that immigration is one of the most important issues on the political agenda (though interesting variations exist for publics and elites on issue salience). The European factor may build on these attitudes for the emergence and consolidation of some type of transnational norms concerning immigration.

This paradoxical portrait of consensus amidst competing national and ideological interests should not be too surprising for scholars following the "new politics" or "new security" debates in comparative politics and international relations. That other patterns of opposition (e.g., materialism/postmaterialism; religious in-groups/out-groups; international/national; pro-/anti-Europe) are operative in European politics today lends credence to the impact of European integration in structuring policy debates. They corroborate the findings of EU researchers (Inglehart 1990a; Carrubba 2001; Noury 2002; Gabel and Anderson 2002; Hix and Lord 1997). One of the notable findings to emerge from my research is the EU cleavage in distinguishing patterns of opposition on issues such as immigration and asylum. The data in chapter 5 identified a pro-/anti-European integration dichotomy in distinguishing those people who want to see a common immigration policy and those who do not. Orientations toward European integration help structure political competition, and provide a map to navigate our way through issues that touch the core of cultural diversity. Given the close connection between a common immigration policy and the ability to move forward with EU integration, it is important to consider how support for integration is organized within the EU.

According to Simon Hix, European political elites must be measured on two dimensions – pro-/anti-Europe and left/right axes (1999b: 158). In cases involving European integration, "the political interests about the question of European integration are more determined by national and cultural factors than by party affiliation" (Hix and Lord 1997: 26).[5] Although Hix claims European integration does not run across the usual ideological continuum, he does not argue, as many scholars have, that the left–right organizing device has simply become irrelevant. One of the reasons given for the failure to "integrate" the issue of integration is that it is simply a new dimension which traditional party families have not yet had time to take stable positions upon (1999b). If, as Hix claims, parties have not yet taken explicit and differing stances on integration issues, should we expect to see the integration issue affect the politics of the EU in a more subtle way? If so, how would such an effect manifest itself on issues related to immigration and asylum policy?

The findings in my study tell us that there is a relationship between preferences on integration and immigration preferences. My data on MEPs and their public constituencies allow us to extend arguments applied to MEP roll-call votes (Hix 2001a: 680–683), to youths in Europe (Nelsen and Guth 2001), to party politicians (Ray 1999; Gabel and Anderson 2002), and to other experts (Hooghe, Marks, and Wilson 2002) about the connection of immigration politics to the EU. The construction of the European Union exposes important cleavages that are relevant to all issues that touch the core of national identity or cultural values. My analysis of public opinion reveals that some individuals think of immigration and asylum as "national" issues, and thus immigration policy is one of those policy areas where conflict between champions of national policy and supporters of the EU occurs. Broadly speaking, those who want more Europe are more receptive to a common immigration regime than those who are more protectionist. But, as I mentioned above, the findings also expose an ideological dimension that orders preferences on EU immigration policy. Those on the left of the spectrum are more prepared to delegate immigration matters to an EU authority than those on the right.

These findings suggest that reality is more complex than can be represented by a two-dimensional axis, since partisanship *and* national/EU interests have strong predictive power over stances toward immigration in the EU. This assertion brings to light our assumption that attitudes toward integration and toward immigration are related, since we could predict attitudes toward a supranationalization of immigration policy using party data, but not on integration. How can we square this with Hix's findings?

According to Hooghe, Marks, and Wilson (2001: 22), party positioning on the new politics dimension (e.g., immigration) is causally prior to party positioning on issues related to European integration, which is why they speak of new politics structuring positions on European integration rather than the reverse. My findings that party affiliation and ideological orientations inform policy preferences also suggest that positions on the immigration issue may alternatively influence which party individuals choose in the EU. These conclusions call for a more nuanced understanding of the left–right heuristic, as it is conditioned by important national and cultural factors.

Hooghe, Marks, and Wilson reason that European integration brings some aspects of the new politics dimension to the fore while deemphasizing others. In this context, they propose that "the interaction between European integration, nationalism, and anti-immigrant attitudes is an important topic for further inquiry" (Hooghe, Marks, and Wilson

2001: 23). Other researchers corroborate the finding of this study of the relationship between immigration and EU attitudes (Nelsen and Guth 2001; De Master and Le Roy 2000) and hint at the complex inter-active effects of country and ideology on policy preferences within the EU. These conclusions take us beyond Hooghe *et al.*'s speculations that "European integration has not only been structured by new politics, but it has shaped it in the process" (Hooghe, Marks, and Wilson 2001: 23).

The European factor perpetuates a dualism that may be applicable to immigration politics. The range of polarizations includes the degrees of cultural homogeneity desirable; the lines between "Europe without frontiers" and "Fortress Europe"; supranational vs. national approaches to decision-making; religious in-groups and out-groups; postmaterialists vs. materialists; or, to put it in old-fashioned terms, the "left" and the "right." The European factor builds on older schisms, but in the context of a world of change and insecurity. Moreover, polarizations in an enlarged Europe continue to distinguish between those who have more to gain and those who have more to lose – from the new European order and from immigration.

As in all political systems, the dominant forces are expected to prevail. For immigration in Europe, this may mean that policy will follow the thinking of the three dominant, most socioeconomically developed EU powers, with the largest immigrant numbers – France, Germany, and the United Kingdom. The policy preferences of these three countries also coincide with those of the mainstream parties. How do these divisions translate institutionally and substantively at the EU level? What do these patterns mean for the contours of an immigration regime?

Institutionalizing immigration interests: intergovernmental vs. supranational Europe

How multilevel interests are organized in the EU not only deter-mines issue attitudes, but also shapes the institutional organization (i.e., intergovernmental or supranational) that structures immigration preferences and norms in the EU. Referring to Lijphart's work (1977, 1996), Gabel suggests that institutional organization and the success of democratic reforms depend crucially on how citizens define their interests regarding EU politics. Lijphart contends that plural societies are generally unstable environments for majoritarian democratic insti-tutions because they inhibit compromise. Based on this reasoning, Gabel argues that, if EU citizens identify their political interests regarding integration solely along national lines, then the introduction of majoritarian democratic institutions (i.e., supranational approaches) may serve to aggravate national political conflicts over EU policy and reduce the proponents for compromise (1998a: 8). My analysis of public opinion reveals that Europeans are equally split about delegating immigration regulation to EU authority or guarding it under national control.

It is therefore fitting to find traces of intergovernmental bargaining coexisting alongside supranational cooperation driving immigration policy-making at the EU level. This is a logical correlate to the divisions we have discovered among the ambivalent public. On a macro level, a Europe *à la carte* model of policy-making provides the option of sitting out for those members who are more supportive of national approaches, while allowing the champions of EU supranational policy to proceed. Countries such as the United Kingdom and Ireland were thus able to opt out of the new area of freedom, security, and justice created by the Amsterdam Treaty. Similarly, Denmark (a member of the Schengen Group) was excused from the incorporation of the Schengen *acquis* as the frame for cooperation on immigration and asylum, and limited its cooperation to a common visa policy.

The construction of Europe poignantly illustrates how, at one time, seemingly contradictory streams of interests between domestic and international constraints may be reconciled at the regional level. That policy thinking at the European level incorporated national (intergovernmental) and supranational tendencies is clearly reflected in the direction that Maastricht has taken, and that Amsterdam has upheld. To a large degree, new guidelines were based on the previous work already undertaken by intergovernmental groups such as Schengen. Yet, at the same time, the Maastricht Treaty created a more active role for the representatives of a "people's and social Europe," the European Parliament. The Treaty was a compromise between those who wanted to move toward a federal Europe with a stronger supranational element (the original EC-6, Portugal, Spain, and Ireland) and those who preferred intergovernmental (national) cooperation. The result was a three-pillar structure that extended the areas of economic policy under supranational control, while strengthening intergovernmental mechanisms for foreign policy and home policy. Although the Amsterdam amendment followed by the Nice Treaty brought much of the third pillar into the supranational EC first pillar, it also institutionalized considerable national impediments (i.e., voting procedures).

As immigration has evolved from the demographic and economic spheres to the social and political domains, decision-making has been increasingly marked by more formal attempts to bring immigration under European competence. In order to overcome the "negative externalities" of EU market integration on migration control, the impetus for coordination has come from states which are looking to avoid the political and substantive repercussions of other states' migration decisions (Hix 1999b: 322–323; Monar 1998). Similar to their strategy in other policy areas, in which states (also known as "principals") coopt "agents" in joint exchange of gains (Pollack 1997), national states have delegated authority over migration to EU actors (Stetter 2000; Guiraudon 2000a) and other third-party agents (Lahav 1998) in order to secure policy goals and reduce costs.[6] These developments suggest that the politicization of immigration bolsters cooperation, as policy-makers seek to shift immigration regulation and liabilities upward to supranational and intergovernmental actors (Guiraudon and Lahav 2000). Europeanization of immigration policy is likely, because more and more nations are looking to restrict immigration, and to increase state effectiveness in controlling migration (Lahav 1998, 2000). The most pressing issues for national harmonization remain those related to immigrants inside the EU.[7]

Such developments draw our attention to the important distinction raised by Hammar regarding immigration policy (admissions) and immigrant (integration) issues. While my conclusions point to an emerging consensus between elites and publics on issues related to immigration policy (admissions), they simultaneously reveal what happens when consensus is lacking, and national supporters prevail, as is the case in areas critically related to culture, such as integration policy.[8] Although the evidence in this book suggests that a public opinion constituency for Europeanizing integration policy may also emerge, the pronounced distribution of policy attitudes on nationally laden models of citizenship and belonging explains why so few policies dealing with integration matters (i.e., education, acculturation, language, etc.) are handled at the EU level.[9] While political interests have converged sufficiently that citizenship of a member-state now confers economic and social rights exercisable throughout the EU, the control over granting nationality and citizenship remains in the hands of the nation-states.

If my speculation that politicization begets more cooperation is found to be true, we may expect increasing convergence of the type one Dutch MEP described with regard to the changes unleashed by Maastricht:

I think that Europe's politicians are trying and groping toward two different but related approaches. One is to reduce the legal scope for immigrants from outside the EC to move into the EC. That is the same – more restrictionist policy. On the other hand, I think they will want to compensate for that by giving the legally established more rights. So that, while you're being more restrictive toward outsiders, you compensate for that psychologically in your own mind, but also in the way you relate to the people. A number of them are living here legally, and it's about time we give them more rights. (interview no. 44; Strasbourg, May 12, 1992: 6)

The attitudinal portrait I draw in this book reveals that these senti-ments toward immigrant policy were embraced much more among elites than among their publics, and varied both nationally and ideologi-cally. This divergence gives some pause about extending my argument to the integration side of the immigration policy equation. Further empirical research on comparative integration dynamics is warranted in order to evaluate the prospects of states overcoming national models of integration. For now, we can conclude that, considering the "external-ities of EU immigration policy" (Lavenex and Uçarer 2002b) and "the unintended effects of incomplete integration, with immigration policy being Europeanized and immigrant and welfare policies not" (Geddes 2002), immigration policies are increasingly interdependent with other policy domains (from foreign affairs to welfare policy), and cooperation here will be mediated by developments in other domains.

Explaining integration: market vs. cultural norms

On January 1, 2002, most national currencies were replaced by the euro, and the first major step toward a true European federation came into place, with hardly any protest or confusion. The relative ease and normalcy of this currency reform draws more attention to the seemingly haphazard and ambivalent policy evolution of migration, exemplified by the controversy surrounding the events that led Austria's extreme-right Freedom Party leader, Jörg Haider, to become part of the government following elections in 2000.[10] With the completion of the main stage of the euro project, and with the experience of ethnic conflict in Kosovo, Europe has awakened to its political, military, and moral identity. Haider's accession to power set up yet another highly charged test of national sovereignty versus the embryonic government of the EU. The political crisis in the EU fueled by one member-state revealed that on such sensitive issues an emergent Europe could possibly interfere in the domestic politics of its constituent parts. This political climate is another reason to reexamine the nature of regional integration in relation to issues of "people."

To what extent can a market's union promote a "people's Europe"? Sociologists of regional integration have concluded that, "although most Europeans support the goals of European economic and, to some extent, political union, they are reluctant to relinquish their national cultural heritages in favor of a common supranational Union or super-state" (Kourvetaris and Kourvetaris 1996: 164). My observations largely confirm these trends. The understated cultural boundaries of policy cooperation help explain why Turkey fares poorly as a candidate for

European expansion. While Europeans have made significant strides toward economic and political integration, they continue to lag behind with respect to cultural and ethnic matters. Immigration and asylum policies are signature case studies in point. This resistance is not unique to the European Union, but is endemic to other regional projects, such as the North American Free Trade Agreement (NAFTA), in which the tension between economic openness and cultural protection is biased against the free movement of persons.

Students of Europe and of immigration politics have become more attentive to the distinction between utilitarian/economic-driven explanations and cultural/identity motivations (also referred to as interest-based vs. identity-based arguments) behind public opinion (Gibson 2002; McLaren 2002; De Master and Le Roy 2000; see also Risse-Kappan 1996; Risse 2002). According to many scholarly accounts, utilitarian or rational (i.e., cost–benefit) concerns dominate the literature on European integration (Eichenberg and Dalton 1997: 6; Nelsen, Guth, and Fraser 2001), and tend to obscure the more affective considerations of belonging and identity that shape cultural boundaries. Elaborate cost–benefit analyses of public support for integration have made a persuasive case for the rational basis of attitudes toward economic integration (Gabel 1998a; Anderson 1995; Anderson and Reichert 1996; Gabel and Palmer 1995). Based on Zaller's thesis that cognitively mobilized or educated persons are more receptive to political messages (1992), Gabel concludes that assessments of personal material self-interest provide a source of distribution of public opinion (1998a: 123).[11] Immigration analysts have similarly adopted this view to argue that, even in cases where most of the political messages on an issue are similar, variation in public opinion on that subject may endure as a result of differences in citizens' levels of political awareness (McLaren 2001).

The results in my study confirm that attitudes toward immigrants or immigration cooperation appear to be not random, but based on informed views. There is sufficient evidence in the aggregate to suspect that knowing the number of immigrants in a country may tell us something about people's attitudes and orientations toward immigration, since perceptions have some basis in reality. Publics are more informed than migration scholars have assumed, but there are multiple aspects to their immigration concerns (e.g., racist, self-interest, or sociotropic assessments), which vary from rational to more emotive evaluations. In assessing attitudinal patterns, it is important to extricate ourselves from reductionist explanations of immigrant rejection. Certainly, unfettered xenophobia or symbolic racism is one version of exclusionism, which may defy "rationality" and distinguish attitudinal patterns. But other more "rational" motivations, such as self-interest and sociotropic considerations, must also be employed to explain immigration norms.

Regardless of levels of cognitive mobilization that we may impute to public opinion, the primacy of sociotropic concerns over self-interest motivations, as the findings in this study strikingly capture, is a testament to the more robust effects of the societal/non-personal dimension of immigration attitudes that exist. While these findings may legitimate immigrant opposition, they overcome the tendency to label all skepticism about immigration as racism.

These observations also underscore the affective–cultural dimension of immigration, and concur with research in the United States, which suggests that people's attitudes about immigration may be crystallized along both non-economic and non-racial lines (Gimpel and Edwards 1999: 314). Evaluations of the data would be incomplete without an understanding of Europeans' abstract beliefs or non-utilitarian calculations about general conditions.

Neither immigrant numbers alone nor opinion leadership, partisan politics, or personal unemployment situations – objective factors – entirely account for public policy preferences. Chapter 3 worked through the discrepancy in aggregate versus individual findings regarding immigrant numbers and rejection. It concluded that while objective indicators, such as immigrant numbers and types, matter it is only in the EU context that these factors assume meaning. One of the primary findings in my study pointed to the role of European integration itself in exacerbating attitudes toward nationally sensitive issues, such as immigration. The cultural/affective dimension of European integration is an intervening variable in discriminating attitudes to immigration. This is the key to unraveling the contradictory findings that numbers matter only in aggregate, not in individual, more personal responses.

A "conjunctural" argument, such as that adopted by Jeannette Money in her analysis of anti-immigrant sentiment at the local level, is useful in explaining the interactive effects of economics and culture or objective and subjective factors more generally (1999: 56–60). In her study, the assumption is that the interactive part of job competition comes not from the mere presence of migrants, but from their presence when unemployment rises (which is what creates labor-market competition). My analysis parallels and extends this logic in arguing that the EU serves as a contextual intervening variable that helps predict conditions under which rejection grows. That is, immigrant numbers and types begin to matter when concerns about community and identity are most prevalent. When attitudes toward Europe are unfavorable, the presence of immigrants and the uncertainty that they exacerbate add sure fuel to the protectionist anti-liberal fire. Empirically, the salience of identity politics has been linked to the increasing politicization of immigration in Europe and the revival in political fortunes of nationalist populist parties (Laffan 1996: 88). But the integration project channels these sensitivities (see Taggart 1998 on the EU's effects on identity politics and populism).

While the utilitarian aspects of European integration undeniably exist in the minds of publics and elites, these explanations neglect the more affective component of attitudes that Easton described as being integral to political stability (1965). This dimension of attitudes tends to underpin cultural factors and has an important effect on certain policy preferences in Europe (Inglehart 1990a; Putnam 1993; Huntington 1996). My analysis on European immigration policy reminds us that rationality is a complex term, and that utilitarian concerns may be more applicable to some issue areas than to others. The data show a European public and a legislative body that understand the benefits and necessity of dealing with immigration supranationally, but an unwillingness to accept the consequences of such an action – abdicating some national sovereignty. This impasse indicates that culture and identity matter to people.

Immigration remains tinged with cultural or societal considerations that correlate with more affective than instrumental evaluations of policy preferences. For example, while it is true that family income – a utilitarian measure of pocketbook self-interest – discriminates attitudes toward immigration for nearly 6 percent of opinion leaders, for the majority of less cognitively mobilized citizens, affective attitudes toward European integration (i.e., feeling European) or other more cultural factors such as religion were most prevalent in determining immigration attitudes (see chapter 5). To the extent that family income is a good operationalization of utilitarian concerns, they do not predict immigration attitudes.

We may infer from these findings that utilitarian aspects tap better into issue attitudes related to economic matters than into those areas related to culture, identity, and community, where affective (i.e., subjective) measures may better predict policy preferences. These distinctions are vividly exposed in chapter 3's breakdown of policy areas European citizens are prepared to delegate authority over to the EU. While a clear preference for either national control or European authority materializes in some policy areas, in others, such as immigration, defense, political asylum, agriculture, and fishing, public opinion is most polarized.

The primacy of cultural values is particularly pertinent to issues related to identity, such as immigration, asylum, and citizenship, and may account for substantial attitudinal variance. Hence, Ole Wæver astutely distinguished between political and cultural identity when he forewarned that "identity is the dangerous area where the [European] project can destruct if it challenges the nations in an overly confrontational manner" (1995: 430). In contrast, establishing a political identity does not threaten cultural identity, and therefore can be assumed to be less volatile.

The import of affective or cultural measures is a point worth articulating given its opaque treatment in the literature. Nelsen, Guth, and Fraser remind us that even economic accounts surreptitiously bring in cultural variables through the "back door" by the use of country variables (2001: 2). The diffuse power of political culture to constrain or promote common policy-making has been taken for granted, though it is rarely directly addressed.[12] Early integration theorists have implicitly referred to the role of diffuse norms and attitudes as a measure of integration and policy preferences (Deutsch *et al.* 1957; Haas 1958). More recently, these factors have been identified by Caporaso and Keeler as "one of the principal directions of theoretically interesting research" (1995: 49). Insofar as integration has prompted a shift in mass loyalties, this is founded on ideas and identity (Risse-Kappan 1996; Risse 2002), culture and sentiment (Sinnott 1995: 23) – though these factors are the most difficult to measure (Wallace 1990b: 9). Analysts of immigration would hardly disagree about the cultural effects on policy-making (Gimpel and Edwards 1999; Money 1999: 27–30; Stalker 1994; Leitner 1995; Zolberg 1981),[13] and face similar methodological challenges.[14] In their final analysis, Gimpel and Edwards conclude that "particularly important, but difficult to measure, are attitudes toward cultural differences among groups that are separable from racial attitudes" (1999: 314).

If regional integration promotes cooperation in the economic sphere, then to what extent can we expect some form of "functional spillover" in the migration domain? As one scholar of European refugee policy well captured, the degree to which such cooperation is likely to occur depends not only on institutional reforms in the sense of a reaffirmation of the "Community method," but also on the Union's ability to develop a "community of values" (Lavenex 2001: 852). These claims return us to March and Olsen's critical distinctions between formal and informal structures (1989), and the notion that Europeanization refers to insitutionalization both of action and of meaning (Olsen 2000). As the European project evolves from a limited project of economic interaction and exchange to a political union and a "community of values," normative frameworks become more essential. For this reason, my study on immigration attitudes in the EU shifts our attention from the more rational/economic models traditionally applied to regional integration to emphasize norms and informal structures as more fruitful avenues of analysis.

Celebrating a Europe emergent?

There is a tendency among the media and even some scholars to declare a festival around a unified Europe. My analysis of immigration attitudes in the EU suggests that it may be appropriate to postpone these celebrations and reconsider some of the obstacles or complexities involved, and the values such Europeanization engenders. That European integration is progressing at a herculean speed cannot be denied. What this means for migration and asylum types of issues – those that touch the core of European identity – requires clarification. What can developments on the immigration front tell us about an integrated Europe, or about theories of integration? The effects of European integration on one policy area of key Europe-wide concern tell an important story about the paradoxical nature of globalization and regional integration more generally.

In attempting to sort through the debate between realist and neofunctional visions of Europe, my study provided enough evidence of supranational policy-making norms to neutralize the strong national interests that drive whatever intergovernmental vestiges of migration and asylum policy remain. Chapter 3 made an important revelation about the nature of public support and opposition. The data show that public support for immigration cooperation does not precede but rather follows policy initiatives. Policy breakthrough on immigration – as it relates to a public constituency – follows the signing of major treaties. Elite and mass opinion follows events. Regional integration seems to strengthen immigration cooperation, and inspires further integration. That a common immigration policy is associated with integration in other policy areas is supportive of the spillover predictions made by neofunctionalists, historical institutionalists, and European integrationists.

It may be argued that, under conditions of regional integration, the weight of issues such as immigration grows as political conflicts shift from socioeconomic redistribution to new security (both social and cultural) concerns. Given the way the EU apparatus has expanded and the growing perception by domestic constituencies of immigration as a threat emanating from the international environment, what is interesting is not that immigration issues have become increasingly politicized but that patterns of regulation are increasingly conforming to national public policy models which are converging in the world.

These observations lend support to the hypothesis that immigration policy is an area in which states may indeed defer to international regimes, defined by Steven Krasner as principles, norms, rules, and decision-making procedures around which actor expectations converge in a given issue area (1982; Ruggie 1982). This of course precipitates questions concerning which actors may be ultimately responsible for overseeing such a regime (as has been the case with the General Agreement on Tariffs and Trade or the International Monetary Fund for trade and finance or the office of the United Nations High Commissioner for Refugees for refugee movement), and what types of substantive values would characterize such a system. Answers to these questions run somewhat counter to our common understanding of regimes, and they account for my tempered enthusiasm about European integration.

The construction of an immigration regime in Europe deviates from both liberal and realist accounts of cooperation. The stereotyping of these camps into state-centric versus supranationally/internationally driven forces undermines the level of compatibility that exists among both explanations of European integration. While the former has neglected the compatibility of national interests, and the prospects for supranational cooperation, the latter has overlooked the fact that cooperation may reinforce national interests and open up new channels and opportunities for control. Transnational regulation may be less than "liberal" – serving to *inhibit* immigration rather than promote it.

Reconsider the evolution of immigration cooperation in the EU. It is noteworthy, for example, that the concept of a "people's and social Europe" first appeared in the early 1970s, when immigration was being halted for the first time in postwar Europe, due to oil crises and ensuing recession. An analogue to this came in the Maastricht Treaty agreed upon in 1991, when the concept of "European citizenship" was officially introduced as the Treaty formally recognized the need for a serious common immigration policy. In earlier days, the rights of EC nationals to free movement within the Community was one of the most contentious items in the enlargement negotiations leading to the accession of Greece, Spain, and Portugal (which were considered the weak link to external frontiers) to EC Treaties. Today, EU membership extension eastward to countries such as Hungary, Poland, and the Czech and Slovak Republics is tied to immigration control considerations as well as economic issues. Similarly, Turkey's admissions calculations augur alarming demographic projections for EU policy-makers (Teitelbaum and Martin 2003).[15]

Negotiations for Schengen membership reveal the same restrictive motivations underlying cooperation. The applications of Italy, Spain, Portugal, and Greece to join the Schengen Group were delayed by the five founding members (also known as the "fast-track countries"), which sought guarantees of serious immigration control before granting full membership (see chapter 2). After 1985, there was a notable trend toward institutionalization of migration at the EU level, especially as the Schengen "lab" was reincarnated to envelop the entire EU. The abolition of internal borders within the EC was explicitly linked to "compensatory measures" in external border control policies, and the fields of immigration and asylum (Guiraudon 2000a: 254). Even as the EU has pushed farther to communitarize the third pillar in the Amsterdam Treaty, it is at the behest of frustrated states, concerned by the "uncertainty" and "enforcement problems" of intergovernmental arrangements (Hooghe and Marks 2001: 22). These trends capture the spirit of cooperative initiatives, and suggest that the analogue to an integrated Europe with open markets for trade is a common immigration policy based on secured borders.

This study reminds us that, insofar as convergence is based on compatible interests to secure effective state control over migration, cooperation may bolster – not compromise – state sovereignty. If one recalls the European Coal and Steel Community, the customs unions, or even the original basis of the Schengen agreements – early attempts to regulate areas of conflict between states, and to ensure effectiveness of free movement by coordinating policies – then the program for a common immigration policy assumes a restrictive character. Indeed, with specific exceptions (e.g., guest-worker programs, the US Bracero program) cooperation on migration has existed predominantly in the form of prevention (Münz 1996: 14; Huysmans 2000: 756; Kostakopoulou 2000). This is also true of refugee matters, which have been shown to be less about establishing a common European asylum system, and more about reducing migration pressures and compensating for the perceived losses of internal security resulting from a frontier-free Europe (Joppke 1998a, 1998c; Lavenex 2001: 869). To consider international and transnational organizations as an *opportunity* for, rather than a *constraint* on, nation-states' regulatory power corroborates the rare but practical view that states may act more effectively by joining transnational institutions (Miall 1993: 52–53) or by delegating authority to supranational actors (Lahav 1998; Guiraudon and Lahav 2000).

The implications expose a converse relationship between European integration and immigration policy that contrasts with the unilinear conceptualizations of globalization and regional integration. It is plausible that globalization assumes diverse patterns in different sectors, depending on the respective asset specificity structures of those sectors (Cerny 1995). In other words, as labor is a specific asset (especially workers as people, as partially distinct from more abstract "labor processes"), states retain and even extend their capability and interests to intervene. In many cases, states may even find their political will to do so increasing as migration issues and other integration costs become more politicized as part of a backlash against globalization and regional integration in other sectors. In nationally sensitive areas such as immigration, cooperation may be marked by more protectionist impulses. This claim goes beyond the conventional understanding of international regimes. It is a prelude to all policy areas, which are particularly relevant to security in a changing Europe.

While there are strong economic and demographic pressures to open borders, the political momentum for greater restriction is paramount. The appeal of migration in light of reemerging concerns about population aging and decline at the turn of the twenty-first century needs to be reconciled with public reservations about migrants – especially in the wake of September 11 – and with the mounting security concerns associated with the movement of persons. These cross-pressures have affected all advanced industrialized democracies, but are particularly salient in Europe, which is simultaneously dealing with deepening and widening (to Central and Eastern Europe) integration. In considering the trends revealed in my study, we may postulate that since policy-makers are relatively mindful of public opinion, and given their inclination to think in short-term frames, it is unlikely that they will impose unpopular measures if they will not harvest the results.

Through a normative prism, then, this book shows how the issue of immigration does not fit the usual assumptions about European integration at all. Growing interdependence and developments associated with Europeanization or globalization do not necessarily lead to expansive or open free movement regimes. The development of a common immigration regime does not preclude, and may even strengthen, the ability of states to maintain their own national and ideological interests on issues as sensitive as immigration. These trends have prospects for the establishment of an international migration regime, one oriented to protectionism and contrary to principles of free trade that govern the regime for capital, goods, services, and information. This argument revises the image offered by conventional theorists of globalization who have overlooked the growing compatibility of transnational norms and domestic interests, more particularly the role of the EU in bolstering national interests.

NOTES

1. For early attitudinal perspectives, see Lerner and Gorden 1969.
2. In Switzerland, for example, citizen initiatives have put migration-related items on referendum ballots. The one scheduled in 2002 was poised to pass as one of the most restrictive immigrant and asylum policies in Europe.

3. Indeed, for some countries, such as France, these groups are far better represented within the European Parliament than in the national legislature. On the basis of garnering 5.7 percent of the national vote for the 1999–2004 assembly of the European Parliament, the Front national gained five MEPs in Brussels. In comparison, although the FN received 11.3 percent of the vote in the French National Assembly elections in 2002, it did not place a single representative.

4. In the broadest sense of the term, I am referring to the representativeness of elite attitudes as measured by their similarity to the overall attitudes of the public (see Weissberg 1978; Dalton 2002; Bardi 1991).

5. "National traditions" have been found to exert a significant impact on support for the EU and for various policy domains, even when a multitude of other factors is included in a multivariate model (Eichenberg and Dalton 1993; Dalton and Eichenberg 1998: 256; Hix 2001a: 677; Deflem and Pampel 1996).

6. This is primarily a principal–agent theoretical model which comes from the work of O. E. Williamson (1975, 1993) on transaction costs. The principal–agent model has been used in political science to understand such diverse phenomena as congressional committees, courts, and regulatory agencies. For a review of that literature in the US case, see Moe 1984; Shepsle and Weingast 1994. For application to European integration, see Garrett 1995; Garrett and Weingast 1993; Pollack 1997. For a critical corrective, see Pierson 1996. See also Bendor, Glazer, and Hammond (2001) for a review of theoretical work on delegation in political science, and Epstein and O'Halloran (1999) for application to US politics.

7. Personal communication with Bill Newton Dunn MEP, substitute minister for the Committee on Citizens' Freedoms and Justice and Home Affairs (February 25, 2000).

8. Institutional dynamics capture the "balancing act" that exists with regard to integration-related issues. Consider for example, the "soft option" taken by the 1989 Report of the European Committee on Racism and Xenophobia (Fekete 1991: 148). In essence, the Report examined the topics in isolation, as extreme movements, rather than within the framework of the European body politic. According to some critics, the latter approach was followed in order to avoid looking at racism in a national context and/or making judgments about each country's immigration policy. An earlier report by the Runnymede Trust, a British non-profit group, sponsored by the European Commission, was abandoned on the grounds that it was "unwilling to enter into conflict with the Member States" (ibid.). The conflict between national and supranational interests affected the resolve of the 1989 Report as well; the Committee had agreed to a compromise whereby the European Commission was asked to "study seriously" the report's recommendations, rather than "endorse" them.

9. Although there has been some success with regard to anti-discrimination legislation, there is clear evidence of a disjuncture between policy adopted at the EU level and national paradigms, including discourse and opinion (Geddes and Guiraudon 2002; see also Bleich 2002 for national frames and anti-race policies).

10. Known best for his comments downplaying the actions of the Nazis and for his anti-immigrant rhetoric, Haider was thought to be a potential roadblock to both EU expansion and immigration. Consequently, EU member-states threatened to isolate Austria.

11. Education, occupational skills, and income level tend to be positively related to level of political awareness and political sophistication. According to Gabel, the evidence in support of the human capital and income hypotheses may be explained by differences in citizens' levels of political knowledge and cognitive skills (1998a: 93).

12. For a useful review of political culture, public opinion, and regimes, see Sinnott 1995: 24–27.

13. According to Stalker, how a country regards itself – its own national mythology – is perhaps the most fundamental factor in defining levels of tolerance (1994: 138).

14. My study attempts to overcome some of these methodological difficulties by operationalizing culture in the immigration equation through national traditions, homogeneity, religious predominance, GDP, and immigrant populations (see appendix A).

15. They include projections of 20 to 30 percent of the country's young people moving to test the EU labor markets, and trepidations that, if it were admitted to the EU, Turkey would become the most populous country of the EU by 2014 (Teitelbaum and Martin 2003).

Appendix A: Data collection and methodology

The opinion data in this research derive from two sources: mass surveys and profiles of elite attitudes. Each is described below.

1. Public opinion data

The public opinion data come from Eurobarometer studies provided by the Inter-university Consortium for Political and Social Research (ICPSR), located at the University of Michigan. In 1974, the Commission of the European Communities initiated the series, designed to provide regular monitoring of social and political attitudes of the publics within the EU. These have generated longitudinal and comparative data on controversial issues, including immigration, xenophobia, and race, as well as European integration. They are used here to provide some comparative context for national, ideological, and other polarizations that have evolved over the post-World War II period. Conducted biannually, these surveys consist of batteries of items repeated each year as well as special topics. Since the special issue on immigration and xenophobia in 1988/89, the spring Eurobarometer has consistently included a few questions related to immigration and immigrant groups. Not all questions are asked each year.[1]

Eurobarometers 30, 35, 36, 37, 38, 38.1, 39, 40, 41, 42, 43.1, 44.2, 46, 47.1, 47.2, 48, 49, and 50 were most useful for this study. They range in date from 1988 to 1998. The questions included: (1) in 1988 (*Eurobarometer* 30), entire survey;[2] (2) 1991 (35), q27; (3) 1991 (36), q93; (4) 1992 (37), q44, q70, q73; (5) 1992 (38), q12B, q34, q40, q52; (6) 1992 (38.1), q19E; (7) 1993 (39), qq31–38, q58A, B; (8) 1993 (40), q35, qq67–70, q72, q77; (9) 1994 (41), q24; (10) 1994 (42), q30, q36, q79A, B, q82, q84, q85; (11) 1995 (43.1), qq28–30, q41; (12) 1996 (44.2), q23, q26; (13) 1996 (46), q13, qq66–67; (14) 1997 (47.1), numbering online *www.europa.int*, questions related to unemployment, well-being, and trust; (15) 1997 (47.2), q50, q53; (16) 1997 (48), q27, q33, q53; (17) 1998 (49), q26, q36; (18) 1999 (50), q39, q50. In addition, a special report commissioned by the European Commission compared general public opinion (based on *Eurobarometer* 45.1, 1996) and "top decision-makers" (Commission of the European Communities 1996) and thus provided for the first time a direct appraisal of mass – elite correspondence.

Despite and because of the reliance here on the Eurobarometer surveys to measure public opinion in Europe, their patent methodological limitations and shortcomings are worthy of comment. First, while many of the study's questions are driven by the scientific concern of its chief investigators (i.e., Inglehart, Rabier), the fact that they are sponsored by the European Communities means that one should be cautious about inferring policy motivations from them (e.g., to promote European integration). Second, these policy orientations may limit the range of subjects covered, and may even affect the wording of questions (see Niedermayer and Sinnott 1995b: 4). Third, word changes throughout the series render some questions incomparable, and make it difficult to discern the source of attitudinal trends. I have noted this problem in the appropriate places in the text. Finally, there are a number of critiques on the use of certain measures, particularly materialist/postmaterialist (see Davis and Davenport 1999; Clarke *et al.* 1999). With these caveats in mind, I proceed cautiously on the positive merits of the instrument. That is, Eurobarometer generates data that are unquestionably strong in terms of the large range of individuals surveyed, and that are analyzable both cross-sectionally and longitudinally (see Niedermayer and Sinnott 1995b for a more detailed critique of the surveys).

2.   Elite data

In addition to a randomly selected sample of national and European elites, the bulk of systematic elite data derives from 167 surveys of members of the European Parliament (MEPs) conducted in 1992–93, and fifty-four one-to-one interviews. There was some overlap between those interviewed and those surveyed, but not all interviewees responded to the questionnaire. With a survey of a sample of European policy-makers, one can make statements about the distribution of attitudes and opinions across party and nation-state lines. With personal interviews, one can inquire into the motivations and expectations that guide behavior (Putnam 1971; Axelrod 1977; Dalton 2002: 2). While we may probe patterns by examining roll-call votes (see Hix 2001a), these are extremely limited because such votes are often not used on important issues facing the European legislature (see Zellentin 1967).

The European Parliament (EP), the legislative organ of the European Union and the only directly elected body in the EU, provides an ideal forum to examine national, partisan/ideological, and transnational allegiances at work. This organ, more than any other in the EU, strives to transcend nation-state lines and promote integration. Here, members represent both nation-state and political parties, but by seating members according to party groups, the Parliament aims to foster some type of consensual thinking based on transnational ideological positions. Even if we agree that the EP is not the quintessential power-holder of the EU system, we cannot overlook the momentum associated with the introduction of the co-decision procedure, adopted by the Treaty of Maastricht and simplified by the Amsterdam Treaty.[3] The drive to reduce the EU's "democratic deficit" bodes well for the only purely representative body of the EU.

The European Parliament represents a microcosm of interests of European leaders, as they discuss the prevailing issues of the day (see also Abélès 1992 for an insightful cultural-anthropological study of the European Parliament). While the influence of members of the European Parliament has been debatable, the factor most pertinent to the analysis here is their role as directly elected deputies. Although the EP does not explicitly create a government, a function typical of other legislatures, it consists of a group of individuals who know each other, communicate in elite dialogue, and work toward promoting certain commonly held viewpoints in parliamentary discussion and voting (Corbett, Jacobs, and Shackleton 2000). Regardless of the strength of the EP, the fact remains that "parliaments are, after all 'talking shop'" (Putnam 1973: 26–27). Like those of traditional parliamentarians, MEPs' discussions and attitudes reflect the parameters of debate. European Parliamentarians provide more than a measure of institutional predominance in the EU; they also provide a crosscultural measure of elite thinking.

The study's questions measured attitudes toward the traditional dimensions of the immigration problem along two policy streams (intake and incorporation), in addition to issues regarding transnational regulation. For ease of comparison, the questions replicated those asked in Eurobarometer public opinion surveys. However, in some cases, wording was modified for sample/subject sensitivity. Thus, while it may be appropriate to gauge public attitudes by asking about immigrant numbers, decision-makers respond better to policy-related questions which may involve policy direction (i.e., increase, decrease, etc. [see also Rockman 1976]). In this way, they are being engaged on policy-based attitudes, rather than being treated as "bricklayers," as opinion researchers have been accused of treating them (see Brown 1969).

In order to probe the issue further, in-depth interviews with fifty-four MEPs were conducted. These open-ended interviews varied in length from forty minutes to four hours. They were taped and coded for content analysis. The questionnaires as well as the oral interviews were conducted in English, French, or Italian.

In order to reduce the distortion of issue salience of immigration, question sequence intentionally interspersed random policy questions. In assessing issue attachments, the assumption of attitudinal research is that what people report on a given issue is as important to the respondent in everyday life as it is to the researcher. For example, the survey question-naires and in-depth interviews on immigration attitudes with MEPs in this study presume that elites consider the issue an important one, an assumption that is borne out by the data. However, MEPs may vary greatly in how attached they are to the issue, regardless of how informed or articulate their responses. Ascertaining the level of impor-tance attached to immigration is crucial for evaluating other related attitudes. Hypothetically, for example, a study on attitudes toward the role of the Roman Catholic Church would need to consider that among a sample of Catholics there is a distinction between practicing members and non-active ones. These differences must be weighed accordingly. Similarly, all MEPs have certain ideas about immigration, but not all start from the same premise; the issue is more important to some than to others. As the previous chapters described, countries vary in their phases of immigration development, and this may affect national perceptions of issue salience. Such attachment determines the tone, depth, intensity, and value of other convictions regarding the issue. Expressions of impor-tance may also suggest where, in the minds of elites and masses, the issue is placed on the political agenda. This factor provides what is referred to as the contextual nature of other answers.

The elite study attempted to measure the importance attached to the immigration issue in two ways: closed-ended questions in a survey; and open-ended questions in an interview. Since the survey question-naire is predominantly concerned with immigration-related questions, respondents are forced to focus on that issue. To overcome this method-ological bias, the oral interviews, conducted weeks after the distribution of the questionnaire, began by first surveying ideas on random issues (see chapters 3–5).

In order to account for the effects of national differences and to facil-itate quantitative analysis, country names were replaced by theoretical concepts (Przeworski and Teune 1970). The analysis of MEP attitudes taps into national *and* partisan interests of EU legislators. The following two sections discuss each in more depth.

A.   National representation

National tendencies are promoted in various ways. First, several MEPs are well-established national politicians.[4] Although dual mandates are not permitted in six member-states, thirty-four MEPs of the third parliamentary session were still members of the national parliaments. In 1990 (the time span of the research sample), approximately 150 MEPs were former national parliamentarians, 7 were former heads of state or government, 73 held ministerial office, 24 held national party leadership, and 60 were involved in regional or local government (Corbett, Jacobs, and Shackleton 1992: 47–48). Second, MEPs are elected directly every five years in each of the EU member-states. They campaign on national issues. Studies have shown that the majority of electorates in EP elections consider the national political situation more than the European issue (Mayer 1993: 7). Many observers have regarded the European elections as "second-order national contests" that are dominated by domestic political concerns and national political actors (van der Eijk and Franklin 1996). In cases where national elections have coincided with EP elections, voting patterns have been similar, suggesting that voters themselves do not make a distinction between them. In sum, the EP seems to mirror national struggles.

B.   Party and ideological representation

In operationalizing party and ideological variables, I consider both ideological self-placement and party identification. Political party groups are defined as coalitions with shared ideological traditions, which also identified themselves as such at the EP. These transnational parties have been grouped according to the way they form links across national frontiers. Parliament in the third assembly was divided into nine political groups (excluding the Independents) which represented nearly eighty different national political parties. These loose party groups represented the traditional European political families. Some, such as the Liberals, Democrats, and Reformists (LDR), Christian Democrats (PPE), and Socialists are parties that go as far back as June 1953, under the Common Assembly established by the European Coal and Steel Community. More recently, electoral reforms and social changes in Western Europe have led to the advent of new political groups to broaden representation of new interests. These include the European Right (DR), Communist groups, and other more nationally based movements.[5] Most of the transnational parties have federations or worldwide organizations, which enhance political affinity among groups and are responsible for promoting party activities (see Pridham and Pridham 1981: 93).

The analysis here focuses on six clusters of party groups: (1) Greens; (2) GUE/CG (Communists); (3) Socialists; (4) PPE/RDE (Christian Democrats and Republican Conservatives); and (5) DR (Radical Right). These groups constitute the most relevant political players in almost all of the national party systems. For ideological and historical reasons, the two communist parties are grouped together even though they do not share the same approaches to communism. Similarly, if not for nationalist reasons, the largely French RDE would be joined with the PPE. They are thus treated here as a party group cluster.

Due to the special nature of institutional structures and other arrangements adopted by the Union (e.g., direct elections and the absence, in some cases, of real constituencies), party discipline and pressure to conform are greatly minimized. One may expect more independence in the EP than in national parliaments because failure to toe the party line does not have the same consequences (i.e., the survival or defeat of the government) as at the national level (Fitzmaurice 1975: 163). The absence of structural and situational constraints that often counterbalance the impact of elite beliefs in other institutional settings facilitates an examination of ideological sources of attitudes.

3.   Survey questionnaire

See appendix C for survey instruments.

The sample group was representative of all countries and parties in the EP (see figures A.1 and A.2). Although in some cases the small size of the cells precluded tests of statistical significance, percentages were suggestive of differences. In addition, the sample size is substantial, considering high rates of absenteeism; in actuality even the 260 votes (required for the EP's second reading amendment power) constituted a two-thirds majority of members present at the time (Tsebelis 1992: 2, 1994).

4.   Statistical methods

Various statistical methods were used to help analyze the data. The most common procedures were bivariate or multivariate regressions. A chi-square test and gamma measures of association were also employed. Regressions proved useful in any context where one or more variable(s) may have had a causal relationship with another variable. These tests yielded information on the statistical and substantive significance of a relationship between the independent variable(s) and a dependent

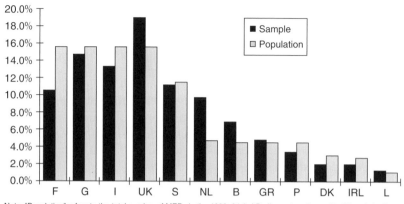

Note: "Population" refers to the total number of MEPs in the 1989–94 3rd Parliamentary Assembly. "Sample" refers to those MEPs who were included in the sample for this study.

Figure A.1 MEP sample, representation by country

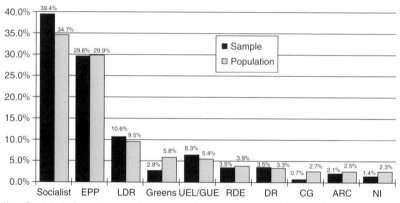

Note: "Population" refers to the total number of MEPs in the 1989–94 3rd Parliamentary Assembly. "Sample" refers to those MEPs who were included in the sample for this study.
EPP = European People's Party; LDR = Liberal, Democratic and Reformist; UEL/GUE = United European Left;
RDE = European Democratic Alliance; DR = Technical Group of the European Right; CG = Left Unity; ARC = Rainbow;
NI = Independent.

Figure A.2 MEP sample, representation by party group

variable. When no causal mechanism was a priori assumed, a chi-square test was used to determine the likelihood that two variables were related in the population. A gamma measure of association was employed to gauge the direction and strength of a relationship between two discrete variables.

At times, running regressions for the MEP data was problematic due to the low n-size (number of respondents in the survey). To overcome

Table A.1 *Nation operationalized*

	Position on level of immigration
GDP	.234[1]
	.026[2]
	(.056)[3]
Non-EU	.242
	.03
	(.042)
Region	.220
	.024
	(.065)
Religion	.125
	.004
	(.462)

[1] OLS coefficient.
[2] r^2.
[3] Significance.

this, dummy variable regressions were often employed. Dummy variables (coded 0 and 1) were used to recode the categories of an independent variable so that the n-size per category in the variable would be sufficiently large for statistical testing.

5.   Nation operationalized

In order to account for national variations, and conduct statistical analysis, an effort was made to operationalize the fifteen European countries (see chapters 3–5). Several approaches were tested. Table A.1 shows the various operationalizations of the nations the MEPs come from. For all regressions on elite data, there was no information for Austria, Finland, and Sweden (nations that entered the EU after completion of the MEP surveys).

This first regression operationalized the nations by GDP per head, with the average GDP being $16,733 across the twelve nations. Therefore, any nation that had a GDP per capita of less than this amount was coded 0 (Greece, Spain, Portugal, and the UK), while nations with a GDP per head of more than this amount were coded 1 (Belgium, Denmark, Germany, France, Ireland, Italy, Luxembourg, and the Netherlands) (Eurostat 1997: 11). The regression proves to be nearly statistically significant with a p-value of .056. However, its real-world significance is small, with only 2.6 percent of the variance in attitudes toward level of immigration being accounted for by whether or not the MEP's nation had above or below the average GDP per head.

In the next regression, the MEPs' nations were coded 0 if less than 2.03 percent of the population were non-EU foreigners (Greece, Italy, Ireland, Luxembourg, Portugal, Spain, UK). Otherwise, the nations were coded 1 (Belgium, Denmark, Germany, France, Netherlands). A slightly stronger relationship is shown here, with a statistical significance at the standard .05 level and an r^2 of 3 percent. Note that OLS coefficients may be signed differently here than was the case in chapter 5, because the dummy variables were coded differently than in the regression shown in table 5.2. The demographic figures were based on the 1992 count (shown in table 4.3) rather than more recent demographic trends (reported in chapters 2 and 3 and appendix E) in an effort to correspond to the timeframe of the elite and public surveys.

The regression for region is broken down according to the core/North and periphery/South countries and the immigration–emigration operationalization. Greece, Italy, Ireland, Portugal, and Spain make up the South/periphery or emigration nations, while Belgium, Denmark, Germany, France, Luxembourg, the Netherlands, and the UK constitute the core/North or immigration nations. This regression is similar in strength to the first regression in which nations were operationalized by GDP per head. Since this regression deals with nominal variables, and is not based on hard numbers, it is easily manipulable. Further, the operationalization of nations using proportions of non-EU foreigners proves slightly stronger.

The weakest regression came about when nations were operationalized by religion. Since MEPs from Austria, Finland, and Sweden could not be represented (because they did not exist in the original MEP data file), only two nations were coded 1 for Protestant (Denmark and the UK). All other nations were coded 0 because, based on the nation profiles, they were either a majority or plurality Catholic (see appendix D). The low n-size for the variable coded Protestant should be noted, as it is likely to partially account for the weakness of this regression.

For some regressions, I have coded nations using the percentage of non-EU foreigners. This is the strongest relationship and among the most easily justified.

6.   European integration operationalized

The literature on public opinion regarding European integration has made use of Easton's "affective" (ideological or non-material beliefs) and "utilitarian" (cost–benefit) distinctions (1965, 1975; see Hix 1999b: 138–139 and Gabel 1998a for fuller discussion) to discern attitudinal patterns (see chapter 5). The Eurobarometer polls have consistently contained questions that tap into both identity and benefit types of support, and have therefore facilitated measurement. Nonetheless, classification of these orientations has been difficult. What exactly they measure has been contentious, and therefore a general index of European integration attitudes is warranted. To gauge attitudes toward European integration that capture both these measures, I created a factor score from a principal-components analysis of the following five questions (*Eurobarometer* 30, 1988):

> v520: "In general, are you for or against efforts being made to unify Western Europe?"
> v521: "Generally speaking, do you think that (your country's) membership of the European Community is (a good thing, neither good nor bad, bad thing)?"
> v522: "Taking everything into consideration, would you say that (your country) has on balance benefited or not from being a member of the European Community?"
> v523: "If you were to be told tomorrow that the European Community had been scrapped, would you be very sorry about it, indifferent, or relieved?"
> v524: "Do you ever think of yourself not only as a (nationality) citizen but also as a citizen of Europe?"

The 1988 survey is used because of the comparability of questions on the immigration theme (see n. 2, appendix A).

7.   Policy analysis

The policy component of the analysis derives from published key texts by the European Communities, Schengen Group, Ad Hoc Group on Immigration, OECD/SOPEMI, reports as well as secondary sources. The original data have been tracked from 1985 to 2000, after the Single European Act, and were obtained from the European Parliament, Commission, Court of Justice, and Schengen libraries in Brussels, Strasbourg, and Luxembourg. Some materials derive from political party headquarters archives in Paris and London.

NOTES

1. A summary of goals and parameters of the series can be found at the ICPSR web site (http://www.icpsr.umich.edu/), archive search for Eurobarometer.

2. This was a prime early database, since it was the first survey dedicated explicitly to the theme of migration. A Eurobarometer Report on Racism, Xenophobia, and Intolerance, published by the Commission of the European Communities, was based on a sample of 11,795 individuals in the then twelve European Community countries.

3. This has given the Parliament the power to adopt instruments jointly with the Council, and has strengthened its legislative powers in the following fields: the free movement of workers, right of establishment, services, internal market, education, health, consumer policy, trans-European networks, environment, culture, and research (Article 251 of the EC Treaty, formerly Article 189b). The Treaty of Amsterdam extended the procedure to new areas such as social exclusion, public health, and the fight against fraud. See www.europa.eu.int.

4. In this sample, for example, Jean-Marie Le Pen, Leon Schwartzenberg, and Franz von Stauffenberg are among a few prominent national figures.

5. While the Italian Communist group (GUE) merged with the Socialist group after the data were collected, this development was anticipated by the findings, as the GUE group consistently converged with the Socialists in their ideological profile. Thus, on an ideological scale from 1 to 9, where 1 represents the extreme left and 9 the extreme right, the average self-placement of the GUE group was 3.11. The mean of the Socialist group was 3.05. The Green party group placed itself further left (mean = 2.50) than both.

Appendix B: Comparing different measures of attitudes

In formulating the relationship between what people think and how they may be expected to behave, attitudinal research on immigration needs to be sensitive to issues such as social desirability, accessibility, and intensity of responses. Building on theories of perceived behavioral control, recent public opinion studies have reaffirmed the view that attitudes predict behaviors when they are highly accessible in the perception process (i.e., they come to mind quickly), independent even of direction and intensity.[1] While it is true that attitudes that are highly accessible are more likely to guide perception and therefore behavior, it is imperative to recognize that there is a myriad of other factors that may inhibit or promote behaviors.

Social norms are especially important in attitudinal studies engaged in sensitive issues. The classic study of the Chinese couple travelling across the United States, conducted by Richard La Piere in the 1930s, revealed how social norms can inhibit behaviors that are thought to derive from attitudes.[2] A thorny problem of all attitudinal research is that of the socially desirable responses. Asking people about issues as politically sensitive as minorities and migrant groups is telling (Hewstone 1986: 50). One way of overcoming the methodological bias of socially desirable responses is to ask people to project about the attitudes of their reference groups. My study on immigration, for example, has considered that publics and elites may more readily report the views of their colleagues and compatriots than their own. It follows the logic captured by a French poll in the mid-1980s, which confirmed that it was easier to label "others" than oneself. While most Frenchmen denied being racist themselves, 71 percent of French polled considered Frenchmen to be racist.[3]

Evidence of this phenomenon exists among the European public as well. Figure B.1 shows that, while only 33 percent of the European public label themselves a 4 to 10 on a 10-point racism scale (where 1 is not at all racist and 10 is very racist), almost twice that number (65 percent) express the racist sentiment that more minority immigration would be problematic for their nation. These respondents believe their

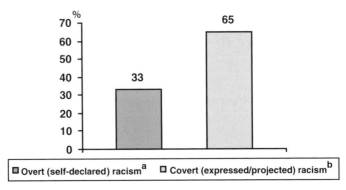

Source (n-size): *Eurobarometer* 47.1, 1997 (16,154).
a. In accordance with a European Commission report, these data include all those respondents who labeled themselves a 4 to 10 on a 10-point racism scale, where 1 is "not at all racist," 2–3 are "a little racist," 4–6 are "quite racist," and 7–10 are "very racist."
b. Those agreeing "our country has reached its limits; if there were to be more people belonging to these minority groups, we would have problems."

Figure B.1 Overt vs. covert expressions of racism

fellow nationals to be much more racist than they readily admit to be themselves. National breakdowns reinforce these discrepancies and expose the chasm between self-declared or overt racism and projections of other compatriots, what may be conceived as covert racism or symbolic racism (see figures B.1–B.3).

The tendency to understate one's own feelings toward minority groups may be compared to broader assessments of intolerance in country context (see figure B.2). Levels of self-declared racism by country are lower than the projections made by national respondents with regard to the positions of minority groups in their national job markets. Indirectly, the response spread in figure B.3 suggests that people can attribute discrimination to their fellow nationals while extricating themselves from feelings of racism.

With the exception of Austria, public opinion in all countries was more likely to sympathize with the plight of immigrants in the national job market than to label themselves racist (figure B.3 above). I explore these contradictions in the text, while being sensitive to methodological difficulties.

Again, we must heed caution about methodological biases (see appendix A). Interpretations generated by the evidence need to be examined on a country-by-country basis. For example, according to the data above, one may conclude that Belgium is one of the most racist

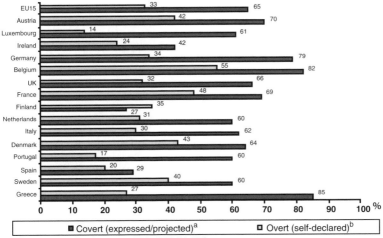

Source (n-size): *Eurobarometer* 47.1, 1997 (16,154).

a. Those agreeing "our country has reached its limits; if there were to be more people belonging to these minority groups, we would have problems."

b. In accordance with a European Commission report, these data include all those respondents who labeled themselves a 4 to 10 on a 10-point racism scale, where 1 is "not at all racist," 2–3 are "a little racist," 4–6 are "quite racist," and 7–10 are "very racist."

Figure B.2 Overt vs. covert expressions of racism, by country

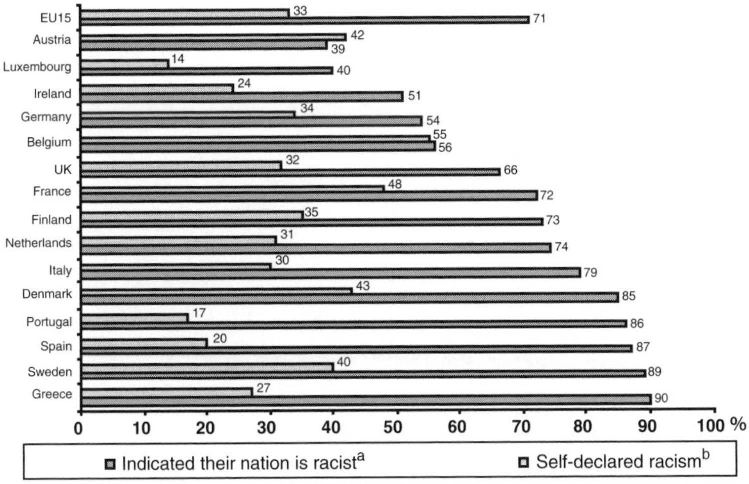

Source (n-size): *Eurobarometer* 47.1, 1997 (16,154).

a. Those agreeing that "people from minority groups are discriminated against in the job market."

b. In accordance with a European Commission report, these data include all those respondents who labeled themselves a 4 to 10 on a 10-point racism scale, where 1 is "not at all racist," 2–3 are "a little racist," 4–6 are "quite racist," and 7–10 are "very racist."

Figure B.3 Self-declared vs. national projections of racism, by country

countries in Europe. This finding needs to be contextualized to consider that Belgians who called themselves racist may do so as a result of their views toward other Belgians (i.e., their rival Flemish or Walloons). It is an example that can be more broadly extended, and hence the comparability of the data needs to be considered carefully.

NOTES

1. See Glynn *et al.* 1999: 129–133; Fishbein and Ajzen 1980; Ajzen 1991.
2. Richard La Piere's classic study (1934) found that a Chinese couple in the 1930s could travel across the country and be accepted without prejudice into all but one of the hotels, camps, and restaurants they visited. This was despite the fact that surveys of the people in those institutions found a vast majority (92 percent) who said they would not accept Chinese people as guests. Respondents did not behave in the way that their attitudes might predict. From this widely cited example, we recognize just one of the factors that make the attitudes/behavior link so elusive.
3. *Paris Match* (November 1984 poll, cited by Diana Geddes, in *The Times*, December 2, 1984). A contrasting version of this was found in a recent experimental psychological study of college students' attitudes toward affirmative action programs (see Van Boven 2000). The study found that respondents were less supportive of affirmative action programs than they believed their fellow students to be. The author concluded that this belief was due to projections of political correctness. This factor may also be involved in the MEP sample in this study, which revealed more favorable attitudes toward immigrants attributed to colleagues than to themselves.

Appendix C: Questionnaire and survey

English-language letter accompanying questionnaire

Dear Member:

The Center for European Studies at the City University of New York is concerned to develop in the United States a greater understanding of the European Community, and especially of the European Parliament. I write to seek your assistance in that endeavor.

In studying the European Parliament at this time, our goal is to build a base from which to trace its development over time. To that end, we are conducting a study of the current members' perspectives and policy preferences regarding one of the most challenging issues facing the Community, i.e., immigration.

As the central emergent leadership institution in the European Community, [what] the Parliament [thinks] seems crucial on this issue. Therefore, the perspectives and policy preferences of the members are essential not only for our understanding of the development of policy, but to our understanding of the development of the Parliament itself.

In pursuit of such understanding, we are asking the cooperation of each member of the European Parliament. Specifically, we ask that you take a few moments of what we know is precious time to share your views on immigration with us by completing the enclosed questionnaire. Your thoughtful and candid answers are essential for our study. They will, of course, be kept completely confidential.

As project director, I will be in Europe during the period 1 April 1992 and 1 June 1992. Should your time permit, I would very much appreciate the opportunity of discussing these issues with you. If you would be willing to have such an interview, please so indicate in the place provided at the end of the questionnaire, and I will be in touch with your office to arrange a specific time.

Thank you very much for your assistance.

Sincerely,

Gallya Lahav
Project Director

English-language questionnaire

Questionnaire for members of the European Parliament

March 1992

Gallya Lahav, Project Director
Center for European Studies   Telephone: [01] (212) 593–5742
Box 555   Bitnet: GAL@CUNYVMSI
Graduate Center
33 West 42 Street
New York, NY 10036-8099, USA

All responses will be kept confidential. Data generated by this study will be used for statistical analysis only.[1]

Questionnaire for members of the European Parliament (MEPs)

This questionnaire focuses primarily on immigration from outside the European Community (EC), although it touches upon intra-EC migration as well. For the following questions, please either circle the number which is closest to your position or rank the categories as requested.

An addressed return envelope is provided for your convenience. All questionnaires or inquiries can be sent to the address listed on the first page. We ask that you kindly give your valuable time to this study, which will not be possible without YOUR cooperation.

Thank you very much for your assistance.

* * * * * * * * * * * * * * * *

Please begin by entering the names of the following:
Country: _____
Political Party: _____

I. On immigration
1. On a scale from 1–5, ranging from not important (1) to very important (5), how important do you think the immigration issue is . . .

	not important			very important	
(a) to your country?	1	2	3	4	5
(b) to the European Community?	1	2	3	4	5
(c) to your party grouping?	1	2	3	4	5
(d) to you?	1	2	3	4	5

2a. Do you think of immigration as an issue that is primarily: (Please circle one)
1. political
2. social

3. economic
4. foreign policy and security
5. cultural
6. demographic
7. other: (please specify)___

2b. When you think of immigration problems, to which other area do you relate them first? (Please circle one)
1. social welfare
2. race relations
3. unemployment
4. education
5. crime
6. citizenship
7. drug trafficking
8. integration
9. other: (Please specify)____

3. Are the problems of immigration in Europe: (Please circle one)
1. greater today than in the past
2. about the same today as in the past
3. lesser today than in the past

4. How optimistic or pessimistic are you that current immigration problems will be resolved?
1. very optimistic
2. optimistic
3. pessimistic
4. very pessimistic

5. Should immigration from each of the following be kept at its present level, increased or decreased?

	increased	present level	decreased
from other EC member countries	1	2	3
from East European countries	1	2	3
from West European *non*-EC countries	1	2	3
from Turkey	1	2	3
from North Africa	1	2	3
from Africa	1	2	3
from Asia	1	2	3
in general	1	2	3

6a. In your opinion, what level of immigration from outside the EC would have the most favorable impact on the standard of living in Western Europe?
1. higher than current level
2. same as current level
3. lower than current level

6b. In your opinion, what level of immigration from outside the EC would have the most favorable impact on the social fabric of Western Europe?
  1. higher than current level
  2. same as current level
  3. lower than current level

II. On immigration policy
  7. In general, when thinking about immigration policy, which of the following considerations should come first? (Please circle one)
    1. humanitarian concerns
    2. economic concerns
    3. social integration concerns
    4. demographic concerns
    5. problems of emigrant countries
    6. other: (Please specify)____
  8. How strongly do you agree or disagree that there should be a common immigration policy for members of the EC?
    1. agree strongly
    2. agree
    3. disagree
    4. disagree strongly
  9. Who should be responsible for regulating immigration policy? (Please circle one)
    1. national governments acting independently
    2. national governments, through prior consultation with other EC governments
    3. EC institutions, with member governments retaining the right to veto
    4. entirely by EC institutions, through majority vote
  10. How do you think immigration regulation should be *primarily* ensured in the European Community? (Please circle one)
    1. by keeping border controls between member-countries intact
    2. by having after-entry border controls
    3. by strengthening border controls between member-countries and non-member countries
    4. other: (Please specify)_____
  11. According to what principle, if any, should immigration be regulated?
    1. number quotas
    2. geographic quotas
    3. professional skill quotas
    4. race and ethnic quotas

   5. it should not be regulated
   6. other (Please specify)_____
12. What should be done about the rights of immigrants?
   1. extend their rights
   2. leave things as they are
   3. restrict their rights
13. What should be the first concern of immigration policy-makers? (Please circle one)
   1. integration of foreigners and their families who have been in an EC country
   2. the limitation of further entry of foreigners
   3. assistance to foreigners who desire to return to their homeland
   4. economic and educational assistance to countries who are sending immigrants
   5. other: (Please specify)____
14. In your opinion, what is the largest obstacle, if any, for the Schengen Group? (Please circle one)
   1. the possible inclusion of certain EC countries that are currently non-members
   2. the exclusion of certain EC countries
   3. its computer data service
   4. resolving "third-national status" issues
   5. other: (Please specify)____

III. On left–right and party groups
15. In your opinion, how clear are party group differences in the European Parliament on the immigration issue?
   1. very clear
   2. somewhat clear
   3. not clear
16. How divisive has the debate been in your party group over the immigration issue?
   1. very divisive
   2. somewhat divisive
   3. not divisive
17. *(If immigration has been very divisive amongst your party group, you may wish to skip this question.)* With regard to immigration from the following areas, which of the following best characterizes the opinions of MEPs from your party grouping, regardless of country? Please use the following scale:
   1. strongly in favor
   2. somewhat in favor

3. somewhat opposed
4. strongly opposed

Developing countries	1	2	3	4
East European states	1	2	3	4
South European EC member-states	1	2	3	4
North European EC member-states	1	2	3	4
West European non-EC member-states	1	2	3	4

18a. In your opinion, how different are left and right positions on most issues:

	very different	somewhat different	not different
in your country?	1	2	3
for you?	1	2	3

18b. In your opinion, how different are left and right positions on immigration issues specifically:

	very different	somewhat different	not different
in your country?	1	2	3
for you?	1	2	3

IV. Country

19a. In your opinion, how important are historical and cultural differences between EC nations in thinking about most issues?
1. very important
2. somewhat important
3. not important

19b. In your opinion, how important are historical and cultural differences between EC nations in thinking about immigration issues?
1. very important
2. somewhat important
3. not important

20. In your opinion, how divisive has the public debate been in your country over the immigration issue?
1. very divisive
2. somewhat divisive
3. not divisive

21. Which of the following statements most accurately represents your view regarding immigration problems?
1. My country faces *more* immigration problems than other EC countries.
2. My country faces *about the same number* of immigration problems as other EC countries.
3. My country faces *fewer* immigration problems than other EC countries.

V.   On integration
22a. Do you think that the movement towards European unification
     should be speeded up, slowed down, or continued at its present
     rate?
     1. speeded up
     2. continued at present rate
     3. slowed down
22b. What position, in your opinion, does your country's present
     government take on this subject?
     1. It favors speeding up
     2. It favors continuing at present rate
     3. It favors slowing down
22c. What position, in your opinion, does public opinion of your country
     take on this subject?
     1. It favors speeding up
     2. it favors continuing at present rate
     3. It favors slowing down

VI. MEPs
 23. There is a lot of talk about the objectives that your country should
     strive to achieve in the next ten to fifteen years. This list includes
     objectives that certain people believe should have priority.
     a. Which of these objectives do you personally believe is the most
        important one in the long-term?
     b. Which do you believe is the second most important objective?
        (Please check just one in each column).

	First	Second
Maintain order in the country	---	---
Increase participation of citizens in government decisions	---	---
Fight rising prices	---	---
Guarantee freedom of expression	---	---

 24. How important, do you think each of the following is in shaping
     your views in regard to immigration issues? (on scale of 1–5 where
     1 = no importance and 5 = great importance, please indicate by
     circling each)

	no importance			great importance	
(a) Ideology	1	2	3	4	5
(b) National and cultural values	1	2	3	4	5
(c) Personal experience	1	2	3	4	5
(d) Concerns about economic competition	1	2	3	4	5
(e) Concerns about intermarriage	1	2	3	4	5
(f) Other: (Please specify) ____	1	2	3	4	5

25. On the ideological spectrum, where do you place yourself from left to right?

left   right
1———2———3———4———5———6———7———8———9

VI. Background information
26. Sex of respondent:
   1. Male
   2. Female
27. Age:
   1. Under 35 years
   2. 35–49 years
   3. 50–64 years
   4. 65 years and above
28. Highest level of education attained: _____
29. Private occupation: _____
   If you feel there is something that you would like to discuss that is not addressed in this survey or if you wish to add any further comments, please feel free to do so in the space provided on the following page.
All responses and comments will be kept confidential.
Comments:

_____
_____
_____
_____
_____
_____

If you would be willing to have a future interview, please indicate: ___ yes ___ no (and list your name below)
If you wish to receive a summary of the findings, please list your name and address below.

_____
_____
_____
_____

Thank you very much for your time and cooperation.

NOTE

1. Identical versions of this survey in French and Italian were also sent (see Lahav 1995 for original data source).

Appendix D: National policy variations in EU countries

Table D.1 *Inflows of foreigners, by legal status (workers, family dependants, refugee asylum), 1999 (thousands)*

Country	Inflows of foreign population[a]	Inflows of foreign workers	Family reunification[b]	Inflows of asylum seekers[c]
Austria	224.2[d]	45.7	178.5	18.3
Belgium	57.8	20.5[e]	37.3	42.7
Denmark	33.0[f]	2.7[d]	30.3	10.1
Finland	7.9	n.a.	n.a.	3.2
France	104.4	11.8	92.6	38.6
Germany	674	262.5[d]	411.5	78.6
Greece	n.a.	n.a.	n.a.	3.1
Ireland	n.a.	3.8[d]	n.a.	10.9
Italy	268	219	49	18.0
Luxembourg	12.8	24.2[g]	n.a.	0.6
Netherlands	78.4	n.a.	n.a.	43.9
Portugal	n.a.	n.a.	n.a.	0.2
Spain	n.a.	36.6[f]	n.a.	7.2
Sweden	34.6	n.a.	n.a.	16.3
UK	354	37.7[d]	316.3	97.9

[a] Data from Austria, France, and the UK are based on residence and work permits; other data come from population registers. According to the OECD, data from population registers are not fully comparable because the criteria governing who gets registered differ from country to country. Counts for the Netherlands and especially Germany include substantial numbers of asylum-seekers.

[b] Family reunification figures were calculated by subtracting foreign worker inflow from total foreign population inflow.

[c] Source: OECD 2001 (reporting 2000 figures).

[d] Source: OECD 1999 (reporting 1996 figures).

[e] Source: OECD 2001 (reporting 1998 figure).

[f] Source: OECD 1999 (reporting 1995 figures).

[g] Luxembourg figure includes the arrival of foreign workers into Luxembourg and foreign residents entering the labor force.

Source: OECD 2001 (reporting 1999 figures) unless otherwise noted.

Table D.2 *Refugee and asylum applications in EU countries (thousands)*

Country	1988	1989	1990	1991	1992	1993	1994	1995	1996	1997
Austria (A)	18	25	24	30	18	6	6	7	8	8
Belgium (B)	6	9	9	16	19	27	14	11	14	14
Denmark (DK)	6	6	6	6	15	15	10	10	7	10
Finland (FIN)	0	0	3	2	4	2	2	1	1	1
France (F)	43	70	68	62	29	28	33	25	21	25
Germany (D)	111	127	200	268	447	339	153	128	130	117
Greece (EL)	9	7	4	3	2	1	1	1	2	4
Ireland (IRL)	0	0	0	0	0	0	0	0	1	2
Italy (I)	1	2	5	26	3	1	2	2	1	2
Luxembourg (L)	9	0	0	0	0	0	0	0	0	0
Netherlands (N)	9	15	22	23	25	45	60	31	32	40
Portugal (P)	0	0	0	0	1	2	1	0	0	0
Spain (E)	5	4	9	8	12	13	12	6	5	5
Sweden (SW)	24	33	31	28	85	39	20	9	6	11
UK	7	19	39	74	33	31	34	45	32	37

Note: Numbers were tabulated by adding figures for asylum applications and figures for refugees. B, I: excluding dependent children; DK: excluding applications outside Denmark and rejected applications at the border; D: including dependent children if the parents requested asylum for them; EL: figures for 1989–92 are the sum of the applications registered with the Greek authorities and those registered with the United Nations High Commission for Refugees; E: excluding dependants; F: excluding children and some accompanying adults; A: excluding displaced persons from former Yugoslavia who benefit from exceptional leave to stay. Refugee numbers are not reported for: Belgium 1994, 1995; France 1992, 1993; Germany 1995; Greece 1988, 1989, 1991; Ireland 1988, 1989, 1990, 1991, 1995; Italy, 1995, 1996; Luxembourg, 1988, 1989, 1994, 1995, 1997; Portugal, 1992, 1993, 1994, 1995; Spain 1988, 1989, 1990, 1991, 1992, 1993, 1995, 1996; Sweden, 1995, 1996.
Source: Eurostat 2000 (calculated from 1997 figures).

Table D.3 *Beneficiaries of family reunification in the European Union*

	Spouse	Minor children	Parents	Other relatives
Belgium	yes	less than 18; dependent		
Denmark	yes (also concubine)	less than 18; living with person with parental responsibility	over 60; dependent	for special reasons or close ties
France	yes	less than 18; less than 21 for member-states to the European Charter	not considered	
Germany	yes	less than 16; unmarried; less than 18 for specific cases	for humanitarian reasons	
Greece	yes	less than 18	dependent	
Ireland	yes	depending on individual circumstances	depending on the circumstances	depending on individual circumstances
Italy	yes	less than 18; dependent	dependent	non-minor children
Luxembourg	yes	less than 18	yes	non-minor children
Netherlands	yes (also concubine)	less than 18; dependent	if non-reunification creates serious difficulties	in exceptional circumstances
Portugal	yes	dependent	dependent	may be considered
Spain	yes	less than 18	dependent	non-minor children
United Kingdom	yes	less than 18; dependent; unmarried	dependent widow mother; widower father over 65; dependent parents if one is over 65	for extraordinary humanitarian reasons

Source: Callovi 1993; Commission of the European Communities 1992c.

Table D.4 *Naturalization of foreigners in selected EU countries, 1999*

Country	Years of residence	Numbers (thousands)	Percentage of foreign population[a]
Austria	n.a.	25.0	3.3
Belgium	5+5[b]	34.0	3.8
Denmark	7	12.4	4.8
France	5	145.4	4.5
Germany	10	248.2	3.4
Greece	8	n.a.	n.a.
Ireland	5	n.a.	n.a.
Italy	5	11.3	0.9
Luxembourg	10	0.6	0.4
Netherlands	5	62.1	9.4
Portugal	6	0.9	0.5
Spain	10	16.4	2.3
UK	5	54.9	2.5

Notes: [a]Percentage of foreign population indicates the number of persons acquiring the nationality of the country as a percentage of the stock of foreign population at the beginning of the year.
[b]Belgium requires an intermediate stage before full naturalization after ten years.
Source: Years of residence: Baldwin-Edwards 1992. Numbers and percentage figures: OECD 2000, reporting 1999 figures (except for Belgium and Luxembourg, for which 1998 figures are reported).

Table D.5 *Citizenship principles:* jus soli *and* jus sanguinis *in EU countries*

Jus soli (by birthplace)	Jus sanguinis (by parental nationality)
Belgium	Austria
France	Belgium
Greece	Denmark
Italy	Finland
Luxembourg	Germany
Netherlands	Ireland
Spain	Portugal
UK	

Acquisition of nationality
by % of foreign population

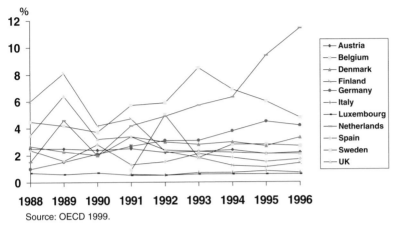

Source: OECD 1999.

Figure D.1 Naturalization rates, by country

Appendix E: EU country profiles

Table E.1 *EU country profiles*

	EU	Austria	Belgium	Denmark	Finland	France	Germany
GEOGRAPHY							
Total area, per 1000 sq. km	3193	84	31	43	338	544	357
National area, as percentage of EU area	–	3	1	1	11	17	11
POPULATION							
Total population, 1998 (1000s)	374586	8075	10192	5295	5147	58727	82057
Age structure (% total population):							
Children (0–14)	17	17	18	18	19	19	16
Workers (15–64)	67	68	65	67	67	65	68
Retired (65+)	16	15	17	15	14	16	16
Total fertility[1]	1.45	1.34	1.53	1.72	1.70	1.75	1.34
Average growth rate %[2]	–	0.5	0.1	0.3	0.3	0.4	0.1
Natural population increase per 1000 inhabitants	0.8	0.4	1.0	1.4	1.5	3.4	0.9
Population density: total inhabitants per sq. km	117	96	334	123	15	108	230
National population as % EU total population	–	2.2	2.7	1.4	1.4	15.7	21.9
Potential support ratio:[3]							
1999	–	5	4	4	5	4	4
2050	–	2	2	2	2	2	2
Chief religions[4]	–	RC 85%, PR 6%	RC 75%; PR and OTH 25%	EL 91%	EL 89%	RC 90%	PR 45%; RC 37%
Language	–	German	Flemish 56%; French 32%; German 1% (all official)	Danish	Finnish, Swedish (both official)	French	German

Table E.1 *(cont.)*

Greece	Ireland	Italy	Luxembourg	Netherlands	Portugal	Spain	Sweden	UK
132	69	301	3	41	92	505	411	242
4	2	9	0	1	3	16	13	8
10511	3694	57567	424	15654	9957	39348	8848	59090
16	23	15	19	18	17	16	19	19
68	67	68	67	67	68	69	64	64
16	11	17	14	13	15	16	18	16
1.30	1.93	1.19	1.68	1.62	1.46	1.15	1.51	1.72
0.3	0.7	0.0	1.1	0.4	0.0	0.0	0.2	0.2
0.0	6.0	−0.9	3.5	3.9	0.7	0.1	−0.5	1.5
80	54	191	164	382	108	78	22	244
2.8	1.0	15.4	0.1	4.2	2.7	10.5	2.4	15.8
4	6	4	5	5	4	4	4	4
2	3	2	2	2	2	1	2	2
GO 98%	RC 93%; AN 3%	RC 98%	RC 97%	RC 34%, PR 25%	RC 97%	RC 99%	EL 94%	AN, RC (together 71%), MU (3%), OTH (3%)
Greek	English, Gaelic	Italian	French, German, Luxem- bourgisch	Dutch	Portuguese	Castilian Spanish	Swedish	English, Welsh, Scottish, Gaelic

Table E.1 (*cont.*)

	EU	Austria	Belgium	Denmark	Finland	France	Germany
Ethnic groups	–	German (99%), Croatian, Slovene.	Flemish 55%; Walloon 33%	Scandinavian, Eskimo	Finn 94%, Swede, Lapp	Celtic and Latin; Teutonic, Slavic, North African, Indo-Chinese, Basque minorities	German 95%, Turkish 2%
POLITICS							
Government type[5]	–	FR	CM	CM	R	R	FR
Independence	–	1156	1830	1849	1917	486	1871
Year acceded to EU	–	1995	1957	1973	1995	1957	1957
# of MEPs[6]	–	21	25	16	16	87	99
Extreme-right parties at last election[7]	–	Freedom Party, 26.9%, 1999	Flemish Bloc (VB), 9.9%, 1999	Danish People's Party, 12%, 2001	n.a.	Front nat'l, 17.9%, 2002	German People's Union (DVU), 1.2%, 1998
Naturalization of foreigners: years of residence[8]	n.a.	5 + 5*	7	n.a.	5	10	
Citizenship principles[9]	*Jus sanguinis*	*Jus sanguinis*, *Jus soli*	*Jus sanguinis*	*Jus sanguinis*	*Jus soli*	*Jus sanguinis*	
Ministries/ agencies dealing with migration issues[10]	Ministry of Domestic Affairs; Ministry of the Interior	Office of Foreign Nationals; Gen. Commission for Refugees and Stateless Persons; Standing Refugees Appeals Board; Conseil d'Etat	n.a.	Min. of the Interior	Office des Migrations Internationales; Office français de protection des refugiés et apatrides; Ministry of the Interior	Ministry of Labor	
Dual nationality permitted?	No	No, except for children born outside of country whose parents are citizens	No, except for children born outside of country whose parents are citizens	Yes, through marriage or birth	Yes	Yes, in certain circumstances[11]	

Table E.1 (*cont.*)

Greece	Ireland	Italy	Luxembourg	Netherlands	Portugal	Spain	Sweden	UK
Greek 98%	Celtic, English minority	Italian; small minorities of German, French, Slovene, Albanian, Greek	French and German	Dutch 96%	Homogeneous Mediterranean stock, small African minority	Mix of Mediterranean and Nordic	Swedish 90%, Finnish 2%	English 81.5%, Scottish 9.6%, Irish 2.4%, Welsh 1.9%, Ulster 1.8%, West Indian, Indian, Pakistani, others 2.8%
PR	PR	R	CM	CM	R	CM	CM	CM
1829	1921	1861	1839	1579	1140	1492	1523	10th century
1981	1973	1957	1957	1957	1986	1986	1995	1973
25	15	87	6	31	25	64	22	86
n.a.	n.a.	Nat'l Alliance, 12%, 2001; North. League, 3.9%, 2001	Nat'l Bewegong, 2.4%, 1994	Centrum-democraten, 1%, 1998	Popular Party, 8.75%, 2002	Independent Liberal Group (GIL), no national rep.	Sweden Democrats, 0.3%, 1998	British Nat'l Party, 11.4%, 2002
8	5	5	10	5	6	10	n.a.	5
Jus soli	*Jus sanguinis*	*Jus soli*	*Jus soli*	*Jus soli*	*Jus sanguinis*	*Jus soli*	n.a.	*Jus soli*
Ministry of Public Order; Ministry of the Interior; Ministry of Labor	Dept of Justice	Ministry of the Interior	n.a.	Ministry of Justice	Ministry of the Interior	Directorate General for Migration	Swedish Immigration Board	Home Office
Yes	Yes	Yes	No	No, except for children born outside of country whose parents are citizens	Yes	n.a.	n.a.	Yes

Table E.1 (*cont.*)

	EU	Austria	Belgium	Denmark	Finland	France	Germany
Colonial relations[12]		Lombardy	Congo Free State (now Zaire); Eupen; Malmedy, St. Vith, Moresnet; Ruanda-Urundi (now Rwanda and Burundi)	Iceland, Greenland, Faeroe Islands	–	Algeria, Indochina, Morocco, Tunisia, Quebec	East Africa, SW Africa, New Guinea, Cameroons, Togo, Samoa
ECONOMY							
Total employment (1000s)	n.a.	3626	3857	2679	2179	22469	35537
% in agriculture	n.a.	6.5	2.2	3.7	7.1	4.4	2.8
% in industry	n.a.	29.6	27.2	26.4	28.2	26.4	34.4
% in services	n.a.	64.0	70.5	69.7	64.5	69.2	62.8
Total unemployment rate	10.0	4.7	9.5	5.1	11.4	11.7	9.4
GDP at market prices, in million ECU	7593142	188453	223142	155789	114792	1297401	1921764
GDP: real growth (% change on previous period)	2.66	2.88	2.91	2.69	5.04	3.16	2.15
MIGRATION							
Number of foreign population (1000s)[13]	–	748	897	259	88	3263	7344
% foreigners/total population[13]	–	9.2	8.8	4.9	1.7	5.6	8.9
Number of EU foreigners (1000s)[14]	–	n.a.	559.6	49	14.1	1321.5	1839.9
% EU foreigners/ total population[15]	–	1.2	5.5	1.0	0.3	2.0	2.3
% EU foreigners/foreign population[15]	–	13.0	62.2	20.5	18.7	36.6	25.1
# non-EU foreigners (1000s)[17]		n.a.	330.7	188.7	59.6	2275.1	5474.2
% non-EU foreigners/ total population[17]		n.a.	3.3	3.6	1.2	4.0	6.7

Table E.1 (*cont.*)

Greece	Ireland	Italy	Luxembourg	Netherlands	Portugal	Spain	Sweden	UK
–	–	Libya; Dodecanese Islands	–	Netherlands Indies (now Indonesia), Ceylon (now Sri Lanka), So. Tip of Africa, Aruba, Netherlands Antilles, New Netherlands (now parts of NY, NJ, CT and DE in the US).	Brazil, Angola, Cape Verde, Guinea-Bissau, Mozambique, São Tomé, Príncipe, Malaysia, Indonesia, China	SW America, Mexico, Western South America, West Indies, Central America, Philippine Islands	–	America, Australia, Canada, New Zealand, So. Africa, India, Pakistan, Sri Lanka, Burma, Brunei, Cyprus, Ghana, Kenya, Malaysia, Malta, Nigeria, Papua New Guinea, Solomon Islands, Sudan, Trinidad & Tobago, Uganda, Zimbabwe
3967	N/A	20065	171	7402	4763	13161	3946	26883
17.7	N/A	6.4	2.9	3.3	13.7	7.9	3.1	1.7
23.0	N/A	31.6	21.6	21.7	36.0	30.4	25.9	26.6
59.2	N/A	61.9	74.9	70.3	50.2	61.7	71.0	71.4
10.7	7.8	12.2	2.8	4.0	5.1	18.7	8.3	6.3
108580	75850	1058697	16389	349675	97637	520196	212003	1252776
3.66	8.93	1.34	5.02	3.66	3.49	3.96	2.95	2.16
238	118	1252	159	652	191	801	487	2208
2.7	3.1	2.2	36	4.1	1.9	2.0	5.5	3.8
45.1	81.3	133.5	127.9	188.4	43.7	251.9	178.2	805.5
n.a.	n.a.	0.3	31.0	1.2	0.5	0.7	2.0	0.7
28[16]	71[16]	13.7	89.0	28.0	26.3	42.7	33.9	18.5
116.2	33.1	751.1	15	491.5	129.2	286.3	348.4	1321.4
1.1	0.01	1.3	3.6	3.2	1.3	0.7	4.0	2.3

Table E.1 (*cont.*)

	EU	Austria	Belgium	Denmark	Finland	France	Germany
% non-EU foreigners/ foreign population[18]		n.a.	37	73	68	70	75
Net migration per 1000 people[19]		0.6	1.3	2.7	0.8	0.7	2.3
Immigration, total 1000s (1997 figures)[20]		70	59	50	14	66	841
Inflows of foreign workers[21]	–	16.3	2.2	2.7	–	16.3	262.5
Inflows of asylum seekers in 1000s[23]	393.8	18.3	42.7	10.1	3.2	38.6	78.6
Acquisition of citizenship (1997 figures)[24]	–	15792	26149	5482	1439	83676	83027
Migrant stock from Eastern European countries[25]		517690	17260♣	47108δ	n.a.	103154κ	2055395ψ
Largest inflows of foreign population by nationality[26]		n.a.	Netherlands; France; Morocco	Former Yugoslavia; Somalia; Iceland	Russia; Estonia; Sweden	Algeria; Morocco; Turkey	Poland; Turkey; Italy
Largest stock of foreign population by nationality[24]			Italy; Morocco; France	Turkey; Former Yugoslavia; UK	Former USSR; Estonia; Sweden	Portugal; Algeria; Morocco	Turkey; Former Yugoslavia; Italy

[1] Total fertility is the average number of children that would be born alive to a woman during her lifetime if she were to experience during her childbearing years the age-specific fertility rates of the respective calendar year or period (source: Eurostat).

[2] Source: United Nations, Population Division 1999b (figures are for 1995–2000).

[3] Source: United Nations, Population Division 1999 (number of persons aged 15 to 64 years for each person aged 65 years or older).

[4] Religion coding: RC=Roman Catholic; PR=Protestant; EL=Evangelical Lutheran; GO=Greek Orthodox; AN=Anglican; MU=Muslim; OTH=Other.

[5] Government type coding: CM=constitutional monarchy; FR=federal republic; PR=parliamentary republic; R=republic.

[6] Source: http://europa.eu.int/ Official website of the European Union, February 2000.

[7] Source: www.irr.org; data provided by the Institute of Race Relations, November 2002.

[8] Sources: OECD 1992 (reporting 1990); Baldwin-Edwards (1992).

* Belgium requires an intermediate stage before full naturalization after ten years.

[9] Citizenship principles are classified as *jus soli* (by birthplace) or *jus sanguinis* (by parental nationality).

[10] OECD 1998.

[11] For example, for children born outside Germany who have at least one parent who is a German citizen and resident for at least eight years; or as a German adult citizen who obtains another country's citizenship but applies for permission to retain German citizenship.

[12] Source: World Book Encyclopedia 1998 (Chicago: World Book).

[13] Source: OECD 2001 (reporting 1999 figures).

[14] Source: Eurostat 2000 (reporting 1997 figures).

[15] Source: OECD 2001 (reporting 1998 figures).

[16] Eurostat 2000 (calculated from 1997 figures).

[17] Eurostat 2000 (calculated from 1997 figures).

[18] Eurostat 2000 (reporting 1997 figures); OECD 2001 (reporting 1999 figures). Figures calculated by dividing # non-EU foreigners by # foreign population to obtain percentages. These estimates are somewhat distorted due to different sources reporting different years. Due to these estimates being taken from different years, the numbers and percentages do not equal 100.

Table E.1 (*cont.*)

Greece	Ireland	Italy	Luxembourg	Netherlands	Portugal	Spain	Sweden	UK
49	28	60	9	75	68	36	72	60
3.3	4.9	2.0	9.4	2.1	1.3	0.9	1	1.6
22	44	n.a.	10	110	3	58	45	285
–	3.8	129.2	18.3	–	–	36.6[22]	–	37.7
3.1	10.9	18	0.6	43.9	4.4	7.2	16.3	97.9
930	355	7442	761	59831	1364	9801	28875	37010
54409	n.a.	328417	2927*	38365[+]	1726[φ]	n.a.	112510[γ]	281200
n.a.	n.a.	Morocco; Albania; Philippines	Portugal; France; Belgium	Turkey, Germany; UK	Cape Verde; Brazil; Angola	n/a	Finland, Iraq; Norway	USA, Australia; India
		Morocco; Albania; Philippines	Portugal Italy; France	Morocco; Turkey, Germany	Cape Verde; Brazil; Angola	Morocco; UK; Germany	Finland, Former Yugoslavia; Norway	Ireland; India; USA

[19] United Nations, Population Division 2002b.

[20] Reporting on immigration varies dramatically between member-countries of the EU. For example, the UK does not record flows with Ireland; France has no statistics on immigration of nationals. Data are therefore not fully comparable (source: Eurostat 2000)

[21] Source: OECD 1998 (reporting 1996 figures unless otherwise noted).

[22] 1995 figure.

[23] Source: OECD 2001 (reporting 1998 figures).

[24] Acquisition of citizenship by non-nationals is handled differently in countries throughout the EU. The data do not include acquisition of citizenship by birth. Data are based on varying national definitions and practices, and are not fully comparable (source: Eurostat). All figures are 1997 except Belgium, Italy and Ireland (1995).

[25] Figures from Eastern Europe, the former USSR, Albania, and the former Yugoslavia. Figures from national population census unless otherwise noted. Source: United Nations, Population Division, 2002a.

♣ Source: Institut National de Statistique; Annuaire Statistique de la Belgique; Institut National de Statistique: Statistiques Démographiques.

δ Source: Denmarks Statistik; Eurostat; Council of Europe.

κ Source: Institut National de la Statistique et des Etudes Economiques (1997).

ψ Source: Statistiches Bundesament; Council of Europe; Eurostat.

* Source: Service Central de la Statistique et des Etudes Economiques (1994).

+ Source: Central Bureau voor de Statistiek; Council of Europe; Eurostat.

φ Source: Council of Europe; Eurostat; Instituto Nacional de Estatistica Portugal.

γ Official Statistics of Sweden, Population Statistics.

[26] Source: OECD 1998 (reporting 1996 figures).

Appendix F: Selected Eastern and Central European country profiles

Table F.1 *Selected Central European country profiles*

Country[1]	BG	CZ	EE	HU	LT	LV	PL	RO	SI	SK
Total area (sq. km.)	110.910	78870	45230	93030	65301	64590	312690	238390	20270	49040
Total population (thousand)[2]	7949	10272	1393	9968	3696	2421	38605	22438	1988	5399
Population density, inhabitants per sq. km.	75	131*	32*	109*	57	38	124*	95	98*	110*
Migrant stock (in thousands)[2]	101	236	365	296	339	613	2088	94	51	32
Life expectancy at birth: boys	67.2	70.5	64.5*	66.5	65.0*	64.1	68.5	65.2	71.0	68.9
Life expectancy at birth: girls	74.4	77.5	75.5*	75.0	76.1*	74.9	77.0	73.0	78.6	76.7
Unemployment rate	15.0	4.7	10.5	8.1	14.1	14.4	11.2	6.0	7.3*	11.6
GDP at current prices and in PPS (billions of dollars)	36.7	123.8	10.3	90.3	21.3	12.7	291.2	131.8	25.8	48.2
Annual GDP growth rates, % (1998 figures)	3.4	-2.3	4.0	5.1	5.1	3.6	4.8	-7.3	3.9	4.4
Chief religion(s)	Bulgarian Orthodox, 85%; Muslim, 13%	Atheist, 39.8%; Roman Catholic 39.2%; Protestant, 4.6%; Orthodox, 3%	Lutheran, Orthodox	Roman Catholic, 67.5%; Calvinist, 20%; Lutheran, 5%	Mostly Roman Catholic	Lutheran, Roman Catholic, Russian Orthodox	Roman Catholic, 95%	Romanian Orthodox, 70%; Roman Catholic, 6%; Protestant, 6%	Roman Catholic, 96%	Roman Catholic, 60%; Protestant, 8%
Date of EU application[3]	December 16, 1995	January 17, 1996	November 28, 1995	March 31, 1994	December 12, 1995	October 27, 1995	April 5, 1994	June 22, 1995	June 10, 1996	June 27, 1995

Sources: UN 2002b; Eurostat 1998, 1999a; *World Almanac and Book of Facts* 1998.
All figures are 1997 numbers, unless otherwise noted.
* = 1996 figures.

NOTES

[1] Country coding: BG = Bulgaria; CZ = Czech Republic; EE = Estonia; HU = Hungary; LT = Lithuania; LV = Latvia; PL = Poland; RO = Romania; SI = Slovenia; SK = Slovakia.

[2] Source: UN 2002a (reporting 2000 figures).

[3] Other countries submitting applications for expansion into the EU include: Cyprus, July 4, 1992; Malta, July 16, 1990; Turkey, April 14, 1987; and Switzerland, May 20, 1992. Switzerland's application is on hold (source: European Union).

Bibliography

Abadan-Unat, Nermin 1992, "East–West vs. South–North Migration: Effects upon the Recruitment Areas of the 1960s," *International Migration Review*, 26 (Summer): 401–412.

1997, "Ethnic Business, Ethnic Communities, and Ethno-politics Among Turks in Europe," in Uçarer and Puchala 1997, pp. 229–251.

Abélès, Marc 1992, *La vie quotidienne au Parlement européen*, Paris: Hachette.

Aberbach, Joel, James Chesney, and Bert A. Rockman 1975, "Exploring Elite Political Attitudes: Some Methodological Lessons," *Political Methodology*, 2 (Winter): 1–28.

Aberbach, Joel D., Robert D. Putnam, and Bert A. Rockman 1981, *Bureaucrats and Politicians in Western Democracies*, Cambridge, MA, and London: Harvard University Press.

Agence Europe (various 1990–92), *Europe Agence Internationale d'Information Pour La Presse*, Brussels: Bulletin.

Ajzen, Icek 1991, "The Theory of Planned Behavior," *Organizational Behavior and Human Decision Processes*, 50: 179–211.

Aleinikoff, T. Alexander, and Douglas Klusmeyer eds. 2000, *From Migrants to Citizens: Membership in a Changing World*, Washington, DC: Carnegie Endowment for International Peace/Brookings Institution Press.

Allen, William Sheridan 1984 [1965], *The Nazi Seizure of Power: The Experience of a Single German Town, 1922–1945*, rev. edn., New York: Franklin Watts.

Allison, Graham, and Morten Halperin 1972, "Bureaucratic Politics: A Paradigm and Some Policy Implications," *World Politics*, 24 (supplement, Spring): 40–79.

Allport, Gordon 1979 [1954], *The Nature of Prejudice*, 25th anniversary edn., Reading, MA: Addison-Wesley.

Almond, Gabriel, and Sidney Verba 1963, *The Civic Culture: Political Attitudes and Democracy in Five Nations*, Princeton: Princeton University Press.

Anderson, Benedict 1991 [1983], *Imagined Communities*, rev. and exp. edn., London: Verso.

Anderson, Christopher 1995, "Economic Uncertainty and European Solidarity Revisited: Trends in Public Support for European Integration," in Carolyn Rhodes and Sonia Mazey, eds., *The State of the European Union*, vol. III, *Building a European Polity?*, Boulder: Lynne Rienner.

1998, "When in Doubt, Use Proxies: Attitudes Toward Domestic Politics and Support for European Integration," *Comparative Political Studies*, 31, 5: 569–601.

Anderson, Christopher, and M. Shawn Reichert 1996, "Economic Benefits and Support for Membership in the EU: A Cross-National Analysis," *Journal of Public Policy*, 15, 3: 231–249.

Anderson, Malcolm, and Monica den Boer eds. 1994, *Policing Across National Boundaries*, London: Pinter.

Andreas, Peter, and Timothy Snyder eds. 2000, *The Wall Around the West: State Borders and Immigration Controls in North America and Europe*, Lanham, MD: Rowman and Littlefield.

Armstrong, John 1982, *Nations Before Nationalism*, Chapel Hill: University of North Carolina Press.

Art, Robert, and Robert Jervis eds. 1992, *International Politics: Enduring Concepts and Contemporary Issues*, 3rd edn., New York: Harper Collins.

Arthur, Brian 1994, *Increasing Returns and Path Dependency in the Economy*, Ann Arbor: University of Michigan Press.

Attinà, Fulvio 1990, "The Voting Behavior of the European Parliament Members and the Problems of Europarties," *European Journal of Political Research*, 18: 557–579.

Axelrod, Robert ed. 1977, *The Structure of Decision: The Cognitive Maps of Political Elites*, Princeton: Princeton University Press.

Baldwin, Peter 1990, *The Politics of Social Solidarity: Class Bases of the European Welfare-State, 1875–1975*, Cambridge: Cambridge University Press.

Baldwin-Edwards, Martin 1991a, "Immigration After 1992," unpublished paper, University of Manchester.

1991b, "Immigration After 1992," *Policy and Politics*, 19 (3): 199–211.

1992, "Recent Changes in European Immigration Policies," *Journal of European Social Policy*, 2 (1): 53–71.

1997, "The Emerging European Immigration Regime: Some Reflections on Implications for Southern Europe," *Journal of Common Market Studies*, 35, 4 (December): 497–519.

Baldwin-Edwards, Martin, and Martin Schain eds. 1994, "Special Issue on the Politics of Immigration in Western Europe," *Western European Politics*, 17, 2.

Barber, Benjamin 1992, "Jihad vs. McWorld," *Atlantic Monthly* (March): 53–55.

Bardi, Luciano 1991, "Representation in the European Parliament and the Building of the European Political System," Paper presented to the 15th World Congress of the International Political Science Association (July).

1994, "Transnational Party Federations, European Parliamentary Groups, and the Building of Europarties," in R. S. Katz and P. Mair, eds., *How Parties Organize: Adaptation and Change in Party Organizations in Western Democracies*, London: Sage, pp. 58–78.

2002, "Parties and Party Systems in the European Union," in Kurt Richard Luther and Ferdinand Müller-Rommel, eds., *Political Parties in a Changing Europe: Political and Analytical Challenges*, Oxford: Oxford University Press, pp. 293–321.

Bartram, David 1998, "Foreign Workers in Israel: History and Theory," *International Migration Review*, 32 (2): 304–325.

Bauböck, Rainer 1994, *Transnational Citizenship: Membership and Rights in International Migration*, Aldershot: Edward Elgar.

Baumgartl, Bernd, and Adrian Favell eds. 1995, *New Xenophobia in Europe*, London: Kluwer Law International.

Beck, Roy, and Steven Camarota 2002, "Elite vs. Public Opinion: An Examination of Divergent Views on Immigration," *CIS Backgrounder*, Washington, DC: Center for Immigration Studies, December.

Bell, Daniel 1962, *The End of Ideology: On the Exhaustion of Political Ideas in the Fifties*, 2nd revised edn., New York: Collier Books, Free Press.

1973, *The Coming of Post-Industrial Society*, New York: Basic Books.

Bendor, J., A. Glazer, and T. Hammond 2001, "Theories of Delegation," *Annual Review of Political Science*, 4: 235–269.

Betts, Katherine 1988, *Ideology and Immigration: Australia 1976–1987*, Carlton, Victoria, Australia: Melbourne University Press.

Betz, Hans-Georg 1990, "Value Change and Postmaterialist Politics: The Case of West Germany," *Comparative Political Studies*, 23, 2: 239–256.

1993, "The New Politics of Resentment: Radical Right-Wing Populist Parties in Western Europe," *Comparative Politics*, 25, 4 (July): 413–427.

1994, *Radical Right-Wing Populism in Western Europe*, New York: St. Martin's Press.

Betz, Hans-Georg, and Stephan Immerfall eds. 1998, *The New Politics of the Right: Neo-Populist Parties and Movements in Established Democracies*, New York: St. Martin's Press.

Bhagwati, Jagdish 2003, "Borders Beyond Control," *Foreign Affairs*, 82, 1: 98–101.

Bigo, Didier 1996, *Polices en réseaux: l'expérience européenne*, Paris: Presses de la Fondation Nationale de Science Politique.

2001, "Migration and Security," in V. Guiraudon and C. Joppke, eds., *Controlling a New Migration World*, London: Routledge, pp. 121–149.

Blalock, Hubert 1967, *Toward a Theory of Minority-Group Relations*, New York: John Wiley and Sons.

Bleich, Erik 2002, "Integrating Ideas into Policy-Making Analysis: Frames and Race Policies in Britain and France," *Comparative Political Studies*, 35, 9 (November): 1054–1076.

Blondel, Jean, Richard Sinnott, and Palle Svensson 1998, *People and Parliament in the European Union: Participation, Democracy and Legitimacy*, Oxford: Oxford University Press.

Bobo, Lawrence 1983, "Whites' Opposition to Busing: Symbolic Racism or Realistic Group Conflict?," *Journal of Personality and Social Psychology*, 45: 1196–1210.

Body-Gendrot, Sophie, and Martin Schain 1992, "National and Local Politics and the Development of Immigration Policy in the United States and France," in Donald Horowitz and Gérard Noiriel, eds., *Immigrants in Two Democracies: French and American Experiences*, New York: New York University Press, pp. 411–438.

Bogardus, Emory 1928, *Immigration and Race Attitudes*, New York and London: D. C. Heath.

Böhning, W. R. 1972, *The Migration of Workers in the United Kingdom and the European Community*, Oxford: Oxford University Press.

Bommes, Michael, and Andrew Geddes eds. 2000, *Immigration and Welfare: Challenging the Borders of the Welfare State*, London: Routledge.

Börzel, Tanja 1999, "Towards Convergence in Europe? Institutional Adaptation to Europeanisation in Germany and Spain," *Journal of Common Market Studies*, 37, 4: 573–596.

Bourdieu, Pierre 1973, "L'opinion publique n'existe pas," *Temps Modernes*, 20: 1292–1309.

Brewer, Marilynn 1979, "In-Group Bias in the Minimal Inter-group Situation: A Cognitive Motivational Analysis," *Psychological Bulletin*, 86: 307–324.

Brochmann, Grete, and Tomas Hammar eds. 1999, *Mechanisms of Immigration Control: A Comparative Analysis of European Regulation Policies*, Oxford and New York: Berg.

Broughton, David, and Mark Donovan eds. 1999, *Changing Party Systems in Western Europe*, London: Pinter.

Brown, Bernard E. 1969, "Elite Attitudes and Political Legitimacy in France," *Journal of Politics*, 31(2): 420–442.

Brown, Rupert 1995, *Prejudice: Its Social Psychology*, Oxford: Blackwell.

Brubaker, William Rogers, ed. 1989, *Immigration and the Politics of Citizenship in Europe and North America*, Lanham, MD: German Marshall Fund, University Press of America.

1992, *Citizenship and Nationhood in France and Germany*, Cambridge, MA: Harvard University Press.

1994, "Are Immigration Control Efforts Really Failing?," in Cornelius, Martin, and Hollifield 1994.

1995, "Comments on "Modes of Immigration Politics in Liberal Democratic States," *International Migration Review*, 24, 4 (Winter): 903–908.

Budge, Ian, Ivor Crewe, and Dennis Farlie eds. 1976, *Party Identification and Beyond*, London and New York: Wiley.

Budge, Ian and Dennis Farlie 1983, "Party Competition – Selective Emphasis or Direct Confrontation?: An Alternative View with Data," in H. Daalder and P. Mair, eds., *Western European Party Systems: Continuity and Change*, Beverly Hills and London: Sage.

Bull, Hedley 1977, *The Anarchical Society: A Study of Order in World Politics*, New York: Columbia University Press.

Bunyan, T. 1991, "Towards an Authoritarian European State," *Race and Class*, 32, 3: 179–188.

Bunyan, Tony, and Frances Webber 1995, *Intergovernmental Co-operation on Immigration and Asylum*, CCME Briefing Paper No. 19, Brussels: Churches' Commission for Migrants in Europe.

Burley, Anne-Marie, and Walter Mattli 1993, "Europe Before the Court: A Political Theory of Legal Integration," *International Organization*, 47, 1 (Winter): 41–76.

Burns, James MacGregor 1979, *Leadership*, New York: Harper and Row.

Butler, David, and Donald Stokes 1969, *Political Change in Britain*, New York: St. Martin's Press.

1974, *Political Change in Britain: The Evolution of Electoral Choice*, New York: St. Martin's Press.

Butt Philip, Alan 1994, "European Union Immigration Policy: Phantom, Fantasy or Fact?," *West European Politics*, 17, 2: 169–191.

Callovi, Giuseppe 1990, "Immigration and the European Community," *Contemporary European Affairs*, 3, 3: 17–38.

1992, "Regulation of Immigration in 1993: Pieces of the European Community Jigsaw Puzzle," *International Migration Review*, 26, 2 (Summer): 353–372.

1993, "Il ricongiungimento delle famiglie straniere nella communità," in *La famiglia in una società multietnica*, Milan: Vita e Pensiero.

Caporaso, James 1996, "The European Union and Forms of State: Westphalian, Regulatory or Post-Modern?," *Journal of Common Market Studies*, 34, 1 (March): 29–52.

2000, "Changes in the Westphalian Order: Territory, Public Authority, and Sovereignty," *International Studies Review*, 2: 1–28.

Caporaso, James, and John Keeler 1995, "The European Union and Regional Integration Theory," in Carolyn Rhodes and Sonia Mazey, eds., *The State of the European Union: Building a European Polity?*, vol. III, Boulder, CO: Lynne Rienner, pp. 29–62.

Carmines, Edward, and James Stimson 1980, "The Two Faces of Issue Voting," *American Political Science Review*, 74: 78–91.

Carrubba, Clifford 2001, "The Electoral Connection in European Union Politics," *Journal of Politics*, 63: 141–158.

Cassell, Mark 1993, "The Intergovernmental Politics of Immigration in the Federal Republic of Germany: A National Crisis," Paper presented at the American Political Science Association Conference, Washington, DC (September).

Castles, Stephen, H. Booth, and T. Wallace 1984, *Here for Good: Western Europe's New Ethnic Minorities*, London: Pluto Press.

Castles, Stephen, and Godula Kosack 1985 [1973], *Immigrant Workers and Class Structure in Western Europe*, 2nd edn., Oxford: Oxford University Press.

Castles, Stephen, and Mark Miller 1998, *The Age of Migration: International Population Movements in the Modern World*, 2nd edn., New York: Guilford Press.

Cerny, Philip G. 1995, "Globalization and the Changing Logic of Collective Action," *International Organization*, 49, 4 (Autumn): 595–625.

Checkel, Jeffrey 1998, "The Constructivist Turn in International Relations Theory: A Review Essay," *World Politics*, 50 (January): 324–348.

1999, "Norms, Institutions, and National Identity in Contemporary Europe," *International Studies Quarterly*, 43: 83–114.

2001, "Why Comply? Social Learning and European Identity Change," *International Organization*, 55, 3 (Summer): 553–588.

Church, Clive, and David Phinnemore 1994, *European Union and European Community: A Handbook and Commentary on the Post-Maastricht Treaties*, Hemel Hempstead, UK: Harvester Wheatsheaf.

Churches' Commission for Migrants in Europe, Briefing Papers 1–24, Brussels.

1991, *Fourth Conference of European Ministers Responsible for Migration Affairs*, Luxembourg: Council of Europe (September).

1993, *The Use of International Convention to Protect the Rights of Migrants and Ethnic Minorities*, Strasbourg (November).

Citrin, Jack, Donald Green, Christopher Muste, and Cara Wong 1997, "Public Opinion Toward Immigration Reform: The Role of Economic Motivations," *Journal of Politics*, 59, 3 (August): 858–881.

Citrin, Jack, Beth Reingold, and Donald Green 1990, "American Identity and the Politics of Ethnic Change," *Journal of Politics*, 52, 4: 1124–1153.

Clarke, Harold D., Allan Kornberg, Chris McIntyre, Petra Bauer-Kaase, and Max Kaase 1999, "The Effect of Economic Priorities on the Measurement of Value Change: New Experimental Evidence," *American Political Science Review*, 93 (September): 637–647.

Coase, Ronald 1937, "The Nature of the Firm," *Economica*, 4 (November): 386–405.

1960, "The Problem of Social Cost," *Journal of Law and Economics*, 3 (October): 1–44.

Collinson, Sarah 1993, *Beyond Borders: West European Migration Policy Towards the Twenty-First Century*, London: Royal Institute of International Affairs.

1994, *Europe and International Migration*, London: Pinter.

Commission of the European Communities, *Eurobarometer: Public Opinion in the European Community*, nos. 9, 10, 12, 20, 21, 35–50, Ann Arbor, MI: Inter-university Consortium for Political and Social Research; Brussels: Directorate-General for Information, Communication, and Culture.

1985a, "Guidelines for a Community Policy on Migration," Commission Communication to the Council, Bulletin of the European Communities Supplement, COM 85 48 final, Commission Decision (July).

1985b, *Migrants in the European Community*, Brussels: Directorate-General for Information (August–September).

1989, *Eurobarometer 30: Public Opinion in the European Community: Special Issue on Racism and Xenophobia*, Brussels: Directorate-General for Information, Communication, and Culture (November).

1990a, "Citizens of the Community: A People's Europe," Brussels: Directorate-General for Information, Communication, and Culture.

1990b, "Completing the Internal Market: An Area Without Internal Frontiers," Progress report required by Article 8B of the Treaty, COM (90) 552, final Brussels, 23 (November).

1991a, "Commission Communication to the Council and the European Parliament on Immigration," PE154, 464, Brussels: Directorate-General for Committees and Delegations (October); also known as "Communication of the Commission on the Possibility of Developing a Common Immigration Policy," Brussels, EC DOC 8811/91.

1991b, "Communication from the Commission to the Council and the European Parliament on the Right of Asylum," Sec (91) 1857 final, Brussels (October); EC DOC 8810/91.

1991c, "Social Europe: Immigration of Citizens for Third Countries into the Southern Member States of the European Community: A Comparative

Survey of the Situation in Greece, Italy, Spain, and Portugal," Supplement 1/91, Luxembourg: Directorate-General for Employment, Industrial Relations, and Social Affairs.

1992a, *Eurobarometer: Public Opinion in the European Community*, Special Issue on "Trends: 1974–1991," Brussels: Commission of the European Communities (April).

1992b, Treaty on European Union: ECSE-EEC-EAEC, *1992*, Brussels and Luxembourg.

1992c, Unpublished Report, V/384/92, Brussels (May).

1993, Report on *Harmonization of National Policies on Family Reunification*, SN 2828/1/93 WGI 1497 Rev. 1 and PE205.496, annexe, Brussels: Ad Hoc Immigration Group (June 3).

1996a, Eurobarometer Special Report, TOP (The European Union: A View from the Top. Top Decision-makers and the European Union). Brussels: EOS (European Omnibus Survey) Gallup Europe (September); available at http://europa.eu.int/comm/public_opinion/archives/top/top_en.htm.

1996b, *The European Union: Key Figures*, Luxembourg: Office for Official Publications of the EC (July).

Converse, Philip 1964, "The Nature of Belief Systems in Mass Publics," in David Apter, ed., *Ideology and Discontent*, New York and London: Free Press, pp. 206–261.

1970, "Attitudes and Non-Attitudes: Continuation of a Dialogue," in Edward R. Tufte, ed., *The Quantitative Analysis of Social Problems*, Reading, MA: Addison-Wesley, pp. 168–189.

1974, "Comment: The Status of Non-Attitudes," *American Political Science Review*, 68: 650–660.

Converse, Philip, and Georges Dupeux 1962, "Politicization of the Electorate in France and the United States," *Public Opinion Quarterly*, 26: 1–23.

Corbett, Richard, Francis Jacobs, and Michael Shackleton 2000 [1992 2nd edn.], *The European Parliament*, London: Catermill, 4th edn.

Cornelius, Wayne, Philip Martin, and James Hollifield eds. 1994, *Controlling Immigration*, Stanford: Stanford University Press.

Council of Europe 1984, "Immigrant Populations and Demographic Developments in the Member States of the Council of Europe, Part I: Analysis of General Trends and Possible Future Developments," *Population Studies*, 12, Strasbourg.

1986, "Exchange of Views on Opinions and Attitudes with Regard to Demographic Problems in the Member States of the Council of Europe," Information document prepared by the members of the European Population Committee, Strasbourg.

1990, "World Demographic Trends and Their Consequences for Europe," *Population Studies*, 20, Strasbourg.

Council of Europe, with John Salt, expert consultant 1991, "4e Conférence des ministres européens responsables des questions de migration," Luxembourg (September).

Cover, Albert, Neil Pinney, and George Serra 1997, "Ideological Cohesion Between Congress and the President: Does the Road to the White House Matter?," *Journal of Legislative Studies*, 13, 2 (Summer): 50–69.

Crewe, Ivor, and David Denver 1985, *Electoral Change in Western Democracies*, New York: Croom Helm.

Cruz, Antonio 1993, *Schengen, Ad Hoc Immigration Group and Other European Intergovernmental Bodies: In View of a Europe Without Internal Borders*, CCME Briefing Paper No. 12, Brussels: Churches' Commission for Migrants in Europe.

Dalton, Russell 2002 [1988], *Citizen Politics: Public Opinion and Political Parties in Advanced Industrial Democracies*, 3rd edn., New York: Chatham House.

Dalton, Russell, and Richard Eichenberg 1998, "Citizen Support for Policy Integration," in Sandholtz and Stone Sweet 1998, pp. 250–282.

Dalton, Russell, Scott Flanagan, and Paul Allen Beck 1984, *Electoral Change in Advanced Industrial Democracies: Realignment or Dealignment?*, Princeton: Princeton University Press.

Davis, Darren W., and Christian Davenport 1999, "Assessing the Validity of the Postmaterialism Index," *American Political Science Review*, 93 (September): 649–664.

Davis, Darren, and Brian Silver forthcoming, "Civil Liberties vs. Security: Public Opinion in the Context of the Terrorist Attacks on America," *American Journal of Political Science*, 48.

De Master, Sara, and Michael Le Roy 2000, "Xenophobia and the European Union," *Comparative Politics*, 32, 4: 419–436.

Dedecker, Renee 1992, "The Right of Asylum in Europe: Some Proposals on Accelerated Procedures for the Twelve Member States," Working Document Prepared with the Support of the United Nations High Commission for Refugees, UNHCR (January).

Deflem, Mathieu, and Fred Pampel 1996, "The Myth of Postnational Identity: Popular Support for European Unification," *Social Forces*, 47, 1: 119–143.

Deheneffe, Jean-Claude 1986, *Europe as Seen by Europeans: European Polling, 1973–1986*, European Documentation Series, Office for Official Publications of the European Communities, Luxembourg.

Delors, Jacques 1989, "Europe: Embarking on a New Course," *Contemporary European Affairs*, Special Issue "1992 and After," 1(1/2): 15–27.

den Boer, Monica, and William Wallace 2000, "Justice and Home Affairs: Integration Through Incrementalism?," in Wallace and Wallace 2000, pp. 493–519.

Deutsch, Karl 1967, "A Comparison of French and German Elites in the European Political Environment," in Deutsch *et al.* 1967, pp. 213–302.

    1981, "The Crisis of the State," *Government and Opposition* (Summer): 331–343.

Deutsch, Karl, S. A. Burrell, R. A. Kann, M. Lee, Jr., M. Lichterman, R. E. Lindgren, F. L. Loewenheim, and R. W. Van Wagenen 1957, *Political Community and the North Atlantic Area: International Organization in the Light of Historical Experience*, Princeton: Princeton University Press.

Deutsch, Karl, Lewis Edinger, Roy Macridis, and Richard Merritt eds. 1967, *France, Germany, and the Western Alliance: A Study of Elite Attitudes on European Integration and World Politics*, New York: Charles Scribner's Sons.

Documents Observateur 1989, "L'Europe Multiraciale," 4 (January/February)

Downs, Anthony 1957, *An Economic Theory of Democracy*, New York: Harper.

Duch, Raymond, and Michael Taylor 1997, "Economics and the Vulnerability of Pan-European Institutions," *Political Behavior*, 18, 1: 65–80.

Duchesne, Sophie, and André-Paul Frognier 1995, "Is There a European Identity?," in Niedermayer and Sinnott 1995b, pp. 193–226.

Dummett, Ann, and Jan Niessen 1993, *Immigration and Citizenship in the European Union*, CCME Briefing Paper No. 14, Brussels: Churches' Commission for Migrants in Europe (November).

Easton, David 1965, *A Systems Analysis of Political Analysis*, New York and London: John Wiley and Sons.

    1975, "A Re-assessment of the Concept of Political Support," *British Journal of Political Science*, 5: 435–457.

ECPR (European Consortium for Political Research) 2000, "Immigration Politics in Europe," *ECPR News*, 11, 2 (Spring).

Eichenberg, Richard, and Russell Dalton 1993, "Europeans and the European Community: The Dynamics of Public Support for European Integration," *International Organization*, 47, 4 (Autumn): 507–534.

    1997, "Convergence and Divergence in Citizen Support for European Integration, 1973–1996," Paper presented to the Annual Meeting of the American Political Science Association, Washington, DC (August).

Eijk, Cees van der, and Mark Franklin eds. 1996, *Choosing Europe? The European Electorate and National Politics in the Face of Union*, Ann Arbor: University of Michigan Press.

Eijk, Cees van der, Mark Franklin, and Michael Marsh 1996, "What Voters Teach Us About Europe-Wide Elections, What Europe-Wide Elections Teach Us About Voters," *Electoral Studies*, 15, 2: 149–166.

Epstein, David, and Sharyn O'Halloran 1999, *Delegating Powers: A Transaction Cost Politics Approach to Policy Making Under Separate Powers*, Cambridge: Cambridge University Press.

Erikson, Kai 1966, *Wayward Puritans: A Study in the Sociology of Deviance*, New York: John Wiley and Sons.

Esman, Milton 1994, *Ethnic Politics*, Ithaca, NY: Cornell University Press.

Espenshade, Thomas, and Charles Calhoun 1993, "An Analysis of Public Opinion Toward Undocumented Immigration," *Population Research and Policy Review*, 12: 189–224.

Espenshade, Thomas, and Katherine Hempstead 1996, "Contemporary American Attitudes Toward US Immigration," *International Migration Review*, 30, 2 (Summer): 535–570.

European Communities, Economic and Social Committee 1991a, "Additional Opinion of the Economic and Social Committee on the Status of Migrant Workers from Third Countries," SOC/217, Brussels (September).

    1991b, "Opinion of the Economic and Social Committee on Immigration Policy," EXT/90, Brussels (November).

European Council 1999, Presidency Conclusions, Tampere (October).

    2001, Presidency Conclusions, Laeken (December), SN 300/1/01 REV 1.

2002, Presidency Conclusions, Seville (June).

European Council on Refugees and Exiles (ECRE) 1999, *Guarding Standards: Shaping the Agenda*, London (April).

European Parliament, Information Memos, Brussels: European Parliament, Various 1983–93.

Session Documents, Strasbourg: European Communities, Various, 1985–93.

1985, Dimitrios Evrigenis, Rapporteur, *Report of the Findings: Committee of Inquiry into the Rise of Fascism and Racism in Europe 1985*, Luxembourg: Directorate-General (December).

1991a, "1993: The New Treaties, European Parliament Proposals," Luxembourg: Office of Official Publications of the European Communities.

1991b, "Migrant Workers from Non-Community Countries," PE 151.064, Luxembourg: Directorate-General (April).

1991c, "One Parliament for Twelve: The European Parliament," 13th edn. (September).

1991d, Glyn Ford, Rapporteur, *Report of the Findings: Committee of Inquiry on Racism and Xenophobia 1991*, Luxembourg: Office for Official Publications of the European Communities.

1991e, "The Work of the European Parliament: July 1988–1989," Brussels: Office of Official Publications of the EC.

Eurostat (Statistical Office of the European Commission) 1990a, *Eurostat 1990: Basic Statistics of the Community*, 28th edn., Luxembourg: Statistical Office of the European Communities.

1990b, "Migration Statistics," *Rapid Reports: Population and Social Conditions Series*, Luxembourg: Office for Official Publications of the European Communities.

1994, *Yearbook 1994: A Statistical Eye on Europe, 1992–1993*, Luxembourg: Office for Official Publications of the European Communities.

1997, *The European Union: Key Figures*, Brussels and Luxembourg: ECSC-EC-EAEC.

1998, *Facts Through Figures: Eurostat Yearbook at a Glance*, Luxembourg: European Communities.

1999a, *Economic Accounts of the European Union, 1998*, 4th edn., Luxembourg: Office for Official Publications of the European Communities.

1999b, *Yearbook 1998–1999: A Statistical Eye on Europe, Data 1987–1997*, Luxembourg: Office for Official Publications of the European Communities.

2000, *Yearbook 2000: A Statistical Eye on Europe 1988–1998*, Luxembourg: Office for Official Publications of the European Communities (May).

Evans, Peter 1998, "The Eclipse of the State? Reflections on Stateness in an Era of Globalization," *World Politics*, 50 (October): 62–87.

Everts, Philip, and Richard Sinnott 1995, "Conclusion: European Publics and the Legitimacy of Internationalized Governance," in Niedermayer and Sinnott 1995b, pp. 431–457.

Falkner, Gerda, and Simone Leiber 2003, "A Europeanization of Governance Patterns in Smaller European Democracies," Paper presented to the Eighth Biannual International Conference of the European Union Studies Association, March 27–29, Nashville, TN.

Favell, Adrian 1997, "European Citizenship and the Incorporation of Migrants and Minorities in Europe: Emergence, Transformation, and Effects of a New Political Field," Paper presented to the European University Institute Forum on International Migrations, Florence, Italy (November).

1998a, "The Europeanization of Immigration Politics," European Integration Online Papers, 2, 10: *http://eiop.or.at/eiop/texte/1998-010.htm*.

1998b, *Philosophies of Integration: Immigration and the Idea of Citizenship in France and Britain*, London: Macmillan.

Fekete, Liz 1991, "Report of the European Committee on Racism and Xenophobia: A Critique," *Race and Class*, 32: 147–149.

Feld, Werner, and John Wildgen 1976, *Domestic Political Realities and European Unification: A Study of Mass Publics and Elites in the European Community Countries*, Boulder, CO: Westview Press.

Feldblum, Miriam 1999, *Reconstructing Citizenship: The Politics of Nationality Reform and Immigration in Contemporary France*, Albany, NY: State University of New York Press.

Feldman, Stanley 1988, "Structure and Consistency in Public Opinion: The Role of Core Beliefs and Values," *American Journal of Political Science*, 32: 416–440.

Feldman, Stanley, and Karen Stenner 1997, "Perceived Threat and Authoritarianism," *Political Psychology*, 18: 741–770.

Fellermaier, L. 1979, *The Work of the Socialist Group in the European Parliament*, Report to the 10th Congress of the Confederation of the Socialist Parties of the European Community, Brussels (January).

Ferguson, Yale, and Richard Mansbach 1999, "Global Politics at the Turn of the Millennium: Changing Bases of 'Us' and 'Them', *International Studies Review*, 1, 2 (Summer): 77–107.

Fetzer, Joel 2000, *Public Attitudes Toward Immigration in the United States, France, and Germany*, Cambridge: Cambridge University Press.

Fieschi, Catherine, J. Sheilds, and R. Woods 1996, "Extreme Right-Wing Parties and the European Union: France, Germany and Italy," in John Gaffney, ed., *Political Parties and the European Union*, London: Routledge: 235–253.

Finnemore, Martha 1993, "International Organizations as Teachers of Norms: UNESCO and Science Policy," *International Organization*, 47, 4: 565–597.

1996, "Norms, Culture and World Politics: Insights from Sociology's Institutionalism," *International Organization*, 50 (Spring): 325–348.

Fiorina, Morris 1981, *Retrospective Voting in American National Elections*, New Haven: Yale University Press.

Fishbein, Martin, and Icek Ajzen 1980, *Understanding Attitudes and Predicting Social Behavior*, Englewood Cliffs, NJ: Prentice-Hall.

Fishel, Jeff 1972, "On the Transformation of Ideology in European Political Systems," *Comparative Political Studies*, 4 (January): 406–437.

Fitzmaurice, John 1975, *The Party Groups in the European Parliament*, Farnborough, England: Saxon House.

Flanagan, Scott C. and Russell J. Dalton 1990, "Models of Change," in Mair 1990, pp. 232–246.

Flanagan, Scott, and Aie-Rie Lee 2003, "The New Politics, Culture Wars, and the Authoritarian–Libertarian Value Change in Advanced Industrial Democracies," *Comparative Political Studies*, 36, 3 (April): 235–270.

Foner, Nancy, Rubén Rumbaut, and Steven Gold eds. 2000, *Immigration Research for a New Century: Multidisciplinary Perspectives*, New York: Russell Sage Foundation.

France, Senate 1991, "Report made on behalf of the Control Committee for the Convention applying the Schengen Agreement," Chairman M. Paul Masson, Paris (June).

Franklin, Mark 1992, "The Decline of Cleavage Politics," in M. Franklin, T. Mackie, and H. Valen, eds., *Electoral Change: Responses to Evolving Social and Attitudinal Structures in Western Countries*, Cambridge: Cambridge University Press, pp. 383–405.

Franklin, Mark, Michael Marsh, and Lauren McLaren 1994, "Uncorking the Bottle: Popular Opposition to European Unification in the Wake of Maastricht," *Journal of Common Market Studies*, 32: 455–72.

Franklin, Mark, and Susan Scarrow 1999, "Making Europeans? The Socializing Power of the European Parliament," in Katz and Wessels 1999, pp. 45–60.

Freeman, Gary P. 1979, *Immigrant Labor and Racial Conflict in Industrial Societies: The French and British Experience, 1945–1975*, Princeton: Princeton University Press.

1986, "Migration and the Political Economy of the Welfare-State," *Annals of the American Academy of Political and Social Science*, 485: 51–63.

1993, "Why the Immigration Intake Is Too Large in Democracies," Paper presented at the 1993 Annual Meeting of the American Political Science Association, the Washington Hilton (September).

1994, "Can Liberal States Control Unwanted Migration?," *Annals of the American Academy of Political and Social Science*, 534: 17–30.

1995, "Modes of Immigration Politics in Liberal Democratic States," in *International Migration Review*, 29, 4 (Winter): 881–908.

1998, "The Decline of Sovereignty? Politics and Immigration Restriction in Liberal States," in Joppke 1998b, pp. 86–108.

2002, "Winners and Losers: Politics and the Costs and Benefits of Migration," in Messina 2002a, pp. 77–96.

Friedland, Roger, and Robert R. Alford 1991, "Bringing Society Back In: Symbols, Practices, and Institutional Contradictions," in Powell and DiMaggio 1991, pp. 232–263.

Fullbrook, Mary ed. 1993, *National Histories and European Histories*, London: University College London Press.

Gabel, Matthew J. 1998a, *Interests and Integration: Market Liberalization, Public Opinion and European Union*, Ann Arbor: University of Michigan Press.

1998b, "Public Support for European Integration: An Empirical Test of Five Theories," *Journal of Politics*, 60, 2: 333–354.

Gabel, Matthew, and Christopher Anderson 2002, "The Structure of Citizen Attitudes and the European Political Space," *Comparative Political Studies*, 35 (8) (October): 893–913.

Gabel, Matthew, and Simon Hix 2002, "Defining the EU Political Space: An Empirical Study of the European Elections Manifestos, 1979–1999," *Comparative Political Studies*, 35, 8 (October): 934–964.

Gabel, Matthew, and John Huber 2000, "Putting Parties in Their Place: Inferring Party Left–Right Ideological Positions from Manifestos Data," *American Journal of Political Science*, 44, 1 (January): 94–103.

Gabel, Matthew, and Harvey Palmer 1995, "Understanding Variation in Public Support for European Integration," *European Journal of Political Research*, 27: 3–19.

Gabel, Matthew, and Guy Whitten 1997, "Economic Conditions, Economic Perceptions and Public Support for European Integration," *Political Behaviour*, 19, 1: 81–96.

Gallagher, Michael, Michael Laver, and Peter Mair 1992, *Representative Government in Western Europe*, New York: McGraw Hill.

Garrett, Geoffrey 1995, "The Politics of Legal Integration in the European Union," *International Organization*, 49, 1: 171–181.

Garrett, Geoffrey, and George Tsebelis 1996, "An Institutional Critique of Intergovernmentalism," *International Organization*, 50, 2: 269–299.

Garrett, Geoffrey, and Barry Weingast 1993, "Ideas, Interests and Institutions: Constructing the European Community's Internal Market," in Goldstein and Keohane 1993, pp. 173–206.

Garson, Jean-Pierre 1992, "International Migration: Facts, Figures, Policies," *OECD Observer*, 176 (June/July): 18–24.

Gatsios, Konstantine, and Paul Seabright 1989, "Regulation in the European Community," *Oxford Review of Economic Policy*, 5, 2: 37–60.

Geddes, Andrew 1998, "The Representation of 'Migrants' Interests' in the European Union," *Journal of Ethnic and Migration Studies*, 24, 4: 695–714.

1999, "The Development of the EU Immigration Policy: Supranationalisation and the Politics of Belonging," in Andrew Geddes and Adrian Favell, eds., *The Politics of Belonging: Migrants and Minorities in Contemporary Europe*, Aldershot: Ashgate, pp. 176–227.

2000, *Immigration and European Integration: Towards Fortress Europe?*, Manchester: Manchester University Press.

2002, "The EU Migration Regime's Effects on European Welfare States," in Lavenex and Uçarer 2002b, pp. 195–208.

Geddes, Andrew, and Virginie Guiraudon 2002, "The Anti-Discrimination Policy Paradigm in France and the UK: Europeanization and Alternative Explanations to Policy Change," Paper presented to the Workshop on "Theorising the Communitarisation of Migration" of the UACES Study Group on the Evolving European Migration Law and Policy, University of Liverpool (May).

Gibson, James 1995, "The Political Freedom of African Americans: A Contextual Analysis of Racial Attitudes, Political Tolerance and Individual Liberty," *Political Geography*, 14: 571–599.

1996, "A Mile Wide but an Inch Deep? The Structure of Democratic Commitments in the Former USSR," *American Journal of Political Science*, 40 (May): 396–420.

Gibson, Rachel 2002, *The Growth of Anti-Immigrant Parties in Western Europe*, Ceredigion, UK: Edwin Mellen Press.

Gillespie, Paul 1996, "Models of Integration," in Brigid Laffan, ed., *Constitution-Building in the European Union*, Dublin: Institute of European Affairs, pp. 140–169.

Gimpel, James, and James Edwards, Jr. 1999, *The Congressional Politics of Immigration Reform*, Boston: Allyn and Bacon.

Giscard d'Estaing, Valéry 2002, "Pour ou contre l'adhésion de la Turquie à l'Union européenne," *Le Monde* (November 9).

Givens, Terri 2002, "The Role of Socioeconomic Variables in the Success of Radical Right Parties," in Schain, Zolberg, and Hossay 2002, pp. 137–158.

forthcoming, "The Radical Right Gender Gap," *Comparative Political Studies*.

Glynn, Carroll J., Susan Herbst, Garret O'Keefe, and Robert Shapiro 1999, *Public Opinion*, Boulder, CO: Westview Press.

Goldstein, Judith, and Robert O. Keohane eds. 1993, *Ideas and Foreign Policy: Beliefs, Institutions and Political Change*, Ithaca, NY: Cornell University Press.

Green, David Michael 2000, "On Being European: The Character and Consequences of European Identity," in M. G. Cowles and M. Smith, eds., *The State of the European Union*, vol. V, Oxford: Oxford University Press, pp. 292–324.

Greenstein, Fred 1987, *Personality and Politics: Problems of Evidence, Inference and Conceptualization*, Princeton: Princeton University Press.

Groenendijk, Kees, Elspeth Guild, and Paul Minderhoud eds. 2002, *In Search of Europe's Borders*, The Hague: Kluwer Law International.

Guendelsberger, J. 1988, "The Right to Family Unification in French and United States Immigration Law," *Cornell International Law Journal*, 21, 1: 1–102.

Guild, Elspeth 1998, "Competence, Discretion and Third Country Nationals: The European Union's Legal Struggle with Migration," *Journal of Ethnic and Migration Studies*, 24, 4 (October): 613–626.

Guild, Elspeth, and Carol Harlow eds. 2001, *Implementing Amsterdam: Immigration and Asylum Rights in EC Law*, Portland, OR: Hart Publishing.

Guild, Elspeth, and Jan Niessen 1996, *The Developing Immigration and Asylum Policies of the European Union: Adopted Conventions, Resolutions, Recommendations and Conclusions*, The Hague: Kluwer Law International.

Guiraudon, Virginie 1997, "Policy Change Behind Gilded Doors: Explaining the Evolution of Aliens' Rights in Contemporary Western Europe," Ph.D. Dissertation, Harvard University.

1998, "Third-Country Nationals and European Law: Obstacles to Rights Expansion," *Journal of Ethnic and Migration Studies*, 24, 4: 657–674.

2000a, "European Integration and Migration Policy: Vertical Policy-Making as Venue Shopping," *Journal of Common Market Studies*, 38, 2 (June): 251–271.

2000b, *Les Politiques d'Immigration en Europe*, Paris: L'Harmattan.

2001a, "The European 'Garbage Can': Accounting for Policy Developments in the Immigration Domain," Paper presented at the European Community Studies Association Conference, Madison, WI (May–June).

2001b, "Weak 'Weapons of the Weak'? Transnational Mobilization Around Migration in the European Union," in Doug Imig and Sidney Tarrow, eds., *Contentious Europeans: Protests and Politics in an Emerging Polity*, Lanham, MD: Rowman and Littlefield, pp. 163–187.

2002a, "Including Foreigners in National Welfare States: Institutional Venues and Rules of the Game," in Rothstein and Steinmo 2002, pp. 129–156.

2002b, "Setting the Agenda on Immigration and the Asylum in the EU: Experts and 'the Public,' " Paper presented at the Annual Meeting of the American Political Science Association, Boston, MA.

2003, "The Constitution of a European Immigration Policy Domain: A Political Sociology Approach," *Journal of European Public Policy*, 10, 2 (April): 263–282.

Guiraudon, Virginie, and Gallya Lahav 2000, "A Reappraisal of the State Sovereignty Debate: The Case of Migration Control," *Comparative Political Studies*, 33, 2 (March): 163–195.

Guiraudon, Virginie, and Martin Schain 2002, "The French Political 'Earthquake' and Extreme Right in Europe," *European Studies Newsletter*, 32, 1/2 (September): 1–5.

Gurr, Ted, and Desmond King 1987, *The State and the City*, Chicago: University of Chicago Press.

Haas, Ernst 1958, *The Uniting of Europe: Political, Social, and Economic Forces 1950–1957*, Stanford: Stanford University Press.

1961, "International Integration: The European and the Universal Process," *International Organization*, 15: 366–392.

1964, *Beyond the Nation-State: Functionalism and International Organization*, Stanford: Stanford University Press.

1968, *The Uniting of Europe*, 2nd edn., Stanford: Stanford University Press.

1970, "The Study of Regional Integration: Reflections on the Joy and Anguish of Pretheorizing," *International Organization*, 24: 607–646.

Habermas, Jürgen 1995, "Comment on the Paper by Dieter Grimm: 'Does Europe Need a Constitution?,' " *European Law Journal*, 1, 3: 303–307.

Hainsworth, Paul ed. 1992, *The Extreme Right in Europe and the United States*, New York: St. Martin's Press.

Hall, Peter 1986, *Governing the Economy*, Oxford: Oxford University Press.

1997, "The Role of Interests, Institutions, and Ideas in the Comparative Political Economy of the Industrialized Nations," in Lichbach and Zuckerman 1997, pp. 174–207.

Hall, Stuart 1992, "Our Mongrel Selves," *New Statesman and Society*, Special Issue on "Borderlands," 19 June.

Hallstein, Walter 1972, *Europe in the Making*, London: George Allen and Unwin.

Hammar, Tomas 1985a, "Dual Citizenship and Political Integration," *International Migration Review*, 19 (3) (Fall): 438–450.

ed. 1985b, *European Immigration Policy: A Comparative Study*, Cambridge: Cambridge University Press.

Hansen, Randall 2000, *Citizenship and Immigration in Post-War Britain*, Oxford: Oxford University Press.

Hansen, Randall, and Patrick Weil eds. 2001, *Towards a European Nationality: Citizenship, Immigration and Nationality Law in the EU*, New York: Palgrave.

Harris, Geoffrey 1994 [1990], *The Dark Side of Europe: The Extreme Right Today*, Edinburgh: Edinburgh University Press.

Haus, Leah 2002, *Unions, Immigration, and Internationalization: New Challenges and Changing Coalitions in the United States and France*, New York: Palgrave Macmillan.

Heisler, Martin 1992, "Migration, International Relations and the New Europe: Theoretical Perspectives from Institutional Political Sociology," *International Migration Review*, 26 (Summer): 596–622.

Henig, Stanley ed. 1979, *Political Parties in the European Community*, London: George Allen & Unwin.

Hennessy, B. 1970, *Public Opinion*, Belmont, CA: Wadsworth.

Hernes, Gudmond, and Knud Knudsen 1992, "Norwegians' Attitudes Toward New Immigrants," *Acta Sociologica*, 35: 123–139.

Hewstone, Miles 1986, *Understanding Attitudes to the European Community: A Social-Psychological Study in Four Member States*, Cambridge and Paris: Cambridge University Press and Maison des Sciences de l'Homme.

Hix, Simon 1999a, "Dimensions and Alignments in European Union Politics: Cognitive Constraints and Partisan Responses," *European Journal of Political Research*, 35, 2: 69–125.

1999b, *The Political System of the European Union*, New York: St. Martin's Press.

2001a, "Legislative Behaviour and Party Competition in the European Parliament: An Application of Nominate to the EU," *Journal of Common Market Studies*, 39, 4 (November): 663–688.

2001b, "Legislator's Ideology or Party Organisational Power? What Drives Voting Behaviour in the European Parliament?," Paper presented to the European Community Studies Association Meeting, Madison, WI, May 31–June 3.

2002, "Parliamentary Behavior with Two Principals: Preference, Parties, and Voting in the European Parliament," *American Journal of Political Science*, 46, 3 (July): 688–698.

Hix, Simon, and Christopher Lord 1997, *Political Parties in the European Union*, London: Macmillan.

Hix, Simon, and Jan Niessen 1996, *Reconsidering European Migration Policies: The 1996 Intergovernmental Conference and the Reform of the Maastricht Treaty*, Brussels: Migration Policy Group/Churches' Commission for Migrants in Europe/Starting Line Group.

Hoffmann, Stanley 1966, "Obstinate or Obsolete? The Fate of the Nation-State and the Case of Western Europe," *Daedalus*, 95: 862–915.

Holland, Martin ed. 1994, *European Integration: From Community to Union*, London: Pinter.

Hollifield, James 1992a, *Immigrants, Markets and States: The Political Economy of Postwar Europe*, Cambridge, MA: Harvard University Press.

1992b, "Migration and International Relations: Cooperation and Control in the European Community," *International Migration Review*, 26, 2 (Summer): 568–595.

Hooghe, Liesbet, and Gary Marks 1999, "Making of a Polity: The Struggle over European Integration," in Herbert Kitschelt, Peter Lange, Gary Marks, and John Stephens, eds., *Continuity and Change in Contemporary Capitalism* Cambridge: Cambridge University Press, pp. 70–97.

2001, *Multi-Level Governance in the European Union*, Boulder, CO: Rowman and Littlefield.

Hooghe, Liesbet, Gary Marks, and Carole Wilson 2001, "Party Positions on European Integration: New Politics vs. Left–Right," Paper presented at the European Community Studies Association Seventh Biennial International Conference, Madison, WI (May–June).

2002, "Does Left/Right Structure Party Positions on European Integration?," *Comparative Political Studies*, 35, 8 (October): 965–989.

Hoskin, Marilyn 1984, "Integration and Nonintegration of Foreign Workers: Four Theories," *Political Psychology*, 5: 661–685.

1991, *New Immigrants and Democratic Society: Minority Integration in Western Democracies*, New York: Praeger.

Hoskin, Marilyn, and Roy C. Fitzgerald 1989, "German Immigration Policy and Politics," in LeMay 1989, pp. 661–685.

1992, "Public Acceptance of Racial and Ethnic Minorities: A Comparative Analysis," in Anthony Messina, Ruis Fraga, Laurie Rhodebeck, and Frederick Wright, eds. *Ethnic and Racial Minorities in Advanced Industrial Democracies*, New York: Greenwood Press.

Hovy, Bela 1993, "Asylum Migration in Europe: Patterns, Determinants and the Role of East–West Movements," in Russell King, ed., *The New Geography of European Migrations*, London: Belhaven Press, pp. 207–227.

Hovy, Bela, and Hania Zlotnik 1994, "Europe Without Internal Frontiers and International Migration," *Population Bulletin*, 36, http://europa.eu.int.

Huber, John 1989, "Values and Partisanship in Left–Right Orientations: Measuring Ideology," *European Journal of Political Research*, 17: 599–621.

Huber, John, and Ronald Inglehart 1995, "Expert Interpretations of Party Space and Party Locations in Forty-Two Societies," *Party Politics*, 1: 73–111.

Huddy, Leonie 2001, "From Social to Political Identity: A Critical Examination of Social Identity Theory," *Political Psychology*, 22: 127–156.

Huddy, Leonie, Stanley Feldman, Gallya Lahav, and Chuck Taber 2003, "Fear and Terrorism: Psychological Reactions to 9–11," in Pippa Norris, Montague Kern, and Marion Just, eds., *Framing Terrorism*, New York: Routledge, ch. 13.

Huddy, Leonie, Stanley Feldman, Chuck Taber, and Gallya Lahav 2002, "The Politics of Threat: Cognitive and Affective Reactions to 9/11," Paper presented at the American Political Science Association, Boston.

Huntington, Samuel 1968, *Political Order in Changing Societies*, New Haven and London: Yale University Press.

1993, "The Clash of Civilizations?," *Foreign Affairs*, 72, 3 (Summer): 22–49.

1996, *The Clash of Civilizations and the Remaking of World Order*, New York: Simon and Schuster.

2000, *Culture Matters: How Values Shape Human Progress*, New York: Basic Books.

Husbands, Christopher 1981, "Contemporary Right-Wing Extremism in Western European Democracies: A Review Article," *European Journal of Political Research*, 9: 75–100.

   1988, "The Dynamics of Racial Exclusion and Expulsion: Racist Politics in Western Europe," *European Journal of Political Research*, 16, 6: 701–721.

   1991, "The Support for the Front National: Analyses and Findings," *Ethnic and Racial Studies*, 14 (July), 382–416.

Huysmans, Jef 1995, "Migrants as a Security Problem: Dangers of 'Securitizing' Societal Issues," in Miles and Thränhardt 1995, pp. 53–72.

   2000, "The European Union and the Securitization of Migration," *Journal of Common Market Studies*, 38, 5: 751–777.

ICPSR (Inter-university Consortium for Political and Social Research) 1980, *Codebook for Eurobarometer 1980*, no. 9, Ann Arbor, MI: ICPSR.

   1985, *Candidates for the European Parliament, April–May 1979*, Jacques-René Rabier, Carsten Sorensen, Ronald Inglehart, and Ian Gordon, eds., Ann Arbor, MI: ICPSR.

Ignazi, Piero 1992, "The Silent Counter-Revolution: Hypotheses on the Emergence of the Extreme Right-Wing Parties in Europe," *European Journal of Political Research*, 22, 1: 3–34.

Immergut, Ellen 1992, *Health Politics: Interests and Institutions in Western Europe*, New York: Cambridge University Press.

"In Europe, Immigrants Are Needed, Not Wanted" (1990), *New York Times* (August): 1.

Inglehart Ronald 1970a, "Cognitive Mobilization and European Identity," *Comparative Politics*, 3, 1 (October): 45–70.

   1970b, "The New Europeans: Inward and Outward Looking?," *International Organization*, 24: 129–139.

   1971, "Value Priorities and European Integration," *Journal of Common Market Studies*, 10, 1 (September): 1–36.

   1977, *The Silent Revolution: Changing Values and Political Styles Among Western Publics*, Princeton: Princeton University Press.

   1979, "Political Action: The Impact of Values, Cognitive Level and Social Background," in Samuel Barnes, Max Kaase, *et al.*, eds., *Political Action: Mass Participation in Five Western Democracies*, Beverly Hills: Sage, pp. 343–380.

   1990a, *Culture Shift in Advanced Industrial Society*, Princeton: Princeton University Press.

   1990b, "From Class-Based to Value-Based Politics," in Mair 1990, 266–282.

   1990c, "The Nature of Value Change," in Mair 1990, 247–252.

   1997, *Modernization and Postmodernization*, Princeton: Princeton University Press.

Inglehart, Ronald, and Paul R. Abramson 1999, "Measuring Postmaterialism," *American Political Science Review*, 93 (13): 665–677.

Inglehart, Ronald, and Wayne Baker 2000, "Modernization, Cultural Change, and the Persistence of Traditional Values," *American Sociological Review*, 65 (February): 19–51.

Inglehart, Ronald, and Hans Klingemann 1976, "Party Identification, Ideological Preference and the Left–Right Dimension Among Western Mass Publics," in Budge, Crewe, and Farlie 1976, pp. 277–284.

Inglehart, Ronald, and Dusan Sidjanski 1976, "The Left, the Right, the Establishment and the Swiss Electorate," in Budge, Crewe, and Farlie 1976, pp. 225–242.

INSEE 2000, *Recensement de la population 1999*. Paris: INSEE.

Ippolito, Dennis, Thomas Walker, and Kenneth Kolson 1976, *Public Opinion and Responsible Democracy*, Englewood Cliffs, NJ: Prentice-Hall.

Ireland, Patrick 1994, *The Policy Challenge of Ethnic Diversity: Immigrant Politics in France and Switzerland*, Cambridge, MA: Harvard University Press.

1995, "Migration, Free Movement, and Immigrant Integration in the EU: A Bifurcated Policy Response," in Stephen Leibfried and Paul Pierson, eds., *European Social Policy: Between Fragmentation and Integration*, Washington, DC: Brookings Institution, pp. 231–266.

Jackman, Robert, and Karin Volpert 1996, "Conditions Favoring Parties of the Extreme Right in Western Europe," *British Journal of Political Science*, 26: 501–521.

Jacobs, Lawrence R., and Robert Y. Shapiro 2000, *Politicians Don't Pander: Political Manipulation and the Loss of Democratic Responsiveness*, Chicago and London: University of Chicago Press.

Jacobson, David 1996, *Rights Across Borders: Immigration and the Decline of Citizenship*, Baltimore: Johns Hopkins University Press.

Jennings, M. Kent 1992, "Ideological Thinking Among Mass Publics and Political Elite," *Public Opinion Quarterly*, 56: 419–441.

Jervis, Robert 1976, *Perceptions and Misperceptions in International Politics*, Princeton: Princeton University Press.

Joint Council for the Welfare of Immigrants 1989, "Unequal Migrants: The European Community's Unequal Treatment of Migrants and Refugees," Policy Papers in Ethnic Relations No. 13, London: JCWI.

Joppke, Christian 1997, *Asylum and State Sovereignty: A Comparison of the United States, Germany and Britain*, Oxford: Oxford University Press.

1998a, "Asylum and State Sovereignty," in Joppke 1998b, pp. 109–151.

ed. 1998b, *The Challenge to the Nation-State: Immigration in Western Europe and the United States*, New York: Oxford University Press.

1998c, "Why Liberal States Accept Unwanted Immigration," *World Politics*, 50, 2: 266–293.

1999, *Immigration and the Nation-State: The United States, Germany and Great Britain*, Oxford: Oxford University Press.

Karapin, Roger 1998, "Explaining Far-Right Electoral Success in Germany," *German Politics and Society*, 16, 3: 24–61.

Kaschuba, Wolfgang 1993, "Volk und Nation: Ethnozentrisus in Geschichte und Gegenwart," in H. Winkler and H. Kaeble, eds., *Nationalismus, Nationalitaten, Supra-nationalitaten*, Stuttgart: Klett-Cotta, pp. 68–80.

Kastoryano, Riva 1994, "Mobilisations des migrants en Europe: du national au transnational," *Revue Européenne des Migrations Internationales*, 10, 1: 169–181.

1996, *La France, l'Allemagne et leurs immigrés: négocier l'identité*, Paris: Armand Colin.

Katz, Richard 1999, "Representation, the Locus of Democratic Legitimation and the Role of the National Parliaments in the European Union," in Katz and Wessels 1999, pp. 21–44.

Katz, Richard, and Bernhard Wessels 1999, *The European Parliament, the National Parliaments, and European Integration*, Oxford: Oxford University Press.

Katzenstein, Peter 1996, *The Culture of National Security: Norms and Identity in World Politics*, New York: Columbia University Press.

Keohane, Robert 1984, *After Hegemony: Cooperation and Discord in the World Political Economy*, Princeton: Princeton University Press.

Keohane, Robert, and Stanley Hoffmann 1990, "Conclusions: Community Politics and Institutional Change," in Wallace 1990a, pp. 276–300.

Keohane, Robert, and Helen Milner eds. 1996, *Internationalization and Domestic Politics*, Cambridge: Cambridge University Press.

Keohane, Robert, and Joseph Nye 1989, *Power and Interdependence*, 2nd edn., Glencoe, IL: Addison-Wesley; 1st edn., 1977, Boston: Little, Brown.

Kessler, Alan 1997, "Trade Theory, Political Incentives, and the Political Economy of American Immigration Restriction, 1875–1924," Paper presented at American Political Science Association Annual Meeting, Washington, DC (August).

Kessler, Alan, and Gary Freeman 2002, "Sovereignty, Public Opinion, and Prospects for a Common European Migration Policy," Paper presented to the Annual Meeting of the International Studies Association, New Orleans, March 24–27.

Key, V. O. Jr. 1961, *Public Opinion and American Democracy*, New York: Knopf.

Kinder, Donald, R. Gordon, S. Adams, and Paul W. Gronke 1989, "Economics and Politics in the 1984 American Presidential Election," *American Journal of Political Science*, 33: 491–515.

Kinder, Donald, and D. Roderick Kiewiet 1981, "Sociotropic Politics: The American Case," *British Journal of Political Science*, 11, 2: 129–161.

Kinder, Donald, and Lynn M. Sanders 1996, *Divided by Color: Racial Politics and Democratic Ideals*, Chicago: University of Chicago Press.

Kinder, Donald, and David O. Sears 1981, "Prejudice and Politics: Symbolic Racism Versus Racial Threats to the Good Life," *Journal of Personality and Social Psychology*, 40, 3: 414–443.

King, Gary 1997, *A Solution to the Ecological Inference Problem: Reconstructing Individual Behavior from Aggregate Data*, Princeton: Princeton University Press.

King, Russell, Gabriella Lazaridis, and Charalambos Tsardanidis eds. 2000, *Eldorado or Fortress? Migration in Southern Europe*, London: Macmillan.

Kitschelt, Herbert 1989, *The Logics of Party Formation*, Ithaca, NY: Cornell University Press.

1994, *The Transformation of European Social Democracy*, New York: Cambridge University Press.

Kitschelt, Herbert, with Anthony McGann 1995, *The Radical Right in Western Europe: A Comparative Analysis*, Ann Arbor: University of Michigan Press.

Klausen, Jytte 1995, "Social Rights Advocacy and State Building: T. H. Marshall in the Hands of Social Reformers," *World Politics*, 47, 2 (January): 244–267.

Klausen, Jytte, and Louise Tilly eds. 1997, *European Integration in Social and Historical Perspective: 1850 to the Present*, Lanham, MD: Rowman and Littlefield.

Klotz, Audie 1995, "Norms Reconstituting Interests: Global Racial Equality and US Sanctions Against South Africa," *International Organization*, 49 (Summer): 451–478.

Knutsen, Oddbjorn 1989a, "Cleavage Dimensions in Ten Western European Countries: A Comparative Empirical Analysis," *Comparative Political Studies*, 21: 495–534.

1989b, "The Priorities of Materialist and Post-Materialist Political Values in the Nordic Countries – A Five-Nation Comparison," *Scandinavian Political Studies*, 12: 221–243.

1995a, "Left–Right Materialist Value Orientations," in Jan Van Deth and Elinor Scarbrough, eds., *The Impact of Values*, Oxford: Oxford University Press.

1995b, "Value Orientations, Political Conflicts and Left–Right Identification: A Comparative Study," *European Journal of Political Research*, 28: 63–93.

1998, "Expert Judgements of the Left–Right Location of Political Parties: A Comparative Longitudinal Study," *West European Politics*, 21: 63–94.

Koch, L. 1989, "Impact of the Reversal of the Migration Situation on the Social Structure of Certain Countries: The Case of Italy," *International Migration*, 27: 191–201.

Kook, Rebecca 2002, *The Logic of Democratic Exclusion: African Americans in the United States and Palestinian Citizens in Israel*, Lanham, MD: Lexington Books.

Koslowski, Rey 1994, "Intra-EU Migration, Citizenship and Political Union," *Journal of Common Market Studies*, 32, 3: 369–402.

1998a, "European Migration Regimes: Emerging, Enlarging and Deteriorating," *Journal of Ethnic and Migration Studies*, 24, 4 (October): 735–749.

1998b, "European Union Migration Regimes: Established and Emergent" in Joppke 1998b, pp. 153–188.

2000, *Migrants and Citizens: Demographic Change in the European State System*, Ithaca, NY: Cornell University Press.

Kostakopoulou, Dora 2000, "The 'Protective Union': Change and Continuity in Migration Law and Policy in Post-Amsterdam," *Journal of Common Market Studies*, 38, 3 (September): 497–518.

Kourvetaris, Andreas, and George Kourvetaris 1996, "Attitudes Toward European Integration," in G. Kourvetaris and A. Moschonas, eds., *The Impact of European Integration: Political, Sociological and Economic Change*, Westport, CT: Praeger, pp. 151–168.

Krasner, Stephen 1982, "Structural Causes and Regime Consequences: Regimes as Intervening Variables," *International Organization*, 36 (Spring): 379–415.

ed. 1983, *International Regimes*, Ithaca, NY: Cornell University Press.

1993, "Westphalia and All That," in Goldstein and Keohane 1993, pp. 235–264.

Kratochwil, Friedrich 1989, *Rules, Norms and Decisions: On the Conditions of Practical and Legal Reasoning in International Relations and Domestic Affairs*, Cambridge: Cambridge University Press.

Kreppel, Amy, and George Tsebelis 1999, "Coalition Formation in the European Parliament, *Comparative Political Studies*, 32: 933–966.

Kurzer, Paulette 2001, *Markets and Moral Regulation: Cultural Change in the European Union*, Cambridge: Cambridge University Press.

La Piere, Richard 1934, "Attitudes vs. Actions," *Social Forces*, 13: 230–237.

Ladrech, Robert 1994, "Europeanisation of Domestic Politics and Institutions: The Case of France," *Journal of Common Market Studies*, 32, 1: 69–88.

Laffan, Brigid 1996, "The Politics of Identity and Political Order in Europe," *Journal of Common Market Studies*, 34: 81–102.

Lahav, Gallya 1991, "Population Movements: An Emerging Concern of American Foreign Policymakers," *American Foreign Policy Newsletter*, 14, 5 (October): 1–6.

1992, "Immigration, Hypernationalism, and European Security," in J. Philip Rogers, ed., *The Future of European Security: The Pursuit of Peace in an Era of Revolutionary Change*, New York and London: St. Martin's Press and Macmillan Press, pp. 74–84.

1995, "Old Values and Changing Frontiers in the European Union: A Study of Attitudes of Members of the European Parliament Towards Immigration," Ph.D. Dissertation, City University of New York.

1997a, "Ideological and Party Constraints on Immigration Attitudes in Europe," *Journal of Common Market Studies*, 35, 3 (September): 377–406.

1997b, "International Versus National Constraints in Family-Reunification," *Global Governance*, 3, 3 (September–December): 349–369.

1998, "Immigration and the State: The Devolution and Privatisation of Immigration Control in the EU," *Journal of Ethnic and Migration Studies*, 24, 4 (October): 675–694.

2000, "The Rise of Nonstate Actors in Migration Regulation in the United States and Europe: Changing the Gatekeepers or Bringing Back the State?," in Foner, Rumbaut, and Gold 2000, pp. 215–241.

2002b, "Threat, Community-Building, and the Politics of Immigration: Some Preliminary Empirical Findings on Security in the EU and US," Paper presented to the Europeanists Conference, Palmer House, Chicago (March).

Lahav, Gallya, and Joseph Bafumi 2001, "The Elite–Mass Connection: Perceptions and Misperceptions in Collective Correspondence," Paper presented to the Midwest Political Science Association, Chicago (April).

Lahav, Gallya, and Virginie Guiraudon 2000, "Comparative Perspectives on Border Control: Away from the Border and Outside the State," in Andreas and Snyder 2000, pp. 55–77.

Lamont, Michèle 2000, *The Dignity of Working Men: Morality and the Boundaries of Race, Class and Immigration*, Cambridge and New York: Harvard University Press and Russell Sage Foundation.

Lane, Jan-Erik, and Svante Ersson 1999, *Politics and Society in Western Europe*, 4th edn., London: Sage.

Lane, Robert E. 1962, *Political Ideology: Why the American Common Man Believes What He Does*, New York and London: Free Press.

Lapid, Yosef 1996, "Culture's Ship: Returns and Departures in International Relations Theory," in Y. Lapid and Friedrich Kratochwil, eds., *The Return of Culture and Identity in IR Theory*, Boulder, CO: Lynne Rienner, pp. 2–20.

Lavenex, Sandra 1999, *Safe Third Countries: Extending the EU Asylum and Immigration Policies to Central and Eastern Europe*, Budapest: Central European University Press.

   2001, "The Europeanization of Refugee Policies: Normative Challenges and Institutional Legacies," *Journal of Common Market Studies*, 39, 5 (December): 851–874.

Lavenex, Sandra, and Emek Uçarer 2002a, "Introduction," in Lavenex and Uçarer 2002b, pp. 1–14.

   eds. 2002b, *Migration and the Externalities of European Integration*, Lanham, MD: Lexington Books.

Laver, Michael, and Benjamin Hunt 1992, *Policy and Party Competition*, London: Routledge.

Layton-Henry, Zig 1978, "Race, Electoral Strategy and the Major Parties," *Parliamentary Affairs*, 31, 3: 268–281.

   1984, *The Politics of Race in Britain*, London: George Allen & Unwin.

   ed. 1990, *The Political Rights of Migrant Workers in Western Europe*, London: Sage.

   1992, *The Politics of Immigration*, London: Blackwell.

Legomsky, Steven 1987, *Immigration and the Judiciary: Law and Politics in Britain and America*, Oxford: Clarendon Press.

Leibfried, Stephan, and Paul Pierson 2000, "Social Policy: Left to Courts or Markets?," in Wallace and Wallace 2000, pp. 267–292.

Leitner, Helga 1995, "International Migration and the Politics of Admission and Exclusion in Postwar Europe," *Political Geography*, 14, 3: 259–278.

LeMay, Michael ed. 1989, *The Gatekeepers: Comparative Immigration Policy*, New York: Praeger.

Lerner, Daniel, and Morten Gorden 1969, *Euroatlantica: Changing Perspectives of the European Elites*, Cambridge, MA: MIT Press.

Levi, Margaret 1997, "A Model, a Method, and a Map: Rational Choice in Comparative and Historical Analysis," in Lichbach and Zuckerman 1997, pp. 19–41.

Levine, R., and D. Campbell 1972, *Ethnocentrism: Theories of Conflict, Ethnic Attitudes and Behavior*, New York: John Wiley.

Lewis-Beck, Michael, and Glenn Mitchell II 1993, "French Electoral Theory: The National Front Test," *Electoral Studies*, 12 (June): 112–127.

Lichbach, Mark, and Alan S. Zuckerman eds. 1997, *Comparative Politics: Rationality, Culture, and Structure*, Cambridge: Cambridge University Press.

Lieberman, Robert 2002, "Political Institutions and the Politics of Race in the Development of the Modern Welfare State," in Rothstein and Steinmo 2002, pp. 104–128.

Lijphart, Arend 1977, *Democracy in Plural Societies*, New Haven: Yale University Press.

1979, "Religious vs. Linguistic vs. Class Voting: The 'Crucial Experiment' of Comparing Belgium, Canada, South African and Switzerland," *American Political Science Review*, 73, 2: 442–458.

1996, "The Puzzle of Indian Democracy: A Consociational Interpretation," *American Political Science Review*, 90, 2: 258–268.

Lindberg, Leon, and Stuart Scheingold 1970, *Europe's Would-Be Polity*, Englewood Cliffs, NJ: Prentice-Hall.

Lippmann, Walter 1922, *Public Opinion*, New York: Macmillan.

1955, *Essays in the Public Philosophy*, Boston: Little, Brown.

Lipset, Seymour Martin 1990 [1960], *Political Man: The Social Bases of Politics*, Baltimore: Johns Hopkins University Press..

Lipset, Seymour M., and Stein Rokkan 1967, "Cleavage Structures, Party Systems and Voter Alignments: An Introduction," in S. M. Lipset and S. Rokkan, eds., *Party Systems and Voter Alignments: Cross-National Perspectives*, New York: Free Press, pp. 1–64.

1990,"Cleavage Structures, Party Systems, and Voter Alignments," in Mair, 1990, pp. 90–138.

Lowi, Theodore 1964, "American Business, Public Policy, Case Studies and Political Theory," *World Politics*, 16: 677–693.

Lu, Chien-Yi 1999, "Harmonization of Migration Policies in the European Union: A State-Centric or Institutionalist Explanation?," Paper presented to European Community Studies Association Conference, Pittsburgh (June).

Lubbers, Marcel, Mérove Gijsberts, and Peer Scheepers 2002, "Extreme Right-Wing Voting in Western Europe," *European Journal of Political Research*, 31, 3: 345–378.

Macdonald, Stuart Elaine, Ola Listhaug, and George Rabinowitz 1991, "Issues and Party Support in Multiparty Systems," *American Political Science Review*, 85 (December): 1107–1132.

Machiavelli, Niccolò 1961 [1514], *The Prince*, Harmondsworth: Penguin.

Mackuen, Michael, Robert Erikson, and James Stimson 1992, "Peasants or Bankers?," *American Political Science Review*, 86: 597–611.

Mair, Peter ed. 1990, *The West European Party System*, Oxford: Oxford University Press.

March, James, and Johan Olsen 1984, "The New Institutionalism: Organizational Factors in Political Life," *American Political Science Review*, 78: 734–749.

1989, *Rediscovering Institutions: The Organizational Basis of Politics*, New York: Free Press.

Marcus, George, John Sullivan, Elizabeth Theiss-Morse, and Sandra Wood 1995, *With Malice Toward Some: How People Make Civil Liberties Judgements*, Cambridge: Cambridge University Press.

Marks, Gary 1993, "Structural Policy and Multilevel Governance in the EC," in Alan Cafruny and Glenda Rosenthal, eds., *The State of the European Community: The Maastricht Debates and Beyond*, Boulder, CO: Lynne Rienner, pp. 391–411.

Marks, Gary, Liesbet Hooghe, and Kermit Blank 1996, "European Integration Since the 1980s: State-Centric Versus Multi-Level Governance," *Journal of Common Market Studies*, 34, 4: 341–378.

Marks, Gary, Fritz Scharpf, Philippe Schmitter, and Wolfgang Streeck eds. 1996, *Governance in the European Union*, London: Sage.

Marks, Gary, and Marco Steenbergen eds. 2002, "Understanding Political Contestation in the European Union," *Comparative Political Studies*, 35, 8 (October): 879–892.

Marks, Gary, Carole Wilson, and Leonard Ray 2002, "National Political Parties and European Integration," *American Journal of Political Science*, 46, 3 (July): 585–594.

Marshall, T. H. 1963, "Citizenship and Social Class," in T. H. Marshall, ed., *Sociology at the Crossroads and Other Essays*, London: Heinemann, pp. 67–112.

1965, *Class, Citizenship and Social Development*, New York: Doubleday.

Martinotti, Guido, and Sonia Stefanizzi 1995, "Europeans and the Nation State," in Niedermayer and Sinnott 1995b, pp. 163–191.

Maslow, Abraham 1954, *Motivation and Personality*, New York: Harper and Row.

Mathew, D. 1980, *Europeanism: A Study of Public Opinion and Attitudinal Integration in the European Community*, Ottawa: Norman Patterson School of International Affairs, Carleton University, Ottawa.

Mayer, Nonna 1993, "Attitudes Towards the Region, Europe, and Politics in 1992 France," Paper presented to the Annual Meeting of the American Political Science Association, Washington, DC (September).

1999, *Français qui votent Front National*, Paris: Librairie-Ernest-Flammarion.

Mayer, Nonna, and Pascal Perrineau eds. 1989, *Le Front National à decouvert*, Paris: Presses de la Fondation des Sciences Politiques.

Mayer, Nonna, and Pascal Perrineau 1992, "Why Do They Vote for Le Pen?," *European Journal of Political Research*, 22, 1 (July): 123–141.

McLaren, Lauren 2001, "Immigration and the New Politics of Inclusion and Exclusion in the European Union: The Effect of Elites and the EU on Individual-Level Opinions Regarding European and Non-European Immigrants," *European Journal of Political Research*, 39: 81–108.

2002, "Public Support for the European Union: Cost/Benefit Analysis or Perceived Cultural Threat?," *Journal of Politics*, 64, 2 (May): 551–566.

Merritt, R. 1967, "Interviewing French and West German Elites," in Deutsch *et al.*, pp. 1–26.

Messina, Anthony 1985, "Race and Party Competition in Britain: Policy Formation in the Post-Consensus Period," *Parliamentary Affairs*, 38, 4 (Autumn): 423–436.

1987, "Postwar Protest Movements in Britain: A Challenge to Parties," *Review of Politics*, 49 (3) (summer): 410–428.

1989, *Race and Party Competition in Britain*, Cambridge: Clarendon Press.

1990, "Political Impediments to the Resumption of Labour Migration to Western Europe," *West European Politics*, 13 (January): 31–46.

1996, "The Not-So-Silent Revolution. Postwar Migration to Western Europe: Review Articles," *World Politics*, 49, 1: 130–154.

ed. 2002a, *West European Immigration and Immigrant Policy in the New Century*, Westport, CT: Praeger.

2002b, "Why Doesn't the Dog Bite? Extreme Right Parties and Euro-Skepticism Within the European Union," Paper presented to the Conference on "The Year of the Euro," University of Notre Dame, Notre Dame, IN (December).

Messina, Anthony, and Colleen Thouez, 2002, "The Logics and Politics of a European Immigration Regime," in Messina 2002a, pp. 97–122.

Meyer, John 1980, "The World Polity and the Authority of the Nation-State," in A. Bergesen, ed., *Studies of the Modern World System*, New York: Academic Press.

Miall, Hugh 1993, *Shaping the New Europe*, London: Pinter.

Miles, Robert, and Dietrich Thränhardt eds. 1995, *Migration and European Integration: The Dynamics of Inclusion and Exclusion*, London: Pinter.

Miller, Arthur, and Martin Wattenberg 1985, "Throwing the Rascals Out," *American Political Science Review*, 79: 359–372.

Miller, Mark 1981, *Foreign Workers in Western Europe: An Emerging Political Force*, New York: Praeger.

Miller, Mark, and Christopher Mitchell 1993, "Comparing Policy-Making Patterns Towards Migration in Industrial Democracies: Western Europe and the United States," Paper presented to the Seminar on Migration, the State, and International Relations, New York University (February).

Milner, Helen 1997, *Interests, Institutions and Information: Domestic Politics and International Relations*, Princeton: Princeton University Press.

Minkenberg, Michael 1992, "The New Right in Germany: The Transformation of Conservatism and the Extreme Right," *European Journal of Political Research*, 22, 1: 55–81.

1994, "The New Right in France and Germany: A Comparative Analysis of Changing Cleavage Structure and New Configurations in European Politics," Paper presented to the Ninth International Conference of Europeanists, Council of European Studies, Chicago (March–April).

2000, "The Renewal of the Radical Right: Between Modernity and Anti-Modernity," *Government and Opposition*, 35, 2 (Spring): 170–188.

2001, "The Radical Right in Public Office: Agenda-Setting and Policy Effects," *West European Politics*, 24, 4 (October): 1–21.

Moe, Terry 1984, "The New Economics of Organization," *American Journal of Political Science*, 28: 739–777.

Monar, Joerg 1998, "Justice and Home Affairs in the Treaty of Amsterdam: Reform at the Price of Fragmentation," *European Law Review*, 23: 320–335.

2000, "Justice and Home Affairs," *Journal of Common Market Studies*, 38 (September): 125–142.

Monar, Joerg, and Roger Morgan eds. 1994, *The Third Pillar of the European Union: Co-operation in the Fields of Justice and Home Affairs*, Brussels: European University Press.

Money, Jeannette 1995, "Two-Dimensional Aliens: Immigration Policy as a Two-Dimensional Issue Space," Paper presented to the American Political Science Association Meeting, Chicago (September).

1998, "Human Rights Norms and Immigration Control," *UCLA Journal of International Law and Foreign Affairs*, 3, 2 (Fall/Winter): 497–525.

1999, *Fences and Neighbors: The Political Geography of Immigration Control*, Ithaca, NY: Cornell University Press.

Monnet, Jean 1962, "A Ferment of Change," *Journal of Common Market Studies*, 1, 1: 203–211.

1978, *Memoirs*, New York: Doubleday.

Moravcsik, Andrew 1991, "Negotiating the Single European Act: National Interests and Conventional Statecraft in the European Community," *International Organization*, 45: 19–56.

1993, "Preference and Power in the European Community: A Liberal Intergovernmental Approach," *Journal of Common Market Studies*, 31: 473–524.

1995, "Liberal Intergovernmentalism and Integration: A Rejoinder," *Journal of Common Market Studies*, 33: 611–628.

1997, "Taking Preference Seriously: A Liberal Theory of International Politics," *International Organization*, 51 (Fall): 177–198.

1998, *The Choice for Europe: Social Purpose and State Power from Messina to Maastricht*, Ithaca, NY: Cornell University Press.

Moser, Peter 1996, "The European Parliament as a Conditional Agenda Setter: What Are the Conditions? A Critique of Tsebelis (1994)," *American Political Science Review*, 90: 834–838.

Müller-Rommel, Ferdinand ed. 1989, *New Politics in Western Europe: The Rise and Success of Green Parties and Alternative Lists*, Boulder, CO: Westview Press.

Münz, Rainer 1996, "A Continent of Migration: European Mass Migration in the Twentieth Century," *New Community*, 22, 2: 201–226.

Nelsen, Brent, and James Guth 2001, "Religion and Youth Support for the European Union: A Country Analysis," Paper presented to the Annual Meeting of the American Political Science Association, San Francisco (September).

Nelsen, Brent, James Guth, and Cleveland Fraser 2001, "Does Religion Matter? Christianity and Public Support for the European Union," *European Union Politics*, 2, 2: 267–291.

Neuman, Gerald 1990, "Immigration and Judicial Review in the Federal Republic of Germany," *New York University Journal of International Law and Politics*, 23, 1: 35–85.

Niedermayer, Oskar 1995a, "Trends and Contrasts," in Niedermayer and Sinnott 1995b, pp. 53–72.

1995b, "Trust and Sense of Community," in Niedermayer and Sinnott 1995b, pp. 227–245.

Niedermayer, Oskar, and Richard Sinnott 1995a, "Democratic Legitimacy and the European Parliament," in Niedermayer and Sinnott 1995b, pp. 277–309.

eds. 1995b, *Public Opinion and Internationalized Governance*, Oxford: Oxford University Press.

Niedermayer, Oskar, and Bettina Westle 1995, "A Typology of Orientations," in Niedermayer and Sinnott 1995b, pp. 33–51.

Niessen, Jan 1992, "European Community Legislation and International Cooperation on Migration," *International Migration Review*, 26, 2 (Summer): 676–
684.

1994, *The Making of European Immigration Policies*, CCME Briefing Paper No.
15, Brussels: Churches' Committee for Migrants in Europe (February).

1999, *EU Policies on Immigration and Integration After the Amsterdam Treaty*,
Brussels: Migration Policy Group (October).

2000, *The Management and Managers of Immigration*, Brussels: Migration Policy
Group (December).

Noury, Abdul 2002, "Ideology, Nationality and Euro-Parliamentarians," *European Union Politics*, 3: 33–58.

OECD (Organisation for Economic Co-operation and Development) 1987, *The
Future of Migration*, Paris: OECD.

1990, *Trends in International Migration: SOPEMI Report for 1989*, Paris:
OECD.

1991, *Trends in International Migration: SOPEMI Report for 1990*, Paris:
OECD.

1992, *Trends in International Migration: SOPEMI Report for 1991*, Paris: OECD.

1995, *Trends in International Migration: SOPEMI Report for 1994*, Paris: OECD.

1999, *Trends in International Migration: SOPEMI Report for 1998*, Paris: OECD.

2001, *Trends in International Migration: SOPEMI Report for 2001*, Paris: OECD.

Official Journal of the European Communities 1999, Debates of the European Parliament, Strasbourg: 1990–1999 Sessions.

Oliver, Eric, and Tali Mendelberg 2000, "Reconsidering the Environmental
Determinants of White Racial Attitudes," *American Journal of Political Science*, 44: 574–589.

Olsen, Johan 2000, "Organizing European Institutions of Governance: A Prelude
to an Institutional Account of Political Integration," ARENA Working Paper,
Oslo.

Olsen, Johan, and Guy Peters 1996, *Learning from Experience?* Oslo: Advanced
Research on the Europeanization of the Nation State.

Oskamp, S. 1977, *Attitudes and Opinions*, Englewood Cliffs, NJ: Prentice-Hall.

Page, Benjamin, and Robert Shapiro 1982, "Changes in Americans' Policy Preference, 1935–1979," *Public Opinion Quarterly*, 46: 24–42.

1983, "Effects of Public Opinion on Policy," *American Political Science Review*,
77: 175–190.

1992, *The Rational Public*, Chicago: University of Chicago Press.

Palmer, Michael 1983, "The Development of the European Parliament's Institutional Role Within the European Community, 1974–1983," *Journal of
European Integration*, 6: 183–202.

Papademetriou, Demetrios 1996, *Coming Together or Pulling Apart? The European
Union's Struggle with Immigration and Asylum*, Washington, DC:, Carnegie
Endowment for International Peace.

Papademetriou, Demetrios, and Mark Miller 1983, *The Unavoidable Issue: US
Immigration Policy in the 1980s*, Philadelphia: Institute for the Study of
Human Issues.

Parsons, Talcott 1951, *The Social System*, New York: Free Press.

Pastore, Massimo 1991, "Fortress Europe," *Strange W-A-Y-S Newsletter*, 12, Edge Hill College of Higher Education, Centre for Studies in Crime and Social Justice, London (Autumn).

1992, "Boundary Conflicts Around and Inside the European Community," Paper presented to the 20th Annual Conference of the European Group for the Study of Deviance and Social Control, Padua (September).

Perlmutter, Ted 1995, "Bringing Parties Back In: Comments on 'Modes of Immigration Politics in Liberal Democratic Societies,'" *International Migration Review*, 30, 1: 375–388.

Perrineau, Pascal 1985, "Le Front National: un électorat autoritaire," *Revue Politique et Parlementaire*, 87: 24–31.

1988, "Front National: l'echo politique de l'anomie urbaine," *Esprit* (March): 22–38.

1997, *Le Symptome Le Pen: radiographie des électeurs du Front National*, Paris: Fayard.

Petrocik, John 1996, "A Theory of Issue Ownership and the 1980 Presidential Election," *American Journal of Political Science*, 40 (August): 825–850.

Pierson, Paul 1996, "The Path to European Integration: A Historical-Institutional Analysis," *Comparative Political Studies*, 29, 2: 123–163.

2000, "Increasing Returns, Path Dependence, and the Study of Politics," *American Political Science Review*, 94, 1: 151–167.

Pieterse, Jan Nederveen 1991, "Fictions of Europe," *Race and Class*, 32, 3: 3–10.

Plender, Richard 1986, "Recent Trends in National Immigration Control," *International and Comparative Law Quarterly*, 35: 530–566.

1988, *International Migration Law*, Dordrecht, Netherlands: Martinus Nijhoff.

Pollack, Mark 1997, "Delegation, Agency, and Agenda Setting in the European Community," *International Organization*, 51, 1: 9–34.

Powell, Walter, and Paul DiMaggio eds. 1991, *The New Institutionalism in Organizational Analysis*, Chicago: University of Chicago Press.

Pridham, Geoffrey, and Pippa Pridham 1979, "Transnational Parties in the European Community I and II," in Henig 1979, pp. 245–310.

1981, *Transnational Party Co-operation and European Integration: The Process Towards Direct Elections*, London: George Allen and Unwin.

Przeworski, A., and H. Teune 1970, *The Logic of Comparative Social Inquiry*, New York: Wiley.

Putnam, Robert D. 1971, "Studying Elite Political Culture: The Case of Ideology," *American Political Science Review*, 65: 651–681.

1973, *The Beliefs of Politicians: Ideology, Conflict, and Democracy in Britain and Italy*, New Haven and London: Yale University Press.

1976, *The Comparative Study of Political Elites*, Englewood Cliffs, NJ: Prentice-Hall.

1983, "Comment," in Tsoukalis 1983.

1993, *Making Democracy Work: Civic Traditions in Modern Italy*, Princeton: Princeton University Press.

Putnam, Robert, and Nicholas Bayne 1987, *Hanging Together: Cooperation and Conflict in the Seven-Power Summits*, revised and enlarged, Cambridge, MA: Harvard University Press.

Quillian, Lincoln 1995, "Prejudice as a Response to Perceived Group Threat: Population Composition and Anti-Immigrant and Racial Prejudice in Europe," *American Sociological Review*, 60, 4 (August): 586–611.

Rabinowitz, George, and Stuart Elaine Macdonald 1989, "A Directional Theory of Issue Voting," *American Political Science Review*, 83: 93–121.

Raunio, Tapio 1997, *The European Perspective: Transnational Party Groups in the 1989–1994 European Parliament*, London: Ashgate.

2000, "Losing Independence or Finally Gaining Recognition? Contacts Between MEPS and National Parties," *Party Politics*, 6, 2: 211–223.

Rawls, John 1971, *A Theory of Justice*, Cambridge: Cambridge University Press.

Ray, Leonard 1999, "Measuring Party Orientations Towards European Integration: Results from an Expert Survey," *European Journal of Political Research*, 36: 283–306.

Reif, Karlheinz 1984, "National Electoral Cycles and European Elections," *Electoral Studies*, 3: 244–255.

1997, "Reflections: European Elections as Member-State Second-Order Elections Revisited," *European Journal of Political Research*, 31, 1–2 (February): 115–124.

Reif, Karlheinz, and Hermann Schmitt 1980, "Nine Second-Order Elections: A Conceptual Framework for the Analysis of European Election Results," *European Journal of Political Research*, 8, 1: 3–44.

Risse, Thomas 2002, "The Euro and Identity Politics in Europe," Paper presented to the Year of the Euro Conference, Nanovic Institute for European Studies, University of Notre Dame, IN (December).

Risse, Thomas, Maria Green Cowles, and James Caporaso 2001, "Transforming Europe: Europeanization and Domestic Change: Introduction," in M. Cowles, J. Caporaso, and T. Risse, eds., *Europeanization and Domestic Change*, Ithaca, NY: Cornell University Press, pp. 1–20.

Risse-Kappen, Thomas 1991, "Public Opinion, Domestic Structure, and Foreign Policy in Liberal Democracies," *World Politics*, 43: 479–512.

1996, "Exploring the Nature of the Beast: International Relations Theory and Comparative Policy Analysis Meet the European Union," *Journal of Common Market Studies*, 34, 1 (March): 53–80.

Rockman, Bert 1976, *Studying Elite Political Culture: Problems in Design and Interpretation*, Pittsburgh: University of Pittsburgh Center for International Studies.

Rogers, E., and F. Shoemaker 1971, *Communication of Innovations: A Crosscultural Approach*, 2nd edn., New York: Free Press.

Rogers, Rosemarie 1985, "Post-World War II European Labor Migration: An Introduction to the Issues," in Rosemarie Rogers, ed., *Guests Come to Stay: The Effects of European Labor Migration on Sending and Receiving Countries*, Boulder, CO: Westview Press.

Rohrschneider, Robert 1988, "Citizens' Attitudes Toward Environmental Issues: Selfish or Selfless?," *Comparative Political Studies*, 21, 3 (October): 347–367.

1990, "The Roots of Public Opinion Toward New Social Movements: An Empirical Test of Competing Explanations," *American Journal of Political Science*, 34: 1–30.

1993, "Environmental Belief Systems in Western Europe: A Hierarchical Model of Constraint.," *Comparative Political Studies*, 26, 1: 3–29.

Rokeach, Milton 1960, *The Open and Closed Mind: Investigations into the Nature of Belief Systems and Personality Systems*, New York: Basic Books.

Rose, Richard 1991, "What Is Lesson Drawing?," *Journal of Public Policy*, 2: 3–30.

Rosencrance, Richard 1986, *The Rise of the Trading State*, New York: Basic Books.

Rothstein, Bo, and Sven Steinmo eds. 2002, *Restructuring the Welfare State: Political Institutions and Policy Change*, New York: Palgrave.

Ruggie, John 1982, "International Regimes, Transactions and Change: Embedded Liberalism in the Post-War Economic Order," *International Organization*, 36, 2 (Spring): 379–415.

1993, "Territoriality and Beyond: Problematizing Modernity in International Relations," *International Organization*, 47 (Winter): 139–174.

Ryner, Magnus 2000, "European Welfare State Transformation and Migration," in Bommes and Geddes 2000, pp. 51–71.

Salt, John 1993, "External International Migration," in Daniel Noin and Robert Woods, eds., *The Changing Population of Europe*, Oxford: Blackwell, pp. 185–197.

1994, *Migration and Population Changes in Europe*, New York: United Nations.

1996, "Current Trends in International Migration in Europe," Paper presented to the Sixth Conference of European Ministers Responsible for Migration Affairs, Warsaw, June 16–18.

2000, *Current Trends in International Migration in Europe*, Strasbourg: Council of Europe.

Sandholtz, Wayne, and Alec Stone Sweet eds. 1998, *European Integration and Supranational Governance*, Oxford: Oxford University Press.

Sassen, Saskia 1991, *The Global City: New York, London, Tokyo*, Princeton: Princeton University Press.

1996, *Losing Control?*, New York: Columbia University Press.

Schain, Martin 1987, "The National Front in France and the Construction of Political Legitimacy," *West European Politics*, 10, 2: 229–252.

1988, "Immigration and Changes in the French Party System," *European Journal of Political Research*, 16: 597–621.

1999, "Immigration, the National Front and Changes in the French Party System," Paper presented to the Annual Meeting of the American Political Science Association (September).

Schain, Martin, Aristide Zolberg, and Patrick Hossay eds. 2002, *Shadows over Europe: The Development and Impact of the Extreme Right in Western Europe*, New York: Palgrave Macmillan.

Scharpf, Fritz 1988, "The Joint-Decision Trap: Lessons from German Federalism and European Integration," *Public Administration*, 66, 3 (Autumn): 239–278.

1996, "Negative and Positive Integration in the Political Economy of European Welfare States," in Marks *et al.* 1996, pp. 15–39.

1999, *Governing in Europe: Effective and Democratic?*, Oxford: Oxford University Press.

Schattschneider, E. E. 1975, *The Semisovereign People: A Realist's View of Democracy in America*, Hinsdale, IL: Dryden Press (1st edn., 1960, New York: Holt, Rinehart and Winston).

Schmidt, Vivien 1996, "Loosening the Ties that Bind: The Impact of European Integration on French Government and Its Relationship to Business," *Journal of Common Market Studies*, 34, 2: 224–254.

Schmitt, Hermann, and Jacques Thomassen eds. 1999, *Political Representation and Legitimacy in the European Union*, Oxford: Oxford University Press.

2002, "Dynamic Representation: The Case of European Integration," in Pascal Perrineau, Gérard Grunberg, and Colette Ysmal, eds., *Europe at the Polls: The European Elections of 1999*, New York: Palgrave, pp. 22–42.

Schmitter, Philippe 1992, "Interests, Powers, and Functions: Emergent Properties and Unintended Consequences in the European Polity," Stanford: Center for Advanced Study in the Behavioral Sciences Working Paper.

1996, "Imagining the Future of the Euro-Polity with the Help of New Concepts," in Marks *et al.* 1996, pp. 1–14.

Schnapper, Dominique 1994, "The Debate on Immigration and the Crisis of National Identity," *West European Politics*, 17, 2: 127–139.

Schuck, Peter 1989, "Membership in the Liberal Polity: The Devaluation of American Citizenship," in Brubaker 1989, pp. 51–65.

1998, *Citizens, Strangers and In-Betweens: Essays on Immigration and Citizenship*, Boulder, CO: Westview Press.

Scully, Roger 1999, "Between Nation, Party, and Identity: A Study of European Parliamentarians," European Parliament Research Group Working Paper, no. 5, London School of Economics.

2002, "Going Native? Institutional and Partisan Loyalty in the European Parliament," in Steunenberg and Thomassen 2002.

Seago, D. W. 1947, "Stereotypes: Before Pearl Harbor and After," *Journal of Social Psychology*, 23: 55–63.

Sears, David 1969, "Political Behavior," in G. Lindzey and E. Aronson, eds., *The Handbook of Social Psychology*, Reading, MA: Addison-Wesley, pp. 315–458.

Sears, David, and Jack Citrin 1982, *Tax Revolt: Something for Nothing in California*, Cambridge, MA: Harvard University Press.

Sears, David, Richard Lau, Tom Tyler, and Harris Allen, Jr. 1980, "Self-Interest vs. Symbolic Politics in Policy Attitudes and Presidential Voting," *American Political Science Review*, 74, 3: 670–684.

Serra, George, Neil Pinney, Albert Cover, and Jim Twombly 1993, "The Changing Shape of Congressional Parties: Ideological Policy Cohesion and Polarization in the US Congress, 1953–1990," Paper presented to the Annual Meeting of the American Political Science Association, Washington, DC (September).

Shaw, Malcolm 1997, *International Law*, Cambridge: Cambridge University Press.

Shepherd, Robert 1975, *Public Opinion and European Integration*, Westmead: Saxon House.

Shepsle, Kenneth, and Barry Weingast 1987a, "The Institutional Foundations of Committee Power," *American Political Science Review*, 81: 84–104.

1987b, "Why Are Congressional Committees Powerful?" *American Political Science Review*, 81: 935–945.

1994, "Positive Theories of Congressional Institution," *Legislative Studies Quarterly*, 19: 145–179.

Sikkink, Kathryn 1993, "Human Rights, Principled Issue-Networks, and Sovereignty in Latin America," *International Organization*, 47 (Summer): 411–441.

Simon, Julian 1989, *The Economic Consequences of Immigration*, Oxford: Basil Blackwell.

Simon, Rita 1985, *Public Opinion and the Immigrant*, Lexington, MA: Lexington Books.

Simon, Rita, and Susan Alexander 1993, *The Ambivalent Welcome: Print Media, Public Opinion and Immigration*, Westport, CT: Praeger.

Sinnott, Richard 1995, "Bringing Public Opinion Back In," in Niedermayer and Sinnott 1995b, pp. 11–32.

Slater, Martin 1983, "Political Elites, Popular Indifference and Community-Building," in Tsoukalis 1983.

Sniderman, Paul, Joseph Fletcher, Peter Russell, and Philip Tetlock 1996, *The Clash of Rights: Liberty, Equality and Legitimacy in Pluralist Democracy*, New Haven: Yale University Press.

SOFRES, *Opinion Publique 1985, "Les Français et les Immigrés" et "L'Extrême Droite,"* Paris: Gallimard.

Soysal, Yasemin Nuhoglu 1994, *Limits of Citizenship: Migrants and Postnational Membership in Europe*, Chicago: University of Chicago Press.

Spinelli, Altiero 1966, *The Eurocrats: Conflict and Crisis in the European Community*, Baltimore: Johns Hopkins University Press.

Stafford, M., and O. Galle 1984, "Victimization Rates, Exposure to Risk and Fear of Crime," *Criminology*, 22: 173–85.

Stalker, Peter 1994, *The Work of Strangers: A Survey of International Labour Migration*, Geneva: International Labour Organization.

2000, *Workers Without Frontiers: The Impact of Globalization on International Migration*, Boulder, CO: Lynne Rienner.

Stetter, Stephan 2000, "Regulating Migration: Authority Delegation in Justice and Home Affairs," *Journal of European Public Policy*, 7 (March): 80–103.

Steunenberg, Bernard 1994, "Decision-Making Under Different Institutional Arrangements: Legislation by the European Community," *Journal of Theoretical and Institutional Economics*, 150: 642–669.

Steunenberg, Bernard, and Jacques Thomassen eds. 2002, *European Parliament: Moving Towards Democracy in the EU*, Lanham, MD: Rowman and Littlefield.

Stevens, Joe B. 1993, *The Economics of Collective Choice*, Boulder, CO: Westview Press.

Stimson, James 1991, *Public Opinion in America: Moods, Cycles and Swings*, Oxford: Westview.

Stimson, James, Michael Mackuen, and Robert Erikson 1995, "Dynamic Representation," *American Political Science Review*, 89 (September): 543–565.

Stone Sweet, Alec, and Wayne Sandholtz 1998, "Integration, Supranational Governance, and the Institutionalization of the European Polity," in Sandholtz and Stone Sweet 1998, pp. 1–26.

Straubhaar, Thomas, and Achim Wolter 1996, "Current Issues in European Migration," *Intereconomics* (November/December): 267–276.

Sullivan, John, J. Piereson, and G. Marcus 1982, *Political Tolerance and American Democracy*, Chicago: University of Chicago Press.

Swank, Duane, and Hans-Georg Betz 2002, "Globalization, the Welfare State, and Right-Wing Populism in Western Europe," Paper presented to the Council of European Studies, Conference for Europeanists, Chicago (March).

Taggart, Paul 1995, "New Populist Parties in Western Europe," *West European Politics*, 18, 1: 34–51.

1998, "A Touchstone of Dissent: Euroscepticism in Contemporary Western European Party Systems," *European Journal of Political Research*, 33, 3: 363–388.

Taggart, Paul, and Aleks Szczerbiak 2002, "The Party Politics of Euroskepticism in EU Member and Candidate States," Sussex European Institute, SEI Working Paper, 51 (April).

Tajfel, Henri, and Turner, J. C. 1979, "An Integrative Theory of Intergroup Conflict," in W. G. Austin and S. Worchel, eds., *The Social Psychology of Intergroup Relations*, Monterey, CA: Brooks/Cole, pp. 33–48.

Taylor, Paul 1990, "Functionalism: The Approach of David Mitrany," in A. J. R. Groom and P. Taylor, eds., *Frameworks for International Co-operation*, London: Pinter, pp. 125–138.

Teitelbaum, Michael, and Philip Martin 2003, "Is Turkey Ready for Europe?," *Foreign Affairs*, 82, 3 (May–June): 97–102.

Thelen, Kathleen, and Sven Steinmo 1992, "Historical Institutionalism in Comparative Politics," in Sven Steinmo, Kathleen Thelen, and Frank Longstreth, eds., *Structuring Politics: Historical Institutionalism in Comparative Analysis*, Cambridge: Cambridge University Press, pp. 1–32.

Thielemann, Eiko 2001, "The Europeanization of Asylum Policy: Overcoming International and Domestic Institutional Constraints," Paper presented to the European Community Studies Association Biennial International Conference, Madison, WI (May–June).

2003, "Burden-Sharing or Free-Riding? Explaining Variations in States' Acceptance of Unwanted Migration," Paper presented to the Eighth European Union Studies Association Biennial International Conference, March 27–29, Nashville, TN.

forthcoming, "The 'Soft' Europeanisation of Migration Policy: European Integration and Domestic Policy Change," *Journal of Ethnic and Migration Studies*, 29, 1.

Thomassen, Jacques, and Hermann Schmitt 1999, "Partisan Structures in the European Parliament," in Katz and Wessels 1999, pp. 129–148.

Thomson, Janice, and Stephen Krasner 1989, "Global Transactions and the Consolidation of Sovereignty," in Ernst-Otto Czempiel and James Rosenau, eds., *Global Changes and Theoretical Challenges*, Lexington, MA: Lexington Books.

Thränhardt, Dietrich ed. 1992, *Europe: A New Immigration Continent*, Hamburg: Lit Verlag.

1997, "The Political Uses of Xenophobia in England, France, and Germany," in Uçarer and Puchala 1997, pp. 175–194.

Thränhardt, Dietrich, and R. Miles 1995, "Introduction: European Integration, Migration and Processes of Inclusion and Exclusion," in Miles and Thränhardt 1995, pp. 1–12.

Tichenor, Dan 2002, *Dividing Lines: The Politics of Immigration Control in America*, Princeton: Princeton University Press.

Tilly, Charles 1990, *Coercion, Capital, and European States: AD 990–1992*, Oxford: Blackwell; 2nd edn., revised, 1992.

1994, "States and Nationalism in Europe, 1492–1992," *Theory and Society*, 23: 13–46.

Tsebelis, George 1992, "The Power of the European Parliament as a Conditional Agenda Setter," Working Paper, Berkeley: Center for German and European Studies, University of California.

1994, "The Power of the European Parliament as a Conditional Agenda Setter," *American Political Science Review*, 88: 128–142.

1996, "More on the European Parliament as a Conditional Agenda Setter: A Response to Moser," *American Political Science Review*, 90: 839–844.

Tsebelis, George, and Geoffrey Garrett 2000, "Legislative Politics in the European Union," *European Union Politics*, 1: 9–36.

Tsoukalis, Loukas ed. 1983, *The European Community: Past, Present, and Future*, Oxford: Basil Blackwell.

Tyler, T. 1984, "Assessing the Risk of Crime Victimization: The Integration of Personal Victimization Experience and Socially Transmitted Information," *Journal of Social Issues*, 40: 27–38.

Uçarer, Emek, and Donald Puchala eds. 1997, *Immigration into Western Societies: Problems and Policies*, London: Pinter.

Ugur, Mehmet 1995, "Freedom of Movement vs. Exclusion: A Reinterpretation of the 'Insider'–'Outsider' Divide in the European Union," *International Migration Review*, 24, 4 (Winter): 965–999.

UNECE (United Nations Economic Commission for Europe) 1997, *International Migration and Integration Policies in the UNECE Region*, Geneva: Population Activities Unit.

UNHCR (United Nations High Commissioner for Refugees) various years, *The State of the World's Refugees*, Oxford; New York: Oxford University Press.

United Kingdom, House of Lords 1990, *1992 Border Controls of People: Report and Evidence, Select Committee on the EC*, London: Her Majesty's Stationery Office.

United Nations, Population Division 1995, *International Migration Policies, 1995*, New York: United Nations.

1997, *International Migration Policies*, New York, United Nations (February).

1999a, *Population Ageing, 1999*, New York: United Nations (June).

1999b, *World Population, 1998*, New York: United Nations (March).

2001, *Report of the Expert Group Meeting on Policy Responses to Population Ageing and Decline*, New York: United Nations.

2002a, *International Migration from Countries with Economies in Transition, 1980–1999*, New York: United Nations (September).

2002b, *International Migration, Wallchart 2002*, New York: United Nations.

Vachudová, Milada Anna 2000a, "Eastern Europe as Gatekeeper: The Immigration and Asylum Policies of an Enlarging European Union," in Andreas and Snyder 2000, pp. 153–172.

2000b, "EU Enlargement: An Overview," *East European Constitutional Review*, 9, 4 (Fall): 64–69.

2001, "The Leverage of International Institutions on Democratizing States: The European Union and Eastern Europe," Robert Schuman Centre for

Advanced Studies Working Paper No. 2001/33, European University Institute, Fiesole, Italy.

Van Boven, Leaf 2000, "Pluralistic Ignorance and Political Correctness: The Case of Affirmative Action," *Political Psychology*, 21, 2 (June): 267–276.

van Outrive, Lode 1990, "Migration and Penal Reform: One European Policy?" Unpublished paper, 18th Annual Conference of the European Group for the Study of Deviance and Social Control, Haarlem, the Netherlands.

Veugelers, John 2000, "Right-Wing Extremism in Contemporary France: A Silent Counterrevolution?," *Sociological Quarterly*, 41, 1 (Winter): 28–29.

von Beyme, Klaus ed. 1988, "Special Issue: Right-Wing Extremism in Western Europe," *West European Politics*, 11, 2 (April).

Wæver, Ole 1995, "Identity, Integration and Security: Solving the Sovereignty Puzzle in EU Studies," *Journal of International Affairs*, 48: 389–431.

1996, "European Security Identities," *Journal of Common Market Studies*, 34, 1: 103–132.

Wallace, Helen, and William Wallace eds. 2000, *Policy-Making in the European Union*, 4th edn., Oxford: Oxford University Press.

Wallace, William ed. 1990a, *The Dynamics of European Integration*, London: Pinter.

1990b, "Introduction: The Dynamics of European Integration," in Wallace 1990a.

Waltz, Kenneth 1979, *Theory of International Politics*, Reading, MA: Addison-Wesley.

Walzer, Michael 1983, *Spheres of Justice: A Defense of Pluralism and Equality*, New York: Basic Books.

Wapner, Paul 1995, "Politics Beyond the State: Environmental Activism and World Civic Politics," *World Politics*, 47: 311–340.

Weaver, Kent 1986, "The Politics of Blame Avoidance," *Journal of Public Policy*, 6, 4: 371–398.

Weber, Max 1958, *The Protestant Ethic and the Spirit of Capitalism*, New York: Scribners.

Weil, Patrick 1991, *La France et ses Etrangers*, Paris: Calman Levy.

1996, "Nationalities and Citizenships: The Lessons of the French Experience for Germany and Europe," in David Cesarani and Mary Fulbrook, eds., *Citizenship, Nationality, and Migration in Europe*, London and New York: Routledge, pp. 74–87.

Weil, Patrick, and John Crowley 1994, "Integration in Theory and Practice: A Comparison of France and Britain," *West European Politics*, 17, 2: 110–126.

Weiner, Myron 1985, "International Migration and International Relations," *Population and Development Review*, 11 (September): 441–455.

1990, *Security, Stability and International Migration*, Cambridge, MA: MIT Center for International Studies.

Weir, M. and T. Skocpol 1985, "State Structures and the Possibilities for 'Keynesian' Responses to the Great Depression in Sweden, Britain, and the United States," in P. Evans, D. Ruewschmeyer and T. Skocpol, eds., *Bringing the State Back In*, Cambridge: Cambridge University Press, pp. 107–168.

Weissberg, Robert 1978, "Collective Versus Dyadic Representation in Congress," *American Political Science Review*, 72: 535–547.

Welsh, Jennifer, and Iver Neumann 1991, "The Other in European Self-Definition: An Addendum to the Literature on International Society," *Review of International Studies*, 17: 327–348.

Wessels, Bernhard 1995a, "Development of Support: Diffusion or Demographic Replacement?," in Niedermayer and Sinnott 1995b, pp. 105–136.

1995b, "Evaluations of the EC: Elite- or Mass-Driven?," in Niedermayer and Sinnott 1995b, pp. 137–162.

Widgren, Jonas 1990, "International Migration and Regional Stability," *International Affairs*, 66, 4 (October): 749–766.

Wihtol de Wenden, Catherine 1987, *Citoyenneté, nationalité et immigration*, Paris: Arcantère Editions.

1988, *Les immigrés et la politique*, Paris: Fondation Nationale de Sciences Politiques.

1999, *L'immigration en Europe*, Paris: La Documentation Française.

Williamson, O. E. 1975, *Market and Hierarchies: Analysis and Antitrust Implications*, Chicago: Free Press.

1993, "Transaction Cost Economics and Organization Theory," *Industrial and Corporate Change*, 2: 107–156.

Yankelovich, Daniel 1991, *Coming to Public Judgement: Making Democracy Work in a Complex World*, Syracuse, NY: Syracuse University Press.

Zaller, John 1990, "Political Awareness, Elite Opinion Leadership, and the Mass Survey Response," *Social Cognition*, 8: 125–153.

1991, "Information, Values, and Opinion," *American Political Science Review*, 85: 1215–1237.

1992, *The Nature and Origins of Mass Opinion*, Cambridge: Cambridge University Press.

Zellentin, Gerda 1967, "Form and Function of the Opposition in the European Communities," *Government and Opposition*, 2, 3 (April–July): 416–434.

Zolberg, Aristide 1981, "International Migrations in Political Perspective," in M. Kritz, C. Keely, and S. Tomasi, eds., *Global Trends in Migration: Theory and Research on International Population Movements*, New York: Center for Migration Studies, pp. 3–27.

1983, "Patterns of International Migration Policy: A Diachronic Comparison," in C. Fried, ed., *Minorities: Community and Identity*, Report of the Dahlem Workshop on Minorities, Berlin: Springer-Verlag, pp. 229–246.

1999, "Matters of State: Theorizing Immigration Policy," in C. Hirschman, P. Kasinitz, and J. DeWind, eds., *The Handbook of International Migration: The American Experience*, New York: Russell Sage Foundation, pp. 71–93.

2000, "The Politics of Immigration Policy: An Externalist Perspective," in Foner, Rumbaut, and Gold 2000, pp. 60–68.

Zolberg, Aristide, and Litt Woon Long 1999, "Why Islam Is like Spanish: Cultural Incorporation in Europe and the United States," *Politics and Society*, 27, 1: 5–38.

Index

ad hoc groups, formation of (AHI, etc.)
41, 61–62, 63–64, 156
administration (immigration procedures)
4, 100
African immigrants, public responses to
89–90, 92, 116, 158
age, relationship with attitude 16, 172, 183
Algeria, migrations from 33–34, 59
Allport, Gordon 111, 112
Amsterdam, Treaty of 5, 28–29, 45–47,
50–51, 65, 100, 156–157, 219, 228
impact on public opinion 56, 187
Title IV 46, 47, 56, 65, 66
anti-immigrant attitudes
in history 84
informal expressions of xiv, 1
linked to Euroskepticism 172–177
(perceived) national variations 81–83,
118–121, 123
among politicians xiii–xiv, 1, 10, 30, 87,
106, 142, 147
among public 10, 31, 80–81, 86, 104,
106, 146, 162–163, 194, 196
related to immigration levels 117–120,
146, 148
statistics 81–82
Asian immigrants, public responses to 90,
116
asylum
attitudes toward 24, 33–34, 42–43
common policy, movements toward 47,
49
jurisdiction over 46, 101
legislation on 62
policies on 38, 42, 66, 156
restrictions on 43
statistics 53, 256
attitude(s)
formation of 73, 105, 118
links with policy/behavior 12, 23, 73–74,
86, 198, 243
to past 84–85

research into 74–76, 181
see also elite groups; public opinion

behavior *see* attitude
Belgium
immigration policy 35–36
in intergovernmental agreements 41
minority rights 37
Berlin Wall, fall of 42–43
Blair, Tony 66
"blame-avoidance" strategies 49, 54
border controls 2, 41–42
abolition of (internal) 50, 228
national variations 42, 61
tightening of 31, 43–44, 48, 51
Brazil, migrations from 63
Brussels xiv, 1, 155, 208
domination of EU activity 50
burden-sharing 42, 62, 65

Central Europe *see* Eastern/Central
European countries
change, processes of 12–13, 163
Christian Democrats 135, 136, 177, 178,
200
citizenship
discrepant 37, 258
European 28, 44, 69, 113, 156, 220, 227
national 37, 113, 157, 197, 220
naturalization 33, 258–259
qualifications for 37
cognitive mobilization 76, 109, 181–182,
201, 223, 231
collective action 2, 50, 57
collective correspondence 13, 105–106,
208, 210, 211
colonialism, aftermath of 29, 33–34, 150
common immigration policy (EC/EU)
movements toward 16, 18, 26, 27, 35,
38, 40, 41, 44, 46, 50, 53–54, 57, 146,
152, 210, 211, 219–220, 226–229
obstacles to 38, 40–41, 144, 210

308